£28.50

A SURVEY OF MANUSCRIPTS
ILLUMINATED IN THE BRITISH ISLES
VOLUME TWO
ANGLO-SAXON MANUSCRIPTS 900-1066

BY ELŻBIETA TEMPLE

Frontispiece: Pentecost. Rouen, Bibl. Mun., Y.7, f. 29ᵛ (Cat. 24)

A SURVEY OF MANUSCRIPTS ILLUMINATED IN THE
BRITISH ISLES~GENERAL EDITOR: J·J·G· ALEXANDER

ANGLO~SAXON MANUSCRIPTS

900~1066

BY ELŻBIETA TEMPLE

WITH 370 ILLUSTRATIONS

 HARVEY MILLER~LONDON

A SURVEY OF MANUSCRIPTS
ILLUMINATED IN THE BRITISH ISLES

General Editor J. J. G. Alexander

Volume One: INSULAR MANUSCRIPTS FROM THE 6TH TO THE 9TH CENTURY

Volume Two: ANGLO-SAXON MANUSCRIPTS 900–1066

Volume Three: ROMANESQUE MANUSCRIPTS 1066–1190

Volume Four: EARLY GOTHIC MANUSCRIPTS 1190–1285

Volume Five: GOTHIC MANUSCRIPTS 1285–1385

Volume Six: LATER GOTHIC MANUSCRIPTS

© 1976 Harvey Miller · 20 Marryat Road · London SW19 5BD · England

ISBN 0 85602 016 8

Designed by Elly Miller

Printed in Great Britain at the University Press, Oxford
by Vivian Ridler, Printer to the University

CONTENTS

Editor's Preface   page 7

Foreword   9

Introduction   11

Notes to the Introduction   30

Glossary   31

List of Abbreviations   32

Catalogue   35

Illustrations   123

Index of Manuscripts   237

Analysis of Manuscripts in the Catalogue   241

General Index   242

In Memory of my Mother
and H. F. T.

Fig. 1. Detail of f. 60ᵛ. London, B.L., Harley 603 (Cat. 64)

EDITOR'S PREFACE

IN the later centuries covered by our SURVEY OF MANUSCRIPTS ILLUSTRATED IN THE BRITISH ISLES there are so many manuscripts surviving that it is necessary to make a selection. From earlier periods less remains, so that Dr. Temple has been able here to describe and illustrate all known Anglo-Saxon manuscripts with figural illustrations, and the majority of those with decorative initials. There is a considerable literature on the art of this period but even in this volume Dr. Temple has been able to track down a little-known Anglo-Saxon Gospel Lectionary to its present location in Warsaw (No. 92), and reproduce it for the first time.

In the 10th and 11th centuries, English art was probably more widely admired than at any time since, and a full study of its influence on the Continent would require a separate book which remains to be written. Dr. Temple's vivid descriptions will enable the reader to understand the reasons for the contemporary reputation of Anglo-Saxon art. Even when so much has perished, what remains to us demonstrates the pictorial inventiveness and the formal originality in the use of colour and line of these artists. It is an astonishing century and a half in its creative vitality.

J. J. G. Alexander

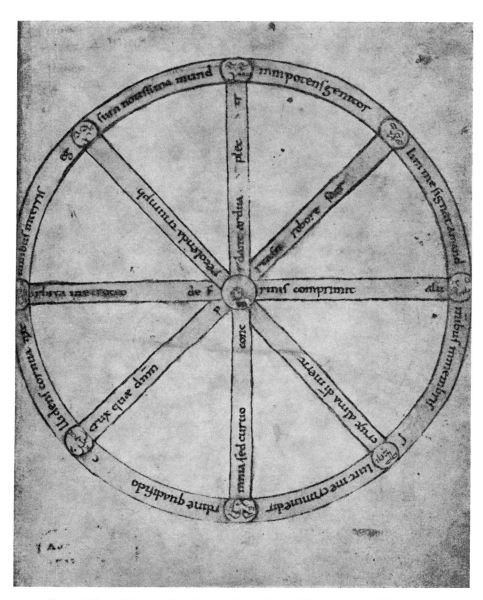

Fig. 2. Wheel-Diagram. London, Lambeth Palace Lib. 204, f. 130 (Cat. 19. x)

FOREWORD

GREAT NAMES in the history of the English nation and of the English church are associated with the art of the Later Anglo-Saxon period (*c.* 900–1066). Kings Alfred (871–99), Aethelstan ('Rex totius Britanniae', 925–39), and Edgar (959–975), responsible for checking the Viking invasions and for reorganizing and expanding the English dominion, pursued a generous patronage of learning and of art; while St. Dunstan, Ethelwold, and Oswald led the tenth-century monastic reform movement conducive to a new artistic flowering.

In this period illuminated manuscripts furnish the bulk of the surviving material for the study of English pictorial art. Not as prolific as in the following centuries, they present, nevertheless, a varied corpus including a number of great liturgical books commissioned for royal or other highly placed patrons, as well as more modestly produced specimens of educational, religious, historical, or scientific interest.

The present survey catalogues and discusses fully all extant manuscripts of importance belonging to the group of great liturgical books which contain miniatures and elaborate decoration. Manuscripts containing mainly penwork initials are grouped separately in two lists which, although incomplete (28 items), are, nevertheless, sufficiently representative of this category.

This book owes its existence to the inspiration and guidance of Dr. J. J. G. Alexander, the editor of the present series. I offer him my grateful thanks for entrusting to me the work on this fascinating period in the history of English illumination. The task would have been much more formidable without the pioneering work of such scholars as, earlier this century, T. D. Kendrick, and especially, somewhat later, Francis Wormald, whose classification of the Anglo-Saxon ornamental initials became the basis of part of this study. The invaluable textbooks of Margaret Rickert and D. Talbot Rice also provided essential support in the field of general research. The recent paleographical discoveries of T. A. M. Bishop, which shattered the accepted attributions of certain manuscripts to their very foundations, proved most illuminating, while N. R. Ker's *Catalogue of manuscripts containing Anglo-Saxon* provided an indispensable criterion for reference. I am greatly indebted to both these scholars for their patient response to my queries and for so readily furnishing information required.

Thanks are also due for their unfailing help to the staff of the Bodleian Library, of the British Library, and of the Conway photographic collection as also to all the many libraries I had to visit in the course of my work. I am especially grateful to the State Public Library in Leningrad for supplying me with most useful information on MS I. 3311, now in Warsaw.

A very special debt must also be acknowledged to Dr. Revel Elliot, formerly of Manchester University, for her encouragement and helpful comments; to Mrs. Isabel Hariades for her kind understanding and patience in preparing the book for publication; and last but not least to Mrs. Elly Miller, the publisher of the series, for her interest and admirable perceptiveness in the production and final presentation of the volume.

Fig. 3. Ose (*propheta*) and Laurentius (*diaconus*), St. Cuthbert's Stole, before 916. Durham, Cathedral Library

INTRODUCTION

THIS SURVEY begins with the reign of King Alfred (871–99) and ends with the Norman Conquest in 1066. The wars with the Danes had brought destruction to numbers of earlier English manuscripts and had also stopped book production; but in 886 Alfred reached a settlement with the invaders. He ensured peace for Wessex and devoted himself to the restoration of art and learning. Scholars were invited to his court from the British Isles and the Continent, among them Grimbald from Rheims, formerly a monk from St. Bertin, whom he installed at Winchester. He also maintained personal contacts with continental courts through his step-mother Judith, daughter of Charles the Bald, and married one of his daughters to Baldwin II, Count of Flanders. The revival of book production at the close of his reign was due not only to his patronage but also to his work in translating important Latin texts. A copy of his translation of St. Gregory's *Cura Pastoralis* which survives (Bodl. Lib. MS Hatton 20, no. 1), was made under his supervision and presented to Werferth, Bishop of Worcester. Although without new ornamental motifs, its initials, decorated with the interlace and animal-headed terminals in the style of the 8th-century Southern English manuscripts (figs. 4–6), are an important link between these and 10th-century Anglo-Saxon ornament. Indications of the changes which English illumination was about to undergo, however, are found in such manuscripts of *c.* 900 as B.L. Royal 5. F. III (Aldhelm from Worcester, no. 2) and Add. 47967 (Orosius, no. 8) or Durham Cathedral Library A. IV. 19 (Durham Ritual, no. 3), which display full-bodied dragons in the letter-structure alongside the earlier Insular motifs. The 'long and short' leaf pattern, another novel continental element in these initials, was later to become a significant feature of Anglo-Saxon decoration.

The first major example of pictorial art of the post-Alfredian era occurs not in manuscript painting but on the embroidered stole and maniples ordered before 916 by Aelfleda, the queen of King Edward the Elder, for Frithestan, Bishop of Winchester (fig. 3).[1] In 934 King Aethelstan presented them to St. Cuthbert's shrine in Chester le Street. The monumental figure style and decoration of the fleshy, three-dimensional acanthus constitute a complete break with Insular art and suggest fresh Byzantine influences perhaps channelled through Mediterranean or Carolingian works. Dependence on similar imported models is shown by two illuminated manuscripts associated with King Aethelstan (924–39): the additions made to a 9th-century continental psalter, B.L. Cotton, Galba A. XVIII (no. 5; a cutting from it is now Bodleian MS Rawl. B. 484), and Bede's Life of St. Cuthbert, Cambridge, Corpus Christi College MS 183 (no. 6). The four miniatures and the calendar added to the Aethelstan Psalter were probably executed at Winchester to which the King presented the book. The frontispiece of the Cambridge manuscript (ill. 29) shows Aethelstan offering the book (probably the one he gave to the see about 934) to St. Cuthbert. It is the earliest presentation picture in English art, stylistically related to such late Carolingian works as the San Paolo Bible in Rome (fig. 12).[2] The surrounding border panels contain an antique candelabrum-like plant ornament and an inhabited scroll pattern, the latter without parallel until the end of the 10th century in the borders of Lambeth Palace Library MS 200 (no. 39) and in examples from St. Bertin, Pierpont Morgan Library MS 333 and St. Omer MS 56 (fig. 19). The initials of Corpus Christi College 183 are ornamented, on the one hand, with motifs deriving from 8th-century Southern English decoration treated in a new, naturalistic manner and, on the other, with classical acanthus patterns and foliated scrolls which anticipate the ornament of later Anglo-Saxon initials. Both miniatures and initials are an entirely new venture in Anglo-Saxon art and are, to quote Kendrick, 'an English essay in the Frankish fashion of the court'.[3]

Aethelstan had, in fact, close family ties with the reigning continental houses, for his five half-sisters married foreign princes, among them the future Emperor Otto I and Charles the Simple, King of the West Franks. Gifts of manuscripts occasioned by these royal marriages may account, in part at least, for the predominance of continental influences in English painting of that time. Some books, known to have been in Aethelstan's possession, have survived, and a Gospel Book of the Metz school, now in Coburg and known as the Gandersheim Gospels, bears the names of Aethelstan and his sister Eadgive in Anglo-Saxon script. Another, a late Carolingian Gospel Book made for Lobbes near Liège, B.L. Cotton, Tiberius A. II (fig. 30), had its St. Matthew copied in the middle of the 10th century in St. John's College MS 194 in Oxford (no. 12). More could be quoted and many more must have perished.

How assiduously, in fact, some of the imported books were copied is shown by a somewhat later Rabanus Maurus (Cambridge, Trinity College MS B. 16. 3, no. 14), which closely follows a continental model, probably from northern France, deriving from a Fulda archetype (fig. 33), and whose monumental frontispiece is vaguely related in style to Corpus Christi College 183.

Decoration of the initials underwent major changes during the first half of the 10th century. Two important manuscripts of this period in the Bodleian Library, Junius 27 (no. 7), a psalter probably from Winchester, and Tanner 10 (no. 9), Bede's Ecclesiastical History, are decorated solely with initials whose rich colouring is one of the many innovations. Insular and continental elements are perfectly balanced in the Junius Psalter where earlier motifs are used alongside the three-dimensional acanthus, busts, and heads; sometimes complete human figures occur and inhabited scroll initials make their first appearance. Human figures are also employed in a novel, strikingly functional, manner in the structure of the Tanner 10 initials, anticipating the later 'clambering' type particularly popular in Canterbury around 1100. Although figure initials were used earlier on the Continent (in Merovingian manuscripts, figs. 9, 10, and especially in the Corbie Psalter, Amiens MS 18, c. 800; figs. 7, 8), this gymnastic type may have been an Anglo-Saxon introduction, for nowhere else was the quality of movement of living creatures exploited to the same degree. The type appears again towards the end of the 10th century in a West Saxon psalter, Salisbury Cathedral Library MS 150 (no. 18), and in a Gospel Book, Cambridge, Trinity College MS B. 10. 4, possibly from Canterbury (no. 65).

The initial letters of less sumptuous manuscripts, mainly non-liturgical books in Latin or the vernacular, derive largely from the varied initials of the Junius Psalter, but they are seldom in colour. They fall into two main groups classified by Wormald as Type I with the letters formed by whole creatures, and Type II where only the heads are employed.[4] This classification will be used in the present Survey in the description of particular manuscripts. Both groups make use of leaf ornament and of the interlace which thickens characteristically at the angular 'elbows'. This 'elbowed' interlace is particularly prominent in the large and heavily coloured initials of the late 10th-century Bosworth Psalter, B.L. MS Add. 37517 (no. 22), believed to have been written for St. Dunstan at Canterbury. Type I initials are represented here by a Gospel Book, Boulogne, Bibl. Mun. MS 10 (no. 10); Type II either in black wiry line (a) or in outline (b) can be seen in Cambridge, Trinity College MS B. II. 2 (no. 21), and Bodl. Lib. MS Auct. F. I. 15 (no. 37), respectively. Both types, most effective as book decoration, become the hallmark of 10th- to 11th-century Anglo-Saxon work. Occurring in manuscripts other than of English provenance (e.g. Pierpont Morgan Library MS 333, Gospels from St. Bertin, ill. 112), they reveal the presence of Anglo-Saxon artists in continental scriptoria.

Meanwhile, in the second half of the 10th century two English, basically classical, figure-styles emerge: the so-called 'first' or 'Winchester' style combining various Carolingian

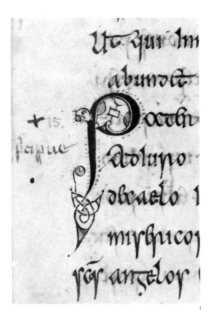

Fig. 4. Zoomorphic Initial.
Mercia (?), 8th century.
London, B.L., Royal 2. A. XX, f. 17

Fig. 5. Initial P.
Book of Cerne, Mercia, early 9th century.
Cambridge, University Lib., Ll. 1. 10, f. 63

Fig. 6. 'In principio' page. Barberini Gospels, Southern England, *c.* 800.
Rome, Vatican Bibl. Apostolica, Barb. lat. 570, f. 125

Figs. 7–8. Initial V, Ps. 76; Initial N, Presentation in the Temple.
Corbie Psalter, *c.* 800. Amiens, Bibl. Mun. 18, f. 67ᵛ, f. 137

Fig. 9. Initial D.
Gellone Sacramentary, Diocese of Meaux, 790-5.
Paris, Bibl. Nat., lat. 12048, f. 113ᵛ

Fig. 10. Detail of a Title-page. Chelles, *c.* 800.
Oxford, Bodl. Lib., Douce 176, f. 62

MUSTUAE ETLOCUMHA   DEXTERAEORUMREPLE   DICAMTEDNE
BITATIONISCLORIAE   TAESTMUNERIBUS
TUAE

XXVI DAUID   PRIUSQUAMLINE   RETUR
DNSINLUMINATIO   TISUNTETCECIDERUNT   OMNIBUSDIEBUSUI

Fig. 11. Psalm 26. Utrecht Psalter, Rheims, c. 820. Utrecht, University Lib. 32, f. 15

Fig. 12. Story of David. San Paolo Bible, c. 870.
Rome, San Paolo fuori le Mura, f. 81ᵛ

Fig. 13. 'In principio' page. Second Bible of Charles the Bald,
Saint-Amand (?), 871–7. Paris, Bibl. Nat., lat. 2, f. 11

Fig. 14. Christ in Majesty. School of Tours, 844–51.
Berlin, Staatsbibliothek, lat. theol. 2°733, f. 17ᵛ

Fig. 15. St. Luke. Ebbo Gospels, Hautvilliers, nr. Rheims,
before 832. Epernay, Bibl. Mun. 1, f. 90ᵛ

Fig. 16. Christ trampling the Beasts. Ivory Book Cover of the Lorsch Gospels,
'Ada' School, early 9th century. Rome, Vatican, Museo Sacro

Fig. 17. Nativity. Ivory Casket. Metz School, 9th century. Paris, Louvre

Fig. 18. Baptism. Ivory Casket. Metz School, 9th-10th century. Brunswick, Herzog Anton-Ulrich Museum

Fig. 19. Detail of Ornamental Border. St. Bertin, *c.* 1000. St. Omer, Bibl. Mun. 56, f. 36

Fig. 20. Initial Q.
Otbert of St. Bertin, 990–1012 (?).
Boulogne, Bibl. Mun. 107, f. 8

Fig. 21. Initial L. Gospels,
Préaux, late 11th century.
London, B.L., Add. 11850, f. 18

Fig. 22. David and the Shulamite.
St. Vaast Bible, Arras, *c.* 1025.
Arras, Bibl. Mun. 559, f. 128ᵛ

Fig. 23. Initial D.
Mont St. Michel Sacramentary, 1040–70.
New York, Pierpont Morgan Lib. 641, f. 66ᵛ

Fig. 24. Ornamental Border.
Mont St. Michel, *c.* 1035–45.
Avranches, Bibl. Mun. 59, f. 1ᵛ

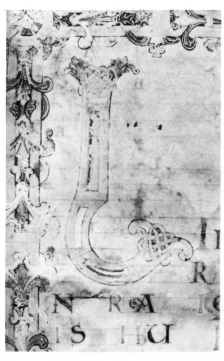

Fig. 25. Initial L (detail).
Gospels, late 11th century
St. Lô, Archives Départmentales de la
Manche, MS 1, f. 5

influences, and that inspired by 9th-century manuscripts from Rheims, in particular by the Utrecht Psalter believed to have reached Canterbury before 1000.

The monumental 'first' style makes its earliest appearance about 950 in an outline drawing of St. Dunstan at the feet of Christ (ill. 41), probably executed at Glastonbury while St. Dunstan was Abbot there between 943 and 957, now prefixed to a 9th-century manuscript, Bodl. Lib. Auct. F. 4. 32 (no. 11). The figure of Christ has a classical solidity of form enhanced by the contrast of firm, rounded contour lines and lightly fluttering draperies. The style and type of the figure suggest a model, perhaps an ivory carving, of the Ada Court School of Charlemagne (e.g. fig. 16). Almost a replica of the figure of Christ is a drawing of excellent quality, probably contemporary, on the flyleaf of St. John's College MS 28 in Oxford (no. 13, ill. 42). Perhaps dependent on the same model are three identical figures of the Trinity in the Pontifical written c. 992–5 for use in Sherborne Abbey, now Bibl. Nat., lat. 943 in Paris (no. 35).[5] This manuscript also contains a monumental Crucifixion remarkable for the economy of its drawing (ill. 134). A certain coarsening of line perceptible in the Sherborne miniatures when compared with the St. John's College manuscript, is more pronounced in the drawings of Bodley MS 155 (no. 59), probably early 11th-century copies of a closely related model.

Allied in style to the St. Dunstan miniature are the drawings in two copies of Aldhelm's *De virginitate*, Bodley MS 577 (no. 57) and Lambeth Palace Library MS 200 (no. 39), both datable to about 1000, the latter containing remarkable initials of Wormald's Type II (ills. 132, 133).

The mid 10th-century appearance of this classical figure-style dominated by Carolingian influences can be explained by direct and repeated contacts with the Continent established by Aethelstan and maintained during the monastic revival which St. Dunstan initiated at Glastonbury. After a year of exile at St. Peter's, Ghent (957–8), St. Dunstan became Archbishop of Canterbury in 960–88. His associates in the monastic reform movement were St. Ethelwold, monk of Glastonbury under Dunstan, Abbot of Abingdon and Bishop of Winchester (963–84), who had close contacts with Fleury, and St. Oswald who studied there before succeeding Dunstan as Bishop of Worcester (961) and becoming Archbishop of York (972–92).

The Glastonbury drawing is doubly important to English art as the first formulation of the new and mature figure style[6] and as the earliest monumental example of the characteristic English technique of outline drawing. This technique, which produced certain variants through the application of colour, was employed from the 10th century onward alongside the rich painting technique of the so-called 'Winchester' school; yet, to quote Wormald, 'it was a case of two media but not of two styles'. The term 'Winchester' school, in fact, denotes no more than the style of certain manuscripts produced in the reformed Benedictine monasteries in England, basically the style of the St. Dunstan drawing elaborated by the use of colour and by characteristic plant decoration. Only a small number of these manuscripts can be securely assigned to Winchester and the problem of their attribution has been further complicated by recent paleographical findings which have shown that manuscripts formerly allocated to different centres may have been written by one and the same scribe. It is significant that the acanthus foliage climbing over trellis-work, typical of 'Winchester' borders, appears early at Glastonbury in one of the illustrations added c. 970 to a continental sacramentary, Bodley MS 579 in Oxford, known as the Leofric Missal (no. 17). This and the other two additions are of particular interest for the history of English painting, being executed in red, green, and blue inks, probably the earliest examples of the coloured outline technique popular in late 10th- and 11th-century English illumination and still occurring after 1100.[7] The Leofric additions already show the influence of the Carolingian Rheims style in the sketchy line of the drawing (ills. 53–56).

Manuscripts executed about 1000 include copies of the Prudentius' *Psychomachia* whose pictorial cycles follow one late classical prototype. Two are in coloured outline: Cambridge, Corpus Christi College MS 23 (no. 48), probably from Canterbury, stylistically close to the

Leofric Missal and B.L. Cotton, Cleopatra C. VIII (no. 49) from Christ Church, Canterbury, as yet unaffected by the Rheims influence. Another copy, B.L. Add. 24199 (no. 51), contains the same cycle of pictures in monochrome drawing and similar in style is also a single leaf in Munich, CLM. 29031b (no. 50).

Coloured outline is also used in parts of two extensively illustrated biblical manuscripts in the vernacular, the 'Caedmon' Genesis (Bodleian MS Junius 11, no. 58), probably a Canterbury work of the early 11th century, and Aelfric's Metrical Paraphrase of the Pentateuch and Joshua (B.L. Cotton, Claudius B. IV, no. 86) from St. Augustine's, Canterbury, of the second quarter of the 11th century. The second of the two groups of drawings in Junius 11 in coloured outline is by the hand of the Cambridge Prudentius (no. 48). The picture cycles of both manuscripts, suggesting the presence in Anglo-Saxon England of illustrated Early Christian Mediterranean models, are at the same time evidence of the existence of an independent English iconographical tradition. The Aelfric illustrations, moreover, executed in firm continuous outline (some left unfinished and showing the progress of work in various stages), are a remarkable example of pictorial invention. They reveal, as Dodwell has shown, the ability of Anglo-Saxon artists to produce new illustrations for a particular manuscript copy, drawing on contemporary English life and customs.

In the meantime, the first manuscript illuminated in the new 'Winchester' manner, the New Minster Charter (B.L. Cotton, Vespasian A. VIII, no. 16), was produced at Winchester shortly after St. Ethelwold became Bishop. It commemorated the introduction of Benedictine monks into the New Minster and may in fact be later than 966, the date it bears. Its painted frontispiece representing King Edgar offering the Charter to Christ (ill. 84), is surrounded by a decorative border of multicoloured acanthus climbing over trellis-work. The illustration, combining certain features of the Aethelstan period (note the stocky, stolid-looking figures of the Virgin and Peter) with the style of the St. Dunstan miniature, is on the whole extremely lively, and a sense of excitement and movement pervades the composition. The source of this style is to be sought in the illumination of the Carolingian 'Ada', Metz, and Tours schools. The rounded Caroline minuscule replacing earlier Insular forms in the script of Cotton Vespasian A. VIII comes from the same sources, a development followed by subsequent 'Winchester' manuscripts.

The most magnificently decorated manuscript of the 'Winchester' school is the Benedictional (B.L. Add. 49598, no. 23) made for Ethelwold at Winchester. It was written at his command between 971 and 980 by Godeman, a Winchester monk and Abbot of Thorney from 981. It contains twenty-six full-page miniatures in decorative borders facing twenty text pages in matching frames (a scheme followed in later 'Winchester' manuscripts) and two historiated initials (one without frame), all painted in rich, opaque body-colours and gold, some with backgrounds of highly stylized cloudy skies, most likely inspired by Carolingian manuscripts from Tours or Rheims, where the late antique feature of airy illusionistic backgrounds is already transformed into formalized patterns (fig. 14). The drawing in the 'first', essentially linear, style is rendered more elaborate by sharply incised surface designs and the drapery folds cascading down across the bodies in zigzagging fluttering hemlines characteristic of the later 10th-century Anglo-Saxon figure-style in painting and in outline drawing. Thus the monumental drawing of the Philosophy in Cambridge, Trinity College MS O. 3. 7 (no. 20) of c. 970, from St. Augustine's, Canterbury (ill. 44) compares closely with St. Etheldreda of the Benedictional, f. 90ᵛ. The miniatures of the main text illustrate the Infancy and the Passion of Christ, introducing entirely new subjects into English art, the prototypes of some being traced by Homburger to certain ivory carvings and illumination of the Metz school (figs. 18, 28, 29).[8] The exuberant frame decoration, an elaboration of the foliate border style of the New Minster Charter, consists of rectangular or arched enclosures, filled with panels of continuous leaf patterns and punctuated by median medallions and corner star-like rosettes of curling acanthus-type foliage.

The structural concepts may have been suggested by the Franco-Saxon school (fig. 13) whose influence on Anglo-Saxon illumination is borne out by the forms of ornamental initials in luxury manuscripts. Ivories and manuscripts from St. Gall and Metz were probably the source of the leaf ornament (fig. 17) though nowhere with its three-dimensional quality so strongly emphasized. Whatever may have been the sources of the decorative elements, their treatment and the final combination are an original English achievement, which had widespread repercussions on the Continent for the next two hundred years, and from which new trends were to spring.

A nearly contemporary pontifical, Rouen, Bibl. Mun. MS Y. 7 (no. 24) known as the Benedictional of Archbishop Robert, executed at Winchester possibly for Ethelwold himself, now contains only three miniatures which are almost a replica of those in the Ethelwold manuscript (Frontispiece, ills. 87, 89). The decoration of another Benedictional, Bibl. Nat., lat. 987 (no. 25), consists of the text pages in 'Winchester' frames (ills. 92, 93); its script, closely similar to that of the St. Ethelwold Benedictional, suggests an origin in the same scriptorium.

A psalter probably made at Winchester for Ramsey Abbey between 974 and 986, B.L. Harley 2904 (no. 41), has initials luxuriantly decorated with 'Winchester' leaf motifs and a monumental Crucifixion (ill. 142) drawn in a delicate, quivering line that could only derive from some manuscripts related to the Ebbo Gospels at Epernay (fig. 15). It introduces a new technique of tinted outline drawing executed in brown and red inks, heightened by quick, black strokes, and shaded with colour. It is also iconographically important as the earliest example with a St. John writing and a Virgin weeping into her mantle (recalling the weeping figure of the Dormition miniatures in the two Winchester Benedictionals). The splendid Beatus initial combining the scrolled acanthus decoration with the Franco-Saxon letter structure became the archetype of the 'great B's of the later English psalters (ill. 141). The drawings of two more manuscripts connected with Fleury, an Aratus, B.L. Harley 2506 (no. 42) and St. Gregory's Homilies, Orléans, Bibl. Mun. MS 175 (no. 43), are in the same technique and style and were, most likely, executed by the artist of the Harley Psalter working on the Continent. To these must be added a Gospel book, Boulogne, Bibl. Mun. MS 11 (no. 44), illuminated at St. Bertin by an Anglo-Saxon artist in the time of Abbot Otbert. It contains besides the Evangelists' portraits and ornamented Canon Tables, a series of Christ's ancestors and scenes of His Infancy unparalleled in England. The decoration, however, employing 'Winchester' elements and certain typically Anglo-Saxon iconographic motifs, points to English sources. The figure style recalling Harley 2904 and even more closely Orléans 175 suggests that all these are by one hand. The same artist may have been responsible for the Evangelists' portraits added in England to an unfinished Carolingian manuscript from the region of Arras, known as the Anhalt Gospels, now Pierpont Morgan Library MS 827 (no. 45). This anonymous English illuminator must have been one of the most influential and forward-looking artists of this early period: the elements of his style and painting technique loom large in Anglo-Saxon illumination throughout the 11th century.

The miniatures added to a Boethius, Bibl. Nat. lat. 6401 (no. 32), show that there was another Anglo-Saxon artist working at Fleury in the later 10th century. He introduces a new type of representation of the Trinity with the Holy Lamb and the Dove (cf. Sherborne Pontifical, no. 35) but his style is rather retrospective being related to such early manuscripts of the 'Winchester' school as the King Edgar Charter.

The Sacramentary known as the 'Missal' of Robert of Jumièges, Rouen, Bibl. Mun. MS Y. 6 (no. 72), written between 1016 and 1023, of uncertain origin, is generally dependent on the iconography and decoration of the St. Ethelwold Benedictional but the sketchy liveliness of its figure-drawing reflects the influence of the Utrecht Psalter and shows an affinity with the Harley 2904 style, while the painterly manner recalls Boulogne 11.

One of the most sumptuous Anglo-Saxon Gospels illuminated in the 'Winchester' style is Cambridge, Trinity College MS B. 10. 4 (no. 65), made for use at Canterbury and probably executed there soon after 1000, containing the Evangelists' portraits with ornamental text pages (ills. 212, 214, 219) and preceded by lavishly decorated Eusebian Canons. The 'Winchester' style may have been introduced to Canterbury by Aethelgar, Abbot of New Minster and Archbishop of Canterbury from 989. The evidence for the Canterbury provenance of the Gospels is two-fold: it entered the Trinity College Library with other Canterbury books as a gift of Thomas Nevile, Dean of Canterbury, and it contains initials of the 'clambering' type unknown in Winchester but common in Canterbury manuscripts around 1100. The patterns of the drapery folds are restless and ragged and the leaf ornament shows a tendency towards emaciation which becomes a feature of later Anglo-Saxon illumination. Roundels with bust figures in certain borders of the Trinity manuscript are an innovation occurring also in B.L. Royal 1. D. IX (no. 70), Gospels of the early 11th century assigned to Canterbury (because it contains King Cnut's Charter conferring privileges on Christ Church), with decoration limited to four initial pages in sumptuous 'Winchester' frames (ill. 222). Stylistically related to the latter is the Kederminster Gospels (no. 71) in the British Library (Loan 11), written by the scribe of Rouen Y. 6 and the Trinity Gospels, now containing only two framed *Incipit* pages whose 'Winchester' borders suggest a date in the early 11th century (ill. 223).

The Gospel Book at Copenhagen (Royal Library, G.K.S. 10, 2°, no. 47), begun before 1000 and completed in the early 11th century, has a St. Matthew accompanied by an inspiring figure of an Angel blowing a horn (ill. 154), very similar to the Matthew in the Lindisfarne Gospels. Hitherto attributed to Durham on account of this analogy it is now believed to have originated in Southern England, possibly Winchester. Angels and Evangelists' symbols blowing horns (a feature of the St. John portrait in the Benedictional of St. Ethelwold) are found also in the Gospel Book at Cambridge, Pembroke College MS 301 (no. 73), decorated by at least two artists, the first probably working in the early 11th century, the second towards the middle of the century.

There are no 'Winchester' borders in the Gospel Book, Pierpont Morgan Library MS 869 (no. 56) formerly in the Arenberg Collection in Brussels, usually assigned to *c.* 1000 but possibly somewhat later, and containing a good deal of coloured outline drawing. The iconography and style of the animated figure drawings decorating the Canon Tables show the unmistakable influence of the Utrecht Psalter (see below). Also inspired by a 'Utrecht' illustration and recalling in style the drawings in Bodley 155 (no. 59), is the portrait of St. Matthew (or St. Mark?) added to a Gospel Book, now Besançon, Bibl. Mun. MS 14 (no. 76). In this the Angel stands behind the Evangelist (ill. 242) and the manuscript is otherwise decorated only with initial pages in foliated 'Winchester' frames.

The origin of a splendid manuscript of the early 11th century, B.L. Add. 34890 (no. 68), known as the Grimbald Gospels (from an appended copy of a letter recommending Grimbald to Alfred), presents a particular problem because, although usually attributed to the New Minster, Winchester, on stylistic and iconographical grounds, it is now said to have been written by a Christ Church, Canterbury monk. This manuscript introduces several innovations including the use of blank vellum behind the figures and of silver in the decoration (colour plate, ill. 215); one also finds figural scenes illustrating theological subjects in the roundels and panels set into the borders of the 'St. John' page instead of the usual leaf ornament. This unprecedented decorative scheme remains unique in England and on the Continent. The figure drawing has a new precision, and the draperies are elaborated by rich patterns of parallel, rope-like folds. In type the Evangelists recall those of the York Gospels. The York Evangelists, however, are less stylized and, set in severely functional frames against airy backgrounds, are remarkably classical in spirit; the manuscript was written in Southern England but known to have been at York *c.* 1020–30.

The important fragments in full colour of an Evangeliary at Damme datable to around 1000 (no. 53), recently published by Boutemy and believed by him to be Anglo-Saxon, show a similar restraint in border decoration and an economy in their figure drawing, the latter in

Initial I. London, College of Arms, Arundel 22, f. 84 (Cat. 26)

the 'first' style and close to St. John's College MS 28 in Oxford although in a less polished, more sketchy version.

Meanwhile, towards the end of the 10th century the impressionistic technique of outline drawing was introduced into England by the illustrations of a psalter from Rheims of about 820, known as the Utrecht Psalter (fig. 11). Its classically inspired and dramatic style, producing an illusion of intense activity by the flickering line of the drawing, had a profound effect on the technique, character, and imagery of Anglo-Saxon painting. Three copies were made in the Canterbury scriptoria. The earliest, which concerns us here, the unfinished B.L. Harley 603 (no. 64) in coloured outline of red, green and blue, was begun in the early 11th century, probably for Christ Church. The work of several hands, it extends over many decades and stops in the early 12th century (ills. 200–207, 210; fig. 1). The early drawings follow the style and the iconography of the Utrecht Psalter, those of the second quarter of the 11th century depart from it and are original Anglo-Saxon introductions, while a later group is in the 'revived Utrecht' style.

The influence of the 'Utrecht' style is apparent in the outline drawings illustrating the occupations of the months in the earliest known English 'occupational' calendar prefixed to an early 11th-century hymnal, B.L. Cotton, Julius A. VI (no. 62). Calendar illustrations in the painting technique in B.L. Cotton, Tiberius B.V. (no. 87), probably about 1030, are a duplication of those in Julius A. VI. This manuscript contains an astronomical text and illustrations copied from a Carolingian Aratus (B.L. Harley 647) known to have been in Canterbury in the 10th century; it also contains an illustrated copy of the Marvels of the East, a treatise whose popularity is witnessed by an earlier copy in Anglo-Saxon, B.L. Cotton, Vitellius A. XV, of c. 1000 (no. 52). B.L. Cotton, Vitellius C. III (no. 63), an illustrated *Herbarium* in the vernacular, another example of scientific literature, is probably of the early 11th century and comes from Canterbury.

B.L. Arundel 155 (no. 66), a psalter of 1012–23, probably from Christ Church, Canterbury and close to the Sacramentary of Robert of Jumièges, has decoration in the 'Winchester' manner and illustrations in outline or fully painted. The latter are influenced by the 'Utrecht' style, but modified on the one hand by the large size of the figures, which are drawn in incisive sweeping lines, and on the other hand by the decorative use of colour, including the emphatic shadow outline. Closely allied to Arundel 155 are the so-called Eadui Gospels in Hanover (no. 67), written by Eadui, a Canterbury monk, about 1020–30, who was also credited with writing the Grimbald Gospels and a leaf in the York Gospels.

It has been suggested that the Utrecht Psalter might have been on loan to libraries outside Canterbury, for the impact of its iconography and style was widespread. Though there is no evidence that it was ever in Winchester, its influence is apparent in the coloured and tinted outline drawings of three manuscripts connected with the New Minster: the *Liber Vitae* (B.L. Stowe 944, no. 78) of between 1020–30 and collections of Prayers and Offices written by Abbot Aelfwin (B.L. Cotton, Titus XXVI and XXVII, no. 77) about 1023–35. The unusual representation of the 'Quinity' in the latter and certain iconographic details of the otherwise typically Anglo-Saxon Last Judgment in Stowe 944 (ills. 244, 247, 248) derive from the illustrations of the Utrecht Psalter. The same indebtedness to the latter in style and partly in iconography is evident in the tiny drawings inserted in the text of Bibl. Nat., lat. 8824 (no. 83), a psalter of unknown provenance containing a Latin version alongside the Anglo-Saxon one.

The two Anglo-Saxon styles, the 'first' and the Utrecht, did not long remain unaffected by each other: their fusion is already apparent in some manuscripts of the first half of the 11th century, e.g. the Arundel Psalter. The 'Winchester' type of decoration is still mainly used, but the impressionistic style, adapted to the inherent Anglo-Saxon need for pattern-making, affects the painting technique as well as the outline drawing. Bodleian MS Douce 296 (no. 79), a psalter from Crowland, probably prior to 1036, contains a figure of Christ triumphant, articulated by soft rhythmic brush strokes, an early example of this new painted style (ill. 259). The Evangelist portraits in Bodleian MS Lat. lit. f. 5 (no. 91), a Gospel lectionary known as St. Margaret's Gospels, are painted in the same impressionistic manner but more firmly modelled. The manuscript can be dated to the second quarter or the middle of the 11th century.

The Gospels which belonged to Judith of Flanders, now Pierpont Morgan Library MSS 709 and 708 (nos. 93, 94) and Monte Cassino Abbey MS BB. 437, 439 (no. 95) are closely allied in style to Douce 296 but are in effect more restless and mannered. Morgan 709, probably made at Winchester in the second quarter of the 11th century, contains a remarkable Crucifixion (ill. 289) equal in dramatic power to that of Harley 2904. It was suggested that the donor —a lady kneeling at the foot of the cross—might be Judith herself and that the miniature is an addition datable after 1051, the year of her arrival in England. The other two Gospels, of uncertain provenance, may have come from Thorney Abbey.

The Psalter (Vatican Library MS Reg. lat. 12, no. 84), made possibly at Canterbury in the second quarter of the 11th century for Bury St. Edmunds Abbey, blends the two styles most happily in monumental and dynamic marginal drawings (ills. 263, 264), a method of psalter illustration employed c. 1000 in part of the Otbert Psalter (Boulogne MS 20; fig. 27) at St. Bertin and possibly contributed by an Anglo-Saxon artist. The richly decorated Gospels, B.L. Harley 76 (no. 75), now sadly mutilated, may also have been produced at Canterbury for Bury Abbey in the same period. In contrast to the highly accomplished drawings of the Bury Psalter, the style of Cambridge University Library MS Ff. 1. 23 (no. 80), a psalter believed to have come from Winchcombe Abbey, is provincial and retrospective. In addition to the miniatures and text pages with 'Winchester' type borders, it contains a wealth of ornamental initials with stringy and emaciated leafwork, reminiscent of the Viking Ringerike style. Other initials, constructed solely of human figures, anticipate the initial style of the 12th century.

The mid-century figure-style reaches an extreme form in B.L. Cotton, Tiberius A. III, *Regularis Concordia* (no. 100), and its copy, Durham Cathedral Library B. III. 32, Aelfric's Grammar (no. 101), both from Christ Church, Canterbury. There the style of Arundel 155 has been carried to its limits and all forms become reduced to pattern, enhanced by the emphatic use of coloured shadow outline and by the extremely vigorous, sweeping lines of the drawing (ills. 313–315). No less animated are the two almost frenzied drawings in the Easter Tables of Christ Church, Canterbury (B.L. Cotton, Caligula A. XV, ff. 120–143; no. 106), executed in the impressionistic 'revived' Utrecht style c. 1073 and iconographically dependent on Arundel 155.

The tendency towards pattern-making predominates also in the illustrations of B.L. Cotton, Tiberius C. VI (no. 98), a psalter from Winchester of about 1050. It is the earliest surviving psalter prefixed with a series of preliminary Bible pictures, a decorative scheme which originated in England to become widely popular in the 12th century in this country and later abroad. The decoration, including initial pages in 'Winchester' frames (ill. 297), consists of two painted miniatures and of drawings with coloured shadow outline, which combine highly ornamental qualities with an animated figure style (ills. 302–311). The Crucifixion (f. 12^v) in B.L. Arundel 60 (no. 103), a psalter of about 1060 from New Minster, Winchester, on the other hand, is formalized to an extreme and its heavy outline, uniformly reinforced with colour, has a hard, rope-like quality (ill. 312). The style of another Crucifixion (f. 52) and of the ornamental pages, believed to be post-Conquest additions to this manuscript, is no longer Anglo-Saxon in spirit and belongs to the Romanesque period.[9]

Rheims, Bibl. Mun. MS 9 (no. 105), a Gospel Book from Southern England, has been identified as a gift, c. 1062–6, from Aelfgar, Count of Mercia, to St. Remi of Rheims in memory of his son Burchard. It contains highly patterned Evangelist portraits on plain vellum backgrounds surrounded by late 'Winchester' borders which recall the Grimbald Gospels (no. 68).

Two mid 11th-century manuscripts, Cambridge, Pembroke College 302 (no. 96), a Gospel lectionary attributed to Hereford, and closely related to B.L. Cotton, Caligula A. XIV (no. 97), a troper, show German or Flemish influences—a new element at work in English painting. The harshly outlined and modelled figures with the sharply incised drapery folds, producing a corrugated effect as yet unknown in English illumination, herald the transition from the Anglo-Saxon to the Romanesque style (ills. 292–295).

To sum up, Anglo-Saxon illumination is remarkable for the richness of its imagery, due on the one hand to the successive influences of Carolingian art with its Mediterranean heritage and, on the other, to the striking ability of English artists not only to assimilate but, above all, to transform those influences into their own pictorial idiom. Thus, there was no question of slavish copying but a notable diversity and independence of interpretation, with a continuous quest for ever new iconographic variants, for originality in the use of colour, and for stylistic modifications. This can no doubt be explained by the fact that the artists, eagerly receptive to classically inspired continental illusionism, were, at the same time, drawing on their own Insular tradition dominated by abstract decorative tendencies. 'The English love', to quote Wormald, 'of reducing everything into a pattern', a pattern of line as well as of colour, kept on asserting itself again and again.

The same tendencies thus predominated in the realm of colour, which was used freely for decorative effect rather than for the sake of naturalistic appearance. The ready adoption of the Late Antique device of coloured shadow outline, and the expressionistic manner in which colour was applied in whorls and splashes to heighten the dramatic context of illustration, went hand-in-hand with an astonishing variety of hue, enriched by over-painting, coloured line shading and a lavish, abstract use of gold and silver. The tonality evolved from somewhat heavy, sombre shades to soft, pale colours lightened by an admixture of white, changing later to a clearer, more vivid palette. Coloured outline technique, a glorious feature of Anglo-Saxon drawing, was a striking innovation, due perhaps to the inherent need for a decorative abstract treatment of the entire page, script as well as drawing, which a monochrome narrative illustration could hardly satisfy.

The search for independence and freedom is further manifested by a number of new iconographic formulas: the Anglo-Saxon portrayal of the Ascension, the Nativity, the Washing of the Feet, and such details as the 'horned' Moses, and the jaw-bone used by Cain as a weapon, etc. (figs. 34–46). In strong contrast to contemporary continental practice, there was also, as Wormald has observed, a very special Anglo-Saxon interest in the depiction of the Trinity, represented in several different ways.

Finally, the introduction of a pictorial cycle from the lives of David and of Christ as a preface to the Psalter text, proved to be of capital importance for the development of European painting. This century-and-a-half of Anglo-Saxon illumination was a great and fruitful period in the history of English art.

After a formative period of assimilation of foreign styles, Anglo-Saxon art began in its turn from the end of the 10th century to influence continental painting. The impact was particularly strong in the Franco-Flemish region where, at St. Bertin, Abbot Otbert not only employed Anglo-Saxon artists whom he copied but himself worked in the English 'first' style.

Anglo-Saxon influences can be detected in the decoration and the figure style of the St. Vaast Bible (Arras, MS 559, fig. 22) and related Arras manuscripts. Towards the end of the 11th century the 'Winchester' decorative style, the source of border ornament of a number of manuscripts from northern and western France,[10] was introduced into the scriptorium of Weingarten Abbey (fig. 49) by the Gospels which were gifts of Judith of Flanders. With the mid 12th-century Evangelist portraits of the Cysoing Gospels at Lille, it had its final flowering.

Anglo-Saxon ornament played a prominent role in the development of Scandinavian styles, and the 'elbowed' interlace and the 'Winchester' acanthus became features of those Scandina-

Fig. 26. Marginal Illustration, Ps. 21.
Bury Psalter, second quarter of 11th century.
Rome, Vatican, Bibl. Apostolica, Reg. lat. 12, f. 36
(Cat. 84)

Fig. 27. Marginal Illustration, Ps. 21.
Otbert Psalter, St. Bertin, 990–1012 (?).
Boulogne, Bibl. Mun. 20, f. 28ᵛ

Figs. 28–29. Nativity: Initial, Drogo Sacramentary, Metz, c. 842,
Paris, Bibl. Nat., lat. 9428, f. 24ᵛ; Ivory Book-cover, Metz, c. 850,
Frankfurt, Stadtbibliothek

Fig. 30. St. Matthew. Late 9th-early 10th century,
made for Lobbes, nr. Liège. London, B.L., Cotton,
Tiberius A. II, f. 24ᵛ

Fig. 31. Trinity. Rome, Vatican,
Bibl. Apostolica, Pal. lat. 834, f. 28

Fig. 32. Rabanus Maurus presenting his Book to
Pope Gregory. 9th century. Amiens,
Bibl. Mun. 223, f. 2ᵛ

Fig. 33. Rabanus Maurus presenting his Book to
Pope Gregory. Fulda, 9th century. Vienna,
Nationalbibliothek, cod. 652 (theo. 39), f. 2ᵛ

Fig. 34. 'Horned Moses'. London, B.L.,
Cotton, Claudius B. IV, f. 139ᵛ (Cat. 86)

Fig. 35. 'Horned Moses'. Bury St. Edmunds, c. 1135.
Cambridge, Corpus Christi College 2, f. 94

Fig. 36. 'Horned Moses'. By Honoré. Paris, end of 13th century.
London, B.L., Add. 54180, f. 5ᵛ

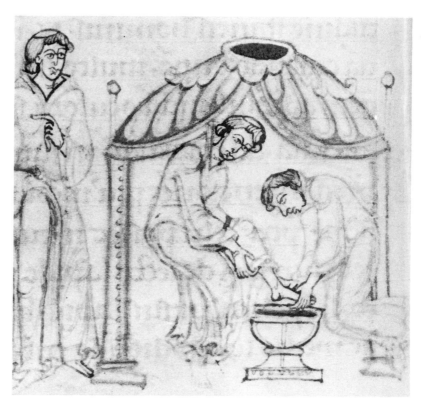

Fig. 37. The Washing of the Feet. Winchester, c. 1150.
London, B.L., Cotton, Tiberius C. VI, f. 11ᵛ (Cat. 98)

Fig. 38. St. Cuthbert washing the Feet of a Monk. Durham, c. 1120.
Oxford, University College 165, p. 58

Figs. 39–40. Ascension: Ingeborg Psalter, early 13th century,
Chantilly, Musée Condé 1695, f. 31; Enamel Plaque from an altar (?),
Mosan, c. 1160, Goluchow Castle (Poland)

Figs. 41–43. Ascension: Border detail, St. Bertin, c. 1000,
New York, Pierpont Morgan Lib. 333, f. 85; Christ ascending:
St. John's page (upper half), Bernward Gospels, early 11th century,
Hildesheim, MS 18, f. 175ᵛ; Breviary of Jean sans Peur, 1413–17.
London, B.L., Harley 2897, f. 199ᵛ

Figs. 44–46. Nativity: Ivory Panel, Anglo-Saxon, early 11th century, Liverpool, Merseyside County Museums;
Detail of Miniature, Winchester, c. 1150, London, B.L., Cotton, Nero C. IV, f. 10; Cysoing Gospels, c. 1150, Lille, Bibl. Mun. 479, f. 14

Fig. 47. St. Mark. Northern France or Flanders, late 11th century. Stuttgart, Landesbibliothek, Cod. Bibl. 4°7, f. 27ᵛ

Fig. 48. St. Matthew. Préaux, late 11th century. London, B.L., Add. 11850, f. 17ᵛ

Fig. 49. Evangelists. 12th century. Fulda, Landesbibliothek, hs. Aa 6, f. 93ᵛ

Fig. 50. St. Mark. Jumièges Gospels, late 11th century. London, B.L., Add. 17739, f. 69

vian monuments datable to the late 10th and early 11th century. This derivation calls in doubt the alleged relevance of such monuments as a basis for dating certain English manuscripts.[11]

Norman illumination was especially affected by the Anglo-Saxon artistic tradition and examples such as the Mont St. Michel Sacramentary[12] (fig. 23) and the Gospels from Préaux and Jumièges[13] show the extent of that indebtedness (figs. 48, 50). Thus Anglo-Saxon influences, absorbed into Norman art throughout the earlier 11th century, return in the wake of the Conquest to shape the English Romanesque.

Figs. 51–55. Initials and Ornamental Border.
Warsaw, Biblioteka Narodowa I. 3311, f. 28, f. 84,
f. 2, f. 1, f. 11 (Cat. 92)

NOTES

1. See R. Freyhan, 'The place of the stole and maniples in Anglo-Saxon Art of the tenth century', *The Relics of St. Cuthbert*, ed. C. F. Battiscombe, 1956, 409–32.

2. Commissioned by Charles the Bald, Rheims(?), c. 870; P. Durieu, 'Ingobert, un grand calligraphe du IXe siècle', *Mélanges offerts à Emile Chatelain*, Paris 1910, 1 ff.; A. M. Friend, 'The Carolingian Art in the Abbey of St. Denis', *Art Studies*, I (1923), 132 ff.; *id.*, 'Two manuscripts of the school of St. Denis', *Speculum*, I, 1926, 59 ff., E. H. Kantorowicz, 'The Carolingian King in the Bible of San Paolo fuori le Mura', *Late Classical and Mediaeval Studies in honor of A. M. Friend, Jun.*, Princeton 1955, 287 ff.; H. Schade, 'Studien zu der karolingischen Bilderbibel aus St. Paul vor der mauern in Rom', *Wallraf-Richartz-Jb.*, XXI, 1959, 99 ff.; XXII, 1960, 13 ff.

3. 'The Viking Taste in Pre-Conquest England', *Antiquity*, XV, 1941, 125.

4. Wormald, *Initials*, 119; in a number of books both types are used side by side, there are also initials of a mixed type.

5. The iconography probably derives from Carolingian sources, cf. Rome, Vat. Pal. lat. 834, probably Lorsch, 9th century, A. Goldschmidt, *German Illumination*, Vol. I. *The Carolingian period*, 2 vols., Florence and Paris 1928.

6. Glastonbury Library founded by St. Dunstan, devastated by the great fire in 1184 but still one of the richest when inspected by Leland in the 16th century, survived in a most fragmentary state, N. R. Ker, *Medieval Libraries of Great Britain* (Royal Historical Society, Guides and Handbooks no. 5, 2nd edn., 1964), 90.

7. Perhaps inspired by a Carolingian model related to Vat. Libr. Pal. lat. 834 (see n. 6), where the two first Persons of the Trinity are in brown outline and the third in blue.

8. The cycle of the Benedictional pictures corresponds largely to that in the initial illustrations of the Sacramentary of Drogo, Bibl. Nat., lat. 9428, Metz, c. 842.

9. The post-Conquest additions to B.L. Arundel 60 are catalogued as no. 1 in Volume III of this Survey, C. M. Kauffmann, *Romanesque Manuscripts 1066–1190*.

10. e.g. Stuttgart, Landesbibliothek, Cod. Bibl. 407, North French or Flemish Gospels, late 11th century, containing remarkable Evangelists' portraits in 'Winchester' frames, fig. 47.

11. For a thorough study of the relationship between Anglo-Saxon illumination and Scandinavian, particularly Ringerike, styles see W. Holmquist, 'Viking art in the eleventh century', *Acta Archaeologica*, XXII, 1951, 1–56; also T. D. Kendrick, 'The Viking taste in pre-Conquest England', *Antiquity*, XV, 1941, 125 ff.; *id.*, *Late Saxon*, particularly, pp. 98 ff.

12. New York, Pierpont Morgan Library MS 641; cf. Alexander, *Norman Illumination*, 127–72, App. VI, pls. 36, 38.

13. British Library MS Add. 11850 and MS Add. 17739, respectively.

Fig. 56. St. Pachomius receiving the Easter Tables.
London, B.L., Arundel 155, f. 9ᵛ (Cat. 66)

GLOSSARY

Benedictional

A liturgical service book containing episcopal benedictions for the great feasts of the Church year.

Calendar

Placed at the beginning of liturgical manuscripts to record, month by month, the feasts and saints' days celebrated locally.

Canon tables

A concordance table of reference to parallel passages occurring in two or more of the four Gospels compiled by Eusebius in the fourth century and usually arranged in columns under arches.

Colophon

Passage appearing at the end of a manuscript recording information comparable to that contained on the title-page of a book.

Easter or Paschal Tables

Charts for the astronomical computations of the date of Easter.

Evangelist Symbols

The four winged creatures derived from Ezekiel's vision (Ezek. I, 5–14; Rev. IV, 6–8) representing the four Evangelists: the Angel (St. Matthew); the Lion (St. Mark); the Calf (St. Luke); the Eagle (St. John).

Gloss

Notes in the margin or between the lines of a book containing comments, interpretations, or explanations of the passages of the text.

Gospel Lectionary

A selection of passages from the Gospels, arranged in order of the liturgical year, to be sung at Mass.

Historiated Initial

Initial letter enclosing a picture which illustrates or refers to the text it introduces.

Homiliary

A collection of homilies or sermons to be used in Church services.

Inhabited Initial

Initial letter enclosing birds, animals, or figures unrelated to the accompanying text.

KL Monograms

A combination of the letters K and L from the Latin *Kalendae*, which stand at the beginning of each month in an ecclesiastical calendar.

Litany

A form of supplicatory prayer consisting of invocations or series of invocations and responses.

Mandorla

An almond-shaped line or series of lines surrounding the body of a person endowed with divine light, usually reserved for Christ or the Virgin.

Missal

The celebrant's book which contains all the recited and chanted texts of the Mass. It gradually replaced the Sacramentary in the eleventh and twelfth centuries.

Pontifical

A book providing for services proper to the Pope and bishops, such as ordinations of the clergy, dedications of churches and altars, blessings of abbots, etc.

Psalter

A service book containing the Psalms and a selection of prayers. Common in the Middle Ages both because Benedictine monks had to sing all Psalms each week and because it was used for private devotion. The present catalogue uses the Vulgate numeration of the Psalms.

Sacramentary

A liturgical service book containing the rites for Mass and the administering of the sacraments; it is the predecessor of the much more complete missal.

Troper

A liturgical service book containing musical interpolations or tropes.

ABBREVIATIONS

Alexander, *Norman Illumination*	J. J. G. Alexander, *Norman Illumination at Mont St. Michel 966–1100*, Oxford, 1970
Anglo-Saxon Illumination	*Anglo-Saxon Illumination in Oxford Libraries* (Bodleian Library Picture Book Special Series no. 1), introductory note by J. J. G. Alexander, Oxford, 1970
Bishop, *Codex Leidensis*	T. A. M. Bishop, *Codex Leidensis Scaligeranus 69* (Umbrae Codicum Occidentalium, X), 1966
Bishop, *English Caroline*	T. A. M. Bishop, *English Caroline Minuscule*, Oxford, 1971
Bishop, *Notes*, I, II, III, IV, V, VI, VII	T. A. M. Bishop, 'Notes on Cambridge Manuscripts. Part I', *Transactions of the Cambridge Bibliographical Society*, I. 5 (1953), 432–41; 'Part II', ib. II. 2 (1955), 185–91; 'Part III', ib. II, 2 (1955), 191–9; 'Part IV', ib. II. 4 (1957), 332–6; 'Part V', ib. III. 1 (1960), 93–5; 'Part VI', ib., III. 5 (1963), 412–13; 'Part VII', ib., 413–23
B.L.R.	*Bodleian Library Record*, 1939–
Dodwell, *Canterbury School*	C. R. Dodwell, *The Canterbury School of Illumination 1066–1200*, Cambridge 1954
Dodwell, *Techniques*	C. R. Dodwell, 'Techniques of manuscript painting in Anglo-Saxon manuscripts', *Settimane di studio del Centro italiano di studi sull'alto medioevo*, XVIII, Spoleto, 1971
(E.E. MSS in facs.)	(Early English manuscripts in facsimile), Copenhagen
E.E.T.S., or ser.	*Early English Text Society*, original series
Freyhan	R. Freyhan, 'The place of the stole and maniples in Anglo-Saxon Art of the tenth century', *The Relics of St. Cuthbert* ed. C. F. Battiscombe, 1956
Gneuss	H. Gneuss, *Hymnar und Hymnen im englischen Mittelalter*, Tübingen, 1968
Goldschmidt, I, II	A. Goldschmidt, *Die Elfenbeinskulpturen aus der Zeit der karolingischen und sächsischen Kaiser*, 2 vols. Berlin, 1914–18
H.B.S.	*Henry Bradshaw Society.*
Holmquist, *Viking Art*	W. Holmquist, 'Viking art in the eleventh century', *Acta Archaeologica*, XXII, 1951
Homburger	O. Homburger, *Die Anfänge der Malschule von Winchester im X. Jahrhundert*. Studien über Christliche Denkmäler, Leipzig, 1912
James, *Ancient Libraries*	M. James, *The Ancient Libraries of Canterbury and Dover*, Cambridge, 1903
J.W.C.I.	*Journal of the Warburg and Courtauld Institutes*
Kendrick, *Late Saxon*	T. D. Kendrick, *Late Saxon and Viking Art*, London, 1949
Ker, *Catalogue*	N. R. Ker, *Catalogue of Manuscripts containing Anglo-Saxon*, Oxford, 1957

Millar, I	E. G. Millar, *English Illuminated Manuscripts from the Xth to the XIIIth Century*, Paris and Brussels, 1926
New Pal. Soc., I and II	*New Paleographical Society. Facsimiles of Ancient Manuscripts, etc.*, 1st and 2nd series, London, 1903–30
Nordenfalk, *Early Medieval*	A. Grabar and C. Nordenfalk, *Early Medieval Painting from the fourth to the eleventh century*, Lausanne, 1957
Pal. Soc., I and II	*Paleographical Society. Facsimiles of Manuscripts and Inscriptions*, 1st and 2nd series, London 1874–94
Pächt and Alexander	O. Pächt and J. J. G. Alexander, *Illuminated manuscripts in the Bodleian Library, Oxford*, III, *British, Irish and Icelandic schools*, Oxford, 1973
Rickert, *Miniatura*	M. Rickert, *La Miniatura Inglese. I. Dalle origine alla fine del seculo XII*, Milan, 1959
Rickert, *Painting in Britain*	M. Rickert, *Painting in Britain, The Middle Ages*. (Pelican History of Art), 2nd edition, 1965
Robb, *Illuminated Manuscript*	D. M. Robb, *The Art of the Illuminated Manuscript*, South Brunswick and New York, 1973
Roosen-Runge	H. Roosen-Runge, *Farbgebung und Technik frühmittalterlicher Buchmalerei*, 1967
St. Albans Psalter	*The St. Albans Psalter, 1. The full-page miniatures*, by O. Pächt. *2. The initials*, by C. R. Dodwell. *3. Preface and description of the manuscript*, by F. Wormald, London, 1960
Saunders, *English Illumination*	O. E. Saunders, *English Illumination*, Florence and Paris, 1928
S.C.	*Summary catalogue of Western Manuscripts in the Bodleian Library*, Oxford, 7 vols., 1895–1953
S.S.	*Surtees Society*, 1835–
Swarzenski, *Monuments*	H. Swarzenski, *Monuments of Romanesque Art. The art of Church Treasures in North-Western Europe*, 2nd edition, London, 1967
Talbot Rice, *English Art*	D. Talbot Rice, *English Art 871–1100* (Oxford History of English Art, II), Oxford, 1952
Warner and Gilson	G. F. Warner, J. P. Gilson, *Catalogue of Western Manuscripts in the Old Royal and King's Collections*, 4 vols., London British Museum, 1921
Westwood, *Facsimiles*	J. Westwood, *Facsimiles of the Miniatures and Ornaments of Anglo-Saxon and Irish Manuscripts*, London, 1868
Wormald, *Angleterre*	L. Grodecki, F. Mütherich, J. Taralon, F. Wormald, in *Le Siècle de l'An Mil*, eds. A. Malraux, A. Parrot, Paris, 1973, 227–254
Wormald, *English Drawings*	F. Wormald, *English Drawings of the tenth and eleventh centuries*, London, 1952
Wormald, *Initials*	F. Wormald, 'Decorated Initials in English MSS from A.D. 900 to 1100', *Archaeologia*, XCI, 1945, 107–35
Wormald, *Style and Design*	F. Wormald, 'Style and design', in *The Bayeux Tapestry*, ed. Sir Frank Stenton, London, 1965
Wormald, *Winchester School*	F. Wormald, 'The "Winchester School" before St. Aethelwold', *England before the Conquest*, eds. P. Clemoes and K. Hughes, 1971

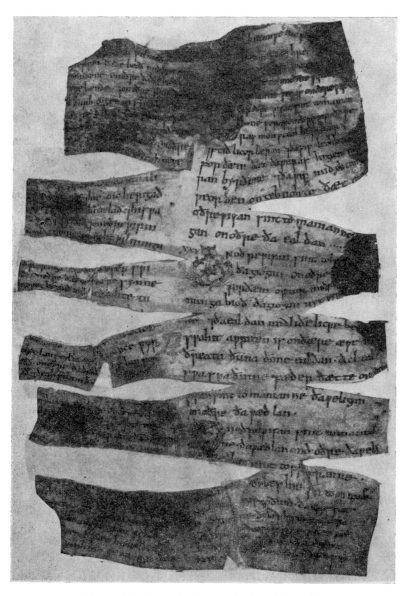

Fig. 57. Page from St. Gregory's *Cura Pastoralis*.
London, B.L., Cotton, Otho B. II, f. 22ᵛ (Cat. 46)

CATALOGUE

1. Oxford, Bodleian Library MS Hatton 20 (S.C. 4113)

Gregory the Great, Pastoral Care
King Alfred's West Saxon version
270 × 220 mm.
c. 890–7

Ills. 2–4

This copy of Alfred's translation, executed under his supervision, was presented to Werferth, Bishop of Worcester, and can be dated *c.* 890–7 (Ker, *Catalogue*, p. 385). Numerous small initials in black outline, their interior space coloured red, olive green, or yellow, are ornamented with summary leafwork, bird and animal heads, and interlace knotwork in the 8th- and 9th-century Southern English initial style (cf. Vat. Barb. lat. 570, Barberini Gospels; Bodl. Lib. Auct. F. 4. 32, ff. 37–47; etc.). Capital letters in the text are parti-coloured in red, green, or yellow; titles to chapters are in red.

PROVENANCE: Annotated at Worcester in the 10th century (f. 98ᵛ) and again possibly by Archbishop Wulfstan (997–1023), in the early 11th century (mainly folios 1 and 1ᵛ), it contains a Latin gloss added by the Worcester 'tremulous hand' in the 13th century. The manuscript seems to have remained *in situ* until 1643. It came into the possession of Christopher, first Baron Hatton, in 1644 and was acquired by the Bodleian Library with Hatton's Collection in 1671.

LITERATURE: H. Sweet, 'King Alfred's West Saxon version of Gregory's Pastoral Care', *E.E.T.S.*, or. ser. XLV, L, 1871; *New Pal. Soc.*, I, pls. 6–8; W. Keller, *Angelsächsische Paläographie*, I, 1906, 23, 34, 36, 41, 50, 51, II, pl. 3; G. F. Warner and H. A. Wilson, *The Benedictional of St. Aethelwold*, 1910, XXXI-XXXII; Millar, I, 2 n. 2; Saunders, *English Illumination*, 15; T. D. Kendrick, *Anglo-Saxon Art to A.D. 900*, 1938, 215, pl. CI; N. R. Ker, 'The provenance of the oldest MS. of the Rule of St. Benedict', *B.L.R.*, II, 1941, 28–9; *Catalogus Manuscriptorum Bibliotecae Wigornensis, 1622–23, by Patrick Young*, eds. I. Atkins and N. R. Ker, 1944, 7, 10, 17; Wormald, *Initials*, 113, 122, 134; Talbot Rice, *English Art*, 176, pl. 42a; N. Denholm-Young, *Handwriting in England and Wales*, 1954, 15 n. 6, pl. 4; N. R. Ker, *The Pastoral Care* (E.E.MSS in facs., VI), 1956; *id.*, *Catalogue*, no. 324; Nordenfalk, *Early Medieval*, 177; Rickert, *Painting in Britain*, 29; T. J. Brown, *The Durham Ritual* (E.E.MSS in facs., XVI), 1969, 38–9; *Anglo-Saxon*

Illumination, pl. 1a, b; Pächt and Alexander, no. 18, pl. 1; Wormald, *Angleterre*, 229, ill. 220; R. Deshman, 'Anglo-Saxon Art After Alfred', *Art Bulletin*, LVI, 1974, 193, fig. 39.

2. London, British Library MS Royal 5. F. III

Aldhelm, De virginitate
235 × 163 mm.
c. 900. (?) Mercia

Ills. 5, 6, 9

Small initials in brown outline showing an elaboration in detail and a tendency towards 'naturalistic' representation (Wormald, *Initials*, 113). They contain a profusion of leaf ornament, dog's head terminals, dragons with foliate tails, birds and lions inhabiting the letters, and also a remarkable spread-eagle dragon initial T (f. 32ᵛ). The characteristic leafy frills on the letter-stems are probably inspired, according to Wormald, by Carolingian initial decoration, perhaps from the Tours or Metz schools. Headings are in red. Though the origin is uncertain, Mercia is suggested by the type of script.

PROVENANCE: At Worcester Cathedral Priory in the Middle Ages. Entered as no. 253 in Patrick Young's Catalogue of Worcester manuscripts of 1622. Belonged to J. Theyer (d. 1673), whose name is inscribed in several places in the margins; his collection, bought by Charles II in 1678, passed with the Royal Library to the British Museum in 1753.

LITERATURE: Warner and Gilson, I, 120; IV, pl. 44; *Catalogus Manuscriptorum Bibliotecae Wigornensis, 1622–23, by Patrick Young*, eds. I. Atkins and N. R. Ker, 1944, 18, 51, 67, no. 253; Wormald, *Initials*, 113 n. 2, 114 n. 1, 118, pl. IIIc; Kendrick, *Late Saxon*, 28, fig. 2a, b; Talbot Rice, *English Art*, 177; Ker, *Catalogue*, no. 253; Rickert, *Painting in Britain*, 220 n. 4; T. J. Brown, *The Durham Ritual* (E.E.MSS in facs., XVI), 1969, 38–9.

3. Durham Cathedral Library MS A. IV. 19 (ff. 1-61)

Collectar (Durham Ritual)
247 × 165 mm.
Early 10th century, additions 970 to 11th century
Southern England, Chester le Street

Ills. 7, 8, 10

Initials of the original manuscript (ff. 1–61), in brown outline, Wormald Type I and II, contain a diversity of motifs mostly occurring in earlier insular illumination (cf. also nos. 1 and 2 above) but here presented in a more robust, 'naturalistic' manner. These include: human, animal, and bird heads, complete creatures, mask heads, and interlace knotwork, fruit and foliage terminals. Two novel elements are the 'long and short' leaf pattern and the hollow leafy calices, both derived from Carolingian acanthus ornament and paralleled on the vestments of St. Cuthbert from Winchester c. 916; remarkable drawings of a mask, dragons, lions, and birds mark the run-overs in the lower margins (ff. 1, 4, 9ᵛ, 15ᵛ, 45, 47ᵛ, 57); drawings of figures decorate a patch in the parchment (ff. 59, 59ᵛ). Some initials were apparently drawn before the text was written; a few at the beginning are partly painted in opaque red or yellow. Rubrics are in red.

PROVENANCE: All initials and drawings in the same brown ink as that of the text (ff. 1–61), were executed by the original scribe in Southern England early in the 10th century. Additions of various dates were made at Chester le Street in the community of St. Cuthbert by a number of scribes, one of whom was Aldred, the glossator of B.L. Cotton, Nero D. IV (Lindisfarne Gospels) and Bodleian Library MS Bodley 819. He supplied initials in red ink in the original part of the manuscript, adding Anglo-Saxon glosses as well as signing the Latin collects for St. Cuthbert (f. 84), with his name, the place, and date: 10 August 970. The manuscript is described in the Durham Cathedral Catalogue by Thomas Rud, 1825, p. 71.

LITERATURE: *Pal. Soc.*, I, pls. 240–1; V. Lindelöf, 'Rituale ecclesiae Dunelmensis', Introduction by A. C. Thompson, *S.S.*, CXL, 1927. pls. I-III; Millar, I, 14 n. 2; E. A. Lowe, *Codices Latini Antiquiores*, 1935, no. 151; R. A. B. Mynors, *Durham Cathedral Manuscripts to the End of the Twelfth Century*, 1939, 25, no. 14, pls. 12, 13; N. R. Ker, 'Aldred the scribe', *Essays and Studies by Members of the English Association*, XXVIII, 1943, 7–12; Wormald, *Initials*, 114–17, 118, pl. IIc; Kendrick, *Late Saxon*, 28, fig. 2 c, d, e, h; Talbot Rice, *English Art*, 177; Freyhan, 424–5, pl. XXXVI, fig. 8; Ker, *Catalogue*, no. 106; *Codex Lindisfarnensis*, ed. T. D. Kendrick, Olten and Lausanne 1960, II, Bk. II, 25–33, pls. 57–60; Rickert, *Painting in Britain*, 30, 33, 220 n. 4; Gneuss, 50, 101–3, 122; T. J. Brown, *The Durham Ritual* (E.E.MSS in facs., XVI), 1969.

4. London, British Library MS Royal 7. D. XXIV

Aldhelm, De virginitate, Epistola Aldhelmi
170 × 120 mm.
Early 10th century to late 10th century
(?) Winchester   *Ills. 11–14, 27*

The initials, numerous and small, are made up of thick, worm-like, ribbon interlace that sometimes ties itself into knots and often terminates in heavy foliage and beasts' heads (one in three-quarter view, f. 86). Two initials contain complete creatures (ff. 104ᵛ, 162ᵛ). In style and colouring of reddish-brown, slate blue, and ochre, the initials closely resemble the small initials of Cambridge, Corpus Christi College MS 183 (no. 6) and were probably executed by the same artist. An unfinished, full-page miniature (f. 85ᵛ) showing Aldhelm (?) seated by a draped desk and writing (cf. no. 57, Bodl. Lib. MS Bodley 577, f. 1), was probably modelled on an Evangelist portrait in type resembling the Evangelists in Rheims MS 9 (no. 105); the miniature is lightly coloured and was partly redrawn in ink in firm outline in the late 10th century.

PROVENANCE: The origin of this manuscript is uncertain. Written in parts by the scribe of no. 6 (Corpus Christi College MS 183; cf. Bishop, 1964–8), probably in the same scriptorium, possibly at Winchester, an attribution corroborated by stylistic connections between the two manuscripts. Belonged to John, Lord Lumley, whose collection passed into the Royal Library after his death in 1609.

LITERATURE: Warner and Gilson, I, 192; IV, pl. 54a; Wormald, *Initials*, 115; Kendrick, *Late Saxon*, 31, pl. XXVIII, 5; Talbot Rice, *English Art*, 178; Wormald, *English Drawings*, 71, no. 38; Ker, *Catalogue*, no. 259; T. A. M. Bishop, 'An early example of the square minuscule', *Transactions of the Cambridge Bibliographical Society*, 1964–8, 247 n. 3.

5. London, British Library MS Cotton, Galba A. XVIII & Oxford, Bodleian Library MS Rawl. B. 484, f. 85

Psalter (Aethelstan Psalter)
128 × 88 mm.
Second quarter of 10th century (before 939)
Winchester, Old Minster

Ills. 15–17, 30–33

English additions to a 9th-century Psalter probably made in the region of Liège consist of a metrical calendar (ff. 3–14ᵛ), computus matter (ff. 15–19), prayers and a litany in Greek (ff. 178–200), and four miniatures probably executed by more than one hand. The miniatures include Christ in Majesty surrounded by implements of His Passion (the sponge, the spear, the cross) and choirs of angels and prophets (f. 2ᵛ); Christ enthroned with choirs of martyrs, confessors, and virgins (f. 21); the Ascension (f. 120ᵛ), which precedes Psalm 101; and the Nativity, originally prefacing Psalm 1 (as shown by the offprint of the Beatus initial on the top of the page), now on a detached leaf in Oxford. The choirs (ff. 2ᵛ, 21) are labelled with invocations from the litany (*omnis chorus angelorum*, etc.) suggesting prayers for intercession as a likely source of the iconography, while the inclusion of the emblems of Christ's Passion (f. 2ᵛ) is perhaps connected with the gift of a priceless relic, Longinus' lance, to Aethelstan from Hugh, Duke of the Franks, in 926 (cf. no. 23, Benedictional of St. Ethelwold, f. 9ᵛ, where this rare feature reappears). The Ascension with Christ frontally enthroned in a mandorla held by the angels (f. 120ᵛ) as well as the Nativity with the bathing of the Child indicate that early 6th- or 7th-century East Mediterranean models may have been available. The representation of Christ in Majesty (f. 21), with the wound in His side uncovered, is a remarkable anticipation of iconographic developments of *c.* 1100. Two miniatures are within plain rectangular enclosures, the other two (ff. 2ᵛ, 21) in frames with ornamental bosses at the angles, in which Insular decorative motifs are combined with fleshy acanthus foliage of Carolingian inspiration foreshadowing the future 'Winchester' style (cf. also f. 9ᵛ). The spindly plant motifs (f. 120ᵛ), already seen in the Barberini Gospels, recur as characteristic features in later Winchester manuscripts. The use made of inscriptions identifying scenes and figures in the pictures is to be noted (cf. St. Cuthbert vestments, fig. 3).

Calendar decoration consists of roundels with signs of the Zodiac and, at the foot of each page on the verso, of bust or full-length figures of saints closely reminiscent of the prophets on the St. Cuthbert vestments. KL monograms, made up of heavy interlace ribbon terminating in beasts' heads with scrolling crests and long tongues (a profiled human head occurs, f. 5), are in the style of 9th-century southern English initials.

The figure style, related to a group of manuscripts of the first quarter of the 10th century (cf. nos. 6, Corpus Christi College 183; 7, Junius Psalter), is a continuation of a predominantly local English style designated by Wormald (1971) as 'early Winchester', which may have become established in the course of the 9th century (cf. fragment of wallpainting discovered in the foundations of New Minster, Winchester). The iconography of the miniatures, inspired by early Mediterranean models, reveals the sources of this style, while the decoration bears evidence of an increasing Carolingian influence. The colours, which are soft but, with the exception of blue, rather dull and heavy, include brown to pinkish-orange, shades of opaque green, yellow, ochre, and blue-black in the background (f. 21).

This Psalter, one of a number of manuscripts of foreign origin which Aethelstan (924–39) gave to various churches, was probably presented by the King to the Old Minster. English additions were no doubt executed at this time and probably at Winchester, an attribution supported by the composition of the calendar which contains obits of King Alfred (26 October) and his consort Ealswith (3 December) in the original hand and clearly derives from a model executed in the West Saxon court (E. Bishop, *Lit. Hist.*; cf. also no. 7, Junius Psalter).

PROVENANCE: Aethelstan's ownership of the Psalter is confirmed by a note (f. 1) of Thomas Dackombe, a Winchester priest, 1542, while its early presence at Winchester is indicated by a verse no longer existing in the manuscript but recorded in *Catalogus Bibl. Cottonianae*, 1696. It tells us of a crucifix gift by Stigand, Bishop of Winchester (1043–52), to a church, in fact Winchester Cathedral, an occasion which was commemorated in the Winchester annals of 1072. In the possession of Sir Robert Cotton, 1621. His library, presented to the nation by his grandson, Sir John Cotton, in 1700, was incorporated into the British Museum in 1753. The Bodleian leaf which belonged to Sir James Ware, 1594–1666, was bequeathed by Richard Rawlinson in 1755.

LITERATURE: R. F. Hampson, *Medii Aevi Kalendarium*, 1841, I, 393–420, frontispiece; J. O. Westwood, *Paleographia Sacra*, 1843–5, no. 22; *id.*, *Facsimiles*, 96, pl. 32; E. M. Thompson, *Catalogue of Ancient Manuscripts in the British Museum*, 1884, 12–13, pl. 28; F. A. Gasquet and E. Bishop, *The Bosworth Psalter*, 1908, 51 ff., 73 n. 1, 148, 153, 176; G. F. Warner and H. A. Wilson, *The Benedictional of St. Aethelwold*, 1910, XV, XXXII; J. A. Herbert, *Illuminated Manuscripts*, 1911, 122–3; *New Pal. Soc.*, II, pl. 62; Homburger, 6, 13 n. 3, 14, 20 n. 4, 21 n. 3, 45 n. 1; E. Bishop, *Liturgica Historica*, 1918, 141 n. 2, 254–5; Millar, I, 2–3, 14 n. 2, no. 1, pl. 2; Saunders, *English Illumination*, 16, pl. 17a; A. Boeckler, *Abendländische Miniaturen*, 1930, 54; Wormald, *Initials*, 115, 118 n. 1; Kendrick, *Late Saxon*, 3, 31, fig. 2 f, g; Talbot Rice, *English Art*, 35, 178, 182; Freyhan, 424; Dodwell, *Canterbury School*, 63, pl. 36c; Nordenfalk, *Early Medieval*, 178; F. Wormald, *The Benedictional of St. Ethelwold*, 1959, 12; D. Tselos, 'English manuscript illustrations and the Utrecht Psalter', *Art Bulletin*, XLI, 1959, 142; A. Watson, 'A 16th-century collector, Thomas Dackombe, *c.* 1496–1572', *The Library*, 5th ser. 18, 1963, 212; Rickert, *Painting in Britain*, 31–2, pl. 20b; Swarzenski, *Monuments*, pl. 54, fig. 123; Roosen-Runge, I, 32, 50; Gneuss, 91, 92, 95; Alexander, *Norman Illumination*, 133, 150, 160, 207, pl. 45e; *Anglo-Saxon Illumination*, pl. 1c; Wormald, *Winchester School*, 305, 308, 310; Pächt and Alexander, no. 19 (Rawl. B. 484, f. 85); Wormald, *Angleterre*, 231–2, ill. 226, pl. 227; Robb, *Illuminated Manuscript*, 145; R. Deshman, 'Anglo-Saxon Art After Alfred', *Art Bulletin*, LVI, 1974, 176–200, figs. 1, 2, 15, 21.

EXHIBITED: Brussels, 1973, *English Illuminated Manuscripts 700–1500*, no. 2.

6. Cambridge, Corpus Christi College MS 183

Bede, Lives of St. Cuthbert, Genealogies
293 × 191 mm.
c. 937. Winchester

Ills. 18, 19, 29

A framed frontispiece (f. 1ᵛ) preceding prose and verse Lives of St. Cuthbert in Latin represents King

Aethelstan offering a book to the Saint who stands in front of a chapel on the right. The miniature is the earliest presentation picture in English art, and its iconography stems from the late antique tradition probably transmitted through Carolingian intermediaries (Bloch, 1962). The composition shows the two figures in an architectural setting with a building in rising perspective and is indebted to Carolingian painting, possibly of the late 9th-century Court school of Charles the Bald (cf. Bible of San Paolo fuori le mura; Coronation Sacramentary, Bibl. Nat., lat. 1141). But the stocky figures with large heads and hands, awkward and stiff in pose, are in Wormald's 'early Winchester' style and recall some of the prophets of St. Cuthbert's vestments (cf. also no. 7, Junius Psalter, f. 118). The background of the picture is plain vellum with figures and details heavily painted in rust brown, pale purple, silvery blue, and some yellow, a colour scheme typical of this early period (cf. no. 4, Royal 7. D. XXIV; no. 7, Junius Psalter).

The miniature is surrounded by a remarkable frame made up of panels with leafy scrolls inhabited by birds and lions and with candelabra-like plant ornaments, originally of the late antique tradition and probably transmitted by Carolingian manuscripts of the Tours school. The designs are reserved on dark red ground and bordered with yellow bands. Besides palmettes and clusters of fruit, the scrolls contain innovations such as hollow calices with protruding tendrils and Wormald's 'long and short' leaf patterns (cf. *Initials*), while birds and beasts which do not dissolve into interlace but preserve their own individual entities, are also a new venture in Anglo-Saxon decoration.

Initial 'd' (f. 2) in orange and yellow, has a naturalistic bird head and bunched acanthus leaves on the two extremities. Another 'd' (f. 42ᵛ) is entirely made up of two birds. Large initial P (f. 6) contains a new type of ornament of Carolingian origin: a leafy scroll filling the upright and a continuous acanthus pattern in the bow. Numerous small initials to chapters are charmingly decorated with beasts' heads (some in three-quarter view), heavy foliage and fruit, mask heads, rings, and knots of interlace. Their colouring of reddish-brown, slate blue, and ochre, as well as their style, are extremely close to no. 4 (Royal 7. D. XXIV). Initials of both books were probably executed by the same artist but those of the present manuscript, being more accomplished, probably belong to a somewhat later period. Rubrics are in coloured or in colour-filled capitals.

PROVENANCE: This version of Bede was written in Southern England, probably Winchester, by a scribe whose hand, according to T. A. M. Bishop (1964-8), appears in parts of Royal 7. D. XXIV (no. 4). The manuscript is identifiable with the book presented by Aethelstan to St. Cuthbert *c.* 937 (Symeon of Durham, *Historia de Sancto Cuthberto*, ed. T. Arnold [Rolls Series, 1882], I, 211). It was in the North in the 10th century, and at Durham, in the second half of the 11th century, as shown by contemporary Old English documents (f. 96ᵛ)

listing church vessels and recording a grant by Walcher, Bishop of Durham (1071-80), to the congregation of St. Cuthbert. Bequeathed to Corpus Christi College by Archbishop Parker: Sub D(5) in 1575.

LITERATURE: Homburger, 6; Millar, I, 3, no. 2, pl. 3a; O. Homburger, 'Review', *Art Bulletin*, X, 1928, 400; T. D. Kendrick, 'An Anglo-Saxon Cruet', *Antiq. Journ.*, XVIII, 1938, 377-81, pl. LXXII; R. A. B. Mynors, *Durham Cathedral Manuscripts*, 1939, no. 16; Wormald, *Initials*, 115-16, pl. IId, IV a, b; Kendrick, *Late Saxon*, 3, 28, 35, 39, pls. XXVIII, 3, 4; XXXIII; Holmquist, *Viking Art*, 6, 29, 31, 32, 34, 46, 52, figs. 25, 27; Talbot Rice, *English Art*, 182 f., 235; *The Relics of St. Cuthbert*, ed. C. F. Battiscombe, 1956, Introduction, 32 n. 5, 33 n. 5; Ker, *Catalogue*, no. 42; Nordenfalk, *Early Medieval*, 178; Rickert, *Miniatura*, 15, 19, pl. 10; P. Bloch, 'Zum dedikationsbild im Lob des Kreuzes des Hrabanus Maurus', *Das erste Jahrtausend*, ed. V. H. Elbern, Dusseldorf 1962, I, 487 no. 66; F. Wormald, 'Continental Influences on English Medieval Illumination', *Fourth International Congress of Bibliophiles*, 1965, 8; T. A. M. Bishop, 'An early example of the square minuscule', *Transactions of the Cambridge Bibliographical Society*, IV, 1964-8, 247 n. 2; Rickert, *Painting in Britain*, 30, 33, pl. 20a; H. Roosen-Runge, I, 43, 50, ill. 1; F. Wormald, 'Anniversary Address', *Antiq. Journ.*, XLVII, 1967, 159-65; Alexander, *Norman Illumination*, 74, 86 n. 3, 116, pl. 17c; Bishop, *English Caroline*, no. 16(b); C. R. Dodwell, *Painting in Europe*, 1971, 81, 221 n. 45; Wormald, *Winchester School*, 309 n. 4, 310; J. Beckwith, *Ivory Carvings in Early Medieval England*, 1972, 28: *English Illuminated Manuscripts 700-1500*, Brussels Exhibition Catalogue, 1973, p. 21; Wormald, *Angleterre*, 231; Robb, *Illuminated Manuscript*, 145; R. Deshman, 'Anglo-Saxon Art After Alfred', *Art Bulletin*, LVI, 1974, 195, 197, figs. 45, 46.

7. Bodleian Library MS Junius 27 (S.C. 5139)

Psalter (Codex Vossianus or Junius Psalter)
242 × 172 mm.
Second quarter of 10th century. Winchester

Ills. 1 (Colour), 20-24, 26

This Psalter in the Roman version with a continuous interlinear Old English gloss is an outstanding example of an early group of manuscripts connected with Winchester. It contains a remarkable series of ornamental initials introducing all the psalms and is preceded by a mutilated, partly metrical calendar with decorated KL monograms (ff. 2-7ᵛ). Large initials and lines of capitals, partly filled in with colour, mark the tripartite division of the Psalter emphasizing Psalms 1 (cut out), 51, 101; smaller initials stress the liturgical eight-fold system prefacing Psalms 26, 38, 52, 68 (cut out), 80 (cut out) 97, 109; in addition Psalms 17, 77, 118, and 119 are also emphasized.

The decoration, a blend of insular and continental elements, is exceedingly varied and includes birds and winged dragons, half-length figures (almost identical with those in the Galba calendar, no. 5, cf. ff. 7ᵛ, 8ᵛ), animal and human heads, interlace and mask heads, elaborate plant motifs (including the characteristic hollow calices issuing tendrils and foliage), and acanthus scrolls in profusion. Beasts' heads in three-quarter view are strikingly realistic and the inhabited scroll initials are an innovation (cf. no. 6, Corpus Christi College 183). Also novel is the quality of all-pervading movement and of transmutation of motifs, features which later become typical of 12th-century Romanesque initials. A large initial D (f. 118) historiated with David and the lion (cf. Cotton Vesp. A. 1, 8th cent.), introduces Psalm 109. A few initials, Wormald Type II(a), are made up of black wiry interlace and bird heads. Figure type and style are a continuation of those in the Aethelstan manuscripts (cf. 5, 6) and belong to Wormald's 'early Winchester' group. The soft and richly varied colouring includes shades of pink, brown, slate blue, ochre, and yellow. Titles and psalm-numberings are in red with verse initials partly filled in with colour.

PROVENANCE: The Psalter can be assigned to Winchester on account of the script related to Winchester manuscripts of the first half of the 10th century (Helmingham Orosius, no. 8; Cambridge, Corpus Christi College 173, ff. 16ᵛ–25ᵛ), an attribution confirmed by the decoration, which derives from that of the Aethelstan manuscripts (cf. nos. 5, 6). Moreover, the composition of the calendar is related to that of 10th- to 11th-century Winchester calendars; and in the metrical part and obits of Alfred (26 October) and his queen Ealswith (3 December), paralleled in the calendar of the Aethelstan Psalter (no. 5), it suggests a dependence on the same archetype. The manuscript belonged to Queen Christina of Sweden, being identifiable in the Antwerp catalogue of her collection, 1655, as *Davidicum Psalterium latino-saxonicum*; it came into the possession of Isaac Vossius, her former librarian, who gave it to his uncle, Francis Junius, 1655. Acquired with Junius' collection in 1678.

LITERATURE: R. F. Hampson, *Medii Aevi Kalendarium*, 1841, I, 393; J. O. Westwood, *Paleographia Sacra*, 1843–5, pl. 41; *id.*, *Facsimiles*, 100, pl. 34; *New Pal. Soc.*, II, pl. 62; Homburger, 6; E. Bishop, *Liturgica Historica*, 1918, 254–6; J. Brønsted, *Early English Ornament*, 1924, 248, 249 n. 1, 250, fig. 175; Millar, I, no. 11; Saunders, *English Illumination*, 19–20, pl. 22 d, e; Wormald, *Initials*, 116–17, 118 n. 2, 119 nn. 1, 2, 133, pls. IIIa, IVc, d; Kendrick, *Late Saxon*, 32, pl. XXVIII, 6; Holmquist, *Viking Art*, 34, figs. 34–5; Talbot Rice, *English Art*, 194; A. Campbell, *The Tollemache Orosius* (E.E. MSS in facs., III), 1963, 17, 19; F. Saxl and H. Meier, *Verzeichnis astrologischer und mythologischer illustrierter Handschriften des lateinischen Mittelalters*, III. *Handschriften in englischen Bibliotheken*, 1953, I, 120; N. Denholm-Young, *Handwriting in England and Wales*, 1954, pl. 5; Freyhan, 424–6. pl. XXXVI, fig. 8; Ker, *Catalogue*, no. 335; T. A. M, Bishop, 'An early example of the square minuscule', *Transactions of the Cambridge Bibliographical Society*, IV, 1964–8, 247; Rickert, *Painting in Britain*, 33, 222 n. 32; D. H. Wright, *The Vespasian Psalter* (E.E.MSS in facs., XIV), 1967, 46–8, 77, 84–5, pl. VI, j; Gneuss, 92, 95; *Anglo-Saxon Illumination*, pl. 2a, b, c; Alexander, *Norman Illumination*, 70 n. 1, 72, 129, 161, 193, pls. 13f, 17d; Wormald, *Winchester School*, 305, 307 n. 3, 310, pls. IIIa, b, IVb, c; Pächt and Alexander, no, 21, pl. II; R. Deshman, 'Anglo-Saxon Art After Alfred', *Art Bulletin*, LVI, 1974, 195.

EXHIBITED: Oxford, Bodleian Library, 1952, *Latin Liturgical MSS*, no. 42; Stockholm, 1966, *Christina, Queen of Sweden*, no. 1341.

8. London, British Library MS Add. 47967 (Helmingham Hall 46)
Orosius, Universal History
King Alfred's translation
282 × 190 mm.
Second quarter of 10th century.
Additions second half of 10th century. Winchester
Ills. 25, 28

Ornamental initials introducing each of the first five Books (a space being left for one at the beginning of Bk. VI, f. 148) are closely reminiscent of the initials in the Junius Psalter (no. 7) and are believed to be by the same illuminator; they are made up of complete creatures, beasts' heads (one horned on p. 28, cf. Junius Psalter, f. 28), foliage and knotwork of a thick, rope-like interlace and a thin wiry one (pp. 8, 39, 60, 94, 128).

Drawings of the four Evangelist symbols added on the fly-leaf (iii) in the second half of the 10th century, are in brown outline with touches of red. Identified by inscriptions, each is copied from a different set of representations: a half-length symbol of John is anthropomorphic (an Eastern iconographic type probably transmitted by manuscripts from Gaul, cf. Poitiers, Bibl. Mun. MS 17, f. 31, 8th century); that of Mark—an *Agnus dei* instead of a lion—is enclosed in a roundel; the ox of Luke is full-length; and Matthew's angel, holding a cup and kneeling, is considerably larger in stature and in posture reminiscent of the Matthew symbol in Bibl. Nat., lat. 9338 (Evangeliary from Metz, 9th century). In addition there are on the same page: a rectangle filled with leaf and scroll ornament labelled *Vinea domini*, a part of the Latin alphabet, and a number of runes, *c.* 1000, while another copy of Matthew's symbol is on the verso. Small drawings in the text conceal defects in the parchment and there are occasional marginal sketches of an interlace motif (pp. 120, 124).

PROVENANCE: Closely related in script and decoration to the Junius Psalter (no. 7), this manuscript is attributable to Winchester on evidence of the script resembling that of the annals for 892–924 in the Anglo-Saxon Chronicle (Cambridge, Corpus Christi College MS 173, ff. 16ᵛ–25ᵛ) and of other Winchester manuscripts of the first half of the 10th century. 'John Davysun' scribbled on the fly-leaf (iii), 16th century. Belonged to the Duke of Lauderdale of Helmingham Hall (d. 1682, cf. Hickes, 1689), from whom it descended to the Tollemache family (signed J. Tollemache, Helmingham Hall, on the front paste-down), hence known as the Tollemache or Helmingham Orosius. Deposited in the British Museum by the Trustees of the Tollemache family in 1948, acquired in 1953.

LITERATURE: G. Hickes, *Catalogus veterum librorum septentrionalium*, 1689, 167; H. Sweet, *King Alfred's Orosius*, E.E.T.S., or. ser. LXXIX, 1885; *New Pal. Soc.*, I, pl. 187; Saunders, *English Illumination*, 19, pl. 22a; Wormald, *Initials*, 118, pl. Va; Kendrick, *Late Saxon*, 33; Wormald, *English Drawings*, 65, no. 22; A. Campbell, *The Tollemache Orosius* (E.E.MSS. in facs., III), 1953; Ker, *Catalogue*, no. 133; Nordenfalk, *Early Medieval*, 177; T. A. M. Bishop, 'An early example of the square minuscule', *Transactions of the Cambridge Bibliographical Society*, IV, 1963–8, 247; Rickert, *Painting in Britain*, 222 n. 32; T. J. Brown, *The Durham Ritual* (E.E.MSS. in facs., XVI), 1969, 37–68; Wormald, *Winchester School*, 305; Pächt and Alexander, no. 21.

9. Oxford, Bodleian Library MS Tanner 10 (S.C. 27694)
Bede, Historia ecclesiastica in Old English version
245 × 165 mm.
First half of 10th century

Ills. 34–37, 39, 40

The remarkable ornamental initials introducing each paragraph (ff. 1–119ᵛ) are mostly painted in minium orange, yellow, green, brown, and pink; a few are left uncoloured and one (f. 104) is in black, wiry interlace (cf. no. 7, Junius Psalter). The initials include the striking gymnastic type constructed of human figures and composite full-bodied creatures (most notable on ff. 54, 68, 93, 115ᵛ). The source of this new initial style is obscure for though figure initials occur in Byzantine and Merovingian manuscripts and appear in the Corbie Psalter *c*. 800, nowhere is the same quality of movement to be found; and these climbing, fighting, lively figures have their closest parallels in later Romanesque initials. Also an anticipation of the Romanesque is the tight interweaving of decorative forms. But the pliancy of the soft, fattish creatures and the way in which several letters of the opening words, not only the initial, are composed of ornamental zoomorphic motifs, suggest features harking back to the 8th- to 9th-century initial style (cf. Bodleian MSS Douce 176 and Laud. misc. 126, north-eastern France). In other initials birds, dragons, quadrupeds (ff. 56, 70,

79) are employed with thick worm-like interlace terminating in beasts' heads, some in three-quarter view (cf. nos. 4, Royal 7. D. XXIV, 6, Corpus Christi College 183).

PROVENANCE: Origin unknown. The medieval binding leaves kept separately since 1898 as MS Tanner 10* were made from the mortuary roll of William, Abbot of Thorney (d. 1293?); records of loans from the book closet at Thorney were added on the blank dorse of the roll, *c*. 1330. The manuscript must have been at Thorney at least from the 14th century. It came into possession of Thomas Tanner, Bishop of St. Asaph (d. 1735), who bequeathed all his manuscripts to the Bodleian Library.

LITERATURE: T. Miller, 'The Old English version of Bede's ecclesiastical history of the English People', E.E.T.S., or. ser. XCV, 1890, XIII-XV; F. Wormald, 'The Survival of Anglo-Saxon illumination after the Norman Conquest', *Proceedings of the British Academy*, XXX, 1944, 134 n. 2; K. W. Humphreys, 'Book distribution lists from Thorney Abbey, Cambridgeshire 1324–30', *B.L.R.*, II, 1948, 205–10; Kendrick, *Late Saxon*, 31, pl. XXVIII, 1, 2; Ker, *Catalogue*, no. 351, pl. 1; Nordenfalk, *Early Medieval*, 177; F. Wormald, 'Anglo-Saxon initials in a Paris Boethius manuscript', *Essais en l'honneur de Jean Porcher*, ed. O. Pächt, 67, 70 n. 12, pl. 7; Rickert, *Painting in Britain*, 49, 226 n. 10; Alexander, *Norman Illumination*, 74 n. 1; *Anglo-Saxon Illumination*, pls. 3a, 4; Wormald, *Winchester School*, 305–6, pl. IIIc; Pächt and Alexander, no. 22, pl. II.

10. Boulogne, Bibliothèque Municipale MS 10
Gospels (2 vols.)
308 × 210 mm.
Mid 10th century

Ill. 38

The Gospels, probably one manuscript originally, are preceded by Canon Tables (ff. 5–20) shown under a series of large double arches superimposed on four smaller ones. The arches are supported on shafts with capitals painted orange or yellow and either perfectly plain or made up of human faces, bird and animal heads, large hollow rings, 'purse-leaves' and a variety of mask-heads.
A faint sketch of St. John seated (Vol. I, f. 21ᵛ) shows him with his symbol—the eagle—spreading its wings immediately above the Evangelist's head (cf. no. 95, Monte Cassino Gospels) being half-concealed by his nimbus (cf. Matthew's angel in the Lindisfarne Gospels).
The manuscript contains large dragonesque initials, Wormald Type I, introducing the first words of each Gospel inscribed on coloured bands or in lines of capitals filled in with yellow, orange, pink, and ochre, a colour scheme reminiscent of no. 4 (Royal 7. D. XXIV). The initials, painted in the same colours and outlined in black, are formed of winged

dragons (their heads with long lappets often shown in three-quarter view and their tails ending in 'long and short' leaf motifs or in deep cup-like flowers, cf. Junius Psalter, no. 7); a particularly splendid initial Q (Vol. II, f. 8) followed by lettering on mauve and ochre bands introduces Luke's Gospel. Some smaller initials in the text are composed of deep-folded leaves with creatures' heads emerging from the hollow. The decoration is also reminiscent of earlier Insular manuscripts in the decreasing size of the initial letters and the shapes of some text-initials; the types of dragon employed and the absence of interlace knotwork recall Tanner 10 (no. 9).

PROVENANCE: The manuscript, written in Anglo-Saxon minuscule possibly in the south or south-west of England, is of uncertain origin. It belonged to St. Vaast, Arras: *Bibliothecae monasterii Sancti Vedasti Atrebatensis, 1628 'A'* (f. 1).

LITERATURE: S. Beissel, *Geschichte der Evangelien-bücher*, Freiburg im Breisgau, 1906, 135 n. 1; Homburger, 4, 47; Wormald, *Initials*, 120, 133; Talbot Rice, *English Art*, 206.

11. Oxford, Bodleian Library MS Auct. F. 4. 32 (S.C. 2176)
'St. Dunstan's classbook'; Part I (ff. 1–9), 9th century;
Part III (ff. 19–36ᵛ), Wales, early 9th century;
Part IV (ff. 37–47), Wales, 9th to 10th centuries
245×179 mm.
Drawing mid 10th century, Glastonbury

Ill. 41

The drawing on f. 1, a leaf originally left blank preceding the text of Part I (Eutyches with Breton glosses), shows a majestic three-quarter-length figure of Christ, represented with rod and book as the Wisdom of God and adored by a kneeling St. Dunstan. Dunstan, who is known to have been an artist, is believed to have been responsible for the drawing since the inscription above the kneeling figure, written in the first person, is probably by his hand (Hunt's Hand 'D', *St. Dunstan's Classbook*, 1961). The miniature, in firm brown outline with red in Christ's halo and in some details, is one of the earliest and most important examples of the so-called 'first style' (cf. Wormald, *Drawings*) and its immediate prototype is to be sought in works, probably ivories, of the Carolingian Ada Court school.
Some initial letters in parts III and IV terminating in animal heads are in the style of the Barberini Gospels, others are filled in with colour.

PROVENANCE: The drawing was probably executed at Glastonbury while St. Dunstan was abbot there, 943–57, for he is still shown as a monk. An inscription across the top of the page, probably of the 16th century, states the authorship of the Saint. Part I was identified in the Glastonbury catalogue of 1248. Parts I, III, IV were domiciled at Glastonbury

from the time of St. Dunstan, the connecting link between them being the annotations in the so-called Hand D (ff. 1, 20, 36, 47). At the foot of the last leaf (f. 47ᵛ) is an inscription: *In custodia fratris H. Langley*, a Glastonbury monk in the second half of the 15th century. There is no evidence to show when Part II (ff. 10–18), second half of the 11th century, was joined with the rest of the manuscript, but it is likely that the whole was bound together in the sixteenth century (cf. Hunt). Donated to the Bodleian by Thomas Allen in 1601 (f. 1).

LITERATURE: R. Ellis, *XII Facsimiles from Latin MSS. in the Bodleian Library*, 1885, pl. 1; *New Pal. Soc.*, I, pls. 81, 82; W. M. Lindsay, *Early Welsh Script*, 1912, 7–10, pl. 3; Millar, I, no. 9; Wormald, *Initials*, 112–13, pl. IIIb; M. T. d'Alverny, 'Le symbolisme de la sagesse et le Christ de Saint Dunstan', *B.L.R.*, 1945–6, 232–44; F. Saxl and R. Wittkower, *British Art and the Mediterranean*, 1948, pl. 21, 1; Kendrick, *Late Saxon*, 4, pl. I; Wormald, *English Drawings*, 24–5, 63, 74, no. 46, pl. 1; Talbot Rice, *English Art*, 177, 180, pl. 43; P. Hunter-Blair, *An Introduction to Anglo-Saxon England*, 1956, 174, pl. IX; Ker, *Catalogue*, no. 297; Nordenfalk, *Early Medieval*, 177; F. Saxl, 'Illuminated Science Manuscripts in England', *Lectures*, 1957, I, 97–9, 107–8, pls. 52a, 53d; Rickert, *Miniatura*, 15, 19, pl. 10; R. W. Hunt, *St. Dunstan's Classbook from Glastonbury* (Umbrae Codicum Occidentalium, IV), 1961 (compl. facs.); Rickert, *Painting in Britain*, 31–2, 203, 220 n. 4, 221 n. 25–6, pl. 22; Bishop, *Codex Leidensis*, p. VI; id., 'An early example of Insular Caroline', *Transactions of the Cambridge Bibliographical Society*, IV, 1968, 400, pl. XXIX (e); M. W. Evans, *Medieval Drawings*, 1969, pl. 24; Alexander, *Norman Illumination*, 120, pl. 21; *Anglo-Saxon Illumination*, pl. 6; Bishop, *English Caroline*, p. xx, nos. 1, 3; Dodwell, *Techniques*, 647–9; J. Beckwith, *Ivory Carvings in Early Medieval England*, 1972, 30, fig. 31; Pächt and Alexander, nos. 10, 17, 24, pls. I, II; Wormald, *Angleterre*, 1973, 240; *English Illuminated Manuscripts 700–1500*, Brussels Exhibition Catalogue, 1973, p. 17; Robb, *Illuminated Manuscript*, 147, fig. 88; C. R. Dodwell, Peter Clemoes, *The Old English Illustrated Hexateuch* (E.E. MSS in facs., XVIII) 1974, 58 n. 4, 59.

12. Oxford, St. John's College MS 194 (f. 1ᵛ)
Gospels
164×140 mm.
Mid 10th century. (?) Canterbury, Christ Church

Ill. 47

The drawing of St. Matthew added on a fly-leaf (now f. 1ᵛ) of a 9th-century Gospel Book, probably Breton, was copied from a St. Matthew portrait in a Gospel Book from Lobbes near Liège of the late 9th to 10th century, now British Library Cotton, Tiberius A. II (it was possibly a gift from the Emperor Otto I of Germany to Aethelstan, who presented it to Christ Church, Canterbury). The drawing in brown ink is shaded with green on the Evangelist's undergarment and on the curtains, and with red on his face and that of the angel. The miniature has been retouched, perhaps when the representation of Edward the Confessor (?) was added on the recto opposite in the 15th century (?). Faint pencil sketches of Evangelist portraits and their symbols (ff. 20ᵛ, 31ᵛ) are datable to the 9th century.

PROVENANCE: The mark GL in the top right-hand corner of the first page is an early pressmark of Christ Church, Canterbury. The manuscript probably remained at Christ Church throughout the Middle Ages.

LITERATURE: James, *Ancient Libraries*, App. D, 527; Wormald, *English Drawings*, 23, 77, no. 52, pl. 40b; *Anglo-Saxon Illumination*, pl. 5.

13. Oxford, St. John's College MS 28
I Miscellaneous texts
II Gregory the Great, Pastoral Care (ff. 7-77ᵛ)
328 × 237 mm.
Mid 10th century to third quarter 10th century.
Canterbury, St. Augustine's

Ills. 42, 43

Part I contains outline drawings added on the fly-leaf (f. 2) and on the end-leaf (f. 81ᵛ) of a gathering of eight. The first miniature executed in reddish-brown ink and representing a full-length youthful figure of Christ holding a cross shaft and a book, is an outstanding example of the earliest phase of English outline drawing. It is related stylistically to the St. Dunstan miniature (cf. no. 11) but shows a freer and more varied pattern in the fluttering and softly zigzagging drapery edges. Closer iconographical and stylistic analogies are provided by representations of the Trinity in the Sherborne Pontifical (no. 35, particularly f. 6). The sketches (f. 81ᵛ), similar in style, show two standing figures (the second on the right being a copy of the first) and below an angel holding out in either hand objects representing 'Day' and 'Night' (Raw, 1955). Wormald has suggested that the Christ (f. 2) and the first figure (f. 81ᵛ) may possibly be connected with a representation of the Trinity (cf. Vatican, Bibl. Apost. Pal. lat. 834, 9th century, Lorsch; and the Sherborne Pontifical, no. 35).

Part II (ff. 7-77) contains ornamental initials (ff. 8, 26, 27) in brown or green inks with touches of red, of a type characteristic of Canterbury manuscripts of the second half of the 11th century; Wormald Type II(b), decorated with beasts' heads; curling acanthus foliage and interlace with prominent 'elbows' and 'hooks'. It also contains a remarkable series of capital letters A(liter) filled in with acanthus leaf patterns. Rubrics are in red.

PROVENANCE: A St. Augustine's, Canterbury, origin has been suggested by T. A. M. Bishop

(1969) for part II on paleographical evidence, an attribution supported by the style of ornamental initials. The origin of the drawings is uncertain but on stylistic grounds they could perhaps be assigned to Glastonbury (cf. no. 11) or, even more likely, to Canterbury (cf. Sherborne Pontifical, no. 35). An invocation to St. Vincent (f. 81) in an early 12th-century hand may mean that the manuscript then passed to Abingdon. It may have belonged later to Southwick Priory like other manuscripts of the same gift from Sir John White of Southwick to St. John's College in 1553 (f. 1).

LITERATURE: Wormald, *English Drawings*, 25, 37, 63, 74, 77-8, no. 51, pl. 2; B. Raw, 'The drawing of an angel in MS. 28, St. John's College, Oxford', *J.W.C.I.*, XVIII, 1955, 318-19; Ker, *Catalogue*, no. 361; Bishop, *Codex Leidensis*, p. xx (25); *Anglo-Saxon Illumination*, pls. 7, 8, 14 a, b; Bishop, *English Caroline*, nos. 5, 10; Wormald, *Angleterre*, 240.

EXHIBITED: Brussels, 1973, *English Illuminated Manuscripts 700-1500*, no. 3.

14. Cambridge, Trinity College MS B. 16. 3 (379)
Rabanus Maurus, De laude crucis
418 × 341 mm.
Mid 10th century. (?) Canterbury, Christ Church

Ills. 45, 46, 48

A frontispiece in full colour (f. 1ᵛ), enclosed by an inscribed, rectangular frame, shows Rabanus Maurus offering his book to Pope Gregory in the presence of three deacons, the scene taking place under three domical arches on columns with acanthus capitals and with curtains draped round them, while the tympana above have identifying inscriptions. The figures with large heads and hands are block-like and stocky and their solemn expression and stiffness of pose and gesture recall the presentation scene in no. 6 (Corpus Christi College, 183). The colours include green, rust brown, ochre, purple, pale lilac, some blue, gold in Gregory's halo and details, and black in the background on the right and left (cf. no. 5, Aethelstan Psalter, f. 21). This dull and heavy colouring is reminiscent of manuscripts of the Aethelstan period but the patterns of stylized, incisive, and repetitive drapery folds derive from continental models (cf. Goldschmidt, *German Illumination*, I, pl. 55A, a 9th-century manuscript from Fulda). Diagrams containing figures represent: Christ with outstretched arms (f. 3), red-winged seraphs and angels (f. 6ᵛ), the Holy Lamb surrounded by the Evangelists' symbols (f. 17ᵛ), and Rabanus Maurus in cowl adoring the Cross (f. 30ᵛ). Iconographically the frontispiece (f. 1ᵛ) and the kneeling figure of the author (f. 30ᵛ) correspond most closely to a 9th-century northern French copy of the same work, now Amiens, Bibliothèque Municipale MS 223. Prochno has shown, however, that this correspondence does not indicate a direct dependence but rather derivation from a distinct common prototype (Prochno, 1929).

PROVENANCE: The origin from Christ Church, Canterbury, was suggested by James (*Ancient Libraries*, no. 379). The name *Eadwine* is inscribed over the top of the frame (f. 1ᵛ).

LITERATURE: James, *Ancient Libraries*, 529; Burlington Fine Arts Club, *Illuminated Manuscripts*, 1908, no. 22, pl. 27; Millar, I, 14, no. 3; O. Homburger, 'Review', *Art Bulletin*, X, 1928, 401; J. Prochno, *Das Schreiber- und Dedikationsbild in der deutschen Buchmalerei* I. Teil, Leipzig and Berlin 1929, 12, no. 7, T. 14*, 16*; P. Bloch, 'Zum Dedikationsbild im Lob des Kreuzes des Hrabanus Maurus', *Das Erste Jahrtausend*, ed. V. H. Elbern, Düsseldorf, 1962, 471; Rickert, *Painting in Britain*, 31, pl. 19; Wormald, *Winchester School*, 309; *id.*, *Angleterre*, 231; R. Deshman, 'Anglo-Saxon Art After Alfred', *Art Bulletin*, LVI, 1974, 183, 190, 197, 199, fig. 12.

15. London, British Library MS Add. 40618
Gospels
127 × 102 mm.
Additions mid 10th century

Ills. 49, 51, 52

The manuscript, an Irish pocket Gospel book of the 8th to 9th century, brought over with its decoration unfinished, contains among other English additions two miniatures painted in the mid 10th century on inserted leaves (ff. 22ᵛ, 49ᵛ). The leaves may have been inserted before the volume reached England since the portrait of St. Luke (f. 22ᵛ) shows faint traces of an erased miniature in a rectangular frame. The Evangelist, shown in three-quarter view leaning to the right, is seated on a massive cushioned throne, writing in a book which he holds in his left hand; the drapery belonging to a book stand (not shown) floats in the air. Over Luke's head there is a tumble of twisted drapery from which emerges an anthropomorphic half-length figure of his symbol—the ox— holding a golden book. The miniature is most unusually framed by two ellipses in structure vaguely resembling the initial S (f. 2) of no. 48 (Cambridge Prudentius); they are joined in the middle by two pairs of gripping heads (one in three-quarter view) with two bosses of curling leafwork at the apices. This work is of a type that appears later in Canterbury initials. The border is filled with a delicate leaf scroll in black that is comparable to the fine brushwork decoration typical of manuscripts from St. Augustine's, Canterbury (cf. no. 21, Trinity Amalarius). The text-page opposite (f. 23) is headed by *Quoniam quidem* painted in gold over a square showing traces of an earlier interlace initial, a modification dating from the 10th century.
St. John (f. 49ᵛ) seated almost frontally on a heavy high-backed throne, is turning slightly to the right with his book in his hand, writing, while above him the bust-figure of the eagle emerges from a tangle of drapery. The miniature is enclosed by a rectangular frame showing some remains of a black scroll pattern between gold edging bands. The animal-headed initial letters of St. John's Gospel on the page opposite (f. 50) were heavily painted in gold over the earlier ones by the 10th-century English illuminator.
Both Evangelist figures and the drapery style derive from Carolingian models probably manuscripts of the Ada Court School (for St. John cf. British Library MS Harley 2788, f. 13ᵛ). The most remarkable feature of the two miniatures is the tangle of drapery separating the symbols from the Evangelists below; unparalleled in Anglo-Saxon illumination, it is also uncommon in Carolingian works, but some parallels are available (e.g. Bibl. Nat., lat. 4, f. 137, 9th to 10th century). The anthropomorphic Evangelist symbols, rare in Anglo-Saxon representations (cf. nos. 8, Helmingham Orosius; 65, Trinity Gospels; 95, Monte Cassino Gospels; also an early Insular example in Rome, Vatican, Barberini Lat. 570, late 8th century) and ultimately perhaps of Coptic origin (cf. Ameisenowa, *J.W.C.I.*, 1949) were probably transmitted by manuscripts from Gaul.
The miniatures are richly painted with a good deal of gold and a range of bright clear colours including orange, blue, green, yellow, pink, and purple. Features and hands are outlined in orange, those of St. John covered with white-silver paste are now oxydized.

PROVENANCE: The origin of the English additions is unknown, probably southern English; some features of the decoration link the manuscript with St. Augustine's, Canterbury. A (?) 13th-century inscription *iste est liber sanct(e)* . . . (f. 66ᵛ) is partly erased. The last page of St. John's Gospel was re-written, as recorded in the colophon (f. 66), by an Anglo-Saxon scribe, Eduardus diaconus, presumably at the time when the English additions were introduced in the mid 10th century. The volume belonged to William Newman, 1538, Robert Lancaster, 1662; unknown before purchase by the British Museum, Sotheby's sale, 1922.

LITERATURE: *New Pal. Soc.*, II, pls. 140-1; British Museum, *Reproductions from Illuminated Manuscripts*, IV, 1928, pl. II; G. L. Micheli, *L'Enluminure du Haut Moyen-Age et les influences irlandaises*, Brussels 1939, 25, 190; Talbot Rice, *English Art*, 194; P. McGurk, 'The Irish Pocket Gospel Books', *Sacris Erudiri*, VIII, 2, 1956, 250, 256, 261, 269; F. Henry, 'An Irish Manuscript in the British Museum', *Journal of the Royal Society of Antiquaries of Ireland*, LXXXVII, 1957, 147 ff.; R. Crozet, 'Les representations anthropo-zoomorphiques des évangelistes', *Cahiers de Civilisation Médiévale*, I, 1958, 187 n. 28; Wormald, *Winchester School* 309-10, pl. V, a, b: *English Illuminated Manuscripts 700-1500*, Brussels Exhibition Catalogue, 1973, p. 29; C. Nordenfalk, 'The Draped

Lectern', *Intuition und Kunstwissenschaft: Festschrift für Hans Swarzenski*, Berlin 1973, 86, 88, fig. 11.

16. London, British Library MS Cotton, Vespasian A. VIII (ff. 2ᵛ-33ᵛ)

New Minster Charter
288 × 162 mm.
After 966. Winchester, New Minster

Ill. 84

The frontispiece preceding the Charter (f. 2ᵛ) is the earliest example of the new Winchester style; painted on a purple-stained ground it is surrounded by a rectangular foliated border with a couplet describing the scene on the opposite page (f. 3). The following two pages, in plain coloured frames, contain the heading of the document (f. 3ᵛ) and the opening line with a Chi Rho monogram (f. 4); the writing on all these pages is in gold lettering.

The miniature represents King Edgar between the Virgin and St. Peter offering the Charter to a youthful Christ enthroned above in a golden mandorla held by four angels. The well-balanced and extremely lively composition contains figures firmly drawn in a vigorous and basically linear style with drapery ends flying, the hemlines fluttering lightly and the sharply incised nested V-folds isolating the thighs, all reminiscent of no. 11 (St. Dunstan drawing). The use of colour is strikingly novel, the miniature being painted in light, clear washes of blue, red, green, pale brown, and purple, with figures outlined in red and the shading executed by contrasting coloured lines (cf. no. 41, Harley 2904, f. 4) while gold is used in profusion in details, and features are drawn in brown on flake white paste.

The stocky and amply-draped figures of the Virgin and St. Peter recall the style of the Aethelstan period (cf. no. 5, Athelstan Psalter, f. 2), while the representation of King Edgar, who is precariously poised on tip-toe in a 'dancing' posture on the edge of the frame, and is shown in rear view with his arms raised, his head flung back and right buttock roundly shaded in, suggests inspiration from the Court school of Charles the Bald (cf. Bible of San Paolo). The miniature is enclosed within a gold trelliswork of two gold rods with candelabra-like acanthus trees growing from the centre of this double frame, the leaves spreading outwards and curling over the edges, while long-stalked palmette and flower leaves project far beyond the frame. The sources of this decoration which, with embellishments and modifications, remains typical of the 'Winchester' school, are to be sought in Carolingian manuscripts from Tours and Metz (cf. Koehler, I, 101-2; III, 71d, 81a; for a different view see Freyhan, 1956).

PROVENANCE: The Charter, written for St. Ethelwold at the New Minster, is a commemoration of the introduction of Benedictine monks into that house. It is witnessed by Edgar and the royal family, St. Dunstan, and various bishops including Ethel-wold himself, and it may be somewhat later than the date 966 inscribed on f. 3ᵛ (Wormald, 1963). The additions (ff. 34-43) are of the post-Conquest period. The manuscript belonged to Sir Robert Cotton (d. 1631). His library, presented to the nation by his grandson, Sir John Cotton, in 1700, was incorporated in the British Museum in 1753.

LITERATURE: Westwood, *Facsimiles*, 130-2, pl. 47; *Pal. Soc.*, I, 46-7; British Museum, *Reproductions from Illuminated Manuscripts*, 1907, I, pl. IV; G. F. Warner and H. A. Wilson, *The Benedictional of St. Aethelwold*, 1910, XXXI, XXXIX; J. P. Herbert, *Illuminated Manuscripts*, 1911, 124-5; Homburger, 17 n. 1, 21 n. 3, 23 n. 1, 43-9, 59, 66; British Museum, *Schools of Illumination*, 1914, I, 9, pl. 8; J. P. Gilson, *Schools of Illumination*, 1918, pl. 8; J. Brønsted, *Early English Ornament*, London and Copenhagen 1924, 249 n. 1, 258, 261, 298 n. 1; Millar, I, 7, no. 4, pl. 3b; Saunders, *English Illumination*, 17, 21, 24, 26; Wormald, *Initials*, 131; Kendrick, *Late Saxon*, 5, pl. II; Talbot Rice, *English Art*, 90, 184-5, pl. 46; Freyhan, 424, 426-7, pl. XXXIX, fig. 20; Nordenfalk, *Early Medieval*, 179; Rickert, *Miniatura*, 15, 19, pl. 11; D. Tselos, 'English manuscript illustrations and the Utrecht Psalter', *Art Bulletin*, XLI, 1959, 137; F. Wormald, *The Benedictional of St. Ethelwold*, 1959, 5, 10; *id.*, 'Late Anglo-Saxon Art; some questions and suggestions', *Studies in Western Art. Acts of the 20th Congress of the History of Art*, ed. M. Meiss, I, Princeton 1963, 19-26; W. Mersmann, 'Das Elfenbeinkreuz der Sammlung Topic-Mimara', *Wallraf-Richartz-Jahrbuch*, XXV, 1963, 13, fig. 6; Rickert, *Painting in Britain*, 27, 32, 36-7, 222 n. 40, pl. 25; G. Duby, *The Making of the Christian West*, 1967, pl. 26; Roosen-Runge, 50 ff., ill. 2; Alexander, *Norman Illumination*, 169 n. 5; Bishop, *English Caroline*, p. XXI; J. Beckwith, *Ivory Carvings in Early Medieval England*, 1972, 38, fig. 40; Wormald, *Angleterre*, 235; pl. 228; Robb, *Illuminated Manuscript*, 147, fig. 89; R. Deshman, 'Anglo-Saxon Art After Alfred', *Art Bulletin*, LVI, 1974, fig. 49.

17. Oxford, Bodleian Library MS Bodley 579 (S.C. 2675)

Sacramentary (Leofric Missal)
195 × 145 mm.
Additions mid 10th century, 969-78, mid 11th century

Ills. 53-56

One of the earlier of the English additions (part 'A') made in the mid 10th century to a 9th-century Sacramentary from the region of Arras/Cambrai contains a fine monochrome initial E (f. 154ᵛ) composed of interlace knotwork, dragons, trefoil and palmette motifs, and a profiled human head with 'antennae' ornament (cf. no. 5, Aethelstan Psalter) recalling the 8th/9th century Southern English initial style (cf. B.L. Cotton, Tiberius C. II).

The second group of additions *c.* 970 (part 'B', ff. 38-58) comprises a calendar for use at Glastonbury and computistical matter with four full-page illustrations in coloured inks of red, green, blue, and purple, also employed in KL monograms, headings, and tables of calculations. A miniature (f. 49) showing the Paschal Hand with dates written on each of its fingers (cf. no. 98, Tiberius C. VI) and with an inscription, *Dextera nam dni fulget cum floribus Paschae* on the top left, contains two figures in the lower corners of the picture, the whole surrounded by an openwork border of curling leaves which project over the corners and are reserved on coloured ground. The personifications of *Vita* (f. 49ᵛ) and *Mors* (f. 50) illustrate a magical text, *Sphaera Apulei* (cf. Heimann, 1966), that contains a formula for calculating a patient's recovery or death; the crowned Christ-like figure of *Vita* is shown holding a scroll displaying propitious numbers, while *Mors*, a winged and horned Satan with seven dragons springing from his head, holds the fatal numbers. A diagram of paschal calculations (f. 50ᵛ) contains a bust figure inscribed *Dionisius* (the inventor of the paschal cycle of 19 years). The Easter Tables (f. 53) extend from 969 to 1006, the former date suggesting a *terminus post quem* for part 'B'. Later additions of the 11th to 12th centuries are partly written on blank leaves of the original portion of the manuscript.

The animated figure drawing with its delicate flickering outline, softly agitated drapery ends, and lightly fluttering hemlines, is the earliest example showing the influence of 9th-century Rheims style and the first to employ the coloured outline technique which, though not necessarily an English invention (cf. Introduction, p. 17), becomes typical of later English drawings.

PROVENANCE: Part 'B', as shown by the calendar, was written at Glastonbury possibly before 978, since St. Edward, king and martyr, is not included. The present volume was probably put together by Leofric, Bishop of Exeter from 1042 to 1072, and, as recorded in Latin and Old English dedicatory notes (f. 1), was presented by him to Exeter Cathedral. Additions of the 11th to 12th century were made at Exeter. The manuscript was given to the Bodleian Library by the Dean and Chapter in 1602.

LITERATURE: Westwood, *Facsimiles*, 99, pl. 33; F. E. Warren, *The Leofric Missal*, 1883; F. A. Gasquet and E. Bishop, *The Bosworth Psalter*, 1908, 15–21 and *passim*; Homburger, 4; E. W. B. Nicholson, *Early Bodleian Music*, 1913, iii, lvi-lx, pl. XXVIII; Millar, I, no. 44; F. Wormald, 'English Kalendars before A.D. 1100', *H.B.S.*, LXXII, 1933, vi n. 3, xiii, no. 4; id., *Initials*, 132; id., *English Drawings*, 29–30, 40, 60, 68, 75–6, 80, no. 49; Talbot Rice, *English Art*, 212, 213 n. 3, pl. 78; F. Saxl and H. Meier, *Verzeichnis astrologischer und mythologischer illustrierter Handschriften des lateinischen Mittelalters*, III, 1953, 119 ff., 315 ff.: S. Schulten, 'Die Buchmalerei des 11. Jahrhunderts im Kloster St. Vaast in Arras', *Münchner Jahrbuch der Bildenden Kunst*, VII, 1956, 53; Bishop, *Notes*, III, 193, 196; Ker, *Catalogue*, no. 315; Rickert, *Painting in Britain*, 33–4, 222 n. 34–6, 226 n. 82, pl. 29a; A. Heimann,

'Three illustrations from the Bury St. Edmunds Psalter and their prototypes', *J.W.C.I.*, XXIX, 1966, 39–43, 50, pl. 7a, c; D. Gremont and L. Donnat, 'Fleury, le Mont Saint-Michel at l'Angleterre à la fin du Xe et au début du XIe siècle à propos du manuscrit d'Orléans No. 127 (105)', *Millénaire monastique du Mont Saint-Michel*, Paris 1967, I, 779; C. M. Kauffmann, 'The Bury Bible', *J.W.C.I.*, XXIX, 1966, 79 n. 97; *Anglo-Saxon Illumination*, pls. 9, 10; Alexander, *Norman Illumination*, 92 n. 4, 207 n. 3; Bishop, *English Caroline*, p. xxiii, nos. 2, 8, 28; Pächt and Alexander, nos. 20, 25, pls. II, III; P. M. Korhammer. 'The Origin of the Bosworth Psalter', *Anglo-Saxon England*, 2, 1973.

18. Salisbury, Cathedral Library MS 150
Psalter with Old English interlinear gloss
Gallican version
287 × 180 mm.
969–78

Ills. 57–61

The Psalter (ff. 12–137ᵛ, *Pusillus eram*, f. 138), followed by canticles (ff. 138ᵛ–151ᵛ) and originally a litany (f. 151ᵛ, erased and rewritten in the 13th century, ff. 152–60), is preceded by lunar tables under arches (ff. 1–2) and a calendar (ff. 3–8ᵛ) decorated with elaborate dragonesque KL monograms and zodiacal signs placed in the right margins, all mainly in red outline with some monograms in green. The Psalter, now badly mutilated and starting imperfectly in Psalm 3, has had whole leaves removed and several initials cut out; full-page illuminations hitherto prefacing Psalms 1, 51, 101, and 109 are also missing—the one still extant introduces Psalm 119 (f. 122).

There are indications that the scribe was also his own illuminator and that, copying page by page from a model, he designed each initial as it came at the head of each psalm and canticle, subsequently inscribing the text round it (Sisam, 1959). Most of the initials are Wormald Type I and are made up of complete dragons (often with heads in three-quarter view); some contain mask heads and lions—a splendid T (f. 62ᵛ) is composed of a spread-eagle lion holding two dragons—and are inhabited by birds. The dragons are of a distinctive variety, having rib-like projections on their backs and often a small leaf protruding from under their bellies. Structurally, the dragonesque initials recall no. 7 (Junius 27) and even more closely no. 9 (Tanner 10) showing the same paucity of leaf and plaited interlace motifs as the latter. Three initials formed wholly (f. 63) or partly (ff. 5, 60ᵛ) of human figures and a few other letters of an inert type (e.g. f. 60) are reminiscent of Merovingian initials but the majority are of a highly animated variety and include remarkable gymnastic initials. The most notable among the latter, a large initial A (f. 122) to Psalm 119, is topped by a mask head, the framework crowded with spirited wriggling dragons twisting their way up the two legs of the letter (cf. no. 65, Trinity Gospels, f. 60), and enclosed within a frame of arch and columns that are decorated with straggly, agitated acanthus leaves and crowned by the figure of a standing Christ; four little legs with paws project downwards from each column and recall the Canon Tables of the 9th-century Cutbercht Gospels (Vienna, Nat. Bibl. Cod. lat. 1224).

Most of the initals are lightly coloured with washes of dull rose pink to red, deep leaf green, ochre, touches of brown, and greyish blue (after f. 108). Verse initials are filled in with patches of red, green, brown, and blue; rubrics inscribed in red. The decoration is in the firm outline of the 'first style' but some of the figure drawings (e.g. f. 6ᵛ) seem to reflect an influence from Rheims in softer and more sketchy drapery patterns.

PROVENANCE: Origin unknown. Internal evidence shows that the volume was prepared and used in a Benedictine house (Sisam, 1959). The calendar, assigned by Wormald (*H.B.S.*, 1933) to the south-west of England, contains slight indications for Shaftesbury Abbey (Sisam, 1959). The manuscript was probably produced after 969, the date indicated by the table of indictions (f. 1ᵛ) containing two cycles (969–87 and 988–1006) and most likely before 978, for the important feast of St. Edward, king and martyr, murdered that year and enshrined in Shaftesbury in 981, is a later addition to the calendar. The Shaftesbury attribution is supported by the end prayer after psalm 151 (f. 138) altered to a feminine form and suggesting probable use by a nun. Obit of 'brictwinus' (perhaps Byrthtwine II, Bishop of Sherborne, 1023–45) added to the calendar in the mid 11th century, and Aldhelm second among confessors, in the litany rewritten in the 12th century (f. 152) connect the manuscript with Sherborne, whence the see was transferred to Salisbury in 1078. It was entered as no. 30 in Patrick Young's list of Cathedral manuscripts in 1622 and no. 83 in an anonymous list of 1670 (Ker, 1950).

LITERATURE: Westwood, *Facsimiles*, 101, pl. 35; *Pal. Soc.*, I, pls. 188–9; F. A. Gasquet and E. Bishop, *The Bosworth Psalter*, 1908, 149–50, and *passim*; Homburger, 6, 47, 66 n. 1; J. Brønsted, *Early English Ornament*, 1924, 246–7, 250, fig. 175; R. Priebsch, *The Heliand Manuscript*, 1925, 30, 32, pls. IV, V; Millar, I, no. 12; F. Wormald, 'English Kalendars before 1100', *H.B.S.*, LXXII, 1934, no. 2; *id.*, *Initials*, 121, 124, 134, pl. Vd; Kendrick, *Late Saxon*, 34, pl. XXIX; N. R. Ker, 'Salisbury Cathedral Manuscripts and Patrick Young's Catalogue', *Wiltshire Archaeological and Natural History Magazine*, LIII, 1949–50, 168, no. 30; Holmquist, *Viking Art*, 16, 21; Wormald, *English Drawings*, 80, no. 58; Talbot Rice, *English Art*, 212, 213 n. 1, pl. 78; Ker, *Catalogue*, no. 379; C. and K. Sisam, 'The Salisbury Psalter', *E.E.T.S.*, 242, 1959, plate (facs. f. 110); D. H. Wright, *The Vespasian Psalter* (E.E.MSS in facs., XIV), 1967, 46 n. 1; T. A. M. Bishop, 'An early example of the Square Minuscule', *Transactions of the Cambridge Bibliographical Society*, IV, 1964–8, 246 n. 1; Alexander, *Norman Illumination*, 54, 56, 69, 80, 189; Bishop, *English Caroline*, no. 5; Wormald, *Winchester School*, 313.

19. MANUSCRIPTS DECORATED WITH INITIALS OF WORMALD TYPE II (a).
Mid 10th to early 11th centuries.
This list is a selection of the more important examples.

(i) Oxford, Bodleian Library MS Bodley 49 (1946)
Aldhelm, De virginitate
198 × 150 mm.
Mid 10th century   *Ill. 62*

(ii) London, British Library MS Cotton, Vitellius A. XIX
Bede, Lives of St. Cuthbert
215 × 145 mm.
Mid 10th century. Canterbury, St. Augustine's
Ill. 63

(iii) London, British Library MS Royal 15. B. XIX
Sedulius, Poems
265 × 165 mm.
Second half of 10th century. Canterbury, Christ Church   *Ill. 64*

(iv) Cambridge, Corpus Christi College MS 326
Aldhelm, De virginitate
220 × 158 mm.
Second half of 10th century. Canterbury, Christ Church

(v) Salisbury Cathedral Library MS 38
Aldhelm, De virginitate
265 × 165 mm.
Late 10th century. Canterbury, (?) Christ Church
Ills. 65–68

(vi) Oxford, Bodleian Library MS Digby 146
Aldhelm, De virginitate
230 × 150 mm.
Late 10th century   *Ill. 70*

(vii) London, British Library MS Harley 110
Prosper, Isidore, etc.
260 × 115 mm.
Late 10th century. Canterbury, Christ Church
Ill. 69

(viii) Oxford, Oriel College MS 3
Prudentius, Peristephanon, etc.
317 × 205 mm.
Late 10th century. Canterbury, Christ Church
Ills. 71, 72

(ix) London, British Library MS Royal 5. E. XI
Aldhelm, De virginitate
218 × 138 mm.
Late 10th century. Canterbury, Christ Church
Ills. 74, 75

(x) London, Lambeth Palace Library MS 204
Gregory the Great, Dialogues; Ephrem
280×180 mm.
Early 11th century. Canterbury, Christ Church

Fig. 2

(xi) Oxford, Bodleian Library MS Bodley 708 (2609)
Gregory the Great, Pastoral Care
300×200 mm.
Early 11th century. Canterbury, Christ Church

Ill. 73

The decoration of this group, related to no. 21 (Trinity Amalarius) and traceable to no. 7 (Junius Psalter), consists mainly of initials designated by Wormald (1945) as Type II(a) in which thin, black, wiry interlace is used in combination with gripping heads, rather sparse foliage, and, occasionally, touches of colour, while the body of the letter, also in black, is split by a fine white line.

In some of the manuscripts, initials of other types occasionally appear: (iii) contains a P (f. 1) with leaf ornament in the framework (cf. no. 6, Corpus Christi College MS 183, f. 6) and an E (f. 7ᵛ) heavily painted in grey and red; while in (v) and (viii)—the former, the most profusely decorated manuscript of the group, containing some initials of a mixed type—a few examples of Type II(b) with heavy double-line interlace also occur. Diagrams of wheels, each with eight spokes inscribed with the same verses are found in (iv) and (x).

PROVENANCE: With the exception of Bodley 49 (i) and Digby 146 (vi) of uncertain origin and containing *ex libris* of Winchester (13th century) and Abingdon (16th century), respectively, all manuscripts of this group come from one of the two Canterbury houses and are interconnected by the hands of common scribes. Corpus Christi College 326 (iv) contains Christ Church, Canterbury, pressmarks (p. ii, 1; cf. James, Catalogue) and was probably entered as no. 47 in Prior Eastry's catalogue of 1130. Lambeth 204 (x) belonged to Ely in the Middle Ages, as shown by the arms of Robert Steward, the last prior (f. 129ᵛ). Bodley 708 (xi) was given to Exeter Cathedral by Bishop Leofric, 1046–72 (gift recorded in Latin and Anglo-Saxon on f. 113).

LITERATURE:

(i) Ker, *Catalogue*, no. 299; Pächt and Alexander, no. 23.

(ii) B. Colgrave, *Two Lives of St. Cuthbert*, 1940, 27, 47, 55; Ker, *Catalogue*, no. 217; Bishop, *Notes*, V, 93; *id.*, *Codex Leidensis*, p. XIX (13).

(iii) Warner and Gilson, II, 159, IV, pl. 90a; Wormald, *Initials*, 134; Ker, *Catalogue*, no. 268; Bishop, *Notes*, VII, 421 (14); *id.*, *Codex Leidensis*, p. XX.

(iv) James, *Ancient Libraries*, 21, 506, no. 47; *id.*, *A descriptive catalogue of the manuscripts in the Library of Corpus Christi College, Cambridge*, 1912, II, 143–6; Wormald, *Initials*, 134; Kendrick, *Late Saxon*, 36 n. 2; Ker, *Catalogue*, no. 61; Bishop, *Notes*, VII, 414, 421, (24).

(v) Wormald, *Initials*, 134; Kendrick, *Late Saxon*, 36 n. 2; N. R. Ker, 'Salisbury Cathedral Manuscripts and Patrick Young's Catalogue', *Wiltshire Archaeological and Natural History Magazine*, LIII, 1949, 167; *id.*, *Catalogue*, no. 378; Bishop, *Notes*, IV, 330, 333, 335; *id.*, *Notes*, VI, 412; *id.*, *Codex Leidensis*, p. XX, no. 26; *id.*, *English Caroline*, p. XXVI.

(vi) Wormald, *Initials*, 122–3, pl. VI, a; Kendrick, *Late Saxon*, 36 n. 2, pl. XXXII, 1; Ker, *Catalogue*, no. 320; R. Derolez, 'Aldhelmus glosatus IV; some "Hapax legomena" among the Old English Aldhelm Glosses', *Studia Germanica Gandensia*, II, 1960, 81–95; Gneuss, 180, 189; Pächt and Alexander, no. 26, pl. II.

(vii) Wormald, *Initials*, 134; Ker, *Catalogue*, no. 228; Bishop, *Notes*, VII, 421(13); Bishop, *English Caroline*, p. xxvi.

(viii) H. Coxe, *Catalogus Codicum Manuscriptorum Colegii Universitatis*, Pars I, 5, 1852, 1; Bishop, *Notes*, VII, 415–16, 420, 421 (25); *Anglo-Saxon Illumination*, pl. 14; Ker, *Catalogue*, no. 358.

(ix) Homburger, 3 n. 3; Warner and Gilson, I, 115; III, pl. 42; Wormald, *Initials*, 134; Kendrick, *Late Saxon*, 36 n. 2; Ker, *Catalogue*, no. 252; Bishop, *Notes*, VII. 414, 419, 420, 421 (20).

(x) M. R. James, *A descriptive catalogue of the manuscripts in Lambeth Palace*, 1930, 325; Wormald, *Initials*, 134; Kendrick, *Late Saxon*, 36 n. 2; Ker, *Catalogue*, no. 277; Bishop, *English Caroline*, p. XVI n. 2.

(xi) *Pal. Soc.*, II, pl. 69; E. W. B. Nicholson, *Early Bodleian Music. Introduction to the study of the oldest Latin Musical manuscripts in the Bodleian Library*, Oxford, 1913, III, p. lx, pl. XXX; Ker, *Catalogue*, no. 316; Bishop, *English Caroline*, p. XXV, no. 10; Pächt and Alexander, no. 35, pl. III.

20. Cambridge, Trinity College MS O. 3. 7 (1179)
Boethius, De consolatione philosophiae
292×227 mm.
c. 970. Canterbury, St. Augustine's

Ills. 44, 76–78

The frontispiece (f. 1) contains an unframed full-page drawing of Philosophy represented as a majestic female figure standing full-face with a book and sceptre in her hands. The drawing, in brown outline lightly accented with red, is an important example of the 'first style' and is closely related to no. 13 (St. John's College MS 28) but shows no suggestion of body structure beneath the ample draperies: their austerely vertical lines are contrasted with the fluttering zigzagging edges and this contrast creates an illusion of vitality in the figure. The drawing is also reminiscent of no. 17 (Leofric Missal, f. 49ᵛ) where the draperies are more agitated however, and the effect less austere. The style of the Trinity drawing derives from the Court School of Charlemagne (cf. Goldschmidt, I, 4, 6, 12) but the influence of Rheims is perceptible in the softening of contours and the sketchy groundline on which the figure stands.

The initials with beasts' heads in three-quarter view are partly painted in brown and yellow; they are mainly Wormald Type II(a), using black interlace (ff. 2, 9), but an 'h' (f. 31) made up of thick soft, ribbon-like strands recalls an earlier initial type in manuscripts of the early 10th century.

PROVENANCE: The manuscript was identified by James (*Anc. Libr.*) with no. 993 in the medieval catalogue of the library of St. Augustine's, Canterbury.

LITERATURE: James, *Ancient Libraries*, 519, no. 993; *id.*, *The Western Manuscripts in the Library of Trinity College, Cambridge*, 1904, III, 188; IV, pl. X; Millar, no. 39; Wormald, *Initials*, 134; Kendrick, *Late Saxon*, 11, 36; Wormald, *English Drawings*, 27–9, 63, no. 17, pl. 3; Holmquist, *Viking Art*, 15; Talbot Rice, *English Art*, 196, pl. 59; Ker, *Catalogue*, Addenda no. 95*; P. Courcelle, *La consolation de Philosophie dans la tradition littéraire*, Paris 1967, 77, pl. 22; J. Beckwith, *Ivory Carvings in Early Medieval England*, 1972, 30–1, ill. 30.

21. Cambridge, Trinity College MS B. 11. 2 (241)
Amalarius, De ecclesiasticis officiis
295 × 225 mm.
c. 975. Canterbury, St. Augustine's

Ills. 79, 80

The manuscript contains numerous fine initials, the earliest examples of Wormald Type II(a); they are in black outline with, unusually in this group, a good deal of colour including shades of grey, green, yellow, blue, pink, and orange. The initials heading each chapter are ornamented with large birds and animal heads in three-quarter view, fine interlace knotwork, and delicate but crisp plant scrolls with fruit and flower-leaves of exquisite workmanship, threading in and out through the shafts of the letters. A splendid large initial P (f. 4) contains besides these motifs a profiled human head at the tip of a knotted strand in the bow (cf. no. 17, Leofric Missal, f. 154ᵛ), a boss of bunched three-dimensional acanthus leaves recalling no. 5 (Aethelstan Psalter, f. 21) and rings of various shapes. The titles and rubrics are inscribed on red, green, and yellow bands and the opening words are in capitals filled in with colour.

PROVENANCE: The manuscript, an outstanding early example of the productions of St. Augustine's, Canterbury, was written in square minuscule by a scribe whose hand appears in a group of manuscripts from the same scriptorium (cf. Bishop, *Notes*, VI, 1963). An inscription in Latin and Old

English records a gift from Bishop Leofric to Exeter in 1072 (f. 121ᵛ). It belonged to 'Johannes Parker' (f. 1), the son of Archbishop Parker and was given to Trinity College Library by John Whitgift, Archbishop of Canterbury 1583–1604.

LITERATURE: M. R. James, *The Western Manuscripts in the library of Trinity College, Cambridge*, 1900–4, I, 327, no. 241, IV, pl. 3; Wormald, *Initials*, 122 n. 2, 134, pl. Ve; Kendrick, *Late Saxon*, 35, pl. XXXI, 1, 2, 3; Talbot Rice, *English Art*, 178, pl. 42b; Bishop, *Notes*, III, 193; *ib.*, IV, 324; Ker, *Catalogue*, no. 84; Bishop, *Notes*, V, 93; *id.*, *Codex Leidensis*, p. XIX (8); Wormald, *Angleterre*, 230, ill. 220.

22. London, British Library MS Add. 37517
Psalter (Bosworth Psalter)
389 × 265 mm.
c. 980. Canterbury, Christ Church

Ills. 81–83

The Psalter is in the Roman version with some 12th- to 13th-century corrections to the Gallican. The Psalms (ff. 4–95), preceded by an almost contemporary calendar (ff. 2–3) are followed by canticles (ff. 96–104), a hymnal (ff. 105–28), and monastic canticles (ff. 129–35). Each psalm is introduced by a graceful brushwork initial of excellent quality in green and, from f. 66ᵛ onwards, in blue and red; some of the initials are ornamented in outline with leafwork and human or animal heads, the latter spitting foliage lightly veined in red.

Unusually large ornamental initials introducing Psalms 1 (f. 4), 51 (f. 33), 101 (f. 64ᵛ), and 109 (f. 74) are accompanied by the opening verses of the text inscribed (with the exception of f. 64ᵛ) on whole pages in lines of capitals of alternating colours, mainly blue, red, and orange. Initials B (f. 4), Q (f. 33), and D (f. 74) are made up of elaborately knotted double-stranded interlace with prominent 'elbows' and three-dimensional acanthus leaves, animal and birds' heads, a mask head (f. 4), and a complete creature (f. 74), and are painted in pale purple, blue, slate grey, dull red, and orange. Initial D (f. 64ᵛ) by a different artist is probably later, and its heavy framework with straggly acanthus on the shaft is painted in bright blue with touches of white, red, and green. The softly scrolling brushwork motifs used in contractions and as line-fillers seem to be typical of Canterbury manuscripts of the second half of the 10th century (cf. no. 30 (xii), Bibl. Nat., lat. 17814). Headings and initials to verses are in red. An unfinished drawing (f. 128) with a seated Christ belongs to the 12th century.

PROVENANCE: The Psalter was written at Canterbury, possibly for Archbishop Dunstan himself (959–88), for it is expressly made for the recitation of the Office according to the Rule of St. Benedict recently introduced into the monastic houses in England. The manuscript is closely related in script to no. 35 (Sherborne Pontifical), both written in a typical Canterbury hand of the late 10th century (cf. *New. Pal. Soc.*, I, 163). The Calendar (ff. 2–3), added after St. Dunstan's death probably between 988 and 1012 and recalling in script and decoration the calendar of no. 17 (Leofric Missal), is liturgically a Canterbury production perhaps originating from St. Augustine's. Latin and Old English glosses to portions of the text, a Litany (f. 104), prayers (ff. 134ᵛ–138ᵛ) and other matters (f. 139) belong to the 10th and 11th centuries. The manuscript belonged in the 16th century to Archbishop Cranmer, Lord Arundel, and finally to Lord Lumley (f. 2); purchased for the Royal Library in 1609 it passed to the family of Turville-Petre. It was bought by the British Museum from O. Turville-Petre of Bosworth Hall, Rugby, in 1907, hence known as the Bosworth Psalter.

LITERATURE: *New Pal. Soc.*, I, pls. 163, 164; G. F. Warner, *Reproductions from Illuminated Manuscripts*, 1907, III, pl. 5; F. A. Gasquet and E. Bishop, *The Bosworth Psalter*, 1908, pls. I–IV; Homburger, 4, 39; G. F. Warner and H. A. Wilson, *The Benedictional of St. Aethelwold*, 1910, XI n. 1, XXXIX; J. Brønsted, *Early English Ornament*, 1942, 245–6, 298 n. 1, fig. 173; Millar, I, 14 n. 1, no. 10; O. Homburger, 'Review', *Art Bulletin*, X, 1928, 400; C. Niver, 'The Psalter in the British Museum, Harley 2904', *Medieval Studies in Memory of A. Kingsley Porter*, ed. W. R. W. Koehler, Cambridge, Mass. II, 1939, 680 n. 54; Wormald, *Initials*, 110–11, 135, pl. IIa; Kendrick, *Late Saxon*, 35, 104, pl. XXX, 1, 3; Holmquist, *Viking Art*, 7, 18, 21, figs, 4, 5; Talbot Rice, *English Art*, 196, pl. 57 b; N. Denholm-Young, *Handwriting in England and Wales*, 1954, 15 n. 8; Dodwell, *Canterbury School*, 27, 34, 40, 53, 123, pl. 24a; Nordenfalk, *Early Medieval*, 185; Ker, *Catalogue*, no. 185; F. Wormald, 'Anglo-Saxon initials in a Paris Boethius manuscript', *Essais en l'honneur de Jean Porcher*, ed. O. Pächt, 1963, 64 n. 4; T. A. M. Bishop, 'An early example of the square minuscule', *Transactions of the Cambridge Bibliographical Society*, IV, 1964–8, 247 n. 1; Rickert, *Painting in Britain*, 33, 62, pl. 21a; Gneuss, 8 n. 12, 18, 45, 50 n. 28, 55, 104–5, 122 and *passim*; J. Beckwith, *Ivory Carvings in Early Medieval England*, 1972, 30, fig. 27; Wormald, *Angleterre*, 230; P. M. Korhammer, 'The Origin of the Bosworth Psalter', *Anglo-Saxon England*, 2, 1973, 173–87, pl. IVa.

23. London, British Library MS Add. 49598
Benedictional of St. Ethelwold

293 × 225 mm.

971–84. Winchester, Old Minster

Ills. 85, 86, 88, 90, 91

This manuscript, a collection of episcopal blessings arranged in the sequence of feasts throughout the liturgical year, is the masterpiece of the Winchester school. It is most sumptuously illuminated with twenty-eight full-page miniatures in foliated borders (f. 118 is unframed), nineteen text-pages inscribed in large square capitals in matching frames, and two full-page historiated initials.

The miniatures fall into two groups. Those of the first group preface the text and represent the heavenly choirs labelled by a *titulus* written across the two facing pages: Confessors (f. 1), with seven crowned standing figures, and virgins (ff. 1ᵛ–2) in two groups of three; the tympana of the intersecting arches of the frames are filled with angels holding books and scrolls. Wormald has shown by an analogy with the choirs in no. 5 (Aethelstan Psalter, ff. 2ᵛ, 21) that probably six leaves are now missing at the beginning of the book and that the lost miniatures included a Christ in Majesty, choirs of angels, patriarchs, prophets, Apostles, and Martyrs, and the first part of the choir of confessors. The twelve Apostles are shown again (ff. 2ᵛ–3) with Paul and Peter in the centre of the two groups of three (ff. 3ᵛ–4) and it seems more likely that the missing leaves (ff. iᵛ–viᵛ) contained three pages with choirs of angels.

The miniatures in the body of the text prefix the important feasts and, with the exception of those marking the Epiphany (ff. 24ᵛ–25), face similarly framed pages with the opening words of the blessings inscribed in large gold square capitals; three miniatures representing the Massacre of the Innocents (f. 20ᵛ), the Nativity of the Virgin (between ff. 105ᵛ and 106) and St. Michael (ff. 106ᵛ–107) have been removed.

Iconographically, some of the illustrations are closely connected with a group of late Carolingian ivory carvings mainly of the 9th- or 10th-century Metz school, and an ivory casket in the Brunswick Museum provides analogies suggesting a common model (cf. Homburger, 1963, 36; for reproductions see Goldschmidt, I, XLIV–XLV). There are also points of contact with certain manuscripts of the same school such as the Drogo Sacramentary in Paris, Bibl. Nat., lat. 9428.

The Annunciation (f. 5ᵛ) shows the Virgin seated under a domed baldachino, her hand resting on an open book by her side, while the announcing angel with a sceptre approaches from the right (cf. Brunswick Casket, Goldschmidt, I, XLV, d). The Second Coming (f. 9ᵛ), prefacing the Third Sunday in Advent, represents Christ descending in a tilted mandorla in thick clouds; He is holding a book and a cross staff over His shoulder and the words *Rex Regum et Dominus Dominantium* (Revelation, XIX, 16) are inscribed on His mantle over His right thigh; He is accompanied by a throng of angels, three of whom carry the instruments of His passion (cf. no. 5, Aethelstan Psalter, f. 2ᵛ). The mandorla, open on one side to enhance Christ's movement, is a striking modification (cf. the Ascension, f. 64ᵛ). The representation of Christ striding vigorously forwards and surrounded by a tilted mandorla recalls certain 9th-century Greco-Italian portrayals of the Descent into Limbo and of the later Byzantine Anastasis.

The illustration of the Nativity (f. 15ᵛ), with the

Virgin reclining on a tilted bedstead and Joseph seated at its foot on the right, introduces two important iconographic features: the crib with the Infant is shown on the nearside of the bed (note the pillow under Christ's head, an unprecedented detail) and a midwife arranges the cushion to make the Virgin more comfortable, both motifs traceable to Carolingian sources, the former becoming a characteristic feature of English Nativities (cf. Goldschmidt, I, XXXI, 75; also I, XLV, c, Brunswick Casket, for a midwife similarly placed).

The Martyrdom of St. Stephen (f. 17ᵛ): the Saint genuflecting on the right and facing a group of his executioners, looks up to Christ who appears above in a mandorla held by two angels, a composition containing some analogies with the Drogo Sacramentary (f. 27). St. John the Evangelist (f. 19ᵛ), seated in three-quarter view on a cushioned throne, a knotted curtain behind him on the left, holds a golden book inscribed *In principio* . . . over a lectern on the right, while above it an eagle emerges from a cloud blowing a horn (cf. no. 47, Copenhagen Gospels; no. 68, Grimbald Gospels; no. 73, Pembroke 301), a motif probably inspired by an Insular model since it is also present in the Lindisfarne Gospels, 8th century (f. 93ᵛ).

The next illustration (f. 22ᵛ) shows on two registers the Virgin reclining on a couch with the Christ Child in her arms and below three seated, conversing figures; this prefaces the blessing for the Octave of Christmas and may represent: 'Jesus increasing in wisdom . . .', Luke, II, 52 (Wormald, 1959).

The Adoration (f. 24) represents the Virgin and Child enthroned under an arched canopy on the right, turning towards the crowned Magi who approach from the left with gifts in their veiled hands. The first King is distinguished by tasselled stockings and by the diadem he is offering to Christ. The figures spill over the frame and the space-filling clouds suggest the adjustment of an originally horizontal composition to the shape of the frame (cf. also f. 25). The Virgin and Child group shown in three-quarters view belongs to the Western tradition, while the veiled hands of the Magi point to ultimate Eastern sources though the crowns on their heads are a most striking innovation simultaneously appearing on the Continent (cf. Egbert Codex, *c.* 980, Trier, Stadtbibl.). The Baptism miniature on the opposite page (f. 25) contains unusual features partly paralleled in Carolingian works and partly of Eastern inspiration: Christ is surrounded by a gold-filled mandorla, and stands waist-deep in swelling water between John the Baptist, clad in skins on the right, and a seated horned Jordan with a pitcher on the left, while an angel with veiled hands assists on either side; the Holy Dove descending from the clouds above carries in its beak a double container with the chrism and is accompanied by four hovering angels holding sceptres and diadems (cf. Goldschmidt, I, XXVII, 66). The mandorla surrounding Christ, an originally Eastern motif, is paralleled on the Brunswick Casket (Goldschmidt, XLIV, a) but otherwise unprecedented in this context. The skins covering the Baptist belong to the early Western

tradition (Arian Baptistery, Ravenna, 6th century), while the horned Jordan probably reflects an influence from Byzantine monastic psalters where horned sea-gods occur (cf. Chludoff Psalter, late 9th century, Moscow, Hist. Cod. Gr. 129). The double container in the Dove's beak, a motif of Carolingian invention, constitutes the most striking and otherwise unparalleled link between the Benedictional and the Brunswick Casket, thus leaving no doubts as to their parentage (cf. also Goldschmidt, I, XXVII, 66, where a single ampulla is shown).

The Presentation scene (f. 34ᵛ) belonging to the Western tradition, takes place within the Temple and shows the Virgin handing the Child over the altar to Simeon followed by the prophetess Anna on the right while behind the Virgin on the left can be seen an attendant maid and Joseph with two turtle-doves; above in the tympanum appears the blessing Hand of God (note a roundel with Franco-Saxon interlace on the apex of the arched frame). The miniature with the Entry into Jerusalem (f. 45ᵛ) shows Christ astride a donkey in the Western manner; He is followed by a group of people (the Apostles?) with golden palm branches, while two youths at the city gate on the right spread mantles under the ass's feet and above them other figures lean out from the city walls or climb a tree on the left to throw flowering branches (cf. no. 98, Tiberius C. VI). Here again the frame partly disintegrates under the horizontally expanding composition (cf. ff. 24ᵛ–25).

The miniature prefacing the Easter blessing (f. 51ᵛ) shows three Holy Women with ointment jars and a censer approaching a basilica-like sepulchre (cf. Goldschmidt, I, XXXV, 84) from the right to be met by a sceptred angel seated by the side; behind the tomb, inside which the grave-clothes can be seen, four guards, bemused, are huddled together. The groups of the Three Marys and the guards spill over the frame which becomes part of the background.

The scene with the Incredulity of Thomas (f. 56ᵛ) represents Christ standing within a gold-filled mandorla between asymmetrically grouped Apostles and raising His bare arm to show the wound in His side to Thomas approaching from the left; Christ's bare arm and side exposed suggest Western, probably Carolingian iconographic sources (Goldschmidt, I, XII, 22).

The Ascension (f. 64ᵛ) shows Christ with a cross staff over His shoulder striding vigorously upwards towards the Hand of God stretching out on the right from a hemisphere in the sky; He is surrounded by a mandorla, the right side open to stress His forward thrust (cf. f. 9ᵛ), and He is flanked by four angels, the two at the bottom addressing a crowd of Apostles below; the latter are shown in two groups, headed by the Virgin on the left, with St. Peter on the right, and all look up to heaven with gestures of amazement. The sense of excitement and movement pervades the whole picture. The miniature showing Christ in profile striding heavenwards blends the Early Christian Western tradition (cf. ivory panel, 5th century, Munich, Nat. Mus.) with such Eastern iconographic features as the mandorla, a combination already established in Carolingian art (cf. Goldschmidt, I, XIV, 17a; XXVII, 65; cf. also the Wirksworth stone panel, England, *c.* 800, for a Christ carrying a cross and surrounded by a mandorla held by the angels, and a closely allied Anglo-Saxon Ascension, ivory, late 10th century, repr. Beckwith, 1972, ill. 50).

The representation of Pentecost (f. 67ᵛ) is Byzantine in type: it shows the twelve Apostles seated on a circular bench in two groups with Peter heading the one on the right, while the Holy Ghost, a golden dove, descends in a mandorla and enters the Apostles' mouths in the tongues of flame. The blessing for Trinity Sunday (f. 70) is introduced by a full-page unframed initial O with Christ in Majesty holding a book and seated on a fragment of the firmament.

The gold-clad majestic figure of St. Etheldreda, Abbess of Ely, (f. 90ᵛ) is shown standing with a book and a flowering branch, accompanied by an identifying inscription in gold uncials on vellum ground and surrounded by a particularly splendid border recalling no. 16 (Vespasian A. VIII); an initial O on the opposite page (f. 91) is similarly framed and contains a half-figure of Christ (cf. f. 70) blessing.

The Nativity of John the Baptist (f. 92ᵛ) is shown on two registers: in the upper one Elizabeth is reclining on a couch with the infant John in a manger on the right, and below, Zacharias seated on the left writes his name on a tablet and is watched by four inquiring figures (cf. f. 22ᵛ). The Martyrdom of St. Peter (f. 95ᵛ) is illustrated in the upper part of the miniature showing the Saint crucified head downwards while two torturers rope his feet to the cross; at the bottom of the same picture St. Paul standing on the right, faces his executioner who brandishes a sword. The composition, though differing in details, broadly recalls the portrayal of the Saints' martyrdom in the Drogo Sacramentary (f. 86).

St. Swithun (f. 97ᵛ) in Mass vestments stands, blessing, in a niche under intersecting arches. St. Benedict (f. 99ᵛ), a golden fillet round his head, is enthroned under a curtained arch and, resting a book on his knee, holds a golden crown in his other hand; the background, filled on either side with architectural motifs, recalls in its crowded abstract effect Insular manuscripts of the 7th to 8th centuries. The miniature with the Death of the Virgin (f. 102ᵛ), showing her at the point of receiving a crown from the Hand of God above, is the earliest known representation of that theme in English art and combines elements of the Byzantine tradition with Italian iconography of the Maria Regina. The Virgin reclines on a draped couch suspended on the capitals of the arched columns and is attended by two weeping women (by then a feature of Winchester manuscripts of the late 10th century) and by a third adjusting the pillows under her head (cf. f. 15ᵛ). Above them four angels (one with a sceptre), flanking the Hand of God, emerge from behind the arched frame, and below stand two groups of the Apostles with Peter at the centre.

The last illustration (f. 118ᵛ), prefacing the blessing for the dedication of a church, represents a bishop standing before an altar assisted by six monks, one of whom holds a golden book, while above them, forming the background, heads look out from a towered building. The miniature is executed in red outline with only the bishop's figure and the altar emphasized, probably deliberately, by colour (see Wormald, 1959; cf. also nos. 58, the Caedmon Genesis, p. 11; 66, Arundel 155, f, 133; 84, Bury Psalter, f. 35) but the suggestion that it may represent the dedication of Winchester Cathedral by Ethelwold in 980 is uncertain. The miniature is unframed and the text from the preceding page continues across the top in three lines of Caroline minuscule.

The differences in figure composition of the miniatures, at times showing adaptation from an originally horizontal format to the vertical shape of the framework, suggest a diversity of models. Close iconographic analogies of certain illustrations with manuscripts and ivories of the Metz school (first observed by Homburger, 1912) point to Carolingian art as the main source of inspiration. The second source was Byzantine and while a number of features belonging to the Greek tradition may have been transmitted through Carolingian intermediaries, the availability of early or perhaps contemporary Greek models is also very likely. Finally, iconographic innovations of lasting importance to English art reveal a highly independent approach and the striking ability of the artists concerned to select rare pictorial motifs from various sources and transform established conventions into a new idiom.

The vigorous and animated figure drawing in firm black outline is in the 'first' style and derives mainly from the Carolingian Ada and Metz Schools but with more emphasis on the incised linear surface patterns and the restless zigzagging drapery edges. The miniatures are fully painted in rich and soft colours of pink to mauve, deep indigo blue, brown, dull red, orange, green, some ochre, and yellow and their range is enriched by overpainting and colour line shading with modelling done in white. Gold is used in great profusion in the draperies, the details, and the framework; coloured shadow outline (ff. 9ᵛ, 67ᵛ), a feature of later Anglo-Saxon painting occurs, as does diaper on the garments; the wavy curls of colour, denoting cloudy skies or rippling water and deriving from the late antique tradition which was probably transmitted through Carolingian works, are prominent in the backgrounds and are treated in a highly ornamental manner. Features and hands, outlined in red, are heavily modelled in white.

The multicoloured foliated framework, the hallmark of Winchester decoration, is extremely varied and includes rectangular and arched borders, the latter supported on columns with capitals and bases of curling foliage, the former ornamented with large median bosses and heavy corner rosettes of acanthus leaves. All borders, except those surrounding the St. Etheldreda miniature (ff. 90ᵛ–91) structurally recalling no. 16 (King Edgar Charter), are composed of acanthus patterns contained within heavy gold panels. Although the structure and the type of leafwork of the 'Winchester' borders are traceable to Carolingian,

Franco-Saxon and Metz works respectively, there are no examples on the Continent blending all the elements into one decorative whole, and their final combination is the great achievement of the Anglo-Saxon artists. Finally, the striking absence of any Insular decorative forms suggests a deliberate choice by the patron for whom the book was made, an impression corroborated by the Caroline minuscule employed in the script throughout. Large plain gold capitals introduce the blessings, while small initials to paragraphs are in gold uncials with rubrics in gold and red.

PROVENANCE: A Latin poem inscribed in golden rustic capitals (ff. 4ᵛ-5) discloses that the manuscript was written for and at the command of Ethelwold, Bishop of Winchester 963-84, by the scribe Godeman, probably a monk of the Old Minster who later became Abbot of Thorney. The book was probably produced after 971 since the blessing for the feast of St. Swithun refers to the miracles which occurred after the Saint's translation in that year. The manuscript remained at Winchester throughout the Middle Ages and was possibly at Hyde Abbey, since a 15th-century list of relics from that house was used to reinforce the binding. It was presented between 1713 and 1720 to the second Duke of Devonshire by General Hatton Compton, the executor of Henry Compton, Bishop of London 1675-1713 (Wright, 1963), to become part of the Chatsworth collection. It was acquired by the British Museum in 1957.

LITERATURE: J. Gage, 'A dissertation on St. Aethelwold's Benedictional', *Archaeologia* XXIV, 1832, 1-117, pls. I-XXXII (outline facs.); Westwood, *Facsimiles*, 132, pl. 45; *Pal. Soc.*, I, pls. 142-4; A. Haseloff, 'École Anglo-Saxonne', in A. Michel, *Histoire de l'art*, Paris 1905, I, 741-2; S. Beissel, *Geschichte der Evangelienbücher*, Freiburg im Breisgau 1906, 138, fig. 38; Burlington Fine Arts Club, *Exhibition of Illuminated Manuscripts*, 1908, no. 11, pl. 17; G. F. Warner and H. A. Wilson, *The Bendictional of St. Aethelwold*, monochrome facs., 1910; J. A. Herbert, *Illuminated Manuscripts*, 1911, 125-7; Homburger, 7-43, 44-6, 48-58, 61, pls. I, II, IV; H. P. Mitchell, 'Flotsam of Later Anglo-Saxon Art', *Burlington Magazine*, XXII, 1923, 304-5, pl. 5; XXIII, 1923, 104, 117, pl. VI, A; J. Brønsted, *Early English Ornament*, London and Copenhagen 1924, 259-60, 298 n. 1, fig. 186; Millar, I, 7-9, no. 5, pls. 4-7; A. Goldschmidt, *Die Elfenbeinskulpturen aus der romanischen Zeit XI-XII Jahrhundert*, Berlin 1926, IV, no. 6, fig. 27; O. Homburger, 'Review', *Art Bulletin*, X, 1928, 401; Saunders, *English Illumination*, 17, 22 ff., 29, 120, pls. 18-21; A. Boeckler, *Abendländische Miniaturen*, 1930, 53-4, pl. 45; J. B. L. Tolhurst, 'An Examination of two Anglo-Saxon Manuscripts of the Winchester School, the Missal of Robert of Jumièges and the Benedictional of St. Aethelwold', *Archaeologia*, 2nd ser., XXXIII, 1933, 27-44; C. Niver, 'The Psalter in the British Museum, Harley 2904', *Medieval Studies in Memory of A. Kingsley Porter*, ed. W. R. W. Koehler, Cambridge, Mass. 1939, II, 681 n. 63, 684; A. Goldschmidt, 'English Influence on Medieval Art', *ib.*, 711; W. Weisbach, *Manierismus in mittelalterlicher Kunst*, Basel, 1942, 21-2, pl. 12; M. Schapiro, 'The image of the disappearing Christ', *Gazette des Beaux Arts*, 6e ser. XXIII, 1943, 142, 145, fig. 2; Wormald, *Initials*, 132; F. Saxl and R. Wittkower, *British Art and the Mediterranean*, 1948, pls. 20 (3), 22 (1); Kendrick, *Late Saxon*, 6-8, pls. III-V; W. Oakeshott, *The Sequence of English Medieval Art*, 1950, 14, 16, 23, 30, 43, pl. 3; G. Zarnecki, 'The Coronation of the Virgin on a capital from Reading Abbey', *J.W.C.I.*, XIII, 1950, 12, pl. 3; Talbot Rice, *English Art*, 162, 175, 185-9, 200, pls. 48-51; Sir Francis Oppenheimer, *The Legend of the Ste Ampoule*, 1953, 124, 140-1, 143, App. I no. 2, 276-7, 285-6, pl. 3; N. Denholm-Young, *Handwriting in England and Wales*, 1954, 15; Dodwell, *The Canterbury School*, 4, 22; A. Boutemy, 'L'Enluminure anglaise de l'époque saxonne (Xe et XIe siècles) et la Flandre française', *Bulletin de la Société nationale des Antiquaires de France*, 1956, 43, 45; Freyhan, 427-8, 430-2, pl. XXXIX, 21-5; Bishop, *Notes*, IV, 333; Nordenfalk, *Early Medieval*, 182, pl. 180; F. Saxl, 'Illuminated science manuscripts in England', *Lectures*, 1957, 97, pls. 52b, 53c; D. Tselos, 'English manuscript illustration and the Utrecht Psalter', *Art Bulletin*, XLI, 1959, 138; F. Wormald, *The Benedictional of St. Ethelwold*, 1959; Rickert, *Miniatura*, 15, 17, 20, pls. 12, 13; R. L. Bruce-Mitford, 'Decoration and miniature', *Codex Lindisfarnensis*, 1960, II, 159 n. 9, pl. 28d; *St. Albans Psalter*, 54, 66, 84, 86, pl. 102b, 118 f.; R. H. Randall jr., 'An eleventh-century ivory pectoral cross', *J.W.C.I.*, XXV, 1962, 164-6, 170; O. Homburger, 'L'art carolingien de Metz et l'école de Winchester', *Essais en l'honneur de Jean Porcher*, ed. O. Pächt, 1963, 36-7, 41-3; C. E. Wright, 'The Benedictional of St. Ethelwold and Bishop Henry Compton', *British Museum Quarterly*, XXVII, 1963, 3-5; F. Wormald, 'Continental influence on English medieval illumination', *Fourth International Congress of Bibliophiles*, London, 1965, 9; *id.*, 'A fragment of a tenth-century English Gospel Lectionary', *Calligraphy and Paleography. Essays Presented to Alfred Fairbank*, ed. A. S. Osley, 1965, 44; Rickert, *Painting in Britain*, 36-8, 223 n. 41, figs. 26, 27; Swarzenski, *Monuments*, 21, pls. 55, fig. 124, 56, fig. 126, 62, fig. 140; Roosen-Runge, 30-50, pl. II, ills. 3-4; F. Deuchler, *Der Ingeborg Psalter*, Berlin, 1967, 42; M. Bourgeois-Lechartier, 'À la recherche du scriptorium de l'Abbaye du Mont Saint-Michel (XIe-XIIe siècles)', *Millénaire monastique du Mont Saint-Michel*, Paris 1967, II, 194; J. Vezin, 'Manuscrits des dixième et onzième siècles copiés en Angleterre et conservés à la Bibliothèque nationale de Paris', *Mélanges offerts a Julien Cain*, Paris 1968, II, 285; Alexander, *Norman Illumination*, 63, 92 n. 1, 101 n. 2, 120-1, 124-5, 129, 132-3, 135, 137-8, 142, 151-2, 154, 155 n. 3, 156, 161-2, 167 n. 5, 169, pls. 23, 32b, 33b, 34h, 39e, 41b; R. Deshman, 'Otto III and the Warmund Sacramentary (*c.* 969-1011), Biblioteca Capitolare MS. LXXXVI', *Zeitschrift für Kunstgeschichte*, 34, 1971, 7, fig. 11; C. R. Dodwell, *Painting in Europe, 800-1200*, 1971, 55, 145; *id.*, *Techniques*,

645–7, 649–50; Bishop, *English Caroline*, pp. XX, XXII, no. 12; G. Schiller, *Iconography of Christian Art*, 1971, I, 137–8, ill. 371; II, 187, ill. 645; J. Beckwith, *Ivory Carvings in Early Medieval England*, 1972, 33–4, ills. 33, 58; Wormald, *Angleterre*, 236, ill. 233, pl. 231; C. Nordenfalk, 'The Draped Lectern', *Intuition und Kunstwissenschaft: Festschrift für Hans Swarzenski*, Berlin 1973, 87, fig. 3; *English Illuminated Manuscripts 700–1500*, Brussels Exhibition Catalogue 1973, pp. 17, 23; R. Deshman, 'Anglo-Saxon Art After Alfred', *Art Bulletin*, LVI, 1974, 179, 197, 199, figs. 47 a, b, 50, 51; Robb, *Illuminated Manuscript*, 147–9, pl. XIV; H. Holländer, *Early Medieval Art*, 1974, 185, ill. 149. C. R. Dodwell, Peter Clemoes, *The Old English Illustrated Hexateuch* (E.E.MSS in facs., XVIII) 1974. 58–9.

24. Rouen, Bibliothèque Municipale MS Y. 7 (369)

Benedictional and Pontifical
(Benedictional of Archbishop Robert)
323×245 mm.
c. 980. Winchester, New Minster

Colour Frontispiece, Ills. 87, 89

The decoration of the manuscript confined to the Benedictional proper (ff. 8–81), now consists of only three miniatures in 'Winchester' frames facing decorative text-pages in matching borders: the Holy Women at the Sepulchre (f. 21ᵛ), Pentecost (f. 29ᵛ), and the Dormition (f. 54ᵛ). Two more unaccompanied text-pages (ff. 9, 28) indicate that the miniatures of the Nativity and the Ascension have been cut out. The three extant illustrations are close copies of the representations in no. 23 (Benedictional of St. Ethelwold) but show, nevertheless, certain changes in their simplified iconography and in their composition which is better adjusted to the vertical format of the frames (cf. Homburger for a view that the two Benedictionals derive independently from a common model).

The first miniature (f. 21ᵛ) surrounded by a rectangular border, shows an angel seated in front of the sepulchre of a compressed shape (its black interior, without the usual grave-clothes, serving as a foil for the angel's figure); the Three Marys, sharply silhouetted on plain vellum ground, are approaching from the right, while the guards lie asleep in the forefront of the picture.

The Pentecost scene (f. 29ᵛ), represented as in no. 23 under an arched frame with architectural motifs in the spandrels and showing two groups of the Apostles seated on a semicircular bench with the Holy Spirit descending in the tongues of fire from above, contains a number of modifications: the Hand of God appears in a roundel on the arch, St. Paul is placed centremost next to St. Peter, and the background, painted in atmospheric streaks of colour, is elaborated by two small arches supported on a spiralled column right down the middle of the picture. The representation of the Dormition (f. 54ᵛ) is a

simplified version of the miniature in no. 23, free of all elements superfluous to the narrative. Set in a similar arched border on plain vellum ground it shows the Virgin lying with hands in an *orans* posture on an austerely plain bed; she is about to receive a crown from the Hand of God appearing in a roundel above, while the four attendant mourners watch and weep into their mantles (note again the hunchbacked weeping female figures, inspired by Carolingian models, an important feature of Winchester manuscripts of the late 10th century). It is one of the two earliest known representations of the Coronation of the Virgin (cf. no. 23). The figure drawing in firm outline is closely related to that of no. 23 but is more ponderous and shows simplification in the patterns of the heavy drapery folds and in their less linear treatment; consequently the figures look more weighty and solid. The same tendency predominates in the decoration with its bold and heavy foliage supported on massive gold trelliswork and sharply set off by black backgrounds. The rich and heavy colours include rust brown, orange, yellow, bluish grey, and mauve with touches of green and white in the highlights; gold is used extensively in the garments, details, and framework. Features, outlined in orange, are shaded rust brown and lightened with white.

The benedictions for Christmas (f. 9), Easter (f. 22), and those for the Ascension (f. 28) and Pentecost (f. 30) are written throughout in gold lettering. Headings and responses are in red and initials in gold.

PROVENANCE: Liturgical evidence shows that the manuscript was made for a bishop of Winchester, possibly Ethelwold himself, and, as it is dependent on the iconography and the decorative style of no. 23 (Benedictional of St. Ethelwold), it is datable to 980–90. It was probably written at the New Minster, Winchester, as suggested by the forms for the festival of SS. Judoc and Grimbald and by their names invoked in the litanies in the Pontifical portion (f. 95ᵛ). Identifiable in a list of the Rouen Cathedral manuscripts from the time of Archbishop Godefredus (1111–28) the manuscript contains a 17th-century inscription: *Benedictionarius Roberti Archiepiscopi*, f. 1, ('Cantauriensis' added on an erasure in a different contemporary hand) which gave rise to a controversy whether the owner was Robert, brot of Queen Emma and Archbishop of Rouen, 990–1037, or Robert of Jumièges, Archbishop of Canterbury, 1051–2. It belonged to the Cathedral library throughout the Middle Ages as indicated by an inscription of 1673 on the inside of the cover.

LITERATURE: J. Gage, 'A description of a Benedictional or a Pontifical called Benedictionarius Roberti Archiepiscopi', *Archaeologia*, XXIV 1832, 118–36, pls. XXXIII-XXXIV; Westwood, *Facsimiles*, 139; H. A. Wilson, 'The Benedictional of Archbishop Robert', *H.B.S.*, XXIV, 1903; G. F. Warner and H. A. Wilson, *The Benedictional of St. Aethelwold*, 1910, pp. XXIV, XXVI, XXXI, XXXIX; J. A. Herbert, *Illuminated Manuscripts*, 1911, 127–8; Homburger, 2, 21 n. 3, 25, 49–57, 59, 61, 62,

53

pls. VI, VII; Millar, I, 9 f., no. 6, pls. 8, 9; J. Brønsted, *Early English Ornament*, 1924, 259; Saunders, *English Illumination*, 18; A. Boeckler, *Abendländische Miniaturen*, 1930, 54–5; H. Labrosse, 'Le benedictionaire de l'archevêque Robert', *Les richesses des bibliothèques provinciales de France*, 1932, II, 134, pl. XXX; V. Leroquais, *Les Pontificaux manuscrits des bibliothèques publiques de France*, 1937, II, 300; III, pls. III-VI; G. Zarnecki, 'The Coronation of the Virgin on a capital from Reading Abbey', *J.W.C.I.*, XIII, 1950, 12; Talbot Rice, *English Art*, 189 f., 212, pl. 52; Nordenfalk, *Early Medieval*, 183; F. Wormald, *The Benedictional of St. Ethelwold*, 1959, 9, 15; Rickert, *Miniatura*, 15, 16, 20, pl. 16; id., *Painting in Britain*, 38, pl. 29b; Roosen-Runge, 56; Alexander, *Norman Illumination*, 132, 152, 169, 237, pl. 40d; Wormald, *Angleterre*, 239, pl. 230; H. Holländer, *Early Medieval Art*, 1974, 186, ill. 150.

EXHIBITED: Brussels, 1973, *English Illuminated Manuscripts 700–1500*, no. 4.

25. Paris, Bibliothèque Nationale MS lat. 987
Benedictional (ff. 1–84)
315 × 225 mm.
Last quarter of 10th century. Winchester

Ills. 92, 93

The manuscript, containing Benedictions identical with those in no. 23 (Benedictional of St. Ethelwold), is also related to the latter in the decoration which is, however, less elaborate and consists only of nine ornamental pages with splendid large initials in gold and text-lines in gold and red within rectangular or arched borders. Some of the former are made up of plain gold, blue, pink and mauve bands (ff. 16, 63, 71; cf. no. 16, King Edgar Charter, ff. 3ᵛ, 4); others are of the 'Winchester' type with corner rosettes and medallions and have curling blue and green foliage climbing over gold trelliswork (f. 31) or contain continuous acanthus patterns within gold panels (f. 41); the long-stalked flower-leaves on the corner recall no. 16 (King Edgar Charter). The arched borders (ff. 26, 43, 65) have round arches in gold and colour supported on columns with acanthus capitals and slender architectural motifs in the spandrels (cf. Pentecost miniatures in nos. 23 and 24, the two Winchester Benedictionals). Finally, a rectangular frame of gold and mauve (f. 68) has within it a plain gold arch on pilasters. Headings and Amens are in red uncials, other initials, standing in the margins, are small gold capitals.

PROVENANCE: The manuscript (ff. 1–84), closely related in script and contents to no. 23 (Benedictional of St. Ethelwold), was written in the same scriptorium, if not by the same scribe, Godeman, and is nearly contemporary with the St. Ethelwold manuscript. Benedictions for the festival and the Translation (1023) of St. Elphege among the additions (ff. 85–111) in a hand close to that of no. 65 (Trinity Gospels, probably from Canterbury),

suggest that the book passed to Canterbury after 1023. A drawing (f. 111) of a king, perhaps the Confessor, between two ecclesiastics, was added in Canterbury early in the 12th century (cf. Dodwell, 1954). The manuscript entered the Royal Library in Paris in 1732 with the collection of J. B. Colbert (no. 1298).

LITERATURE: M. L. Delisle, *Mémoire sur d'anciens sacramentaires*, Paris 1886, XXII, 216; G. F. Warner and H. A. Wilson, *The Benedictional of St. Aethelwold*, 1910, pp. XI, XXIV, LVIII; *New Pal. Soc.*, I, pls. 83, 84; Homburger, 48, 51, 57–65, pls. VIII, IX; Millar, I, no. 19; Saunders, *English Illumination*, 18, 21, pl. 17b; Talbot Rice, *English Art*, 195; Dodwell, *Canterbury School*, 21, 121, pl. 12c; Freyhan, 428; F. Wormald, *The Benedictional of St. Ethelwold*, 1959, 9, 10; J. Vezin, 'Manuscrits des dixième et onzième siècles copiés en Angleterre en minuscule caroline et conservés à la Bibliothèque nationale de Paris,' *Mélanges offerts à Julien Cain*, Paris, 1968, II, 287; Alexander, *Norman Illumination*, 238 n. 6; Bishop, *English Caroline*, no. 12.

26. London, College of Arms MS Arundel 22
Fragment of a Gospel Lectionary (ff. 84–85ᵛ)
335 × 235 mm.
c. 980. (?) Winchester

Colour Plate p. 21

Two conjoined but not consecutive leaves from a Gospel Lectionary (ff. 84–85ᵛ) contain a framed page (f. 84) with a splendid initial I of Franco-Saxon type made up of two gold-edged panels with confined acanthus patterns in dull green and yellow, and two loosely-knit interlace terminals on clear yellow ground, the one at the bottom ending with two birds' heads. The initial introduces the opening words of the reading for the vigil of Christmas, inscribed in gold capitals and uncials, the whole being surrounded by a border of running leaf patterns contained within two heavy gold bars with acanthus rosettes in gold roundels at the corners. On all four sides of the frame are median medallions of thick ribbon interlace knotwork, adorned with four birds' heads; this particular motif has no parallel in Anglo-Saxon book painting. All elements of the decoration are traceable to Franco-Saxon sources, though, as shown by Wormald, no single model containing them all together is known. The colouring, including bright, clear yellow, cool green, blue, pale purple, and a profusion of gold, is also strongly reminiscent of Franco-Saxon illumination. Minor initials in the text (ff. 84ᵛ–85ᵛ) are in gold and rubrics in red.

PROVENANCE: Written by the scribe of no. 23 (Benedictional of St. Ethelwold), Godeman, no doubt in the same scriptorium, the fragment is an important example of English Caroline minuscule datable *c*. 980 (Wormald, 1965). Inscribed 'John Betts: his Booke: 1606' (f. 84), the leaves are bound with miscellaneous 14th-century manuscripts, the whole having been given to the College of Arms by the Duke of Norfolk in 1678.

LITERATURE: Wormald, *Initials*, 108 n. 4; *id.*, *The Benedictional of St. Ethelwold*, 1959, 10; *id.*, 'Late Anglo-Saxon Art: some questions and suggestions', *Studies in Western Art. Acts of the 20th Congress of the History of Art*, ed. M. Meiss, I, Princeton 1963, 20; *id.*, 'A fragment of a tenth-century English Gospel Lectionary', *Calligraphy and Palaeography. Essays presented to Alfred Fairbank*, ed. A. S. Osley, London 1965, 43–6; Bishop, *English Caroline*, no. 12; Wormald, *Angleterre*, 231, ill. 224.

27. London, British Library MS Cotton, Cleopatra A. VI (ff. 2-53)
Grammatical treatises, miscellanea
180 × 113 mm.
Second half of 10th century

Ill. 96

The manuscript contains numerous initials, Wormald Type I, in black outline with the exception of a large P (f. 2) which is painted in slate blue with some green and yellow. The initials, of rather rough execution, are ornamented with a great variety of motifs: complete birds, their necks interlacing and recalling the Insular manuscripts of the 8th to 9th centuries, dragons, mask-heads (the one on f. 19ᵛ being reminiscent of those in the Book of Cerne), much rudimentary leafwork, some double-line 'elbowed' interlace, etc. A 'b' (f. 23) is topped with a profiled human head and an I (f. 31) contains a 'spread eagle' lion. The full bodied birds and dragons are vaguely related to nos. 9 (Tanner 10) and 18 (Salisbury 150).

PROVENANCE: Origin unknown, possibly West Country. The manuscript belonged to Sir Robert Cotton (d. 1631). His library, presented to the nation by his grandson, Sir John Cotton, in 1700, was incorporated in the British Museum in 1753.

LITERATURE: Wormald, *Initials*, 120 n. 6; Kendrick, *Late Saxon*, 33 n. 1; Talbot Rice, *English Art*, 206.

28. Vercelli, Cathedral, Codex CVII
Homilies and Poems in Anglo-Saxon
310 × 205 mm.
Second half of 10th century. (?) Worcester

Ills. 97–99

The manuscript contains one initial, an 'h' (f. 49), Wormald Type I, composed of two dragons, a mask-head, and some foliage; two more initials (ff. 106ᵛ, 112) are examples of an early form of Wormald Type II belonging to the mixed group: the body of the letter is black and is split by a line down the middle, and besides a mask-head and some rudimentary plant motifs, a knotwork of double-line

interlace is introduced at the extremity. An outline sketch of a quadruped occurs (f. 49ᵛ). The other initial letters are plain black capitals.

PROVENANCE: The origin is uncertain; Worcester was suggested (Förster, 1913) on account of the dialect employed in the text, an attribution supported by the decoration of a rather rough type (cf. no. 30.ix, Vat. lat. 1671). A neumed response (f. 24ᵛ) added in the 11th to 12th century indicates that the manuscript was in North Italy by that date. Probably included in a list of Vercelli manuscripts of 1602 compiled by Giovanni Fr. Leone, it was seen at Vercelli by Giuseppe Bianchini in 1748.

LITERATURE: M. Förster, *Il Codice Vercellese con Omelie e Poesie in lingua Anglosassona*, facsimile ed., Rome 1913; Wormald, *Initials*, 120 n. 1, 134; K. Sisam, *Studies in Old English Literature*, 1953, 113–16; P. Hunter Blair, *An Introduction to Anglo-Saxon England*, 1956, 337–8; Ker, *Catalogue*, no. 394; Nordenfalk, *Early Medieval*, 177; D. G. Scragg, 'The compilation of the Vercelli Codex', *Anglo-Saxon England*, 2, 1973, 189–207.

29. Boulogne, Bibliothèque Municipale MS 82
Amalarius, De ecclesiasticis officiis
205 × 140 mm.
Second half of 10th century

Ills. 101, 102

The numerous small initials, mainly in outline, are of Wormald Type I, though Type II(b) also occurs; they are made up of complete dragons with large foliated tails and contain a good deal of leafwork and animal and profiled human heads which appear on the tips of thick interlace strands or emerge from hollow 'sleeves' recalling no. 7 (Junius Psalter). An initial P (f. 2), repeated in an outline sketch on the fly-leaf, is painted in yellow, green, and minium orange.

PROVENANCE: Of unknown origin. The manuscript is written in Anglo-Saxon minuscule. It probably belonged to St. Bertin Abbey.

LITERATURE: Wormald, *Initials*, 120 n. 4, 133, pl. Vb; Talbot Rice, *English Art*, 206; Alexander, *Norman Illumination*, 62 n. 2.

30. MANUSCRIPTS WITH INITIALS WORMALD TYPE II(b).
Second half of 10th century to early 11th century. The list is a selection of the more important examples.

(i) Cambridge, Trinity College MS O. 1. 18 (1042)
Enchiridion Augustini
182 × 140 mm.
Second half of 10th century
Canterbury, St. Augustine's

Ill. 103

(ii) Paris, Bibliothèque Nationale MS lat. 7585
Isidorii Ethymologia
325×205 mm.
Second half of 10th century. Canterbury,
St. Augustine's   *Ill. 104*

**(iii) London, British Library MS
Royal 12. C. XXIII**
Julian, Aldhelm, etc.
238×145 mm.
Second half of 10th century. Canterbury,
Christ Church   *Ill. 113*

(iv) Oxford, Bodleian Library MS Rawl. C. 570
Arator, Historia apostolica
205×161 mm.
Second half of 10th century. Canterbury,
St. Augustine's   *Ills. 100, 106*

**(v) Leiden, Rijksuniversiteit
Codex Scaligeranus 69**
Aethici Istrici Cosmographia
175×100 mm.
Second half of 10th century. Canterbury,
St. Augustine's   *Ill. 105*

**(vi) Cambridge, Trinity College MS O. 2. 31
(1135)**
Prosper, Cato, etc.
208×132 mm.
Second half of 10th century. Canterbury,
Christ Church   *Ill. 107*

**(vii) London, British Library MS Harley 1117
(ff. 2-42ᵛ, 45-62ᵛ)**
Bede, Lives of St. Cuthbert (i), (ii)
255×175 mm.
Second half of 10th century. Canterbury,
Christ Church   *Ills. 108, 109*

**(viii) Paris, Bibliothèque Nationale,
MS lat. 6401 A**
Boethius, De consolatione philosophiae
265×215 mm.
Late 10th century. Canterbury, Christ Church
                                                   Ill. 119

**(ix) Vatican, Biblioteca Apostolica
MS Reg. lat. 1671**
Virgilii, Opera
290×210 mm.
(?) Second half of 10th century. (?) Worcester

(x) Cambridge, Corpus Christi College MS 57
Rule of St. Benedict, Martyrology, etc.
328×254 mm.
Late 10th century. Abingdon

**(xi) London, British Library MS
Royal 6. A. VI**
Aldhelm, De virginitate
285×160 mm.
Before 995. Canterbury, Christ Church   *Ill. 117*

**(xii) Paris, Bibliothèque Nationale
MS lat. 17814**
Boethius, De consolatione philosophiae
295×200 mm.
Late 10th century. (?) Canterbury, Christ Church
                                                   Ill. 110

**(xiii) New York, Pierpont Morgan Library MS
M. 333**
Gospels
270×182 mm.
Early 11th century. St. Bertin   *Ill. 112*

**(xiv) Oxford, Bodleian Library MS Bodley 718
(S.C. 2632)**
Penitential of Egbert, Halitgar
326×204 mm.
Early 11th century. (?) Exeter   *Ill. 111*

**(xv) Boulogne, Bibliothèque Municipale
MS 189**
Prudentius, Carmina, Miscellanea
280×195 mm.
Early 11th century. Canterbury, Christ Church
                                                   Ill. 121

**(xvi) Paris, Bibliothèque Ste Geneviève MS
2410**
Iuvencus, Sedulius, etc.
260×195 mm.
Early 11th century. (?) Canterbury, Christ Church
                                                   Ill. 122

**(xvii) Oxford, Bodleian Library MS
Bodley 340, 342 (S.C. 2404-5)**
Homiliary
315×220 mm.
Early 11th century. Rochester   *Ill. 118*

**(xviii) London, British Library MS Cotton,
Tiberius B.I.**
Orosius (King Alfred's Translation),
Menologium, etc., Anglo-Saxon Chronicle
280×195 mm.
Early to mid 11th century. (?) Abingdon   *Ill. 116*

A considerable number of manuscripts from the
second half of the 10th to the early 11th century
were decorated with initials of Wormald Type II(b)
composed of snapping heads, interlace drawn in
outline, and acanthus foliage. In none of the specimens on the list, however, is the decoration as homo-
geneous as in no. 37 (Auct. F. 1. 15) for in most of
them other types of ornament are also used. Fine
early examples of this initial style are found in (i),
(iii), (iv), the latter closely recalling the Auct F. 1.
15 manuscript in the lay-out of the title-pages and in
the high quality of its initials (ff. 2, 3, 44); it contains, in addition, a foliage initial V and an I made
up of a standing dragon (f. 44ᵛ). Also extremely close
to no. 37 (Auct. F. 1. 15) are three of the initials (ff.
1, 57ᵛ, 79) in (viii), where the letter 'h' (f. 57ᵛ) is
almost a replica of the same letter in the Bodleian
manuscript; the other two initials in (viii) contain:

a lion climbing up the shaft of a P (f. 15) and a bird with a fish inhabiting its bow (both anticipate the Romanesque initial decoration in 12th-century Christ Church manuscripts), and two dragons flanking an I (f. 32). A similar type of I (f. 46) with one appended bird occurs in (xii), which also contains an H (f. 78) inhabited by a lion and a bird; the text columns (ff. 24ᵛ, 46) and two diagrams (ff. 2, 63) in this manuscript are ornamented with delicate plant scrolls in brushwork of exquisite quality with a fine initial D (f. 106) in the same technique which can be associated with Canterbury manuscripts (cf. no. 22, Bosworth Psalter). Manuscripts (ii) and (iii) have each one initial of Wormald Type II(a) with black wiry interlace (ff. 3 and 84 respectively); a dragon climbs between snapping heads in an I (f. 1) of (xiv) which also contains a fine marginal drawing in the 'first' style of a figure kneeling before the Hand of God (f. 28ᵛ).

PROVENANCE: With the exception of the six books from Worcester (ix), Abingdon (x), (xviii), St. Bertin (xiii), (?) Exeter (xiv) and Rochester (xvii), all the manuscripts listed above are of Canterbury origin where also the earliest and the finest extant examples of Wormald Type II(b) initials were produced (cf. no. 37, Auct. F. 1. 15). These Canterbury manuscripts are inter-related by having common scribes who have been identified by T. A. M. Bishop and appear in examples with a firm Canterbury attribution (cf. *Notes*, IV, VI, VII).
Trinity College O. 1. 18 (i) contains an acrostic on St. Dunstan (f. 2) which led James to ascribe the manuscript to Glastonbury; an imperfect copy is found in no. 34 (Trinity College B. 14. 3) from St. Augustine's. Bibl. Nat., lat. 7585 (ii), an imperfect 9th-century continental manuscript, was completed by Canterbury scribes with quires written in English Caroline minuscule (Bishop, 1971); it belonged to C. Dupuy in the 16th century. Rawl. C. 570 (iv) is no. 1433 in St. Augustine's late 15th-century catalogue; the same scribe also wrote Scaliger 69 (v). Two lines (ff. 41, 42ᵛ) in honour of St. Etheldreda in Trinity College O. 2. 31 (vi) suggest that the manuscript may have been at Ely in the 11th century. Harley 1117 (vii) was a gift to Harley from John Anstis (f. 1ᵛ). Bibl. Nat., lat. 6401 A (viii), written in part by the glossator of Royal 6. A. VI (xi) from Christ Church, was on the Continent at least from the 16th century, for a note of this period (f. 94ᵛ) records its purchase by an Augustinian canon of Seyssel, Savoie, from one Philip Molliard de le Burg. Bibl. Nat., lat. 17814 (xii) belonged to President Bouhier, Codex C. 45 of his collection, in 1721.
The attribution of (ix), (x), (xiv), (xvii), and (xviii) rests on internal or paleographical evidence. Morgan 333 (xiii) was produced at St. Bertin where Anglo-Saxon illuminators are known to have been working under Abbot Otbert (986–1007; cf. no. 44, Boulogne Gospels), who himself produced work under strong English influence. (xvi) is ascribed to Christ Church on the style of its ornamental initial (f. 126) and the brushwork initials throughout.

LITERATURE:

(i) James, *Ancient Libraries*, 506; *id.*, *The Western Manuscripts in the Library of Trinity College, Cambridge*, 1900–4, III, 19–22; Homburger, 3 n. 3; Bishop, *Notes*, IV, 323, 326, 329–30, 334; Ker, *Catalogue*, no. 92; Bishop, *Notes*, VII, 418; *id.*, *Codex Leidensis*, p. XIX (9).

(ii) M. Forster, 'Die altenglischen Texte der Pariser Nationalbibliothek', *Englische Studien*, hrsggb. von Johannes Hoops, 62, I, 1927, 130–1; Ker, *Catalogue*, no. 366; J. Vezin, 'Aethici Istrici Cosmographia . . .', *Bibliothèque de l'Ecole des Chartes*, CXXIV, 1966, 534; J. C. Pope, 'Homilies of Aelfric', *E.E.T.S.*, or. ser. 259, 1967, 87; J. Vezin, 'Manuscrits des dixième et onzième siècles copiés en Angleterre en minuscule caroline et conservés a la Bibliothèque nationale de Paris', *Mélanges offerts à Julien Cain*, Paris 1968, II, 286; Bishop, *English Caroline*, p. XXV, no. 6.

(iii) Warner and Gilson, III, 35–6, IV, pl. 72; Homburger, 3 n. 3; Wormald, *Initials*, 135; Ker, *Catalogue*, no. 263; Bishop, *Notes*, VII, 421 (3).

(iv) James, *Ancient Libraries*, 364; Homburger, 3 n. 3; Millar, I, no. 15; Wormald, *Initials*, 124 n. 1, 135, pl. VIc; Talbot Rice, *English Art*, 178, pl. 42c; Holmquist, *Viking Art*, 21 n. 31; Bishop, *Notes*, IV, 329, *Notes*, VI, 413, 418; *id.*, *Codex Leidensis*, pp. V, VIII, XX(24), pl. D; Roosen-Runge, 84; Alexander, *Norman Illumination*, 63 n. 1; *Anglo-Saxon Illumination*, pl. 12b; Pächt and Alexander, no. 38, pl. IV.

(v) Bishop, *Notes*, VI, 412; F. Wormald, 'Anglo-Saxon initials in a Paris Boethius manuscript', *Essais en l'honneur de Jean Porcher*, ed. O. Pächt, 63–4; Bishop, *Codex Leidensis*; J. Vezin, 'Aethici Istrici Cosmographia . . .', *Bibliothèque de l'École des Chartes*, CXXIV (1966).

(vi) James, *Ancient Libraries*, x add.; *id.*, *Catalogue of the Western Manuscripts in the Library of Trinity College, Cambridge*, 1900–4, III, 129–31, IV, pl. III; Homburger, 3 n. 3; Wormald, *Initials*, 135; Kendrick, *Late Saxon*, 37; Talbot Rice, *English Art*, 197; Ker, *Catalogue*, no. 95; Bishop, *Notes*, VII, 413–14, 416, 421.

(vii) B. Colgrave, *Two Lives of St. Cuthbert*, 1940, 28, no. 14; Ker, *Catalogue*, no. 234; Bishop, *Notes*, VII, 414, 417, 419–20, 421 (4), (15), pls. XIIIc, XV.

(viii) E. J. Daly, 'An early ninth-century manuscript of Boethius', *Scriptorium*, 1950, 216; F. Wormald, 'Anglo-Saxon initials in a Paris Boethius manuscript', *Essais en l'honneur de Jean Porcher*, ed. O. Pächt, 63–70, figs. 1, 2, 5; Bishop, *Notes*, VII, 416 n. 1, 421 (19); Bishop, *English Caroline*, p. XXII.

(ix) Bishop, *English Caroline*, no. 19.

(x) Wormald, *Initials*, 134.

(xi) Homburger, 3 n. 3; Warner and Gilson, I, 129, IV, pl. 45b; Ker, *Catalogue*, no. 254; Bishop,

Notes, VII, 415, 417, 421 (12); *id.*, *English Caroline*, no. 9; Pächt and Alexander, no. 37.

(xii) E. J. Daly, 'An early ninth-century manuscript of Boethius', *Scriptorium*, 1950, 216; J. Vezin, 'Aethici Istrici Cosmographia . . .', *Bibliothèque de l'École des Chartes*, LXXIV, 1966, 535; *id.*, 'Manuscrits des dixième et onzième siècles', *Mélanges offerts à Julien Cain*, Paris 1968, II, 286; Bishop, *English Caroline*, pp. XIII n. 2, XXVI; Wormald, *Winchester School*, 310.

(xiii) The Pierpont Morgan Library, *Exhibition of Illuminated Manuscripts*, New York 1933-4, no. 21; F. Wormald, 'The Survival of Anglo-Saxon illumination after the Norman Conquest', *Proceedings of the British Academy*, XXX, 1944, 133 n. 1; Wormald, *Initials*, 123 n. 1; Paris, Bibliothèque Nationale, *Les Manuscrits à peintures en France du VIIe au XIIe siècle*, 1954, no. 116; F. Wormald, 'Anglo-Saxon initials in a Paris Boethius manuscript', *Essais en l'honneur de Jean Porcher*, ed. O. Pächt, 1963, 67-8, 70 no. 13, fig. 4; Swarzenski, *Monuments*, pl. 69, fig. 160; C. R. Dodwell, *Painting in Europe, 800-1200*, 1971, 80-2, pl. 98.

(xiv) M. Bateson, 'The supposed latin penitential of Egbert and the missing work of Halitgar of Cambrai', *English Historical Review*, IX, 1894, 320-6; Homburger, 3; Millar, I, no. 14; O. Homburger, 'Review', *Art Bulletin*, X, 1928, 401; Wormald, *Initials*, 135; Kendrick, *Late Saxon*, 18, 131, pl. XIX, 2; Holmquist, *Viking Art*, 6, fig. 3, 1-3; Talbot Rice, *English Art*, 178; *Anglo-Saxon Illumination*, pl. 12a; Pächt and Alexander, no. 36, pl. III.

(xv) Bishop, *Notes*, VII, 415, 420 n. 1, 421 (21); Ker, *Catalogue*, no. 7; Gneuss, 104, 122.

(xvi) C. Kohler, *Catalogue des Manuscrits de la Bibliothèque Sainte-Geneviève*, Paris 1896, II, 340-4.

(xvii) K. Sisam, 'MSS Bodley 340 and 342: Aelfric's Catholic Homilies', *Review of English Studies*, VII, 1931, 7-22; VIII, 1932, 51-68; IX, 1933, 1-12; Ker, *Catalogue*, no. 309; J. C. Pope, 'Homilies of Aelfric', *E.E.T.S.*, or. ser. 259, 1967, 20; Gneuss, 116; Pächt and Alexander, no. 42, pl. V.

(xviii) B. Thorpe, *The Anglo-Saxon Chronicle* (R. S., XXIII, 2 vols., 1861), pl. 3; *Pal. Soc.*, I, pl. 242; C. Plummer, *Two of the Anglo-Saxon Chronicles parallel*, 1899, I, pl. XI, II, pp. XXX-XXXI; Ker, *Catalogue*, 191; *The Anglo-Saxon Chronicle*, ed. D. Whitelock, 1961, pp. XI-XXXII.

31. Orléans, Bibliothèque Municipale MS 105 (127)
Sacramentary (Winchcombe Sacramentary)
267 × 218 mm.

Second half of 10th century, additions early 11th century. (?) Winchcombe

Ill. 139

The Sacramentary, imperfect at the beginning, contains a large ornamental initial D (p. 8) with a small 's' inside the bowl and decorated with a fleuron. Structurally the initial, painted in red, leaf green, and pale purple, recalls ornamental initials of no. 41 (Harley 2904) its loop being made up of two panels and the shaft adorned at the top and bottom with animal-headed interlace terminals; a medallion composed of bunched acanthus leaves of 'Winchester' type is placed half-way up the shaft. An initial O is in gold (p. 11), other initials are alternately in red, green, and blue. The titles are in lines of red and green capitals, rubrics in red.

PROVENANCE: The manuscript, written in English Caroline minuscule related to the script of Winchester manuscripts of the third quarter of the 10th century, was destined for a Benedictine abbey which especially honoured SS. Peter and Kenelm (Canon of the Mass, prayers, litanies), and, on account of the prominence given to the latter was generally assigned to Winchcombe Abbey, Glos. It has recently been suggested (Gremont and Donnat, 1967), however, that in view of the total absence of any other English saints, the Sacramentary, possibly produced at Winchcombe itself, was not written for Winchcombe or any other English church. A marginal dedicatory inscription of the 10th to 11th century (pp. 63-4) reveals in fact that a benefactor whose name is obliterated (probably Richard, the fugitive count of Avranches) commissioned the volume in England for Fleury. An epitaph for Gauzlin, abbot of Fleury from 1005 to 1030, shows (p. 331) that the manuscript reached St. Benoit by the early 11th century, perhaps by way of Normandy, for a list of monks of Mont St. Michel was added in the 10th to 11th century on the end leaves (cf. also Alexander, *Norman Illumination*, 8 n. 5). The manuscript, probably entered as no. A. 32 in the Fleury catalogue of 1656, remained at Fleury throughout the Middle Ages.

LITERATURE: L. Delisle, *Mémoire sur d'anciens Sacramentaires*, Paris 1886, no. lxxix, 211-15 and App. XVI, 389-91; Homburger, 5, 40 n. 3; V. Leroquais, *Les Sacramentaires et les missels manuscrits des bibliothèques publiques de France*, Paris 1924, I, 89-91; Millar, I, no. 36; O. Homburger, 'Review', *Art Bulletin*, X, 1928, 401; C. Niver, 'The Psalter in the British Museum, Harley 2904', *Medieval Studies in Memory of A. Kingsley Porter*, 1939, II, 667-87; D. Gremont and L. Donnat, 'Fleury, Le Mont-Saint-Michel et l'Angleterre à la fin du Xe et au début du XIe siècle à propos du manuscrit d'Orléans n. 127 (105)', *Millénaire monastique du Mont-Saint-Michel*, Paris 1967, I, 751-93, pl. XIX; Alexander, *Norman Illumination*, 8 n. 5, 38 n. 1, 39, 56 n. 6, 86, 213, 227, 238, pl. Ic; Bishop, *English Caroline*, no. 14.

32. Paris, Bibliothèque Nationale, MS lat. 6401

Boethius, De consolatione philosophiae,
Institutio arithmetica; other miscellaneous texts
275 × 195 mm.
Last quarter of 10th century. Fleury

Ills. 94, 95

The manuscript, written at Fleury, contains three miniatures by an English artist. The first, an unfinished drawing (f. 5ᵛ) no doubt intended as a frontispiece for the *De consolatione* (ff. 15–86), was meant to head the introductory matter of the treatise which was replaced by an entirely unconnected text (ff. 1–11ᵛ), a correspondence between two scholars copied in the 11th century. The drawing, placed over a rectangular border devoid of ornament, is in the firm outline of the 'first style' and shows Boethius in a gabled prison, reclining in bed and writing; his vision of Philosophy, a tall, imposing female figure with a book and sceptre, stands on the left, while three Muses file in from the right (the rectangular prison building and the three figures vaguely recall the Holy Women picture in no. 23, Benedictional of St. Ethelwold, f. 51ᵛ). The miniature, containing certain elements common to earlier continental illustrations (cf. Vienna, Nat. Bibl. MS 271, f. 1ᵛ, 9th century), is largely independent of them and probably derives from a different late antique model. A large initial C (f. 15) introducing the main text of the *De consolatione* contains curling acanthus foliage within a framework terminating in interlace knotwork, the whole painted in ochre, orange, mauve, and green.

A full-page painted miniature (f. 158ᵛ), coming after the *Institutio arithmetica* (ff. 87–158), shows a nimbed figure enthroned under an arched canopy elaborately decorated with acanthus patterns, in the tympanum of which is a mandorla flanked by two seraphs and containing Christ in Majesty, Alpha and Omega on either side of His head and a book and symbol of authority in His Hand (for this figure of Christ, cf. no. 23, Benedictional of St. Ethelwold, f. 91). The figure below flanked by two looped curtains, dips his pen into an inkpot on the left, his other hand resting on a book supported by a stand on the right. Iconographically close to certain Evangelist portraits of the Ada Court School of Charlemagne (cf. St. Mark, Trier, Stadtbibliothek cod. 22), the composition recalls Anglo-Saxon representations in some of its details (note the draped lectern) while the style of the drapery folds is reminiscent of no. 23 (Benedictional of St. Ethelwold) and no. 65 (Trinity Gospels). The figure can be identified as Boethius, the theologian, since the book on the stand bears the opening words of his 'De Trinitate': *Inves(tigatam) diutissime . . .*, an identification brought to my notice by Signor F. Troncarelli (Rome). An historiated initial I on the page opposite (f. 159) is a further indication that the picture (f. 158ᵛ), an apotheosis of Boethius, was to serve as a frontispiece to his treatise which was to follow but was never inscribed. The initial is made up of four narrow vertical rectangles with the Lord in Majesty at the top (cf. Christ, f. 158ᵛ), below it, the *Agnus Dei* in a circle, below that, another circle with the Holy Dove and, at the bottom, a nimbed genuflecting figure, probably the author. The initial is one of the earliest Anglo-Saxon representations of the Trinity (cf. no. 35, Sherborne Pontifical) and, together with the miniature (f. 158ᵛ), an early and rare portrayal of Boethius as a saint. The colours are dull and include pale ochre, brown to mauve, slate blue, green, and white in the highlights, recalling early 10th-century Anglo-Saxon manuscripts (cf. no. 7, Junius Psalter; no. 9, Tanner 10, etc.).

PROVENANCE: The manuscript was produced at Fleury in the last quarter of the 10th century, and contains among later additions the epitaph of Gauzlin, abbot of St. Benoît 1005–30 (f. 171) and a full-page picture (f. 13ᵛ) of the mid 11th century by a continental illuminator. The miniatures (ff. 5ᵛ, 158ᵛ, 159), therefore, were executed by an Anglo-Saxon artist working at Fleury. The manuscript remained *in situ* until the 16th-century despoliation of the Fleury library by P. Daniel.

LITERATURE: L. Delisle, *Le Cabinet des Manuscrits*, Paris 1874, II, 364; P. Tannery, 'Une correspondance d'écolâtres du XIe siècle', *Notices et Extraits des Manuscrits*, XXXVI, 2, 1901, 487–543; id., *Mémoires Scientifiques*, Toulouse 1901–12, V, 230–3; Paris, Bibliothèque Nationale, *Les Manuscrits à peintures en France du VIIe au XIIe siècles*, 1954, no. 122; Nordenfalk, *Early Medieval*, 179; P. Courcelle, *Histoire littéraire des grandes invasions germaniques*, Paris 1964, 369, pl. 40a; C. Nordenfalk, 'Miniature ottonienne et ateliers capétiens', *Art de France*, IV, 1964, 64, fig. 11; A. Vidier, *L'historiographie à Saint-Benoît-sur-Loire*, 1965, 52; Swarzenski, *Monuments*, 50, pl. 70, fig. 164; P. Courcelle, *La Consolation de Philosophie dans la tradition littéraire*, Paris 1967, 91; Wormald, *Winchester School*, 311–13, pls. IIId, Vc, VI; id., *Angleterre*, 239, pl. 232.

33. London, British Library MS Cotton, Caligula A. VII (ff. 11–176)

Poem on the Life of Christ (Heliand)
in Low German
215 × 130 mm.
Second half of 10th century

Ills. 123, 124

Initials made up of elaborately crested and winged dragons introduce sections of the text (ff. 11, 21ᵛ, 35, 36ᵛ, 39, 41ᵛ, 43ᵛ, 46, 132) and in addition coloured bands, serving as backgrounds to the heading inscribed in rustic capitals, mark the beginning (f. 11) and the last section (f. 132) of the poem. The initials, mainly of Wormald Type I, are painted in slate blue, pale purple, and bright yellow; they recall no. 7 (Junius Psalter) in the interlacing of dragons' necks which turn into knotwork of 'elbowed 'strands, and show affinity with no. 58 (Junius 11) in the type of beasts.

PROVENANCE: Origin unknown. The manuscript containing the Old Saxon poem known as Heliand and written in Caroline minuscule of English type was, as shown by the decoration, probably produced in Southern England in the late 10th century. It belonged to Cotton in 1621 and was bound by him with other manuscripts of various dates, now separated, while a charm in Anglo-Saxon, which follows the Heliand text (ff. 176–8) probably belongs to the original part of the manuscript (Ker, *Catalogue*). Sir Robert Cotton died in 1631. His library, presented to the nation by his grandson, Sir John Cotton, in 1700, was incorporated into the British Museum in 1753.

LITERATURE: G. F. Warner, *Illuminated Manuscripts*, 1903, pl. 17; British Museum, *Reproductions from Illuminated Manuscripts*, ser. III, 1923–8, pl. 12; R. Priebsch, *The Heliand MS. Caligula A. VII in the British Museum*, 1925, pls. IV, V; Wormald, *Initials*, 120 n. 2, 134; Kendrick, *Late Saxon*, 33; Holmquist, *Viking Art*, 21 n. 31; Talbot Rice, *English Art*, 179–80; Ker, *Catalogue*, 137.

34. Cambridge, Trinity College MS B. 14. 3 (289)

Arator, Historia apostolica
245×175 mm.
Last quarter of 10th century. Canterbury,
Christ Church   *Ill. 125*

A remarkably large initial Q (f. 5) in full colour (scarlet, dark red, deep blue, green) is elaborately constructed of two dragons, foliage, and interlace, with an appended bird forming the tail of the letter; it is accompanied by the opening line of the text in large green, dark red, and blue capitals and by lines of rustic capitals using the same colours in alternation. Other initials (ff. 1ᵛ, 3, 34ᵛ), Wormald Type II(b), of excellent quality, are in black outline with touches of red, and contain characteristic bulbous rings, 'elbowed' interlace, and snapping heads. Rubrics are in red, green, and black rustic capitals.

PROVENANCE: The manuscript was written at Christ Church, Canterbury; it is identified by the mark 'FF' (f. 5) with an entry in the Christ Church catalogue of the 12th century, bears a class-mark of that house (D. iiᵃ Gra. XXXᵘˢ), 13th century, and contains marginalia (f. 21ᵛ) in a script of the Christ Church type. This attribution is fully supported by stylistic evidence. The volume was given to Trinity College by George Willmer (d. 1626).

LITERATURE: James, *Ancient Libraries*, pp. lxxxiii, 506, no. 79; *id., The Western Manuscripts in the Library of Trinity College, Cambridge*, 1900–4, I, 404, IV, pl. II; Homburger, 3 n. 3; Millar, I, 14 n. 3, no. 17; Wormald, *Initials*, 135; Talbot Rice, *English Art*, 197; Ker, *Catalogue*, no. 85; Bishop, *Notes*, VII, 414–15, 418–19, 421(9); *id., English Caroline*, no. 9.

35. Paris, Bibliothèque Nationale, MS lat. 943

Pontifical (Sherborne Pontifical)
315×205 mm.
Last quarter of 10th century. (?) Canterbury,
Christ Church

Ills. 134–138

The manuscript contains four full-page illustrations, probably not all by the same hand. The first miniature, a hieratic, monumental Crucifixion (f. 4ᵛ), is drawn in firm brown and red outline and shows the dead Christ on a broad, massive cross with the Virgin and St. John on either side. The Hand of God emerges from a cloud at the top of the picture, while two angels with filleted heads and veiled hands hover above the cross bar; a chalice (rarely shown in Anglo-Saxon crucifixions, cf. no. 56, Arenberg Gospels) stands at the foot of the cross, and the whole is surrounded by a frame with contained acanthus leaf patterns. The composition as well as iconographic details closely resemble the Crucifixion in no. 56 (Arenberg Gospels; cf. also an Anglo-Saxon ivory plaque, 10th to 11th century, Beckwith, *Ivory Carvings*, 1972, pl. 38) and, though differing in style, seem to derive from the same model. There are also striking analogies, particularly in the head-types and the gestures, with the drawings in the Cambridge Prudentius (no. 48, probably from Canterbury) which, however, are more sketchy and free. The remaining illustrations, showing three almost identical standing figures, presumably represent the Trinity (cf. Vatican Libr. Pal. lat. 834, 9th century, A. Goldschmidt, *German Illumination*, I, 1928, pl. 61; no. 68, Grimbald Gospels, f. 114). The first two Persons (ff. 5ᵛ, 6), each with a cross shaft and a cross-marked book, are within plain linear frames, while the third, the Holy Ghost, holding a book and a *virga*, is surrounded by an acanthus-filled border (cf. 4ᵛ). The three figures, and particularly that of God the Son (f. 6), are closely related to the representation of Christ in no. 13 (St. John's College MS 28) and derive, no doubt, from the same model. The figure drawing, in the firm outline of Wormald's 'first style', is extremely close to that representation but is perhaps less fluid, and is also more repetitive and harder in the patterns of the drapery folds.

The only initial, an A (f. 10), Wormald Type II(b), contains 'elbowed' interlace knotwork, beasts' heads, bulbous rings and flat acanthus foliage in the initial style of late tenth-century manuscripts from both Canterbury houses (cf. nos. 37, Auct. F. 1. 15; 30 (vii), Harley 1117).

PROVENANCE: The manuscript containing a copy of an 'epistola privilegii' from Pope John XII (959–64) to Dunstan (Archbishop 959–88) in the original hand and supposed to be the Pontifical of Dunstan himself (Mabillon), is attributable to Christ Church, Canterbury, at least on stylistic evidence (cf. Homburger, Talbot Rice). Written in a square Anglo-Saxon minuscule hand datable, according to Ker, after 960 and related by him to that of Bodley MS,

718 (no. 30 (xiv), cf. also Homburger, 1928), the Pontifical was dated by Wormald *c.* 992–5; but it is possibly earlier, before 988 (?) since its decoration is unaffected by the influence of the Utrecht Psalter. An added list of the bishops of Sherborne, Dorset (f. 1ᵛ), ending with Aethelric (1001–9), indicates that the volume was at Sherborne not later than the early 11th century, and probably earlier, since a hortatory letter (f. 2) in a hand close to the original one is addressed by an unnamed archbishop, probably Aelfric of Canterbury (995–1005), to Wulfsin, bishop of Sherborne (992–1001). A list of '. . . *librorum Sancte Marie* . . .' added on an originally blank leaf (f. 154ᵛ) shows that the manuscript belonged to the Cathedral of Notre-Dame in Paris by the end of the 11th century. Bequeathed by Antoine Faure (d. 1689) to Leonard de Jayac, Rheims, the book was purchased from the latter by the Bibliothèque Royale in 1701.

LITERATURE: J. Mabillon, *Acta SS. Ordin. S. Benedicti*, Paris 1703–13, V, 239; Westwood, *Facsimiles*, 128–9; L. Delisle, *Le Cabinet des manuscrits*, Paris 1881, III, 268–70, pl. XXX, 5; *New Pal. Soc.*, I, pls. 111–12; G. Warner and H. A. Wilson, *The Benedictional of St. Aethelwold*, 1910, p. XXXIX; D. de Bruyne, 'Le plus ancien catalogue des manuscrits de Notre Dame de Paris', *Revue Bénédictine*, XXIX, 1912, 481–5; Homburger, 3 n. 1, 39, 57; J. Brønsted, *Early English Ornament*, 1924, 245, fig. 172; Millar, I, no. 13; O. Homburger, 'Review', *Art Bulletin*, X, 1928, 400; V. Leroquais, *Les Pontificaux manuscrits des bibliothèques publiques de France*, Paris 1937, II, 6–10, pls. VII–X; Wormald, *Initials*, 135; F. Saxl and R. Wittkower, *British Art and the Mediterranean*, 1948, pl. 21 (2–4); Kendrick, *Late Saxon*, 45, 137; Wormald, *English Drawings*, 25, 37, 64, 75, 77, 78, no. 54, pls. 4a, b, 5a; Talbot Rice, *English Art*, 162, 197, 209, 212–13, pls. 42d, 64b; Dodwell, *Canterbury School*, 9, pl. 5a; S. Schulten, 'Die Buchmalerei des 11. Jahrhunderts im Kloster St. Vaast in Arras', *Münchner Jahrbuch der bildenden Kunst*, VII, 1956, 55, fig. 12; Ker, *Catalogue*, no. 364; Rickert, *Miniatura*, 15, 22, pl. 9; F. Wormald, 'Late Anglo-Saxon art: some questions and suggestions', *Studies in Western Art. Acts of the 20th Congress of the History of Art*, ed. M. Meiss, I, Princeton 1963, 21; Rickert, *Painting in Britain*, 32 n. 3, 225 n. 65, pls. 23, 24; J. Vezin, 'Manuscrits des dixième et onzième siècles copiés en Angleterre en minuscule caroline et conservés à la Bibliothèque Nationale de Paris', *Mélanges offerts à Julien Cain*, 1968, II, 287; T. A. M. Bishop, 'An early example of the Square Minuscule', *Transactions of the Cambridge Bibliographical Society*, IV, 1964–8, 246 n. 1; Alexander, *Norman Illumination*, 92 n. 1, 115–16, 182, pl. 17a; Bishop, *English Caroline*, pl. XXII; J. Beckwith, *Ivory Carvings in Early Medieval England*, 1972, 48 n. 32, 50; Wormald, *Angleterre*, 240, ill. 235.

EXHIBITED: Brussels, 1973, *English Illuminated Manuscripts 700–1500*, no. 6.

36. Cambridge, Corpus Christi College MS 389

Vita S. Pauli Eremitae (ff. 2–16ᵛ)
Felix, Vita S. Guthlaci (ff. 18–66)
225 × 145 mm.
End of 10th century, additions *c.* 1070.
Canterbury, St. Augustine's

Ills. 130, 316

The original decoration consists of four ornamental initials, Wormald Type II(b) in black and red outline with touches of colour, and composed of heavy double line interlace, bulbous rings, and dragons' heads: an initial H (f. 2) to the Preface of the *Vita Pauli* followed by lines of red and green capitals; a large initial J (f. 4); a J (f. 18) heading the opening line of the *Vita Guthlaci* in green lettering; and a magnificent initial F (f. 22ᵛ). Titles of chapters are in red rustic capitals with minor initials in purple and green.

A full-page framed drawing added *c.* 1070 (f. 1ᵛ) represents St. Jerome in a highly ornate chair writing at a desk on the right, while the Holy Dove whispers into his ear. The crossed legs, the feet in a dancing posture and the windswept drapery folds suggest ecstatic rapture. The scene is set under an arched and towered canopy supported on slender shafts with acanthus capitals and a looped curtain is hanging on the right. The drawing, in a somewhat hesitant and scratchy outline in brown ink with green tinting in the draperies and touches of red and purple in details, shows a notable awareness of the body-forms beneath the softly moulded folds of the garments. It is in the 'revived Utrecht' style of the third group of drawings in Harley 603 (no. 64) and has been related by Wormald to no. 106 (Caligula A. XV). A faint sketch (f. 17ᵛ), probably of the same period as the drawing (f. 1ᵛ), shows a king enthroned full-face, possibly Aelwald, king of the East Angles, to whom Felix on the left is offering his Life of St. Guthlac, with another figure standing on the right. Part of an alphabet is inscribed in green capitals (f. 66ᵛ).

PROVENANCE: The manuscript, written at St. Augustine's, Canterbury, contains a pressmark 'D IX. Gradu tertio. V' (f. 1) and a 14th-century inscription 'Liber S. Aug. Cant.' The same scribe also wrote St. John's College MS 28 (no. 13), according to T. A. M. Bishop. The manuscript is entered as G(2) in the list of Archbishop Parker's gifts to the library of Corpus Christi College in 1575.

LITERATURE: James, *Ancient Libraries*, 533; Wormald, *Initials*, 135; *id., English Drawings*, 55–6, 61, 67, no. 10, pl. 36; Dodwell, *Canterbury School* 27–8, 122, pl. 16c; Ker, *Catalogue*, no. 66; Bishop, *Codex Leidensis*, p. XIV n. 24, p. XIX(4); *id., English Caroline*, no. 5.

37. Oxford, Bodleian Library MS Auct. F. 1. 15 (S.C. 2455)

Boethius, De consolatione philosophiae (ff. 5–77)
375 × 250 mm.
Late 10th century. Canterbury, St. Augustine's

Ill. 114

Each of the five Books of the treatise is introduced by a large ornamental initial, Wormald Type II(b), accompanied by the first words of the text in coloured capitals, silver, green, pale purple, and orange-red. The initials C (f. 5), P (f. 16), I (f. 29), 'h' (f. 48), and D (f. 65), executed in fine brown ink with touches of red, are composed of double-line interlace, snapping heads, and acanthus ornament. The interlace in these initials is particularly characteristic with its 'elbow' thickenings (cf. no. 22, Bosworth Psalter), and its delicate plaited basket-work which provides an intricate background for large bird and animal heads, three-dimensional foliage, and bulbous rings. The decoration is of outstanding quality, of a type particularly popular in, though not limited to, the two Canterbury scriptoria during the second half of the 10th century, with the earliest examples to be found, according to T. A. M. Bishop, in manuscripts from St. Augustine's.
Fine brushwork initials to paragraphs are in green or purple, and minor initials in red.

PROVENANCE: The manuscript was written by the scribe of Harley 5431 (no. 38), who also wrote part of Bodleian MS Auct. D. inf. 2. 9, both from St. Augustine's. Glosses (ff. 66ᵛ–72ᵛ) were added in the late 10th century by the Christ Church scribe of British Library MS Royal 6. A. VI, no. 30 (xi), which shows the close co-operation existing between the two Canterbury houses. The Boethius is now bound together with a copy of Persius' Satires of the same date and origin (ff. 78–93), undecorated but for a sketch probably added in the 11th century (f. 78). Given to Exeter Cathedral as two distinct volumes by Bishop Leofric (1046–72), each manuscript contains dedicatory inscriptions in Latin and Old English (ff. 77ᵛ–78); they were presented in one volume by the Dean and Chapter, 1602.

LITERATURE: R. Ellis, *XII Facsimiles from Latin MSS. in the Bodleian Library*, 1895, pl. 5; E. Chatelain, *Paléographie des classiques latins*, II, 1894–1900, pl. CXXVI; Homburger, 3 n. 3; Millar, I, no. 18; Wormald, *Initials*, 123 nn. 2, 3, 124, pl. VIb; Kendrick, *Late Saxon*, pl. XXX, 2; Holmquist, *Viking Art*, 7, fig. 3, 4–5; Talbot Rice, *English Art*, 178, pl. 44 a, b; Ker, *Catalogue*, no. 294; Bishop, *Notes*, IV, 324, 326, 331, 335; VI, 413, 415, 418, 421–2; F. Wormald, 'Anglo-Saxon initials in a Paris Boethius manuscript', *Essais en l'honneur de Jean Porcher*, ed. O. Pächt, 1963, 64 n. 2, 65, fig. 3; Bishop, *Codex Leidensis*, p. XX (22), (23); Roosen-Runge, I, 84; Alexander, *Norman Illumination*, 57; *Anglo-Saxon Illumination*, pl. 13; Bishop, *English Caroline*, no. 9; Pächt and Alexander, no. 37, pl. III.

38. London, British Library MS Harley 5431 (ff. 6–126ᵛ)

Regula S. Benedicti, Statuta antiqua, etc.
230 × 85 mm.
Last quarter of 10th century. Canterbury, St. Augustine's

Ills. 115, 120, 126, 127

The manuscript, another example bearing witness to the high quality of the St. Augustine's, Canterbury, production (cf. no. 21, Trinity Amalarius), is extensively decorated with initials of various types which include: Wormald Type I composed of complete bird-headed creatures recalling no. 7 (Junius Psalter) and no. 9 (Tanner 10) but crisper in design; Type II(a) employing black, wiry interlace; a mixed type in which a double-line 'elbowed' interlace appears; and some foliage and mask-head initials. All these initials are in fine black outline with touches of red and occasionally patches of mauve or blue filling the inside of the letters. The title (f. 6ᵛ) is in alternate lines of red and green capitals and the first page of the text opposite (f. 7) is inscribed in lines of blue, mauve, and red.

PROVENANCE: The manuscript, preceded by unrelated calendarial matter (ff. 4–5ᵛ), is bound up with works of the 13th and 14th centuries. It bears a St. Augustine's press-mark (f. 2), 'Dist. XIII. G. I' of the 14th century, followed by a list of contents of the same date and an inscription '*Et iste liber Sancti Augustini Cant.*' which show that all the contents were bound up together as early as the 14th century. The scribe of the present volume also wrote part of the Bodleian MSS D. inf 2. 9 and Auct. F. 1. 15 (no. 37), both from St. Augustine's (Bishop, *Notes*, IV).

LITERATURE: James, *Ancient Libraries*, 246, 517, no. 462; *New Pal. Soc.*, II, pl. 63; Homburger, 3 n. 3, 22 n. 2; Millar, I, 17; Wormald, *Initials*, 119 n. 4, 120 n. 5, 134; Kendrick, *Late Saxon*, 33 n. 1, 36 n. 1, pl. XXXI, 4; Talbot Rice, *English Art*, 206; Bishop, *Notes*, IV, 329; F. Wormald, 'Anglo-Saxon initials in a Paris Boethius manuscript', *Essais en l'honneur de Jean Porcher*, ed. O. Pächt, 1963, 64, 69 nn. 6, 8; Bishop, *Codex Leidensis*, pp. X, XII, XIX (17); *id.*, 'An early example of insular Caroline', *Transactions of the Cambridge Bibliographical Society*, IV, 1968, 396 n. 2; *id.*, *English Caroline*, no. 20; Pächt and Alexander, no. 37, pl. III.

39. London, Lambeth Palace Library MS 200 (Part II)

Aldhelm, De virginitate
275 × 200 mm.
Late 10th century. Canterbury, St. Augustine's

Ills. 131–133

The prologue to Aldhelm in the upper part of the page (f. 68ᵛ) is introduced by a large initial R in brown ink, Wormald Type II(b), with the opening words in green and red capitals. A drawing below shows Aldhelm seated on a cushioned chair, presenting his book to the nuns of Barking who form a compact group on the right. The vigorous and animated drawing in firm brown outline is stylistically close to the St. Dunstan miniature (cf. no. 11) but shows a marked elaboration and hardening of line in the drapery folds. On the title page opposite (f. 69) is a large and elaborate initial I with a rosette pattern on dark ground in the shaft and interlace knotwork with bird heads at the extremities, accompanied by lines of green and red lettering. The whole is surrounded by a frame composed of panels with double-stranded interlace plaited into tight basketwork and, in the four angles, with intricate plant scrolls inhabited by birds and quadrupeds (cf. Corpus Christi College 183, no. 6); the scrolls having their closest parallel in stone carvings of *c.* 1000 (cf. Tympanum at Knook, Wilts., Kendrick, *Late Saxon*, pl. XXXV).

The manuscript contains numerous and mainly monochrome initials of excellent quality, Wormald Type II(a) and (b), prefacing each section of the text; they contain large snapping heads, leafwork, and interlace knotwork with prominent acanthus 'elbows' recalling no. 22 (Bosworth Psalter), and are accompanied by the first line of the text in green capitals. A fine initial I (f. 1) to the prologue of a Life of St. Guthlac, Cambridge, Corpus Christi College MS 307 (part I), composed of knotwork of 'elbowed' interlace, snapping bird heads, and a mask on the shaft, which is filled with flat leaf pattern on dark ground, is closely allied in style to the I of the present manuscript (f. 69) and was most likely executed by the same artist.

PROVENANCE: Part II (ff. 66ᵛ–112), now bound with works of various dates (15th, 10th, 13th to 14th centuries), was written at St. Augustine's, Canterbury, by a scribe whose hand appears in no. 30 (iv) (Rawl. C. 570) and a group of manuscripts from the St. Augustine's scriptorium. It belonged at one time to Waltham Abbey (press-mark on f. 66ᵛ, and an inscription on f. 67, '*Aldhelmus de virginitate dor-(mitorii) pri(oris)*', both 14th century).

LITERATURE: H. J. Todd, *Manuscripts and Records in Lambeth Palace*, 1812, frontispiece (f. 68ᵛ); Westwood, *Facsimiles*, 103, pl. 31; *Pal. Soc.*, II, pl. 191; Burlington Fine Arts Club, *Exhibition of Illuminated Manuscripts*, 1908, no. 8, pl. 15; Homburger, 3, 47; J. Brønsted, *Early English Ornament*, 1924, 244–5, 249 n. 1, 255–7, 265, figs. 171, 184; Millar, I, no. 40; O. Homburger, 'Review', *Art Bulletin*, X, 1928, 400; Saunders, *English Illumination*, pl. 22 b, c; M. R. James, *A Descriptive Catalogue of the Manuscripts in Lambeth Palace*, 1930, 315; A. Clapham, *English Romanesque Architecture before the Conquest*, 1930, 137; G. L. Micheli, *L'Enluminure du Haut Moyen Age et les influences irlandaises*, Brussels 1939, 158 n. 1; Wormald, *Initials*, 119 n. 4, 134–5; Kendrick, *Late Saxon*, 36, 39, pls. XXXII, 2, XXXIII, 2; Holmquist, *Viking Art*, 15, fig. 8; Wormald, *English Drawings*, 73, 75, no. 43; Talbot

Rice, *English Art*, 197, 219, 235; S. Schulten, 'Die Buchmalerei des 11. Jahrhunderts im Kloster St. Vaast in Arras', *Münchner Jahrbuch der bildenden Kunst*, VII, 1956, 53, 61, fig. 8; Rickert, *Painting in Britain*, 43, pl. 38a; Bishop, *Notes*, IV, 323–6; *id.*, *Codex Leidensis*, pp. VIII n. 15, IX n. 16, X n. 19, XI, XVII, XX (20), pl. E; Alexander, *Norman Illumination*, 74; *Anglo-Saxon Illumination*, pl. 11; H. Holländer, *Early Medieval Art*, 1974, 186, ill. 152.

40. Cambridge, Corpus Christi College MS 411
Psalter
223 × 153 mm.
Last quarter of 10th century.
Canterbury, St. Augustine's

Ills. 128, 129

The Psalter is preceded by a frontispiece (f. 1ᵛ) and contains three decorative pages introducing Psalms 1 (f. 2), 51 (f. 40), and 101 (f. 81ᵛ). The frontispiece with an outline drawing of a standing bearded figure holding a book (David?) is surrounded by a border in Franco-Saxon style composed of framed panels with stopped-knot interlace reserved on a black ground and ornamented with four large corner bosses of interlace and bird heads; these are heavily painted in pale green, purple brown, ochre, and orange. The opening words of Psalm 1 inscribed in red and green on the opposite page (f. 2) are headed by a large gold initial B. The first verse of Psalm 51 (f. 40) in red and green is accompanied by a splendid initial Q of Franco-Saxon type containing in the bowl a medallion of knotted interlace on a red-spotted ground of milky blue; the whole is bordered by panels of interlace between green edging bands with quadrilobate rosette motifs in ochre-framed squares on the corners. A partly finished large initial D in red outline and the opening words of Psalm 101 (f. 81ᵛ) are enclosed by a similar interlace panelled border. Psalm 109 (f. 94ᵛ) is emphasized by a large plain initial D in green. Large red or green capital letters introduce the psalms, smaller ones head the verse-lines.

The drawing (f. 1ᵛ), executed in delicate brown outline, is of high quality and combines the calm monumentality of the 'first style' with the lightness and vividness of the Rheims manner, while the decoration, suggesting the presence in the British Isles of illuminated Franco-Saxon books, shows, to quote Wormald (1963), 'how greatly the Franco-Saxon style was valued and copied in tenth-century England' (cf. no. 26, Arundel 22).

PROVENANCE: The Psalter, hitherto believed on account of its decoration to be of 9th-century continental origin with the drawing (f. 1ᵛ) and a litany (f. 140) added in England in the late 10th or early 11th century, has now been assigned to St. Augustine's by Wormald (1967) since a prayer in the original hand (f. 138ᵛ) refers to both St. Gregory and St. Augustine of Canterbury. It may have been written by a Christ Church scribe as his hand appears also in Cambridge, Corpus Christi College MS 214 (Bishop, *Notes*, II), possibly from Christ Church, Canterbury (James, *Catalogue*, 298). A litany (140), added in the 11th century, with emphasis on St. Vincent, suggests that the manuscript may have passed through a house dedicated to the Saint. Corrections by a Christ Church scribe (f. 130) and a gospel reading for the feast of St. Elphege (f. 142) among the liturgical gospels in a Christ Church hand of the 11th or 12th century confirm the tradition that the Psalter was at Canterbury in the Middle Ages and came into possession of Thomas Becket (d. 1170) as indicated by a 16th-century inscription (f. 140ᵛ).

LITERATURE: James, *Ancient Libraries*, 528; *id., A descriptive catalogue of the Manuscripts in the Library of Corpus Christi College, Cambridge*, 1912, II, 296–8; Wormald, *English Drawings*, 36, 62, no. 12, pl. 17a; Talbot Rice, *English Art*, 200, pl. 61a; Bishop, *Notes*, II, 187; F. Wormald, 'Late Anglo-Saxon Art: some questions and suggestions', *Studies in Western Art. Acts of the 20th Congress of the History of Art*, ed. M. Meiss, I, Princeton, 1963, 20, pl. VIII (1); *id.*, 'Continental influence on English medieval illumination', *Fourth International Congress of Bibliophiles*, London 1965, 9.

41. London, British Library MS Harley 2904

Psalter (Gallican version)
285 × 242 mm.
Last quarter of 10th century. Winchester

Ills. 140–142

The Psalter, one of the most important manuscripts in the history of Anglo-Saxon illumination, introduces a number of features which are a break with the earlier English tradition in book painting. One of these innovations is the use of the impressionistic tinted outline technique in the full-page monumental drawing of the Crucifixion (f. 3ᵛ) which precedes the psalms. The miniature shows an imposing figure of Christ, dead on the cross, with a *titulus* over His head and the Virgin and St. John on either side. The Virgin on the left, weeping, her head bowed and half-concealed in her mantle, is modelled on the mourners' figures in the two Winchester Benedictionals (nos. 23, 24) and ultimately derives from Carolingian sources (cf. Goldschmidt I, XLIVb).

The portrayal of St. John on the right, inscribing his testimony on a scroll, introduces a new iconographic type recurring in later Anglo-Saxon representations (cf. nos. 77, Titus D. XXVII; 80, Winchcombe Psalter; 93, Judith Gospels). The drawing is in fine brown outline shaded pale red and blue; it is firmer in the figure of Christ while more flickering and broken and accented with quick, black strokes in the figures of the Virgin and St. John. The draperies are shaded with blue or brown and some of the garments are diapered in blue and red (cf. no. 23, Benedictional of St. Ethelwold). The drawing, rooted in the tradition of Wormald's 'first style' but strongly

affected by the influence from Rheims, is technically an entirely new venture and has no parallel in earlier Anglo-Saxon and continental illumination. The style of the Harley artist, who can be credited with the decoration of four more manuscripts (nos. 42, Harley 2506; 43, Orléans 175; 44, Boulogne Gospels; 45, Anhalt Gospels), had a profound influence on future developments in Anglo-Saxon painting, particularly at Canterbury.

The magnificent initial B introducing Psalm 1 (f. 4) and combining the Franco-Saxon letter-form with the luscious leafwork of the 'Winchester' school, was fundamental to the development of English initial decoration and became the archetype of the great B's in the following centuries. The B has animal-headed interlace at the top and bottom of the shaft, its gold-panelled framework contains acanthus leaf patterns while the bows, clasped by a mask head, are filled with multicoloured plant scrolls; the whole is heavily painted in shades of pink, blue, yellow, and green, enriched by overpainting and shading in lines of contrasting colours. The accompanying verses of the Psalm are inscribed over the whole page in gold capital letters. The initial to Psalm 51 is missing. The other initials, all in gold and with the same type of splendid leaf decoration, preface Psalms 51 (f. 125), 109 (f. 144), and 119 (f. 164), while less elaborate ornamental letters emphasize Psalms 118 (f. 151ᵛ) and 143 (f. 181). Large plain initials to all psalms and smaller ones to verses are in gold with rubrics inscribed in red. Small marginal acanthus ornaments and bracket marks are a characteristic feature.

PROVENANCE: The manuscript, which clearly shows Winchester connections in its decoration and certain iconographic features, was hitherto assigned to Ramsey by Niver (1937) on liturgical grounds. The Winchester attribution, suggested by Sisam (1959) on internal evidence—Psalm 77 being divided at v. 40 by a large initial letter, a peculiarity limited to four other psalters from Winchester, all in the British Library, Cotton Vitellius E. XVIII, Tiberius C. VI (no. 98), Stowe 2 (no. 99), and Arundel 60 (no. 103) and postulated by Wormald (1965)—is now further supported by T. A. M. Bishop's identification of the scribe with the one who wrote Cambridge, Sidney Sussex College MS 100 (ii), probably from Winchester. The manuscript in possession of Robert Harley, Earl of Oxford (1661–1724), was acquired with his collection for the nation in 1753.

LITERATURE: Westwood, *Facsimiles*, 115, pl. 43; E. M. Thompson, *English Illuminated Manuscripts*, 1895–6, 23, pl. 6; G. F. Warner, *Illuminated Manuscripts in the British Museum*, 1903, p. IV, pls. 7, 8; British Museum, *Reproductions*, II, 1907, pls. 4, 5; G. F. Warner and H. A. Wilson, *The Benedictional of St. Aethelwold*, 1910, p. XXXI; J. A. Herbert, *Illuminated Manuscripts*, 1911, 116; Homburger, 5; British Museum, *Schools of Illumination*, 1914, I, 10, pls. 9, 10; Millar, I, 10–11, no. 7, pls. 10–11; Saunders, *English Illumination*, 26; Homburger, 'Review', *Art Bulletin*, X, 1928, 401; C. Niver,

The Psalter in the British Museum, Harley 2904', *Medieval Studies in Memory of A. Kingsley Porter*, ed. W. R. W. Koehler, Cambridge, Mass. 1939, II, 667–87, figs. 1–2; F. Wormald, 'The Survival of Anglo-Saxon Illumination after the Norman Conquest', *Proceedings of the British Academy*, XXX, 1944, 129–30; *id.*, *Initials*, 108–9, 125, 132, pl. Ia; Kendrick, *Late Saxon*, 11, 27, 49, 136, pls. VIII, XXVII, 1, 2; H. Swarzenski, 'The Anhalt-Morgan Gospels', *Art Bulletin*, XXXI, 1949, 77–8; Holmquist, *Viking Art*, 16, 21, figs. 12–15; Wormald, *English Drawings*, 29, 32–4, 36, 41, 46, 50–2, 70–1, 73, no. 36, frontispiece, pls. 8, 9; Talbot Rice, *English Art*, 162, 208–10, 217, pls. 73a, 74a; Dodwell, *Canterbury School*, 10; A. Boutemy, 'L'enluminure anglaise de l'époque saxonne (Xe et XIe siècles) et la Flandre française', *Bulletin de la Société nationale des Antiquaires de France*, 1956, 43, 48; Freyhan, 432 n. 1; Nordenfalk, *Early Medieval*, 188; A. Boutemy, 'Un monument capital de l'enluminure anglo-saxonne: le manuscrit 11 de Boulogne-sur-mer', *Cahiers de Civilisation Médiévale*, I, 1958, 181 n. 3, 182; Rickert, *Miniatura*, 18, 21–2, pl. 14; D. Tselos, 'English manuscript illustrations and the Utrecht Psalter', *Art Bulletin*, XLI, 1959, 142; C. and K. Sisam, 'The Salisbury Psalter', *E.E.T.S.*, 242, 1959, 5, 75 n. 2; F. Wormald, *The Benedictional of St. Ethelwold*, 1959, 10; W. Mersmann, 'Das Elfenbeinkreuz der Sammlung Topic-Mimara', *Wallraf-Richartz-Jahrbuch*, XXV, 1963, 26, fig. 18; F. Wormald, 'A fragment of a tenth-century English Gospel Lectionary', *Calligraphy and Paleography. Essays presented to Alfred Fairbank*, ed. A. S. Osley, 1965, 44; Rickert, *Painting in Britain*, 33–5, 54, 58, 64, 200, 223 n. 51, pls. 21b, 30; Wormald, *Style and Design*, 32, fig. 12; *id.* 'Continental Influence on English Medieval Illumination', *Fourth International Congress of Bibliophiles*, 1965, 9; three articles in *Millénaire monastique du Mont Saint-Michel*, Paris 1967: D. Gremont and L. Donnat, 'Fleury, le Mont Saint-Michel et l'Angleterre à la fin du Xe et au début du XIe siècle à propos du manuscrit d'Orléans No. 127 (105)', I, 775 n. 184, 776, 777 nn. 191–5; F. Avril, 'La décoration des manuscrits au Mont Saint-Michel (XIe–XIIe siècles)', II, 209–10; M. Bourgeouis-Lechartier, 'À la recherche du scriptorium de l'Abbaye du Mont Saint-Michel', II, 195; Alexander, *Norman Illumination*, 59, 60–3, 67, 70–3, 91, pl. 9e; Bishop, *English Caroline*, no. 16; J. Beckwith, *Ivory Carvings in Early Medieval England*, 1972, 46, 48, ill. 46; F. Wormald, *The Winchester Psalter*, 1973, 24; *English Illuminated Manuscripts 700–1500*, Brussels Exhibition Catalogue, 1973, p. 25; Wormald, *Angleterre*, 231, 240–2, ills. 225, 236; Robb, *Illuminated Manuscript*, 151, fig. 92.

42. London, British Library MS Harley 2506 (ff. 36–44ᵛ)

Cicero, Aratea
293 × 212 mm.
Late 10th century. (?) Fleury

Ill. 143

The manuscript contains a late classical astronomical poem (ff. 36–44ᵛ) illustrated with twenty-one drawings of personifications of the constellations (three spaces are left blank) which were copied by the Anglo-Saxon artist of no. 41 (Harley 2904) from a Carolingian model, now British Library MS Harley 647. The drawings, in brown ink with touches of red and blue and light sepia washes, are in delicate and, at times, broken and quivering outline characteristic of this artist's style. The text they illustrate is the same as in Harley 647 but the commentaries, which are written in the margins and do not form part of the drawing, are different.

PROVENANCE: The manuscript, containing treatises of Abbo of Fleury which precede the *Aratea*, was probably produced at Fleury and illustrated by the Anglo-Saxon artist referred to above, who was working on the Continent at that time. It was written by several hands, some continental and some possibly English (Bishop, *Engl. Caroline*) and was attributed to Fleury on account of the name of Abbo replaced in the prefatory astronomical texts by that of Berno, a German monk known to be at Fleury *c.*994. Acquired for the nation with the Harley collection in 1753.

LITERATURE: W. Y. Otley, 'On a MS of Cicero's translation of Aratus', *Archaeologia*, XXIV, 1836, 146–7, pl. XI; Westwood, *Facsimiles*, 100, pl. 48; Homburger, 5; A. Van de Vyver, 'Les oeuvres inédites d'Abbon de Fleury', *Revue Bénédictine*, XLVII, 1935, 141–4; C. Niver, 'The Psalter in the British Museum, Harley 2904', *Medieval Studies in Memory of A. Kingsley Porter*, ed. W. R. W. Koehler, Cambridge, Mass. 1939, II, 681 n. 66; F. Wormald, 'The Survival of Anglo-Saxon Illumination after the Norman Conquest', *Proceedings of the British Academy*, XXX, 1944, 130, pl. Ib; F. Saxl and R. Wittkower, *British Art and the Mediterranean*, 1948, pl. 30, b, (4–6); Kendrick, *Late Saxon*, 24, pl. XXIII, 2; H. Swarzenski, 'The Anhalt-Morgan Gospels', *Art Bulletin*, XXXI, 1949, 77, 78 n. 9; Wormald, *English Drawings*, 32–3, 70–1, 73, no. 35, frontispiece, pls. 8, 9; F. Saxl and H. Meier, *Verzeichnis astrologischer und mythologischer illustrierter Handschriften des lateinischen Mittelalters, III. Handschriften in englischen Bibliotheken*, 1953, I, p. XVII, 157–60, figs. 2–4; A. Boutemy, 'Un monument capital de l'enluminure anglo-saxonne', *Cahiers de Civilisation Médiévale*, I, 1958, 182 n. 7; Rickert, *Miniatura*, 15–16, 18, 21–2, pl. 16; *id.*, *Painting in Britain*, 62, 223 n. 51, 224 n. 59; D. Gremont and L. Donnat, 'Fleury, le Mont Saint-Michel et l'Angleterre', *Millénaire monastique du Mont Saint-Michel*, 1967, I, 775, 776 n. 186, 777 n. 195; F. Saxl, 'Illuminated Science Manuscripts in England', *Lectures*, 1967, 1, 102–8, pls. 55b, 56a, b, c, 57b, 59d; M. W. Evans, *Medieval Drawings*, 1969, 22, pl. 13; Bishop, *English Caroline*, p. XII n. 2, nos. 18 n. 1, 20; Wormald, *Winchester School*, 312–13; *English Illuminated Manuscripts 700–1500*, Brussels Exhibition Catalogue, 1973, p. 25; Wormald, *Angleterre*, 240–2, ills. 240–1.

43. Orléans, Bibliothèque Municipale MS 175
St. Gregory, Homilies on Ezekiel
360 × 260 mm.
Late 10th century. Fleury

Ill. 144

A full-page drawing which comes at the end of the Homilies (f. 149ᵛ) shows Christ in a mandorla enthroned between St. Gregory and St. Benedict with a small figure of a monk kneeling at the feet of the latter. The composition, monumental yet of great simplicity, drawn in brown ink with some blue and sepia tinting, is by the artist of nos. 41 (Harley 2904) and 42 (Harley 2506), an Anglo-Saxon working on the Continent. The picture shows all the characteristics of his style, blending firmness and clarity of definition with the expressive animation of the Rheims manner: the draperies fall in long, straight folds with softly zigzagging edges and the outlines are enlivened by quick short strokes (note also the typically rich diaper on Christ's robe, the huge hands and the tiny feet).

PROVENANCE: The manuscript, as shown by the dedicatory inscription (f. 150), was written at Fleury where it remained throughout the Middle Ages; it was entered as no. 201 in the Fleury catalogue of 1552 published by Delisle (1883).

LITERATURE: M. L. Delisle, *Notices sur plusieurs manuscrits d'Orléans*, Paris 1883, 70–83; C. Cuissard, *Inventaire des manuscrits de la Bibliothèque d'Orléans. Fonds de Fleury*, Orléans 1885, 88; Homburger, 5; Millar, I, 17; C. Niver, 'The Psalter in the British Museum, Harley 2904', *Medieval Studies in Memory of A. Kingsley Porter*, ed. W. R. W. Koehler, Cambridge, Mass. 1939, II, 681–3, fig. 3; H. Swarzenski, 'The Anhalt-Morgan Gospels', *Art Bulletin*, XXXI, 1949, 78; Wormald, *English Drawings*, 32–3, 50, 70–1, 73, no. 45, pls. 14, 35b; Talbot Rice, *English Art*, 214; A. Boutemy, 'L'enluminure anglaise de l'époque saxonne (Xe et XIe siècles) et la Flandre française', *Bulletin de la Société nationale des Antiquaires de France*, 1956, 43, 45; id., 'Un monument capital de l'enluminure anglo-saxonne; le manuscrit 11 de Boulogne-sur-mer', *Cahiers de Civilisation Médiévale*, I, 1958, 181; Rickert, *Miniatura*, 15, 16, 18, 21, 29, pl. 15; id., *Painting in Britain*, 222 n. 39; D. Gremont and L. Donnat, 'Fleury, le Mont Saint-Michel et l'Angleterre', *Millénaire monastique du Mont Saint-Michel*, 1967, I, 775, n. 185; Alexander, *Norman Illumination*, 239; Wormald, *Winchester School*, 313; *English Illuminated Manuscripts 700–1500*, Brussels Exhibition Catalogue, 1973, p. 25; Wormald, *Angleterre*, 240–2.

44. Boulogne, Bibliothèque Municipale MS 11
Gospels (Boulogne Gospels)
330 × 260 mm.
Late 10th century. St. Bertin

Ills. 145, 147–150

This is the most copiously illuminated of the surviving Anglo-Saxon Gospel Books. It is preceded by fifteen decorated Canon Tables (ff. 2–9) shown under round or pointed, and often intersecting arches, the whole crowned with one large arch, a rectangular lintel on pilasters, or a superimposed row of small arches on colonettes. The varied decoration of the tympana includes multi-winged Evangelist symbols, a Christ in a mandorla adored by angels, the Holy Lamb, the Hand of God, and hunting scenes, while the spandrels are ornamented with birds, beasts, and musicians playing their instruments, most of these motifs traceable to Carolingian illumination of the Ada, Rheims, and Metz schools.

The Gospels contain a series of full-page miniatures, some of which have no iconographic parallel. Christ in Majesty (f. 10) preceding St. Matthew's Gospel has counterparts in insular manuscripts (cf. Book of Kells; Trinity Gospels, no. 65). The Evangelist portraits (except that of Matthew) are followed by the *Incipit* pages inscribed in gold lettering and containing ornamental initials and elaborate figural compositions, a type of decoration unprecedented in Anglo-Saxon painting but occurring in German manuscripts from Reichenau and Trier (cf. Boutemy, 1958) and from Fulda (cf. Dodwell, 1971). Matthew (f. 10ᵛ), Mark (f. 55ᵛ) and John (f. 107), all hunchbacked, are shown seated frontally in identical poses under domed canopies, turning to the right and leaning heavily over their desks writing. Matthew, unaccompanied by his symbol, appears on one page with four seated conversing figures (a king and three prophets with palms) shown in two registers on the right, and the miniature is followed by two pages containing rows of Christ's ancestors in arched niches (ff. 11, 11ᵛ), with the Annunciation and Visitation at the bottom of the second page (f. 11ᵛ). A Nativity of Anglo-Saxon type (cf. no. 23, Benedictional of St. Ethelwold) and an Annunciation to the Shepherds occupy the left side of the following page (f. 12), with a choir of angels (a feature of German painting of the 10th and 11th centuries) at the top and a splendid Franco-Saxon initial L with text-lines on the right.

Besides the tabernacles of Mark (f. 55ᵛ), Luke (f. 61ᵛ) and John (f. 107) elaborate groups of small buildings are shown (cf. Bible of San Paolo, Boinet, pl. CXXVII), architectural motifs being a prominent feature of the decoration of the present manuscript. Mark and John are accompanied by their symbols on the right, and John is also inspired by the Holy Dove perching on his shoulder (cf. no. 95, Monte Cassino Gospels). Luke, seated frontally, torso erect and one elbow pressed to his side, rests a book on his knee and dips a pen into an inkpot on the left; he is shown under a roofed porch with two curtains looped round the columns. All the Evangelist figures are strong and massive; they have large hands and feet and softly curling hair and beards, closely resembling the Evangelists in no. 45 (Anhalt-Morgan Gospels), undoubtedly executed by the same artist.

Christ in a mandorla held by two angels is shown in

the tympanum of Mark's *Incipit* page (f. 56) and below that on the left, under two smaller arches on columns, John the Baptist and Isaiah holding long wavy inscribed scrolls (figures with undulating scrolls are prominent in Canterbury decoration in the first half of the 11th century); and an ornamental initial I with luscious 'Winchester' foliage on the right. The initial Q to Luke's Gospel (f. 62) is historiated with the Annunciation to Zacharias, an iconography of Carolingian derivation (cf. British Library MS Harley 2788; also Morgan 333, Gospels, executed for Abbot Otbert at St. Bertin, *c.* 1000). The initial page to John (f. 107ᵛ) displays in the stem of the I a Christ in a mandorla under heavy interlace knotwork and adored by two angels.

The figure drawing is extremely vivid and expressive, showing mastery and freedom in the treatment of draperies with some suggestion of the bodily forms beneath. Features and hands are drawn in orange (cf. no. 23, Benedictional of St. Ethelwold) and garments, some diapered, are painted in light washes. Soft and clear, the principal colours include pale blue, pink, and purple with touches of red, orange and ochre, and gold in details. The backgrounds are mainly green and inscribed in white lettering with characteristic deep blue shadow outline, the latter becoming a feature of 11th-century Anglo-Saxon manuscripts, particularly those from Canterbury (cf. nos. 66, Arundel 155; 67, Eadui Codex). The framework of the miniatures is highly varied and some borders are of 'Winchester' type of two gold parallel bands with foliated bosses and corner ornaments, others are plain panelled enclosures in gold and colour or arched frames on columns. The decoration, executed by the (probably) Winchester artist of no. 41 (Harley 2904; responsible also for nos. 42, Harley 2506; 43, Orléans 175; 45, Anhalt-Morgan Gospels), has all the hallmarks of his lively and sensitive style but shows a firmer and less quivering line than that seen in the Harley Crucifixion. The iconographic sources are complex and features typically Anglo-Saxon (e.g. the Nativity) are combined with elements preponderantly Carolingian and with motifs reflecting contemporary developments in German painting.

PROVENANCE: Illuminated by an Anglo-Saxon working on the Continent, the manuscript was produced at St. Bertin under Abbot Otbert (990–1007) who participated in its decoration by executing two ornamental initials, an M (f. 53ᵛ) and an 'h' (f. 104ᵛ), drawn in red ink (cf. his Psalter, Boulogne, Bibl. Mun. MS 20). The Gospels belonged to St. Bertin Abbey throughout the Middle Ages as shown by an inscription on the verso of the fly-leaf: '*Scti Bertini*' and an *ex-libris* of Momelin, Abbot of St. Bertin (1706–23).

LITERATURE: Westwood, *Facsimiles*, 101, pl. 36; Homburger, 5 n. 8; Dom A. Wilmart, 'Les livres de l'abbé Otbert', *Bull. hist. de la Société des Antiquaires de la Morinie*, XIV, 1922–4, 169–88; Millar, I, 17; Saunders, *English Illumination*, 23; H. Swar-

zenski, 'The Anhalt-Morgan Gospels', *Art Bulletin*, XXXI, 1949, 78–9; figs. 8–10; Talbot Rice, *English Art*, 215; A. Boutemy, 'La Miniature', in E. Moreau, *Histoire de l'Église en Belgique*, 1945–52, II, 324; Paris, Bibliothèque Nationale, *Les Manuscrits à peintures en France du VIIe au XIIe siècle*, 1954, no. 110; A. Boutemy, 'L'enluminure anglaise de l'époque saxonne (Xe et XIe siècles) et la Flandre française', *Bull. de la Société nationale des Antiquaires de France*, 1956, 43; *id.*, 'Un monument capital de l'enluminure anglo-saxonne: le manuscrit 11 de Boulogne-sur-mer', *Cahiers de Civilisation Médiévale*, I, 1958, 178–82; J. Porcher, *French Miniatures*, 1960, 17, pl. V; R. H. Randall jr., 'An eleventh-century ivory pectoral cross', *J.W.C.I.*, XXV, 1962, 167, 170; W. Mersmann, 'Das Elfenbeinkreuz der Sammlung Topic-Mimara', *Wallraf-Richartz-Jahrbuch*, XXV, 1963, 57, fig. 44; A. Heimann, 'A twelfth-century Manuscript from Winchcombe and its Illustrations', *J.W.C.I.*, XXVIII, 1965, 88, pl. 14 c, d; D. Gremont and L. Donnat, 'Fleury, le Mont Saint-Michel et l'Angleterre à la fin du Xe et au début du XIe siècle à propos du manuscrit d'Orléans No. 127 (105)', *Millénaire monastique du Mont Saint-Michel*, Paris 1967, I, 775 n. 183; Alexander, *Norman Illumination*, 239; C. R. Dodwell, *Painting in Europe 800–1200*, 1971, 80, 82, pl. 96; Wormald, *Angleterre*, 240–2, ill. 238.

EXHIBITED: Brussels, 1973, *English Illuminated Manuscripts 700–1500*, no. 5.

45. New York, Pierpont Morgan Library MS 827
Gospels (Anhalt-Morgan Gospels)
356×254 mm.
English additions *c.* 1000

Ill. 146

The additions made to an unfinished continental Gospel Book of the later 10th century consist of Evangelist portraits painted by the Anglo-Saxon artist of no. 41 (Harley 2904), known to have been working at Fleury (cf. nos. 42, Harley 2506; 43, Orléans 175) and at St. Bertin (cf. no. 44, Boulogne Gospels). The portraits were added within the original frames of a Franco-Saxon type and are, though without the elaborate architectural backgrounds, almost exact copies of those in the Boulogne manuscript.

All the Evangelists are shown seated frontally and, with the exception of Luke (f. 66ᵛ), are turned to the right. Matthew (f. 17ᵛ) and Mark (f. 40ᵛ), perhaps represented originally on blank vellum (cf. no. 68, Grimbald Gospels), are now on blue and purple backgrounds which are a later addition, while Luke is surrounded by a zigzag-covered ground and John (f. 98ᵛ) is shown on a curtained one, both paralleled in the Boulogne Gospels. Matthew, writing in an open book on a draped stand, is identical with the Matthew in the Boulogne manuscript; Mark is inscribing a scroll he holds in his hands;

Luke, holding a book and a palm branch and turning to the left, closely recalls the prophets of the Matthew miniature in the Boulogne Gospels (f. 10ᵛ); John, sitting by a lectern and writing in an open book, his head supported on his left hand, is modelled on his Boulogne counterpart though without the Holy Dove at his ear.

The figures are of the same massive and imposing type in both books and the similarity extends to their features with curly beards and hair. But the patterns of the drapery folds are more repetitive and less fluid in the present manuscript, showing a certain tendency towards formalization which seems to suggest that the added portraits may have been produced after those in the Boulogne Gospels (cf. Boutemy, 1958, for a different view). Technically, the miniatures show all the hallmarks of the artist's painterly manner with soft brushstrokes marking the deeply shaded drapery folds, bold coloured shadow outline around the figures, and a zigzaggy background.

The decoration of the Canon Tables and of the framed pages with titles and ornamental initials is not by the Anglo-Saxon artist and belongs to the original part of the manuscript: it is in Franco-Saxon style and has its closest analogies in books produced at St. Vaast, Arras, in the 9th century. An *opus interrasile* copper plaque, attached to the lower cover of the original binding boards, is datable to the mid 11th century and is also of continental workmanship.

PROVENANCE: The Gospel Book, written in continental Caroline minuscule of the later 10th century, was probably produced in the region of Arras, perhaps at St. Vaast, though Corbie has been also suggested as its place of origin (cf. Swarzenski, 1949). The Anglo-Saxon additions may have been executed in either of those two places or at St. Bertin where the artist is known to have worked. Though remote, the possibility that the volume was brought over, perhaps as a gift, and the portraits added in England (cf. Swarzenski, 1949) cannot be entirely ruled out: the impact of this Anglo-Saxon artist's style on English illumination, particularly felt in manuscripts produced at Canterbury in the first half of the 11th century, suggests that he may have returned and worked in this country. The manuscript was at Moenchen-Nienburg in Magdeburg diocese, since the marginal figures of its Canon Tables were copied in outline drawings in an unfinished Gospel Book of the second quarter of the 12th century, which came from that house and is now in the Anhalt Museum at Dessau. The present volume is believed to have belonged to Prince George II, Duke of Anhalt-Dessau (born 1507), whose collection was for the most part assembled from the library of Moenchen-Nienburg. Included in Sotheby's sale, 1927, it was acquired by the Pierpont Morgan Library in 1948.

LITERATURE: A. Haseloff, 'École du Nord-Est', in A. Michel, *Histoire de l'art*, 1906, I, Bk. 2, 748; Hom-

burger, 5 n. 9; A. Boeckler, *Abendländische Miniaturen*, 1930, 60; D. Minor, *Illuminated Books from the Middle Ages and the Renaissance* (Exhibition Catalogue, Walters Art Gallery, Baltimore), 1949, 15 ff., no. 15, pl. VII; H. Swarzenski, 'The Anhalt-Morgan Gospels', *Art Bulletin*, XXXI, 1949, 77–83, figs. 4–7; A. Boutemy, 'L'enluminure anglaise de l'époque saxonne (Xe et XIe siècles) et la Flandre française', *Bulletin de la Société nationale des Antiquaires de France*, 1956, 43; F. Adams, *Treasures from the Pierpont Morgan Library* (50th Anniversary Exhibition), 1957, no. 10; A. Boutemy, 'Un monument capital de l'enluminure anglo-saxonne, le manuscrit 11 de Boulogne-sur-mer', *Cahiers de Civilisation Médiévale*, I, 1958, 181; R. H. Randall jr., 'An eleventh-century ivory pectoral cross', *J.W.C.I.*, XXV, 1962, 165; F. Wormald, 'Continental Influence on English Medieval Illumination', *Fourth International Congress of Bibliophiles*, 1965, 9; Swarzenski, *Monuments*, pl. 57, fig. 130; D. Gremont and L. Donnat, 'Fleury, le Mont Saint-Michel et l'Angleterre à la fin du Xe et au début du XIe siècle à propos du manuscrit d'Orléans No. 127 (105)', *Millénaire monastique du Mont Saint-Michel*, Paris 1967, I, 775; C. R. Dodwell, *Painting in Europe 800–1200*, 1971, 82 nn. 55–7, 83, pl. 99; *English Illuminated Manuscripts 700–1500*, Brussels Exhibition Catalogue, 1973, p. 25; Wormald, *Angleterre*, 240–2.

46. London, British Library MS Cotton, Otho B. II

Gregory the Great, Pastoral Care
220 × 175 mm.
c. 1000

Fig. 75

This copy of King Alfred's translation of Gregory's *Cura Pastoralis* (cf. no. 1, Hatton 20) derives from an exemplar sent to Hehstan, Bishop of London, in 897; damaged in the fire of the Cottonian Library in 1731, it now contains only 52 leaves remaining out of the original 82. The decoration consists of three small zoomorphic initials (f. 22ᵛ), Wormald Type I, of rough execution, made up of full-bodied composite creatures and a mask head; they are lightly painted in ochre, yellow, brown, and green, with touches of slate blue. Numerous other initials, of an archaic type, in black outline with fillings of slate blue and yellow, have terminals with animal or bird heads and are sometimes surrounded by dots.

The manuscript is assigned by Ker to *c.* 1000, but the extremely retrospective style of the initials suggests that they may have been closely copied from the 9th-century model for this manuscript.

PROVENANCE: The manuscript belonged to Henry Ellzing from whom it was acquired in 1597 by Sir Robert Cotton; his library, presented to the nation by his grandson, Sir John Cotton, in 1700, was incorporated in the British Museum in 1753.

LITERATURE: Ker, *Catalogue*, lvi, no. 175.

47. Copenhagen, Royal Library
G.K.S. 10, 2°
Gospels (Copenhagen Gospels)
385 × 285 mm.
Late 10th century to first quarter of 11th century
Ills. 151–154

The Gospels are prefaced by fifteen richly decorated Canon Tables (ff. 1–8) shown in corresponding pairs under round and occasionally gabled arches which are either embraced by a large arch flanked by figures of angels, architectural motifs, and plant scrolls, or surrounded by heavy rectangular frames with round or square corner bosses. The arches and shafts are in gold and colour and rest on acanthus leaf capitals with foliage at times markedly agitated and dishevelled.

A hard point sketch for the St. Matthew portrait (f. 8ᵛ) is followed by Jerome's *Epistula ad Damasum* (f. 9) with a large pen-and-ink initial N of Franco-Saxon type and lines of display script of excellent quality in red lettering.

Only two Evangelist portraits (Matthew and Luke) with corresponding initial pages and the opening page to John's Gospel now survive. The Evangelists (ff. 17ᵛ, 82ᵛ) sit in side view and write in open books supported on tall stands on the right, and both recall in pose and gesture the figure of Ezra in the Codex Amiatinus (Florence, Laurenziana Am. I) and its derivative, the Matthew in the Lindisfarne Gospels (B.L. Cotton, Nero D. IV). The Copenhagen portrait of Matthew, moreover, is of the same 'accompanied' type as the latter and contains, besides the Evangelist symbol, a third figure, probably Christ, whose head emerges from behind a curtain on the right. Matthew looks up as if listening to this 'inspiring' figure, while an angel blowing a trumpet flies down from the upper left corner brushing past the Evangelist's nimbus. The scene, nearly identical with that in the Lindisfarne manuscript, was said to have been a faithful copy of it, but certain divergencies in the Copenhagen Matthew (the stool, the desk, the angel flying), suggest that both manuscripts may have been served by a common model.

Luke (f. 82ᵛ), differentiated from Matthew by his crossed feet, is also accompanied by a trumpet-blowing symbol—the ox—which, shown charging from right to left across the picture, is of an early Insular type and recalls the trumpeting lion of Mark in the Lindisfarne Gospels (for symbols blowing trumpets or horns cf. nos. 23, Benedictional of St. Ethelwold; 68, Grimbald Gospels; 73, Pembroke 301).

The portraits on green (f. 17ᵛ) and pink (f. 82ᵛ) backgrounds are surrounded by panelled rectangular frames with sparse leaf decoration in the centre of each side which are vaguely reminiscent of 'Winchester' borders. The miniatures are painted in shades of pink to mauve, red, tan, blue to grey, with gold in details and touches of silver. Features are outlined in reddish ochre and lights are laid on in white patches.

The beginning of each Gospel, inscribed in gold capitals on unframed pages, is introduced by a large ornamental initial of excellent quality containing panels of leafwork and colour within gold framework. An initial 'I' (f. 18) of Franco-Saxon type has interlace terminals on green ground, the bottom one ending in an animal head; the Q (f. 83) is filled with multicoloured leafwork on violet ground, its tail pinned to the bowl by a large crimson and black mask-head; the I (f. 124) contains a large square boss with geometrical pattern, placed diagonally halfway up the shaft.

PROVENANCE: The original part of the manuscript including the display script with the initial N (f. 9), prefatory matter and capitula (ff. 9–16) and most of the text (cf. Bishop, 1967), was written before 1000 in an early type of English Caroline minuscule that can be associated with one of the Ethelwoldian monastic foundations, possibly New Minster, Winchester. The writing of the text and all the decoration were completed in the 11th century by a scribe who may have been domiciled, according to T. A. M. Bishop, in Peterborough and who was also responsible for no. 65 (Trinity Gospels) and no. 72 (Robert of Jumièges Sacramentary) and appears in other manuscripts associated with Christ Church, Canterbury. Neumed liturgical matter (ff. 16, 16ᵛ) added by an apparently English hand in the late 12th century, indicates that the Gospels did not leave England in the time of King Cnut as suggested by Westwood (*Facsimiles*). It belonged in the mid 16th century to Niels Hemmingsen, a Danish theologian, and entered the Royal Library with Gersdorff's collection in 1661.

LITERATURE: J. O. Westwood, 'Archaeological notes of a tour in Denmark, Prussia and Holland', *Archaeological Journal*, XVI, 1859, 144; *id.*, *Facsimiles*, 117, pl. 41; G. F. Warner and H. A. Wilson, *The Benedictional of St. Aethelwold*, 1910, p. XXI; Homburger, 15 n. 3; F. Mackeprang, V. Madsen, C. S. Petersen, *Greek and Latin Illuminated Manuscripts, X–XIII centuries, in Danish Collections*, Copenhagen 1921, 7–10, pls. V–X; Millar, I, 16–17, no. 20; F. Saxl and R. Wittkower, *British Art and the Mediterranean*, 1948, 14 (3); Kendrick, *Late Saxon*, 9; Talbot Rice, *English Art*, 207; Bishop, *Notes*, IV, 333; R. L. S. Bruce-Mitford, 'Decoration and Miniatures', *Codex Lindisfarnensis*, ed. T. D. Kendrick, Olten Lausanne 1960, II, 149–57, 158 n. 11, 159 nn. 7–9, pls. 22d, 23a, 27a, b; Rickert, *Painting in Britain*, 217 n. 32; Swarzenski, *Monuments*, pl. 57, fig. 129; T. A. M. Bishop, 'The Copenhagen Gospel Book', *Nordisk Tidskrift för Bok- och Biblioteksväsen*, 1967, 33–41; *id.*, *English Caroline*, pp. XV, XXII, no. 13; C. Nordenfalk, 'The Draped Lectern', *Intuition und Kunstwissenschaft: Festschrift für Hans Swarzenski*, Berlin 1973, 86.

48. Cambridge, Corpus Christi College MS 23
Prudentius, Psychomachia and other poems
365 × 287 mm.
Late 10th century. (?) Canterbury, Christ Church
Ills. 50, 155–158

The *Psychomachia* (ff. 1ᵛ–40), a poem on the fight between the Virtues and Vices, is illustrated with a series of 89 drawings after originals going back to the fifth century which served as models to the three (nos. 49, 50, 51) other extant illuminated Anglo-Saxon copies. The prologue, containing as usual the story of Abraham, Lot, etc. (ff. 1ᵛ–2ᵛ), is introduced by a large ornamental initial S (f. 2) and the first lines of the text in green and red capitals. The initial composed of plant motifs, interlace knotwork, and two large snapping bird heads at the extremities (cf. no. 15, Add. 40618, f. 22ᵛ), is inhabited by a bird and is an example of the high quality of 10th- to 11th-century initials that are found in Canterbury manuscripts.

The drawings in sepia, green, red, and blue inks are placed within the text-column, mostly two to a page, and are in rectangular frames of double lines; they are by a single artist responsible also for the second group of illustrations in the 'Caedmon' Genesis (no. 58); stylistically they recall the Leofric Missal (no. 17) and the miniature of Philosophy (no. 20) by the striking contrast between the long, swift strokes of the contours and the fluttering drapery edges. The lightness, spontaneity, and animation of the drawing and also, at times, its almost sketchy outline show considerable Rheims influence. The strikingly tall and graceful yet firmly poised figures move with great freedom and ease; they have tiny feet and small heads which, though often in profile, show also the second eye. The miniatures occasionally contain delicate, stylized plant motifs in fine brush-work which occur frequently in Canterbury manuscripts of *c.* 1000 (cf. no. 30. xii, Bibl. Nat. lat. 17814). Initials to verses are in green or red with rubrics in the same colours. Titles describing the illustrations, some translated into Anglo-Saxon, are in red rustic capitals. A figure is faintly sketched in pencil (f. 1).

PROVENANCE: The manuscript was associated by Homburger with Canterbury on stylistic grounds (cf. also Boeckler, 1930); certainly, the decoration executed by the second hand of the 'Caedmon' Genesis (no. 58), which is attributable to Christ Church, favours this suggestion. The volume was at Malmesbury by the mid 11th century, as shown by a dedicatory poem (iib) naming one Athelward (probably the abbot, 1040–50) as the donor of the book to St. Aldhelm; the lines have been tampered with, however, and the variants of Aldhelm's names are crowded in and over erasure (cf. Ker, *Catalogue*). This poem gave rise to the attribution of the manuscript to Malmesbury and to its identification as the 'Malmesbury Prudentius'. It was bequeathed to Corpus Christi College by Archbishop Parker.

LITERATURE: Westwood, *Facsimiles*, 108; M. R. James, 'On Fine Art as applied to the illustrations of the Bible', *Proceedings of the Cambridge Antiquarian Society*, VII, 1888–91, 51–3, pls. X–XI; R. Stettiner, *Die illustrierten Prudentius-Handschriften*, Berlin 1905, 17, pls. 31–2, 49–66; Homburger, 3 n. 3, 5; H. P. Mitchell, 'Flotsam of Later Anglo-Saxon Art',

Burlington Magazine, XLIII 1923, 113, 117, pl. VIII, G, H; Millar, I, 20, 21, n. 4, no. 53; Saunders, *English Illumination*, 29–30, pls. 31–2; O. Homburger, 'Review', *Art Bulletin*, X, 1928, 400–1; H. Woodruff, 'The illustrated Manuscripts of Prudentius', *Art Studies*, 7, 1929–33, 38, no. 3, fig. 7; A. Boeckler, *Abendländische Miniaturen*, 1930, 56; A. Goldschmidt, 'English influence on medieval art on the continent', *Medieval Studies in Memory of A. Kingsley Porter*, ed. W. R. W. Koehler, Cambridge, Mass., 1939, II, 719–20, pl. 11; Wormald, *Initials*, 134; Kendrick, *Late Saxon*, 19, pl. XX, 1; Wormald, *English Drawings*, 29, 35, 40, 60, 76, 80, no. 4, pl. 6b; Talbot Rice, *English Art*, 213, pl. 80; S. Schulten, 'Die Buchmalerei des 11. Jahrhunderts im Kloster St. Vaast in Arras', *Münchner Jahrbuch der bildenden Kunst*, VII 1956, 57; Nordenfalk, *Early Medieval*, 187; Rickert, *Miniatura*, 15, 22, pl. 17; Ker, *Catalogue*, no. 31; Rickert, *Painting in Britain*, 43, 225 nn. 71–2, pl. 38b; M. W. Evans, *Medieval Drawings*, 1969, 21, pl. 9; Pächt and Alexander, no. 34; H. Holländer, *Early Medieval Art*, 1974, 186, ill. 151.

49. London, British Library MS Cotton, Cleopatra C. VIII

Prudentius, Psychomachia (ff. 1–34ᵛ)
215 × 135 mm.
Late 10th century. Canterbury, Christ Church

Ills. 159–162

The pictorial cycle of no. 48 (Cambridge Prudentius) is reduced here to eighty-two drawings, because two leaves are missing. These are in coloured outline and, for the most part, surrounded by rectangular frames with verticals in double lines on a basis suggesting a column (cf. no. 62, Julius A. VI) and with single lines at the bottom; the illustrations, however, showing a tendency to spill over the enclosures, are seldom contained within the picture space.

The drawings are by two artists both working in the 'first style'. Those by Hand I (ff. 1–16ᵛ, 27ᵛ–33ᵛ) resemble the first group of illustrations in the 'Caedmon' Genesis (no. 58) in their elaborate and greatly agitated hemlines but their outline in brown and red inks is much more delicate, while the ample and loosely hung draperies with softly fluttering edges and animated and expressive gestures, show a considerable degree of influence from Rheims. Mostly incomplete, the drawings of Hand II (ff. 18–27), with their hard and heavy contours (in which a good deal of green is used), and with their rope-like and sharply marked nested V-folds, are closely related in style to no. 57 (Bodley 577). The opening line of the prologue (f. 4) is inscribed in metallic red on a coloured band. Initials to sections, standing in the margins, are in blue or red and verse initials in green. Descriptive Latin and Old English titles accompany the pictures.

PROVENANCE: The Prudentius belongs to a group of manuscripts of the late 10th to the early 11th century, assigned by T. A. M. Bishop to the Christ Church, Canterbury scriptorium and interconnected by having common scribes and illuminators (cf. *Notes*). The manuscript inscribed 'Robertus Cotton Bruceus' (f. 4) was lent by Cotton to Usher before April 1621; his collection, presented to the nation by his grandson, Sir John Cotton, in 1700, was incorporated in the British Museum in 1753.

LITERATURE: Westwood, *Facsimiles*, 108; *Pal. Soc.*, I, pl. 190; M. R. James, 'On Fine Art as applied to the illustrations of the Bible', *Proc. of the Cambridge Antiquarian Society*, VII, 1888-91, 53; E. M. Thompson, *English Illuminated Manuscripts*, 1895, 21-2, pl. 4; R. Stettiner, *Die illustrierten Prudentius-Handschriften*, Berlin 1905, 19, pls. 36, 43-6, 49-66; Homburger, 5 n. 1; British Museum, *Schools of Illumination*, 1914, pl. 12a; *id.*, *Reproductions from Illuminated Manuscripts*, 1923, I, pl. VII; H. P. Mitchell, 'Flotsam of Later Anglo-Saxon Art', *Burlington Magazine*, XLIII, 1923, 113, 117, pl. VIII, D, E, F; Millar, I, 20 n. 1, no. 52, pl. 26; O. Homburger, 'Review', *Art Bulletin*, X, 1928, 400; Saunders, *English Illumination*, 30, pl. 33; H. Woodruff, 'The Illustrated Manuscripts of Prudentius', *Art Studies*, 7, 1929, 39, no. 5; Wormald, *English Drawings*, 37, 67, 75, no. 29; Talbot Rice, *English Art*, 208, pl. 71b; Ker, *Catalogue*, no. 145; Bishop, *Notes*, VII, 421 (7); F. Wormald, *Style and Design*, 32, fig. 15; Rickert, *Painting in Britain*, 43, 225 n. 73; *Anglo-Saxon Illumination*, no. 11; Pächt and Alexander, no. 33.

50. Munich, Staatsbibliothek CLM. 29031b (fragment)
Prudentius, Psychomachia
260 × 180 mm.
Late 10th century

Ill. 165

The one remaining leaf of a copy of unknown origin of Prudentius' poem contains (on its recto and verso) three drawings in black and red inks executed in firm, vigorous outline; their iconography and style are closely related to no. 49 (Cleopatra C. VIII) but the drawings are not of the same fine quality.

PROVENANCE: The leaf, folded across the middle, was used in binding in Germany. The name Johannes Marckhart, 1479, is scribbled on the verso (see Ker).

LITERATURE: R. Stettiner, *Die illustrierten Prudentius-Handschriften*, Berlin 1905, 20, pls. 47-8; H. Woodruff, 'The Illustrated Manuscripts of Prudentius', *Art Studies*, 8, 1929-33, 10, no. 6, fig, 120; Wormald, *English Drawings*, 29, 37, 73, no. 44; Ker, *Catalogue*, no. 286.

51. London, British Library MS Add. 24199
Prudentius, Psychomachia
320 × 240 mm.
Late 10th century

Ills. 163, 166

The manuscript contains an unfinished cycle of ninety-one pictures (ff. 2-38) which comprises a series of eighty-nine drawings occurring in no. 48 (Cambridge Prudentius) with an addition of two new ones.

The illustrations in brown ink with touches of green, mauve, and blue in details are by three artists and are of various dates. Those by Hand I (ff. 2-26), of the late 10th century, are in the 'first style' and are reminiscent of certain miniatures in no. 23 (Benedictional of St. Ethelwold), recalling also no. 35 (Sherborne Pontifical) in the firmly drawn, statuesque, and narrow-shouldered figures and in the long, vertical strokes of the drapery folds. But the tendency towards pattern-making is more pronounced in their intricate, multiple-fold designs contrasted with the elaborately zigzagging edges and in the ornamental, highly formalized treatment of the ground and sky (cf. no. 23, Benedictional of St. Ethelwold; no. 86, Aelfric's Pentateuch, second quarter of the 11th century). The linear rectangular frames, often with chamfered corners, occasionally contain ornamental panelling, mostly incomplete; the overflowing of the boundary of the frame by details of the compositions is a characteristic feature (cf. Wormald, *Draw.*, p. 28; cf. also no. 49). A few of the miniatures are more fully coloured (e.g. ff. 12ᵛ, 20ᵛ). The drawings by Hand II (ff. 26ᵛ-27ᵛ, 28ᵛ, 29ᵛ, 31ᵛ, 33ᵛ), second half of the 11th century, include some in the 'revived Utrecht' style. The remaining drawings, by Hand III, datable to *c.* 1100, are rather rough. A scrolled initial S (f. 2) is in red and green, minor initials are in the same colours, and verse-initials in silver.

PROVENANCE: The origin of the manuscript is uncertain; it belonged to Bury St. Edmunds Abbey in the 14th century (press-mark 'P. 123', f. 2), but since Bury was not founded until 1020, it could not have been produced there. The volume was acquired from the library of Archbishop Tenison in 1861 (f. 2).

LITERATURE: Westwood, *Facsimiles*, 107, pl. 44; E. M. Thompson, *English Illuminated Manuscripts*, 1895-6, 18-21, pl. 4; M. R. James, *On the Abbey of St. Edmund at Bury*, 1895, 71; *id.*, 'On Fine Art as applied to the Illustration of the Bible', *Proc. Cambr. Antiq. Soc.*, VII, 1888-9, 53; W. H. St. John Hope, *English Altars* (Alcuin Club Collection, I), 1899, pl. 1, fig. 2; R. Stettiner, *Die illustrierten Prudentius-Handschriften*, Berlin 1905, 19, pls. 37-8, 39-40, 41-2, 49-66; J. A. Herbert, *Illuminated Manuscripts*, 1911, 111; Millar, I, 21, n. 2, no. 54; H. Woodruff, 'The Illustrated Manuscripts of Prudentius', *Art Studies*, 7, 1929, 39, no. 4, fig. 60; Wormald, *English Drawings*, 28-9, 35, 55, 66-7, no. 24, pl. 6a; Talbot Rice, *English Art*, 168, 208; Rickert, *Painting in Britain*, 43, 225 n. 74; F. Wormald, *Style and Design*, 32; A. Heimann, 'Three illustrations from the Bury St. Edmunds Psalter and their prototypes', *J.W.C.I.*, XXIX, 1966, 46, 59 n. 102, pls. 8c, 13c; Bishop, *English Caroline*, p. XXII; Dodwell, *Techniques*,

653; J. Beckwith, *Ivory Carvings in Early Medieval England*, 1973, 31, 33, figs. 32, 37; Wormald, *Angleterre*, 248, ills. 249, 250.

52. London, British Library MS Cotton, Vitellius A. XV

Marvels of the East. In Anglo-Saxon
195 × 115–30 mm., ff. 98ᵛ–106ᵛ
Late 10th century

Ill. 185

The treatise, imperfect at the end, contains 29 framed and unframed pictures executed in brown ink and coloured in blue, ochre, shades of brown, and yellow. The drawings, placed within the text-column, represent fabulous people, monsters, animals, plant and architectural motifs with one large composition on two-thirds of a page (f. 101ᵛ) illustrating the accompanying story of the gold-digging ants and the gold-seekers. The pictorial cycle, probably based on an illustrated Latin version of a Greek prototype, does not derive from the original on which another later Anglo-Saxon copy depends (no. 87, Tiberius B. V). Rather rough and incompetent but not without their own fascination, the drawings, in firm outline, are vaguely reminiscent of manuscripts of the Aethelstan period and, in the highly formalized vegetation, resemble the first group of illustrations in the 'Caedmon' Genesis (no. 58).

PROVENANCE: The manuscript, of unknown origin, forms part of a composite volume bound together by Sir Robert Cotton; the margins suffered in the fire of the Cottonian Library of 1731. The treatise is in a portion which contains Beowulf and other Anglo-Saxon poems and which belonged to Laurence Nowell in 1563 (f. 94); it was in Cotton's possession by 1621. Sir Robert Cotton died in 1631. His Library, presented to the nation by his grandson, Sir John Cotton, in 1700, was incorporated in the British Museum in 1753.

LITERATURE: G. C. Druce, 'An account of the *ΜΥΡΜΗΚΟΛΕΩΝ* or Ant-lion', *Antiquaries Journ.*, III, 1923, 356–7, pl. XXXIX; S. Rypins, 'Three Old English prose texts', *E.E.T.S.*, or. ser. 161, 1924, 51–67, 101–7; M. R. James, *Marvels of the East*, Roxburghe Club, 1929, 1–2, monochr. facs. 63–70; R. Wittkower, 'Marvels of the East', *J.W.C.I.*, 1942, 172 nn. 5, 6, 7, 173, pl. 43b; Talbot Rice, *English Art*, 224; P. Hunter-Blair, *An Introduction to Anglo-Saxon England*, 1956, 338–9; Ker, *Catalogue*, p. li, no. 216.

53. Damme, Belgium, Musée van Maerlant

Gospel Lectionary (fragment)
315 × 183 mm.
c. 1000. Canterbury (?)

Ills. 173–175, 176 (Colour)

The fragment consists of two badly mutilated leaves containing Gospel lections (Matthew VIII, 23–8, leaf I recto) and three miniatures illustrating subjects rarely encountered in early medieval painting and without parallel in Anglo-Saxon illumination. The miniature on leaf I verso represents in continuous narrative the Miracle of the Gadarene demoniacs as narrated in Matthew VIII, 28–34; it shows Christ with His disciples confronted in a landscape setting by two men possessed by the devil approaching from the right, a herd of swine rushing into the Lake of Gennezareth in the foreground, and two armed figures, presumably the swineherds, running across the top of the picture towards a walled city in the far left corner. The iconography points to Eastern sources, for although the subject was represented from the Early Christian period onwards, the text illustrated in the West was either that of Mark V, 1–14, or of Luke VIII, 26–34, with only one demoniac shown. Thus though certain Ottonian portrayals (cf. Otto III Gospels, Aachen Cathedral, 983–1002) recall in composition the scene on the Damme leaf, iconographically and stylistically they have little in common. A nearer parallel for the Damme picture is found in Middle Byzantine Gospel Books such as Paris, Bibl. Nat. gr. 74, late 11th century (f. 16), which thus correspond in most of the iconographic elements to the former. But there are also important divergencies of detail between the Damme and the Byzantine representations, for example: the omission of the walled city, the inclusion of the devils and the tombs, etc., in the latter, in which the horizontal strip composition replaces the three-tiered upright format of the Damme illustration. These modifications strongly suggest a development from related models but within a different pictorial tradition. The miniature is enclosed by a rectangular frame containing a continuous pattern of lozenges with star-like leaf motifs between two gold bands.

The picture on leaf II recto which, according to Boutemy, represents the Transfiguration (?) is iconographically unusual for it shows Christ, a book in His hand and rays issuing from His head, seated on a rocky mountain peak between two groups of three Apostles and silhouetted against a great expanse of impressionistic greyish-blue sky. On the analogy of Syriac and Greek Gospels (e.g. Florence, Bibl. Laur. Plut. I, 56, f. 11; Florence, Laur. VI. 23, f. 35, 11th–12th centuries), its subjects might rather be Christ teaching His Apostles. The miniature is surrounded by a frame with patterns of acanthus foliage between oblique and horizontal bands reminiscent of certain Carolingian manuscripts (e.g. Paris, Bibl. Nat., lat. 261, Le Mans Gospels) and recalling initial ornament in Canterbury examples of the late 10th century (cf. no. 22, Bosworth Psalter).

A similarly framed miniature on the verso of leaf II illustrates the episode of the Didrachm (Matthew, XVII, 24–7) on two registers with Christ instructing Peter on the Tribute Money above, a scene shown under a domed canopy on columns (reminiscent of the arched frames in no. 58, the 'Caedmon' Genesis) with the spandrels painted in zigzags to suggest cloudy sky, and below, the same Apostle standing knee deep in water drawing up a fish on his rod. This episode is an extremely rare subject with no known examples in Western manuscript painting. The iconographic sources are again Eastern, for the episode is represented in Syriac and Greek Gospels (e.g. Florence, Laur. Plut. I, 56, f. 9, and Laur. VI. 23, f. 36ᵛ) and the only parallel in the West is provided by an Ottonian ivory plaque, possibly part of an antependium from Magdeburg Cathedral. But here again, though the inspiration must have come ultimately from related Early Christian works, the representation in all these examples of Peter kneeling rather than standing and holding a fish, points to a different recension from that in the Damme fragment.

Thus, from the examination of the three miniatures a strong possibility emerges that, though no suitable example survives, their immediate model may have been a late Carolingian manuscript, a conjecture supported by the figure drawing and by striking stylistic affinities.

The figure drawing, related to Wormald's 'first style', shows certain analogies with no. 35 (Sherborne Pontifical), particularly in the head types with their large bulging eyes, slender shoulders, and gaunt, narrow feet; but the softer, more sensitive outline recalls in its delicacy and freshness the Cambridge Prudentius (no. 48) and other Canterbury manuscripts of c. 1000 (e.g. no. 56, Arenberg Gospels). The source of this style, which in the Damme fragment becomes pre-eminently linear, is to be sought in Carolingian painting, primarily perhaps in manuscripts of the Court School of Charles the Bald (cf. San Paolo Bible), while the lightness and vivacity of the drawing, recalling initial illustrations of the Drogo Sacramentary (Bibl. Nat., lat. 9428), seem to point also to influences from the Metz group of manuscripts. The lively portrayal of the rushing beasts in the Miracle of the Healing should be compared with an illustration for September in no. 62 (Julius A. VI), but the rendering of water, sky, and rocks with illusionist colour effects suggests a Late Antique inspiration with hardly any parallel in early medieval painting. The scrolly plant motifs in delicate brushwork terminating the initial I and appearing in the first picture recall certain Canterbury manuscripts of c. 1000 (e.g. nos. 30. xii, Bibl. Nat., lat. 17814; 56, Arenberg Gospels).

Soft yet varied, the colouring includes pearl grey to pale blue, lilac, clear and dull green, yellow, ochre, and rust brown with some gold in the framework, in the details, and in the main initials of the text. Christ has throughout a white blue-shaded robe under a pale mauve mantle, an orange book, and a gold nimbus outlined in red.

PROVENANCE: The two leaves must have been part of a richly illuminated manuscript of which it is difficult to determine the type. The text page contains Matthew VIII, 23–7 and 28, with the rubrics *In illo tempore* beginning each paragraph. Thus the book may have been a Gospel Lectionary. These readings, however, are not usually consecutive in a Lectionary, where instead of Matthew VIII, 28–34, a version of Mark or Luke is generally used. Moreover, Dr. Alexander has recently observed (1974) that the text page contains the Ammonian sections in the margin unusual in a Lectionary, and that the two leaves are more likely to have belonged to a Gospels marked with the Lections (cf. Bodmin Gospels, B.L. Add. 9381, 9th century). On the evidence of certain stylistic analogies a Canterbury origin for the Damme fragment can be tentatively suggested (cf. Alexander, *English Illuminated Manuscripts*) but there are no indications in the script, which is in the Caroline minuscule of Anglo-Saxon type datable between 975 and 1015, that the manuscript was produced in either of the two Canterbury houses (an opinion kindly communicated by T. A. M. Bishop). The two leaves came to light at the sale of the De Tracy Collection at Ghent where they were acquired by the Musée van Maerlant in 1952.

LITERATURE: A. Boutemy, 'Les feuillets de Damme', *Scriptorium* 20, 1966, 60–5, pls. 7b, 8–10; J. J. G. Alexander, 'Some aesthetic principles in the use of colour in Anglo-Saxon art', *Anglo-Saxon England*, 4, 1975, 150–3, figs. IVd, VIII.

EXHIBITED: Brussels, 1973. *English Illuminated Manuscripts 700–1500*, no. 7.

54. London, British Library, MS Royal 6. B. VIII
Isidore, De fide catholica (ff. 1–26)
290 × 195 mm.
10th to 11th century.
(?) Canterbury, St. Augustine's   *Ill. 164*

The manuscript contains a most remarkable initial S (f. 1ᵛ) heading the prefatory matter to Isidore and composed of two monks' figures shaped into the curves of the letter: the one on the top, carrying a cross-shaft, bends forward making the sign of the cross, while the bottom one leans backwards and, a book in his veiled hand, makes with the other a gesture of allocution. The drawing is an outstanding and early example of an anthropoid initial (cf. nos. 9, Tanner 10; 80, Winchcombe Psalter); it foreshadows developments in the early 12th-century initial style, not least by the dynamic 'Romanesque' countermovement of the two figures and by the humorous irreverent treatment, a trait typical of early 12th-century Canterbury initials and a feature in the Stephen Harding manuscripts from Citeaux. Vigorous and extremely lively, the drawing is in firm, fine outline; and though this outline is less delicate than in certain illustrations in the Prudentius manuscripts, of which it is reminiscent (cf. no. 48, Cambridge Prudentius), there is nevertheless a close stylistic similarity, particularly in the exceedingly tall figures with small profiled heads. The initial I (f. 2ᵛ) in brown outline, Wormald Type II(a), is composed of fine interlace, a large bird head and a dainty, wiry plant scroll of a type closely recalling no. 21 (Trinity Amalarius) from St. Augustine's, as well as other Canterbury manuscripts of the second half of the 10th century; the style of the initial suggests a date for the manuscript not later than *c.* 1000. Other initials are in metallic orange with rubrics inscribed in red.

PROVENANCE: The manuscript (ff. 1–26), bound together with other undecorated texts of the 11th and 12th centuries, is attributable to Canterbury on stylistic evidence of the anthropoid initial as well as the other initial. The volume belonged to John, Lord Lumley (d. 1609), bearing his name (f. 1ᵛ) and being listed in his catalogue of 1611 (f. 69); the bulk of his collection passed into the British Museum with the Royal Library in 1753.

LITERATURE: Warner and Gilson, I, 136–7; Wormald, *Initials*, 125–6, pl. VIId.

55. London, British Library MS Royal 1. E. VI (f. 30ᵛ)
Gospels
470×345 mm.
c. 1000 (?). Canterbury, St. Augustine's   *Ill. 172*

The miniature added on one of the purple pages of a late 8th-century Gospel Book from St. Augustine's, Canterbury, shows the Evangelist Mark (f. 30ᵛ) enthroned frontally in an arched, curtained tabernacle and turning to the right to grasp with both hands a scroll held by the Hand of God above and winding right down to the bottom of the picture. A winged lion with a book is shown in a quatrefoil placed at the top of the frame at the apex of the arch. The miniature is enclosed by a rectangular frame which is partly filled with confined slanting leaf patterns in various colours and decorated with round bosses. Iconographically, the picture is unusual and without close parallel among Evangelist portraits. Seated figures holding long wavy scrolls are not uncommon, however, in Canterbury manuscripts of the early 11th century (cf. no. 67, Eadui Codex, f. 147ᵛ, St. John; also no. 66, Arundel 155, f. 133, where the scroll is lowered by the Hand of God) and are prominent in the somewhat later Bury Psalter (no. 84), while an earlier comparison is provided by no. 44 (Boulogne Gospels, f. 56) from St. Bertin.
The drawing in long, firm, sweeping strokes is extremely vigorous and the monumental, powerful Evangelist figure is a fine example of the dynamic style typical of Canterbury manuscripts from the late 10th century onwards (cf. nos. 56, Arenberg Gospels; 66, Arundel 155; 84, Bury Psalter), culminating in such mid 11th-century examples as no. 100 (Tiberius A. III, f. 117) The miniature is fully painted and the thickly laid colours include yellow, dull apple green, greyish-white, orange, pink, and brown, with the characteristic coloured shadow outline in part of the picture. The face, hands, and feet are in flesh tint with white highlights.

PROVENANCE: The Gospel Book was at St. Augustine's, Canterbury, in the Middle Ages, as shown by

an ownership inscription 'Liber S. Aug. Cant.' and two 13th–14th century press-marks (f. ii). The date of the added miniature is controversial: generally believed to be of the late 10th century (of the 8th by Saunders and Oakeshott), it has been assigned by Homburger (1928) to *c.* 1050; certainly, it has close comparisons in manuscripts from Canterbury of that period. The volume belonged to John, Lord Lumley (f. iᵛ), whose collection was incorporated into the Royal Library after his death in 1609.

LITERATURE: J. G. Westwood, *Paleographia sacra*, 1843–4, 70, pl. 21; *id.*, *Facsimiles*, 41, pl. 15; *Pal. Soc.*, I, pl. VII; British Museum, *Catalogue of Ancient Manuscripts*, 1884, II, 21; James, *Ancient Libraries*, pp. lxv, 516; S. Beissel, *Geschichte der Evangelienbücher*, Freiburg im Breisgau 1906, 131–2; Warner and Gilson, I, 20; Millar, I, no. 8; Saunders, *English Illumination*, 14, pl. 15; O. Homburger, 'Review', *Art Bulletin*, X, 1928, 401; T. D. Kendrick, *Anglo-Saxon Art to A.D. 900*, 1938, 162; Wormald, *Initials*, 112 n. 1; W. Oakeshott, *Classical Inspiration in Medieval Art*, 1959, 39, 61, pl. 53 (A); P. McGurk, 'An Anglo-Saxon Bible Fragment in the British Museum', *J.W.C.I.*, 1962, 21, 33; Rickert, *Painting in Britain*, 19–20, 219 n. 52.

56. New York, Pierpont Morgan Library MS 869
Gospels (Arenberg Gospels)
300×185 mm.
c. 990–1000. Canterbury, Christ Church
Ills. 167–171

The decoration of the Gospels consists of a frontispiece, eight pages of ornamented Canon Tables, and four Evangelist portraits with corresponding texts headed by large initials on facing pages. The prefatory picture (f. 9ᵛ), a monumentally conceived Crucifixion, shows the dead Christ on a mighty cross, His body sagging heavily to the right and the blood from His feet flowing into a chalice below. The Virgin and John, the two witnesses, standing on either side of the cross look up to Him, a blessing Hand of God is shown emerging from a cloud overhead, and two angels with veiled hands hover above the cross bar. Iconographically the miniature is almost identical with the Crucifixion in no. 35 (Sherborne Pontifical) but the scene is dramatized and gives more emphasis to the emotional involvement of the supporting figures. The drawing is executed in coloured outline of red, green, and blue with a pale ochre wash in the cross and a deep purple background. Stylistically, the miniature shows close affinity with manuscripts affected by the Rheims influence, in particular no. 48 (the Cambridge Prudentius), where similar tall, small-headed figures occur.

The Canon Tables (ff. 10–13ᵛ) are placed under plain double or triple arches and decorated with a series of remarkable, figural compositions, which are centred on Christ. He is shown as a child cradled on the arm of the Virgin holding a palm branch (f. 11); surrounded by a circular Glory (f. 11ᵛ) He is placed between the Virgin with the Holy Dove perched on her head on the left, and the Holy Lamb on the right (iconography derived from the Utrecht Psalter illustrations to the *Credo* and the *Gloria in Excelsis*, cf. also no. 77, Cotton, Titus D. XXVII); He is adored by the Apostles Peter and Paul (f. 12), by two saints (f. 12ᵛ), and, finally, accompanied by angels, He is shown (f. 13ᵛ) treading the beasts and transfixing the basilisk with a spear, an iconographic variant inspired by Carolingian sources (cf. Utrecht Psalter, Psalms 64 and 90, ff. 36 and f. 53ᵛ).

The Evangelists are shown seated working in their cells or studies within elaborate architectural surroundings of multi-storeyed buildings with turrets, columns, curtained doorways, and staircases (cf. no. 44, Boulogne Gospels); their symbols with scrolls and books are placed overhead, and verses of Sedulius are inscribed round the top of each rectangular enclosure. Matthew (f. 17ᵛ), pen in hand, opens a book placed on a draped desk on the right. Mark (f. 57ᵛ) is seated in three-quarter view and leans forward writing in a book on a stand on the right. Luke (f. 83ᵛ), pen in hand and head in profile turning to the right, holds a book supported on a draped lectern, while a scroll lowered by his symbol —the ox—from above, touches his nimbus. John (f. 126ᵛ), pen in hand, opens a book laid on a stand on the right and turns to the left looking over his shoulder to the Hand of God emerging from above. The figure drawing in swift, vigorous outline is extremely lively, and the immediacy of the excited gestures, the hunched backs and heads poked forward, the agitated hemlines and flying drapery ends, point to an unmistakable influence of the Utrecht Psalter. The style of the illustrations with their nervous, 'staccato' contours and the characteristic 'accordion' pleats closely resembles the earlier hands of Harley 603 (no. 64). The similarities are much less obvious in the Evangelist portraits executed in animated but firmer outline which gives a sense of solidity and power to the massive figures. The illustrations above the Canon Tables as well as the Evangelist portraits are drawn in coloured outline with partly tinted backgrounds and painted framework and the colour range comprises light green, blue, dull red, and mauve with gold used for haloes, scrolls, books, and crosses.

The beginning of each Gospel is written in lines of capitals in gold and alternating colours which are headed by a large initial in brushwork of excellent quality, embellished with scroll flourishes and reminiscent of no. 22 (Bosworth Psalter). Minor initials throughout the text are in the same style and technique and relate to those in no. 64 (Harley 603).

PROVENANCE: The manuscript can be assigned to Christ Church, Canterbury, on account of the general aspect of its script, an opinion kindly communicated by T. A. M. Bishop who dates it probably

c. 990–1000. This attribution is confirmed by the analogies of the iconography and style with the Utrecht Psalter and its copy Harley 603 (no. 64). The use of the coloured outline technique, occurring in the latter and traceable to the Leofric Missal (no. 17), is also found in no. 48 (Cambridge Prudentius) for which a Canterbury origin has likewise been suggested. The present volume had left England for Cologne by the early 12th century (f. 14), and, as shown by the additions of various dates (forms of oath, 14th to 15th centuries, ff. 1–9, 14, 124–5, etc.), was kept at the church of St. Severin throughout the Middle Ages. In 1802 it came into the possession of the Dukes of Arenberg from whom it was acquired by the Pierpont Morgan Library in 1954.

LITERATURE: S. Beissel, *Geschichte der Evangelienbücher*, Freiburg im Breisgau 1906, 132–3, 349, figs. 35–6; Homburger, 2, 4, 21 n. 3; H. Ehl, *Die Ottonische Kölner Buchmalerei*, Köln 1922, 26, pl. 16; A. Goldschmidt, *Die Elfenbeinskulpturen aus der romanischen Zeit, XI-XII Jahrhundert*, Berlin 1926, IV, fig. 26; O. Homburger, 'Review', *Art Bulletin*, X, 1928, 400; F. Saxl, 'The Ruthwell Cross', *J.W.C.I.*, VI, 1943, 12 n. 6, fig. 14; Wormald, *English Drawings*, 76, 80, no. 59; M. Schapiro, *Illuminated Manuscripts from the Bibliothèque of Their Highnesses the Dukes d'Arenberg* (J. Seligman & Co. Inc., New York 1952), 10, no. 2, pls. 11–13; G. Zarnecki, 'The Winchester Acanthus in Romanesque Sculpture', *Wallraf-Richartz-Jahrbuch*, XVII, 1955, 211–12, pls. 154–5; Bishop, *Notes*, IV, 333; Nordenfalk, *Early Medieval*, 185; id., 'The Apostolic Canon Tables', *Essais en l'honneur de Jean Porcher*, ed. O. Pächt, 24 n. 19, fig. 8; F. Wormald, 'Anglo-Saxon initials in a Paris Boethius manuscript', *ib.*, 64, 69 n. 5; Alexander, *Norman Illumination*, 107 n. 1, 148 n. 3, 171 n. 6; *English Illuminated Manuscripts 700–1500*, Brussels Exhibition Catalogue, 1973, p. 28; C. Nordenfalk, 'The Draped Lectern', *Intuition und Kunstwissenschaft: Festschrift für Hans Swarzenski*, Berlin 1973, 86, 96, figs. 16–17; Wormald, *Angleterre*, 246–8, ill. 244.

EXHIBITED: Düsseldorf 1904, *Kunsthistorische Ausstellung*, 178, no. 522.

57. Oxford, Bodleian Library MS Bodley 577 (S.C. 27645)

Aldhelm, De virginitate

200 × 140 mm.

c. 1000. Canterbury, Christ Church

Ills. 179, 180

The illumination consists of two drawings. The miniature (f. 1), showing a nimbed figure of St. Aldhelm seated at a draped reading-desk, is modelled on an Evangelist portrait and resembles the St. Mark in the York Gospels (no. 61; cf. also no. 73, Pembroke College 301, f. 44ᵛ). The drawing is in brown outline with some patches of colour probably added later. The second drawing (f. 1ᵛ) with St. Aldhelm standing and presenting his book to the nuns of Barking grouped on the right, recalls the same scene in no. 39) Lambeth 200), where, however, the Saint is shown seated.

Both drawings, in hard, wiry outline, with the stiff draperies heavily marked by incised, repetitive nested 'V'-folds, are a late version of Wormald's 'first style' and recall the second hand of no. 49 (Cotton, Cleopatra C. VIII, cf. Wormald, *English Drawings*, 75).

PROVENANCE: The manuscript is listed by T. A. M. Bishop as one of a large group of books produced *c*. 1000 at Christ Church, which include the Canterbury Prudentius, no. 49 (Cleopatra C. VIII). The present volume was owned consecutively by William Ryffe and William Seller (f. 76ᵛ) and by William Brewster of Hereford, 1697 (f. 1), who presented it to the Bodleian Library in 1715.

LITERATURE: Wormald, *English Drawings*, 75, no. 48; Ker, *Catalogue*, no. 314; Bishop, *Notes*, VII, 420, 421 (2); *Anglo-Saxon Illumination*, pl. 11; Pächt and Alexander, no. 33, pl. III.

58. Oxford, Bodleian Library MS Junius 11 (S.C. 5123)

'Caedmon' Genesis, Exodus, etc. In Old English
318 × 195 mm.
c. 1000. Canterbury, Christ Church

Ills. 189–196

This metrical paraphrase of biblical narratives contains the Old English poems of Genesis (pp. 1–142), Exodus (143–74), Daniel (175–212), and Christ and Satan (213–29). The first of these, which is ascribed to Caedmon, and is known as Genesis A, is a close paraphrase in alliterative verse of the biblical text and is datable to *c*. 700. It contains an interpolation from the so-called Genesis B or Later Genesis (pp. 11–40), a mid 9th-century Old Saxon poem on the Fall of the Angels and of Man, transposed into Old English. The date of the translation is controversial but is thought not to be earlier than the late 9th century and the Junius MS is believed to be the first in which this interpolation occurs. The Genesis is the only poem illustrated with an extensive but incomplete series of full- and half-page pictures (pp. 1–88), executed by two artists. This pictorial cycle belongs to a different recension from the one illustrating no. 86, Aelfric's Paraphrase of the Pentateuch and Joshua (British Library MS Cotton, Claudius B. IV); as shown by Henderson (1963), however, both manuscripts preserve part of the iconography of ancient models and in certain original compositions anticipate unusual features in a twelfth-century Genesis cycle at Saint-Savin-sur-Gartempe, suggesting that sources of the latter may have been English manuscripts of the Caedmon–Aelfric type. According to Gollancz, the present manuscript was probably copied from an unillustrated exemplar; thus it can be assumed that the two Anglo-Saxon artists were responsible for the composition of the pictorial cycle. The miniatures include vast monumental representations, often in strip narrative of Late Antique inspiration; some reflect the tradition of the fifth-century Cotton Genesis (cf. Henderson, 1962) or adapt Early Christian iconographic themes to the expanded text of the poem (cf. Ohlgren, *Mediaevalia*); others suggest acquaintance with apocryphal or Anglo-Saxon literature (cf. Gollancz, p. xxxiv) while a few, which closely follow the Old English Genesis text, are entirely the invention of the two English illuminators.

The thirty-eight drawings by the first hand (pp. 1–62) are in brown and red inks with occasional light red, ochre, or brown washes and include one figure (representing the Almighty, p. 11) fully painted in shades of olive green and mauvy brown, a colour scheme recalling early tenth-century manuscripts (cf. nos. 5, Rawl. 484; 7, Junius Psalter, etc.; cf. also nos. 23, Benedictional of St. Ethelwold, f. 118ᵛ; 66, Arundel 155, f. 133; 84, Bury Psalter, f. 35, for examples in outline drawing where the main figures are emphasized by colour). The illustrations represent: 1 (p. 1)—The Lord enthroned above chaos; 2 (p. 2)—The Lord addressing a haloed angel (Lucifer ?); 3 (p. 3)—Fall of the rebel angels; 4 (p. 6)—The Spirit of God on the surface of the deep; 5 (p. 7)—Creation of the world (3rd–6th days in an incorrect sequence, cf. Gollancz, p. xl); 6 (p. 9)—Creation of Eve; 7 (p. 10)—God blessing Adam and Eve; 8 (p. 11)—Adam and Eve adoring Him; 9 (p. 13)—Adam and Eve in the Garden of Eden; 10 (p. 16)—God hurling the rebellious angels into the open jaws of Hades; 11 (p. 17)—God in Majesty; below, Satan and his angels; 12 to 18 (pp. 20–39)—Temptation and fall of Adam and Eve, their shame and repentance; (note the tempter in the guise of an angel); 19 (p. 41)—God, above, condemning the serpent, below, addressing Adam and Eve; 20 (p. 44)—God pronouncing separate sentences on them; 21 (p. 45)—Expulsion from Paradise; 22 (p. 46)—An angel locking the door of Paradise; 23 (p. 47)—Birth of Abel; 24 (p. 49)—The Cain and Abel episode showing Abel slain with a club, and, below, his blood crying to the Lord; 25 (p. 51)—Above, Cain sentenced by God; below, Enoch in his city; 26 (p. 53)—Birth of Irad's son and Lameh with his two wives; 27 (p. 54)—Tubal Cain depicted as a smith and forger, and, below, Adam and Eve with the infant Seth; 28 (p. 56)—Seth in his palace; 29 (p. 57)—Cainan enthroned; 30 (p. 58)—Malalehel in front of an altar; 31 (p. 59)—His burial; 32 (p. 60)—Enoch, holding a book, is addressed by an angel; 33 (p. 61)—Enoch's translation; 34 (p. 62)—Matusaleh with his kinsmen and birth of Lameh; 35 (p. 63)—Birth of Noah, Noah with his kinsfolk, and on the left with his three sons; 36 (p. 65)—Noah, warned by God of the flood, beginning to build the Ark; 37 (p. 66)—God closing the door of the Ark, a three-tiered, dragon-headed vessel (the shape of its prow had perhaps been suggested by the Viking ship presented to King Aethelstan (925–39) by Harold 'Fairhair' King of Norway); 38 (p. 68)—above, the Ark floating; below, God about to open its door.

The drawings in this group, in firm outline, are in

Wormald's 'first style' and copy earlier, probably English models; but the large-headed, somewhat wooden figures with awkward gestures are invigorated by the richly varied patterns of the garments flaring out stiffly at the bottom in wildly agitated but strangely frozen and formalized hemlines, the latter a rougher version of the same feature in no. 49 (Cleopatra C. VIII), a manuscript from Christ Church, Canterbury. The pictures are often shown under elaborate, canopied frames on columns characteristic of this artist (a similar frame occurs also in no. 53, Damme fragment). The translation of Enoch (p. 61), which represents him standing on the ground between two angels and, above, vanishing into heaven, may have inspired the Anglo-Saxon iconography of the Ascension with 'the disappearing Christ' whose legs alone are shown (for a different opinion cf. Schapiro, 1943). The episode of Enoch is an unusual subject and its presence in the Saint-Savin Genesis cycle points to English influences in the latter (cf. Henderson, 1963).

The first artist is also responsible for a bust figure in a roundel (p. 2) labelled 'Aelwine' (a fact which gave rise to suggestions that the manuscript originated in Winchester), and for twenty-two ornamental initials marking the sections of the poem (pp. 2–73, 79, 143; the last one on p. 236 is not by him). Drawn apparently before the text, they are rather retrospective in style and, composed of full-bodied dragons, interlace, beasts' and mask heads, they recall no. 7 (Junius Psalter). An unfinished design for a repeating pattern (p. 225) and two sketches, possibly models for bracelets (p. 230), are probably by the same illuminator.

The ten drawings of the second group (pp. 73–88), in red, blue, and green inks, are by the artist of the Cambridge Prudentius (no. 48, C.C.C. 23) and show all the lightness and the spontaneity of his sketchy, impressionistic style, in which the influence from Rheims, perhaps of the Utrecht Psalter, is strongly felt. The drawings represent: 39 (p. 73)—Disembarkation of Noah; 40 (p. 74)—Noah offering sacrifice; 41 (p. 76)—God's covenant with Noah; 42 (p. 77)—Noah ploughing; 43 (p. 78)—Noah's drunkenness; 44 (p. 81)—Nimrod sending out his princes from Babylon, and, below, speaking to the Lord; 45 (p. 82)—Building of the tower of Babel, and dispersal; 46 (p. 84)—Call of Abraham and his departure to Canaan; 47 (p. 87)—Abraham between two buildings, and, below, offering incense, then speaking to the Lord; 48 (p. 88)—Abraham and his household approaching Egypt.

A sketch of a lion (p. 31) and an unfinished drawing (p. 96) are additions of the later twelfth century. Hard point sketches, recently discovered under ultra-violet light (pp. 12, 55, 70, 99), are of various and uncertain dates (cf. Ohlgren, *Speculum*). The decoration is incomplete and a number of leaves now lost (six out of eight in the 2nd quire, two between pages 22 and 23, etc.) may have contained miniatures; there are also blank picture-spaces in the later part of the manuscript (cf. Henderson, 1962, p. 191). Large plain capital letters replace ornamental initials after p. 73, with some spaces for initials unfilled after p. 144. The manuscript is written in the main part (pp. 1–212) in one hand assigned by Ker to *c.* 10th to 11th centuries (cf. also Gollancz).

PROVENANCE: Once believed to be from Winchester (cf. Herbert; Gollancz) on account of the portrait of Aelfwine (p. 2), confused with the New Minster abbot (1035–57), the manuscript is probably identical with the one described 'genesis anglice depicta' in Prior Eastry's catalogue of Christ Church, Canterbury, early 14th century (James, *Ancient Libraries*, no. 304), where it was most likely produced, an attribution supported by stylistic evidence. Inscribed 'genesis in anglice' (p. ii), 14th century; 'genesis in lingua saxania' (p. i), 16th century, it was variously dated between *c.* 1000 and 1035, while Wormald assigned it to the second quarter of the 11th century on account of 'Scandinavianisms' in its decoration. It is likely, however, to be of the earlier period since these Scandinavian ornamental features derive from England rather than vice versa (cf. Holmquist) and are typical of Anglo-Saxon initial decoration, particularly in Canterbury manuscripts, from the mid 10th century onwards (cf. nos. 22, Bosworth Psalter; 37, Auct. F. 1. 15; etc.). The volume, in medieval binding of white skins over boards, was probably in the library of Sir Symonds D'Ewes, *c.* 1637(?). It belonged to Archbishop Usher, who gave it to Francis Junius in 1651 and it has borne Caedmon's name since its first publication by Junius in 1655 under the title: *Caedmonis Monachi Paraphrasis . . .* Entered the Bodleian Library with Junius's collection in 1678.

LITERATURE: H. Ellis, 'Account of Caedmon's Metrical Paraphrase of Scripture History', *Archaeologia*, XXIV, 1832, 329–40, pls. 52–104; Westwood, *Facsimiles*, 111; W. W. Skeat, *Twelve Facsimiles*, 1892, 16, pl. 11; *Pal. Soc.*, II, pls. 14–15; James, *Ancient Libraries*, pp. XXV, 51, 509, no. 304; J. A. Herbert, *Illuminated Manuscripts*, 1911, 118–19; Homburger, 5, 21 n. 1; C. R. Morey, 'The illustrations of Genesis', in W. C. Kennedy, *The Caedmon Poems*, 1916, 175–95, frontispiece, pls. 197–245; H. P. Mitchell, 'Flotsam of Later Saxon Art', *Burlington Magazine*, XLII, 1923, 152, 167 n. 1, pl. III(B); J. Brønsted, *Early English Ornament*, 1924, 247, 249 n. 1, 250, 280; R. Priebsch, *The Heliand MS.*, 1924, 31–2, pls. IV, V; I. Gollancz, *The Caedmon Manuscript*, 1927 (complete facsimile); M. R. James, 'Illustrations of the Old Testament', in *A Book of Old Testament Illustrations*, Roxburghe Club, 1927, 21–2; Millar, I, 18–19, no. 41, pl. 23; M. Schapiro, 'The image of the disappearing Christ', *Gazette des Beaux Arts*, 6e ser. XXIII, 1943, 145 n. 39, 152; Wormald, *Initials*, 120 n. 1, 134, pl. Vc; F. Saxl and R. Wittkower, *British Art and the Mediterranean*, 1948, pl. 21c; Kendrick, Late Saxon, 33, 104, 131, fig. 3, pls. LXXII, LXXIII, 2; Holmquist, '*Viking Art*, 3 ff., 14 ff., 47–8, figs. 2, 6, 7; Wormald, *English Drawings*, 39–41, 76, no. 50, pl. 18; Talbot Rice, *English Art*, 129, 191, 201, 203–5, pls. 68, 69 a, b; B. Raw, 'The drawing of an angel in *MS. 28*, St. John's College, Oxford', *J.W.C.I.*, XVIII, 1955, 318; P. Hunter-Blair, *An Introduction to Anglo-Saxon England*, 1956, 337–8; Dodwell, *Canterbury School*, 9, 11, 37, pls. 5f, 9a; Nordenfalk, *Early Medieval*, 186–7, pl. 176; Ker, *Catalogue*, no. 334; Rickert, *Miniatura*, 15, 22, pl. 21; *St. Albans Psalter*, 56 n. 4, 57, 80 n. 1, 81, 122, pl. 108 b, c; O. Pächt, *The Rise of Pictorial Narrative in twelfth-century England*, 1962, 5, 8, pl. I (1); G. Henderson, 'Late-antique influences in some English mediaeval illustrations of Genesis', *J.W.C.I.*, XXV, 1962, 172–98, pls. 34c, 36a; *id.*, 'The sources of the Genesis cycle at Saint-Savin-sur-Gartempe', *Journal of the British Archaeological Association*, XXVI, 1963, 11–26, pls. VII (3), VIII (2), X (2), XI (4), XII (2), (5); W. Mersmann, 'Das Elfenbeinkreuz der Sammlung Topic-Mimara', *Wallraf-Richartz-Jahrbuch*, XXV, 1963, 40, 102, fig. 30; Rickert, *Painting in Britain*, 45, 75, 225 nn. 79–80, 226 n. 82, pl. 44; Wormald, *Style and Design*, 31, fig. 8; Swarzenski, *Monuments*, pl. 47, fig. 105; *English rural life in the Middle Ages* (Bodleian Library Picture Book no. 14), 1965, pl. II; M. C. Morell, *A manual of Old English biblical materials*, 1965, 18–31; M. W. Evans, *Medieval Drawings*, 1969, 24, pl. 25; *Anglo-Saxon Illumination*, pls. 15–20; Alexander, *Norman Illumination*, 57, 62 n. 2; T. H. Ohlgren, 'Five new drawings in the MS. Junius 11: their iconography and thematic significance', *Speculum*, 47, 1972, 227–45, figs. 1–6; *id.*, 'The illustrations of the Caedmonian Genesis', *Mediaevalia et Humanistica*, n. ser. 3, 1972, 199–212, figs. 1–2; Pächt and Alexander, no. 34, pl. IV; Wormald, *Angleterre*, 248, fig. 248; *English Illuminated Manuscripts*, Brussels Exhibition Catalogue, 1973, p. 28; R. Deshman, 'Anglo-Saxon Art After Alfred', *Art Bulletin*, LVI, 1974, 181 n. 24; H. Holländer, *Early Medieval Art*, 1974, 186.

59. Oxford, Bodleian Library MS Bodley 155 (S.C. 1974)
Gospels
260×198 mm.
Early 11th century

Ills. 177, 178

This copy of the four Gospels, partly mutilated, contains two full-page drawings of seraphim replacing the usual Evangelist portraits before the texts of St. Luke and St. John. The first angel (f. 93v), a calm, statuesque figure, firmly poised on the edge of the frame, bears a scroll inscribed 'Fuit in diebus herodis regis Judaeae sacerdos' (Luke, I, 5). The angel introducing St. John (f. 146v) supports a similar scroll with an inscription added in the 16th century (possibly by the antiquary Stephen Batman to whom the manuscript belonged); shown in light contraposto and surrounded by wind-puffed drapery ends, he turns slightly to the right looking up at the Hand of God above, and appears to be less static than the first figure. The two representations, deriving from a figure type of the Early Christian period with many descendants in Anglo-Saxon

painting (cf. Saxl and Wittkower), closely recall the Three Persons of the Trinity in the Sherborne Pontifical (no. 35), but show modifications of the original type, especially in the second angel (f. 146v); executed in black and brown inks in firm outline, the two figures are latish examples of Wormald's 'first style' with the drawing hardened and, particularly in St. John's angel, becoming heavy and schematic. The manuscript is defective: the beginning of St. Matthew's Gospel was supplied in the 16th century by Stephen Batman (d. 1584), who also sketched a figure of an angel (f. iii), possibly copying the lost original; the leaves with the end of St. Mark's preface which are missing may have contained the fourth representation.

PROVENANCE: A list of liturgical gospels throughout the year (f. 182v) may have been copied from a 10th-century Breton Gospel Book, Bodleian Library MS Auct. D. 2. 16, given to Exeter by Bishop Leofric (1046–72). The manuscript was at Barking Abbey as shown by a charter of Abbess Aelfgiva copied in the 12th century (f. 196v). Owned by the antiquary Stephen Batman in the 16th century, it passed into the Bodleian Library not later than 1602.

LITERATURE: Westwood, *Facsimiles*, 123; Millar, I, no. 45, pl. 24d; O. Homburger, 'Review', *Art Bulletin*, X, 1928, 400, fig. p. 402; F. Saxl and R. Wittkower, *British Art and the Mediterranean*, pl. 21b; Wormald, *English Drawings*, 37, 75, no. 47, pls. 5b, 7; Talbot Rice, *English Art*, 218, pl. 70b; Ker, *Catalogue*, no. 303; *Anglo-Saxon Illumination*, pls. 21, 22; Pächt and Alexander, no. 41, pl. IV.

EXHIBITED: Bodleian Library 1952, *Latin Liturgical Manuscripts and Printed Books*, no. 6

60. London, British Library MS Royal 6. A. VII
Life of St. Gregory
280×193 mm.
Early 11th century. (?) Worcester   *Ill. 257*

The manuscript contains one splendid initial B (f. 2), Wormald Type I, with a large mask head midway up the shaft. The initial derives structurally from the great B of Harley 2904 (no. 41) in having a panelled shaft with bird-headed interlace terminals and another mask head clasping the bows; the latter, however, are made up of spirited scrolling dragons instead of plant scrolls and recall a B (p. 246v) in C.C.C. 41 (no. 81) as well as certain initials in the Salisbury Psalter (no. 18) where a similar small leaf protrudes from some of the dragons' bellies. The initial, in brown outline with touches or red, accompanies a title in metallic red. Minor initials are in silver or red.

PROVENANCE: The manuscript written, according to T. A. M. Bishop, by a Worcester hand was probably produced at Worcester. It belonged to J. Theyer (d. 1673) whose books were commonly from the West of England; it was acquired in 1678 for the Royal collection, no. 77 in Theyer's sale.

LITERATURE: Warner and Gilson, I, 125–6; Wormald, *Initials*, 134; Bishop, *English Caroline*, p. XX, no. 22.

61. York Minster, Chapter Library, MS Add. 1
Gospels (York Gospels)
265 × 210 mm.
Late 10th to early 11th century. Canterbury,
Christ Church

Ills. 181–184

The Gospels are preceded by general prefaces with a title-page in alternating lines of coloured capitals (f. 10) and by eight pages of Eusebian Canons (ff. 15ᵛ–19). These are shown under arches in unusual and diverse combinations and supported on columns with geometrical patterns, often with spiral bands around them; the whole is painted in mauve, leaf green, brown, some blue, and touches of gold.

The three Evangelist portraits (St. John's is missing), shown in rectangular enclosures, face unframed pages with the opening lines of the texts headed by ornamental initials. Matthew (f. 22ᵛ), Mark (f. 60ᵛ), and Luke (f. 85ᵛ) are without their symbols but identifiable by inscriptions and are shown blessed by the Hand of God emerging from the clouds in the upper right corner. Matthew and Mark sit frontally, Luke in profile, on massive draped thrones, pen in hand, writing in open books supported on draped stands on the right. The airy backgrounds are in washes of different shades suggesting atmospheric depth (ff. 22ᵛ, 60ᵛ), and each portrait is surrounded by an austerely functional frame; two are panelled in olive green and mauve (ff. 22ᵛ, 60ᵛ), and one has a wavy line pattern (f. 85ᵛ). Soft and harmonius, the colouring includes shades of grey to blue, pale purple, mauve, olive green, and brown to orange, with touches of gold in details.

A splendid gold initial L (f. 23), introducing St. Matthew's Gospel, is topped by an interlace knotwork terminating in the heads of a lion and an eagle (the symbols of Mark and John), and below it a roundel containing the angel of Matthew holding a scroll, closely reminiscent of the one in the Arenberg Gospels (no. 56, f. 14ᵛ). A heavy 'elbowed' interlace joins the vertical to the horizontal shaft of the letter, the horizontal being adorned with a blue bull's head (the symbol of Luke) at its extremity, resembling the decoration of the Canon Tables in no. 67 (Eadui Codex). The elaborate lay-out of this page differs from the other three initial pages in the volume, and the inclusion of all four Evangelist symbols has no parallel in Anglo-Saxon illumination. A gold-panelled initial I (f. 61) has animal-headed interlace knotwork at the top, an acanthus rosette on the shaft, and a foliated base with leafwork recalling Canterbury initials of c. 1000 (cf. no. 30. xv, Boulogne 189). An initial Q (f. 86) is panelled in gold and mauve and the letter-tail is formed by a dragon biting its foot (cf. no. 79, Douce 296) with the characteristic small leaf protruding from under its belly. Initial I (f. 127) is made up of heavy gold

panels outlined in black and filled with green and brown. Initials to paragraphs are in green, mauve, and red.

The Evangelists, shown without symbols but with their names inscribed in the background (cf. no. 91, St. Margaret's Gospels), suggest ultimate Greek models perhaps transmitted through Carolingian painting (cf. Bibl. Nat., lat. 265, Boinet, pl. LXXII); the motif of the Hand of God, however, is unusual in this context for, though rare in Greek manuscripts, it does occur occasionally in the portraits of John (cf. no. 56, Arenberg Gospels). The figures, serenely majestic and composed, are strikingly independent of Rheims and Winchester influences, being clothed in draperies with restrained hemlines and patterns of softly moulded, rippling, linear folds, which suggest the human forms beneath. Like no. 68 (Grimbald Gospels) in their youthful filleted heads, their pose, and their gestures (cf. Oakeshott, 1950, pls. 16 and 17) they perhaps depend on related models, but they are less formalized, less mannered.

PROVENANCE: This manuscript, of uncertain origin, was written by several scribes in English Caroline minuscule with an addition (ff. 10–14), after completion, in Anglo-Saxon minuscule. Wormald (1944) has assigned the main hand (ff. 24–156) to the late 10th century, while T. A. M. Bishop has identified the scribe of the first leaf of Matthew's text (f. 23ᵛ) with Eadvius Basan, a monk of Christ Church, Canterbury, active c. 1010–30. Prof. Ker (*Catalogue*) has suggested that this page (the leaf being conjugate with f. 30 inscribed in the main hand) was possibly left blank 'until the scale of the decoration and of the writing in majuscules which fill the recto had been decided upon'. The participation of Eadui as well as certain stylistic and iconographic considerations indicate that the manuscript may have been produced at Christ Church, Canterbury before 1020, since, as shown by the additions in Old English (ff. 156ᵛ–161ᵛ), it was at York c. 1020–30. The additions contain a copy of King Cnut's writ of 1020–1 in a hand nearly contemporary with its promulgation (ff. 160, 160ᵛ), together with surveys of Yorkshire lands, sermons, etc. (first half, 11th century), and other items (second half, 11th century). The volume served as an oath-book for the Chapter in the 13th to 15th centuries.

LITERATURE: J. Raine, 'Fabric Rolls of York Minster', *S.S.*, 35, 1858, 142; F. Lieberman, *Die Gesetze der Angelsachsen*, Berlin 1903, III, 186; Homburger, 56 n. 1; W. H. Stevenson, 'Yorkshire Surveys and Other Eleventh-century Documents in the York Gospels', *English Historical Review*, XXVIII, 1912, 1; J. P. Gilson, *Description of the Saxon Manuscript of the Four Gospels in the Library of York Minster*, York 1925; *New Pal. Soc.*, II, pls. 163–5; Millar, I, no. 30; F. Wormald, 'The Survival of Anglo-Saxon Illumination after the Norman Conquest', *Proceedings of the British Academy*, XXX, 1944, 129–30, pl. 1a; Kendrick, *Late Saxon*, 10; W. Oakeshott, *The Sequence of English Medieval Art*, 1950, 44, pl. 16; Wormald, *English Drawings*,

41, 75; Talbot Rice, *English Art*, 207, 210 f., pl. 76a; Bishop, *Notes*, II, 186; Ker, *Catalogue*, no. 402; Rickert, *Painting in Britain*, 225 n. 66; T. A. M. Bishop, 'The Copenhagen Gospel Book', *Nordisk Tidskrift för Bok- och Biblioteksväsen*, 1967, 31 n. 1; Swarzenski, *Monuments*, 24, fig. 5; Alexander, *Norman Illumination*, 61, 69, 110–11, pls. 16d, 27e; Bishop, *English Caroline*, p. XV, no. 24; Wormald, *Winchester School*, 310; C. Nordenfalk, 'The Draped Lectern', *Intuition und Kunstwissenschaft: Festschrift für Hans Swarzenski*, Berlin 1973, 86; fig. 4; Wormald, *Angleterre*, 240, ill. 234.

EXHIBITED: Brussels 1973, *English Illuminated Manuscripts 700–1500*, no. 8.

62. London, British Library MS Cotton, Julius A. VI

Calendar (ff. 2–17ᵛ); Hymnal with Old English gloss (ff. 18–90)
196 × 126 mm.
Calendar early 11th century; Hymnal mid 11th century
(?) Canterbury, Christ Church

Ills. 197–199

The Calendar in metrical verse (ff. 3–8ᵛ), accompanied by computistical matter (ff. 2, 9–17ᵛ), is the earliest known English 'occupational' calendar; it is illustrated with drawings of the labours of the months set across the bottom of each page and with signs of the Zodiac in roundels placed above gold KL monograms. The drawings represent: January—Ploughing (f. 3); February—Pruning vines (f. 3ᵛ); March—Digging and sowing (f. 4); April—Feasting (f. 4ᵛ); May—Tending sheep (f. 5); June—Cutting wood (f. 5ᵛ); July—Mowing (f. 6); August—Reaping (f. 6ᵛ); September—Feeding hogs (f. 7); October—Hunting with falcon (f. 7ᵛ); November—Stacking firewood (f. 8); December—Threshing (f. 8ᵛ). Charming and vivacious, the drawings are in delicate brown outline with occasional red or green tinting; they show a blend of the 'first' and the Utrecht styles, with the sketchiness and exuberance of the latter somewhat calmed down by firmer and more clean-cut contours, and by a marked degree of ornamental patterning in certain details (noteworthy is the tree motif transformed into a highly formalized decorative feature). Nevertheless, the pictures retain the atmospheric quality and informality of the agricultural scenes in the Utrecht Psalter with iconographic analogies which, without indicating direct dependence, suggest an inspiration from closely related models, in turn indebted to late antique prototypes (note the type of couch in the scene for April, the genre fragment of the gossiping shepherds in May, etc.). These models may have also served a later 'occupational' calendar (no. 87, Cotton, Tiberius B. V) whose painted illustrations are almost duplicates of those in Julius. The miniatures of the present manuscript are surrounded on three sides by double lines and the verticals of the frames often terminate in large bunched acanthus leaves reminiscent of those in no. 58 ('Caedmon' Genesis, pl. 78). Details of the calendar are in blue, red, and silver. The Easter Tables contain cycles for 969–87, 988–1006, and 1007–14 (ff. 13ᵛ, 14, 16ᵛ).

The Hymnal (ff. 18–90), a basic collection of 95 hymns used in the English Church in the 11th century, contains one ornamental initial O (f. 72ᵛ) introducing the canticles which is embellished with straggly acanthus foliage and a dragon appended across the top, the whole being painted in green and ochre. Other initials are plain red or green capital letters.

PROVENANCE: The Calendar is attributable to Christ Church, Canterbury, on stylistic evidence, an attribution referred to by T. A. M. Bishop (*Notes*, II). The Hymnal, written in a different and somewhat later hand, with interlinear Old English glosses probably by the scribe of the text, contains late 11th-century additions (ff. 18, 19, 90), accompanied by musical notations. The volume, at Durham in the Middle Ages and identified in the catalogue of the Priory of 1391, contains a title in the hand of a Durham librarian, late 15th century (f. 2), preceded by a letter-mark 'a', and another title (f. 20). It belonged to Henry Savile of Banke (1568–1617) and was entered as no. 111 in his catalogue where the Hymnal precedes the Calendar, a sequence perhaps later upset by Cotton (1621), who was in the habit of re-arranging his manuscripts. The library of Sir Robert Cotton was presented to the nation by his grandson, Sir John Cotton, in 1700 and incorporated in the British Museum in 1753.

LITERATURE: R. T. Hampson, *Medii Aevi Kalendarium*, 1841, I, 394–420; J. Stevenson, 'Latin Hymns of the Anglo-Saxon Church', *S.S.*, 23, 1858, p. IX; Westwood, *Facsimiles*, 113; H. D. Traill and J. S. Mann, *Building of Britain*, 1901, II, ills. 177, 179, 181; J. R. Green, *Short History of the English People*, 1901, I, ills. 155, 157, 159; J. A. Herbert, *Illuminated Manuscripts*, 1911, 113; Homburger, 68 n. 2; J. Mearns, *Early Latin Hymns*, p. XI; Millar, I, 20, no. 47, pl. 24c; O. Homburger, 'Review', *Art Bulletin*, X, 1928, 400; J. C. Webster, *The Labours of the Months*, Evanston and Chicago 1938, 53 ff., 99, 134–5, no. 33, pls. XVII, XVIII; R. A. B. Mynors, *Durham Cathedral Manuscripts*, 1939, 28, no. 21; Kendrick, *Late Saxon*, 24, pl. XXIV, 1; Wormald, *English Drawings*, 36, 39, 68, no. 30, pl. 17b; Talbot Rice, *English Art*, 218, 225, pl. 85a; Bishop, *Notes*, II, 187; T. S. R. Boase, *English Art 1100–1216*, 1953, 87; Ker, *Catalogue*, no. 160; Nordenfalk, *Early Medieval*, 191; Rickert, *Painting in Britain*, 40–1, 59, 224 n. 58, pl. 34a; Gneuss, 8 n. 12, 55, 91–7, 122, 197–8 and *passim*; A. G. Watson, *The Manuscripts of Henry Savile of Banke*, 1969, no. 111; M. W. Evans, *Medieval Drawings*, 1969, 24, pl. 22; P. M. Korhammer, 'The origin of the Bosworth Psalter', *Anglo-Saxon England*, 2, 1973, 181; Wormald, *Angleterre*, 242.

63. London, British Library MS Cotton, Vitellius C. III

Herbarium Apulei, Dioscorides (ff. 11–74ᵛ)
Medicina de quadrupedibus (ff. 75–82ᵛ)
290 × 190 mm.
Early 11th century. Canterbury, Christ Church

Ills. 186–188

This Anglo-Saxon translation of the enlarged *Herbarium*, a treatise associated with the name of Apuleius (in fact a Latin compilation perhaps of the 5th century), and of *Medicina de quadrupedibus* by Sextus Placitus (an author of whom nothing is known) is extensively illustrated with hundreds of coloured drawings of plants and creatures added after the text was written. The manuscript also contains two full-page miniatures (ff. 11ᵛ, 19), damaged, like most of the other illustrations, in the fire of the Cottonian Library in 1731.

The first picture (f. 11ᵛ), prefacing the table of contents of the Herbal (ff. 12–18ᵛ), is in soft blue, brown, and green outline and partly painted in the same colours; it represents in the centre a lofty and amply-draped figure of an ecclesiastic treading upon a lion whom he transfixes with a spear (a crozier?) and modelled on a portrayal of Christ triumphant; he is flanked by two smaller figures, a soldier with a round shield on the left, and a monk on the right, presenting him with a book and awkwardly poised on a scroll ornament in delicate brushwork (of a type associated with Christ Church manuscripts); there are two curtains drawn aside in the background and the whole is surrounded by a 'Winchester' frame with four corner rosettes and patterns of attenuated acanthus leaves reminiscent of no. 17 (Leofric Missal); veined in red they are contained within green and orange bands.

A full-page frontispiece to the Herbal (f. 19), with a caption beneath it 'Escolapius, Plato, Centaurus', shows in the centre a majestic figure of Apuleius Platonicus (here called Plato) draped in blue over green over brown and holding a large open book supported on either side by Escolapius, the god of medicine, and Chiron, a centaur skilled in drugs, both isolated within yellow panels. The green background of the picture is crowded in the top part with animal species and filled with reptiles in the forefront, and the miniature is enclosed by an acanthus border similar to that described above. The title to the Herbal (*Herbarium Apulei Platonici quod accepit ab Escolapio et a Chirone Centauro magizro Achillis*) inscribed overleaf (f. 19ᵛ) in green, blue, and red capitals within a wreath-like blue fillet, explains the meaning of the frontispiece.

The illustrations are in fine, delicate outline; the agitated drapery ends and the garments richly patterned with fluttering edges of the folds, particularly prominent in the first picture, are so close stylistically to a Prudentius from Christ Church, Canterbury (Cotton, Cleopatra C. VIII, no. 49) as to suggest not only the same workshop but possibly the same artist (cf. also the profiled head of the monk in Vitellius, f. 11ᵛ, with the heads in the Prudentius manuscript).

The drawings of herbs, snakes, and winged creatures accompanying the 185 descriptive chapters of the Herbal (ff. 20–74ᵛ), and those illustrating the text of Sextus Placitus (ff. 75–82ᵛ), are heavily painted in deep blue, green, ochre, and magenta brown. The pictures, in spite of their free drawing, are not portrayals of actual living models and reveal the Mediterranean parentage of their distant prototypes in that they include representations of Southern instead of English species. Initials to chapters are in red, green, and blue.

PROVENANCE: The manuscript was identified with the 'Herbarius anglice depictus' (Wanley, 1705), no. 308 in Prior Eastry's Christ Church, Canterbury, catalogue of the 14th century (James, *Ancient Libraries*), an attribution supported by stylistic evidence. The script of the 12th-century additions (ff. 82ᵛ–85), however, is not, according to Ker, of the Canterbury type, which may mean perhaps that the manuscript was on loan to another house at that time. It belonged to Richard Hollond (f. 76) in the 16th century; then to 'elysabeth colmore' (f. 11); and subsequently to Sir Robert Cotton (d. 1631) whose library, presented to the nation by his grandson Sir John Cotton in 1700, was incorporated in the British Museum in 1753.

LITERATURE: T. O. Cockayne, *Leechdoms, Wortcunning and Starcraft of Early England* (Rolls Series, XXXV, 1864–6), I, pp. LXXV–LXXXI, frontispiece; James, *Ancient Libraries*, pp. XXVI, 509, no. 308; C. Singer, 'Early English magic and medicine', *Proceedings of the British Academy*, IX, 1919–20, 365 fig. 8; id., ed., *Studies in the History and Method of Science*, II, 1921, pls. IV, XVI, XXV(b); E. S. Rohde, *Old English Herbals*, 1922, 9–11; R. T. Gunther, *The Herbal of Apuleius Barbarus*, Roxburghe Club, 1925, pp. XVII, XXVI, XXXIII–XXXIV, 130, pl. 7; Millar, I, no. 50; C. Singer, 'The Herbal in Antiquity and its Transmission to Later Ages', *Journal of Hellenistic Studies*, XLVII, 1927, 35–9, fig. 37, pls. III, IV; G. T. Flom, 'Old English Herbal of Apuleius, Vitellius C. III', *Journal of English and German Philology*, XL, 1941, 29–37; F. Saxl and R. Wittkower, *British Art and the Mediterranean*, 1948, pl. 31 (1–3); Kendrick, *Late Saxon*, 28, pl. XXV; O. Pächt, 'Early Italian nature studies and the early calendar landscape', *J.W.C.I.*, 1950, 37 n. 3; Talbot Rice, *English Art*, 225, pl. 88; T. S. R. Boase, *English Art 1100–1216*, 1953, 85; Ker, *Catalogue*, 219.

64. London, British Library MS Harley 603

Psalter (Roman version except Psalms 100–105 v. 25 which are Gallican)
380 × 309 mm.
Early 11th century with later additions. Canterbury, Christ Church

Ills. 200–207, 210, fig. 1

This highly important manuscript is the earliest of the three surviving English copies of the Utrecht

Psalter, the Gallican Psalter from Rheims, c. 820, known to have been in England by the end of the 10th century. The Harley copy is written by three scribes: the first (ff. 2–27ᵛ and 54–73ᵛ); the second (ff. 28–49ᵛ); the third (ff. 50–54 line 20). The second of these is Eadvius Basan, a monk of Christ Church, Canterbury, active between 1010 and 1030. Inscribed in three columns, the Psalter ends incomplete at Psalm 143 with a number of spaces for miniatures left blank.

The illumination consists of large and spacious compositions, each with several scenes in literal illustration of the text and set across the written space before each psalm as in the Rheims manuscript. Unlike the monochrome illustrations of the latter, the Harley miniatures are in green, blue, pale sepia, and red inks (cf. nos. 17, Leofric Missal; 48, Cambridge Prudentius; etc.); they are also less illusionistic and more decorative in effect, not only by virtue of their coloured outline and a firmer, less impressionistic drawing, but because of their tendency towards an ornamental treatment of details and an emphasis on an overall pattern, a tendency inherent in Anglo-Saxon art (note modifications in the landscape setting, the abstract forms of the vegetation, the prominence of the pressed 'accordion' pleats in the draperies, etc.).

Wormald has divided the Harley drawings into three groups. The four early hands of Group I (Wormald's 'A' to 'D'), of the first quarter of the 11th century, copy the illustrations and largely the style of the Utrecht Psalter. These drawings, executed mostly before the script, are in the earlier sections of the manuscript written by the first and third scribes (ff. 2–27ᵛ and 50–57ᵛ) where the layout of the pages is, for the most part, identical with that in the Utrecht model. Two later hands (Wormald's 'E', ff. 15, 15ᵛ, 53, 58ᵛ–72ᵛ, and 'F', ff. 58–73ᵛ), added drawings after the script which are mostly independent of the Utrecht illustrations: Hand 'E' inserted a number of sketchy vignettes, unrelated to the text, into the blank spaces of the manuscript (ff. 53–73), while Hand 'F' worked in an intensely expressionistic yet formalized style which is encountered in a group of Canterbury manuscripts of the second quarter of the 11th century and later (cf. Tiberius A. III, no. 100; Caligula A. XV, no. 106).
The drawings in Group I, though sometimes departing in varying degrees from the composition and style of the original, preserve a great deal of the tense vitality, intimacy, and vibrant sketchiness of outline of the Utrecht drawings, while the extremely active attenuated figures with dramatic gestures and wildly agitated draperies become a feature of later Anglo-Saxon illumination.
The later drawings of the Harley Psalter (Wormald's Group II, ff. 17ᵛ, 28, 29ᵛ), probably of the third quarter of the 11th century, are in the 'revived Utrecht' style (cf. Wormald, English Drawings, 55 ff., 70) and only partly depend on the Utrecht illustrations.

Finally, drawings added in the second quarter of the 12th century (Wormald's Group III, ff. 29–35), some left unfinished, appear in the section written by the scribe Eadui and are based on the Utrecht miniatures.

In addition to the illustrations of the psalms the manuscript contains a full-page composition by Hand 'E' (f. 1) representing the Three Persons of the Trinity supported in a mandorla by four angels on a green coloured ground; a frontispiece (f. 1ᵛ) by Hand 'A' with the Psalmist writing which is copied from the Utrecht Psalter; two historiated initials, a B (f. 2) introducing Psalm 1 and showing Christ standing upright and adored by an archbishop prostrate at His feet and a Q (f. 2) to Psalm 51 with Christ in Majesty which is an addition of the second quarter of the 12th century. A sketch in hard point (f. 10ᵛ) with three figures seated under three arches has many counterparts in Canterbury manuscripts of the mid 11th century (cf. Tiberius A. III, no. 100). Initials to psalms are in green, red, and blue brushwork of high quality, occasionally containing interlace knotwork and beasts' heads, while those introducing Psalms 101, 118, 119 are enriched with multi-coloured leafwork. There are leaves missing (after ff. 28, 33, 45, 49, 73) which may have contained some more elaborate initials.

PROVENANCE: The Psalter was produced at Christ Church, Canterbury, as shown by the initial B (f. 2) in which an archbishop wearing a pallium is represented, and by the script of Hand II (ff. 28–49ᵛ) identified by T. A. M. Bishop as being that of Eadvius Basan, the leading Christ Church Canterbury scribe who also wrote no. 67 (Eadui Codex), no. 66 (Arundel 155, between 1012 and 1023), and who appears in no. 61 (York Gospels) and various Christ Church Charters. The original work on the Psalter has usually been dated c. 1000 and although the participation of Eadui (active between 1010 and 1030) may seem to favour a slightly later date, the fact that the work on the manuscript was done in instalments, and that the drawings in the earlier sections were largely executed before the script, suggests the date of c. 1000 or soon after. Belonged to Robert Harley, Earl of Oxford (1661–1724).

LITERATURE: Westwood, *Facsimiles*, 145; W. de Gray Birch, *The Utrecht Psalter*, 1876, 114–21, pl. 2; E. M. Thompson, *English Illuminated Manuscripts*, 1895–6, 16–18, pl. 3; A. Goldschmidt, *Der Albanipsalter in Hildesheim*, Berlin 1895, 13, 15; James, *Ancient Libraries*, lxix, 532; J. A. Herbert, *Illuminated Manuscripts*, 1911, 110, 115; Homburger, 5 nn. 2, 3, 26, 65; British Museum, *Schools of Illumination*, I, 1914, pl. 11; H. Farquhar, *Royal Charities*, I, 1919, (repr. from *British Numismatic Journal* vol. XII), frontispiece, 23–5; Millar, I, 18, no. 38, pl. 22; O. Homburger, 'Review', *Art Bulletin*, X, 1928, 400–1; Saunders, *English Illumination*, 28, pl. 30; British Museum, *Reproductions from Illuminated Manuscripts*, series IV, 1928, pl. V; A. Boeckler, *Abendländische Miniaturen*, 1930, 56, 113, pl. 47; M. R. James, *The Canterbury Psalter*, 1935, 4 ff.; Wormald, *Initials*, 128 n. 3; E. H. Kantorowicz, 'The Quinity of Winchester', *Art Bulletin*, XXIX, 1947, 84–5, fig. 35; Kendrick, *Late Saxon*, 12–16, pls. IX, X, 1, XIV; Wormald, *English Drawings*, 30–1, 36, 39, 44–5, 54–6, 67, 69, 72 no. 34, pls. 10 a, b, 11 a, b, 12 a, b, 25b, 35a; Talbot Rice, *English Art*, 182, 191, 202, pls. 65a, 66; Dodwell, *Canterbury School*, 1–3, 27 ff., 42, 47, 92, 122–3, pl. 1 a, b, c; Freyhan, 431; Nordenfalk, *Early Medieval*, 186; W. Oakeshott, *Classical Inspiration in Medieval Art*, 1959, pl. 65(A); D. Tselos, 'English manuscript illustration and the Utrecht Psalter', *Art Bulletin*, XLI, 1959, 137–49, figs. 3, 10, 11; C. and K. Sisam, 'The Salisbury Psalter', *E.E.T.S.*, 242, 1959, 48 n. 1, 75 n. 2; Rickert, *Miniatura*, 14, 21–2, pl. I; Bishop, *Notes*, V, 94 n. 1; *Notes*, VII, 413, 420–3; *St. Albans Psalter*, 158 n. 1, 198, pl. 162 a, b; W. Mersmann, 'Das Elfenbeinkreuz der Sammlung Topic-Mimara', *Wallraf-Richartz-Jahrbuch*, XXV, 1963, 73; F. Wormald, 'Late Anglo-Saxon Art', *Studies in Western Art. Acts of the 20th Congress of the History of Art*, ed. M. Meiss, I, Princeton, 1963, 21; S. Dufresne, 'Les copies anglaises du Psautier d'Utrecht', *Scriptorium*, 18, 1964, 185–97, pls. 18, 21 a, e, 22 a, b; F. Wormald, 'Continental influence on English medieval illumination', *Fourth International Congress of Bibliophiles*, 1965, 8; Rickert, *Painting in Britain*, 40, 59, 71, pls. 32, 33, 48 b; J. H. A. Engelbregt, *Het Utrechts Psalterium*, Utrecht 1965, 9–11, etc., pls. 19, 21, 23, 25–6, 33–5; Wormald, *Style and Design*, 32; A. Heimann, 'Three illustrations from the Bury St. Edmunds Psalter and their prototypes', *J.W.C.I.*, XXIX, 1966, 39–59, pls. 8 a, b, 12c, 13 a, b; Swarzenski, *Monuments*, pl. 2, fig. 3; M. W. Evans, *Medieval Drawings*, 1969, 8, 23, pl. 19; Bishop, *English Caroline*, nos. 24, 25; Dodwell, *Techniques*, 653; J. Beckwith, *Ivory Carvings in Early Medieval England*, 1972, 43, 48, 53, fig. 58; Wormald, *Angleterre*, 240, ill. 237; Robb, *Illuminated Manuscript*, 149, fig. 91.

EXHIBITED: Brussels, 1973, *English Illuminated Manuscripts 700–1500*, no. 8.

65. Cambridge, Trinity College MS B. 10. 4 (215)

Gospels (Trinity Gospels)
328×235 mm.
First quarter of 11th century. (?) Canterbury, Christ Church

Ills. 212, 214, 219

This is one of the most magnificent surviving Anglo-Saxon Gospel Books. The illumination consists of fifteen pages with lavishly decorated Eusebian Canons (ff. 9–16), a miniature with Christ in Majesty (f. 16ᵛ), four Evangelist portraits, and an initial page to each Gospel. The Canon Tables are shown under splendid gold arches of varying shapes, triangular, horseshoe, and trefoil, supported on golden shafts with acanthus capitals and bases; the tympana contain bust figures of angels, of a blessing

Christ between Alpha and Omega (f. 13), of saints, Apostles, and Evangelist symbols (ff. 15ᵛ–16), while the spandrels are decorated with peacocks and eagles, lions, griffins, plant scrolls, and architectural motifs.

The full-page miniature (f. 16ᵛ) preceding St. Matthew's Gospel shows Christ in a gold mantle over lilac over white, holding a book and enthroned in a blue-rimmed mandorla under a double gold arch profusely ornamented with plant scrolls and 'Winchester' acanthus foliage; the latter includes characteristic knobbed flower-leaves and long-stalked palmette motifs reminiscent of no. 16 (King Edgar Charter).

The Evangelist portraits and corresponding text-pages are in matching 'Winchester' frames of multicoloured leaves with corner medallions, roundels, and quatrefoils containing bust figures of angels, Apostles, or saints (the borders to St. Luke's Gospel excepted, these being decorated solely with foliage and recalling in composition the King Edgar Charter, no. 16). The Evangelists Matthew (f. 17ᵛ) and John (f. 132ᵛ) are enthroned frontally in arched tabernacles with their symbols holding gold scrolls in the lunettes above (that of John is human with an eagle's head). Mark (f. 59ᵛ) and Luke (f. 89ᵛ), shown on wide sofa-like seats, are separated by gold bars from their similar anthropomorphic symbols overhead (cf. no. 15, Add. 40618; no. 95, Monte Cassino Gospels). Matthew and Mark dip their pens into inkhorns on the left; Luke leans forward to the right inscribing 'Quoniam' in an open book on a draped stand; while John, pen in hand, holds an open book with the caption 'In pricipium' (the miniature has suffered badly from damp).

The figure drawing in firm, vigorous outline is in Wormald's 'first style'; it shows extremely rich patterns in the drapery folds whose fluttering edges and agitated hemlines are, however, markedly rugged in effect, their restlessness suggesting a Rheims influence.

Large ornamental initials heavily outlined in gold and followed by the opening lines in gold capitals introduce each of the Gospels. The L (f. 18) is of Franco-Saxon type with animal-headed interlace terminals, acanthus panels, and a round boss on the shaft; the I (f. 60) is an early and outstanding example of the 'clambering' type with lions, dragons, and a bird making their way up the shaft (cf. no. 18, Salisbury Psalter); the Q (f. 90) is made up of beast-filled panels and is inhabited by a bird with the tail of the letter in the form of a large dragon; the I (f. 133) is another example of the 'clambering' initial type. Titles throughout are in large gold capitals with the explicits in narrow rustic ones.

PROVENANCE: The manuscript was probably produced at Christ Church, Canterbury. The scribe, identified by T. A. M. Bishop as hand B of no. 47 (Copenhagen Gospels), active about 1020, was apparently domiciled at Peterborough; he was also responsible for no. 72 (Robert of Jumièges Sacramentary, with Peterborough connections but probably produced at Canterbury) and largely for no. 70

(Royal I. D. IX) which is ascribed to Christ Church. The evidence for Canterbury is supported by the decoration of the present manuscript with its parallels in early 11th-century Canterbury books (though a general dependence on 'Winchester' ornament is evident); by the two 'clambering' initials of a type which became typical of Canterbury manuscripts of the late 11th and 12th centuries; and by the fact that the present volume entered Trinity College Library with other books of Thomas Nevile, Dean of Canterbury (1597–1615), whose collection contained a great number of Canterbury manuscripts.

LITERATURE: Westwood, *Facsimiles*, 140, pl. 42; *New Pal. Soc.*, I, pls. 11, 12; M. R. James, *The Western Manuscripts in the Library of Trinity College, Cambridge*, 1900, I, 287–92; S. Beissel, *Geschichte der Evangelienbücher*, Freiburg im Breisgau, 1906, 135 n. 3; G. F. Warner and H. A. Wilson, *The Benedictional of St. Aethelwold*, 1910, XXVII; J. A. Herbert, *Illuminated Manuscripts*, 1911, 128–9; Homburger, 23 n. 1, 36, 38, 44 n. 2, 55, 65–6; J. Brønsted, *Early English Ornament*, 1924, 248–9, 249 n. 1, 250, 257 n. 1, 265, 297–8, fig. 207; Millar, I, 12, no. 22, pls. 14–15; Saunders, *English Illumination*, 18, 23; Wormald, *Initials*, 109, 121, 132; Kendrick, *Late Saxon*, 16, 34, 103, pls. XV, 2, LXXI, 1; Talbot Rice, *English Art*, 198, pls. 60, 62; Dodwell, *Canterbury School*, 10, 12, 13, 18, 19, 23, 27, pls. 7 b, c, 11a, 14a; A. Boutemy, 'L'enluminure anglaise de l'époque saxonne', *Bull. de la Soc. Nat. des Antiquaires de France*, 1956, 49; Ker, *Catalogue*, LVII, i, 449; Nordenfalk, *Early Medieval*, 185; R. Crozet, 'Les représentations anthropo-zoomorphiques des évangelistes', *Cahiers de Civilisation Médiévale*, I, 1958, 187; Rickert, *Painting in Britain*, 38, 59, 223 n. 48, pl. 28a; T. A. M. Bishop, 'The Copenhagen Gospel Book', *Nordisk Tidskrift för Bokoch Biblioteksväsen*, 1967, 39; Roosen-Runge, I, 62 f., ill. 6; Alexander, *Norman Illumination*, 61 n. 1, 70, 72–3, 80–1, 107 n. 1, 110, 111 n. 1, 114, 124 n. 2, 167 n. 1, 169, pls. 11e, 13d, 15e, 37c; Bishop, *English Caroline*, pp. XV, XXIII, no. 24; C. R. Dodwell, Peter Clemoes, *The Old English Illustrated Hexateuch* (E.E. MSS in facs., XVIII) 1974, pl. Vb.

EXHIBITED: Brussels, 1973, *English Illuminated Manuscripts 700–1500*, no. 9.

66. London, British Library MS Arundel 155

Psalter (Roman version with Gallican corrections)
292 × 170 mm.
1012–23. Canterbury, Christ Church
Ills. 213, 216, 217, 220, fig. 5b

This very important and finely illuminated manuscript was written for Christ Church by the leading scribe of that house, Eadvius Basan. The Psalter is preceded by a calendar (ff. 2–7ᵛ) with KL monograms in gold and various colours and by computistical tables shown under arched frames in red outline (ff. 8ᵛ–11). Two of these contain illustrations in the tympana which represent St. Pachomius receiving the Easter tables from an angel (f. 9ᵛ), and St. Benedict (?) between two adoring monks (f. 10), the former drawn in red and black outline reinforced with green, the latter in black outline drawing.

The opening lines of Psalm 1 in red and green capitals (f. 12) are introduced by a large initial B structurally derived from that in Harley 2904 (no. 41); composed of heavy gold panels, it has two tightly-woven interlace terminals, each with four animal heads, and leafy scrolls filling the bows which are clasped by a mask head. The whole is enclosed by a 'Winchester' frame of two heavy gold bands with climbing foliage and large corner bosses of jutting leaves; arranged in strict symmetry and markedly restrained, the leaf-motifs bear a close resemblance to those in the Eadui Codex (no. 67). The opening verses of Psalm 51 (f. 53) begin with a large 'q' made up of heavy gold panels with bird and dog-headed interlace knotwork and a bulky leaf ornament filling the loop (note the grotesque human face sketched in the D of 'QUID'); the frame is of the same modified 'Winchester' type as that described above but has two roundels on the laterals with bust symbols of Luke and John holding books.

The beginning of Psalm 101 (f. 93), in alternating lines of red and green lettering, is marked by a splendid gold initial D historiated with a representation of David slaying Goliath, in which the contrast between the frail figure of the youth and the sagging body of the giant, partly cut off by the letter-frame, is admirably portrayed. The 'Winchester' border on this page shows further modifications in the meagreness of the foliage and the odd, nearly oval shape of the enclosure composed of heavy gold panels and intersecting gold bands, a variant of the frames in the Eadui Codex (no. 67). Psalm 109 (f. 105) is emphasized by a gold initial 'd' with a bird-headed terminal and by a line of blue capitals.

A full-page miniature (f. 133) framed by an arch on columns in gold and colour enclosing two smaller arches shows an imposing figure of St. Benedict enthroned on the left; clad in pale lilac under gold, the rim of his nimbus inscribed with his name, he is giving the Rule to the monks approaching hurriedly in a crowd from the right with an open book; one of them is kneeling and embracing the Saint's feet, while above in the sky streaked with colour to suggest clouds, the Hand of God appears holding an inscribed scroll.

The decoration of the Psalter is decidedly experimental. It includes the two drawings, one in coloured outline (f. 9ᵛ); the historiated initial with David and Goliath (f. 93), fully and extremely freely painted in gold and colour and containing the characteristic deep blue shadow outline on a light green background (cf. Boulogne Gospels, no. 44; Eadui Codex, no. 67); and the miniature of St. Benedict (f. 133) employing two techniques side by side, painting and tinted outline drawing, with the Saint's figure emphasized by colour and the group of monks on the right executed in outline only (cf. nos. 23, Benedictional of St. Ethelwold, f. 118ᵛ; 58, the 'Caedmon' Genesis, p. 11; 84, Bury Psalter, f. 35).

Remarkably free and vigorous, and stylistically close to the Eadui Codex (no. 67), the decoration was very likely the work of the same artist with figure drawing becoming sharper and with the drapery folds marked by long, straight, more sweeping lines, while the gestures and postures reflect to a greater degree the influence of the Utrecht style.

Initials to psalms are alternately in green, gold, blue, or metallic red; those on the leaves inserted in the 12th century (ff. 136ᵛ–170ᵛ), are blue, red, green, or buff, with rubrics throughout in red and blue. A great deal of gold is used in the decoration and the colours, which include bluish green, pink, blue, ochre, and purple, recall those in the Eadui Codex (no. 67).

PROVENANCE: The Psalter was written at and for Christ Church, Canterbury, by Eadvius Basan, the scribe of the Eadui Codex (no. 67), who also wrote some Christ Church charters and a number of other manuscripts (or parts of manuscripts) in the early 11th century (cf. nos. 61, 62, 68, 69). The approximate date of the present volume between 1012 and 1023 is indicated by the feast of Alphege, Archbishop of Canterbury (martyred 1012), inscribed in the calendar in the original hand, while that of his Translation (1023) is a 12th-century addition. Further evidence for Canterbury is provided by the feast of the dedication of Christ Church (4 May), prayers to SS. Alphege and Dunstan (ff. 186–8), and a reference to Dunstan's relics. The Psalms (ff. 12–132ᵛ) are followed by canticles (ff. 133ᵛ–5), collects (f. 171), and prayers (ff. 171–93ᵛ), with various mid 12th-century additions and alterations (after f. 135) (cf. Ker, Catalogue); there is a continuous interlinear gloss, in part Old English (ff. 171–92). In the custody of the Christ Church monks William Richmond and William Ingram (ff. iᵛ, 8), the Psalter was given subsequently to John Waltham, another monk, by the sub-prior William Hadley (f. 1ᵛ); it was in possession of William Howard, 1592 (ff. 2, 12, 133), passed to his nephew Thomas Howard, Earl of Arundel, and was acquired for the British Museum with other Arundel manuscripts in 1831.

LITERATURE: James, Ancient Libraries, 525; G. F. Warner, Illuminated Manuscripts in the British Museum, 1903, pl. 10; F. A. Gasquet and E. Bishop, The Bosworth Psalter, 1908, 76–118 and passim; G. F. Warner and H. A. Wilson, The Benedictional of St. Aethelwold, 1910, p. XXVIII; J. A. Herbert, Illuminated Manuscripts, 1911, 129; Homburger, 25 n. 1, 65; H. W. C. Davis, Medieval England, 1924, 346, fig. 263; Millar, I, 13 n. 4, no. 25; O. Homburger, 'Review', Art Bulletin, X, 1928, 401; F. Wormald, 'English Kalendars before A.D. 1100', H.B.S., LXXII, 1934, no. 13; id., Initials, 132; Kendrick, Late Saxon, 16, pl. XV (1); R. Schilling, 'Carolingian and Ottonian manuscripts in the exhibition at Berne', Burlington Magazine, XCII, 1950, 82; Wormald, English Drawings, 17, 43, 46, 48, 63, 66, 68, 79, no. 26, pls. 22, 24 a, b; Talbot Rice, English Art, 198, pl. 57a; C. R. Dodwell, Canterbury School, 1954, 4, 18, 26, 31, 35, 85, pls. 2a, 19a; Ker, Catalogue, no.

135; Nordenfalk, Early Medieval, 179; Rickert, Miniatura, 13, 22, pl. 19; R. H. Randall jr., 'An eleventh-century ivory pectoral cross', J.W.C.I. XXV, 1962, 166, pl. 32c; W. Mersmann, 'Das Elfenbeinkreuz der Sammlung Topic-Mimara', Wallraf-Richartz-Jahrbuch, XXI, 1963, 71, ill. 57; Rickert, Painting in Britain, 43–4, 48–9, pls. 40, 41; Roosen-Runge, I, 64 ff., ill. 7; Gneuss, 171 n. 32, 176, 182–3, 185, 189, 241, 250; Alexander, Norman Illumination, 61 n. 1, 169 n. 3; Bishop, English Caroline, p. XV, no. 24; Dodwell, Techniques, 650; English Illuminated Manuscripts 700–1500, Brussels Exhibition Catalogue, 1973, 31, 38; P. M. Korhammer, 'The origin of the Bosworth Psalter', Anglo-Saxon England, 2, 1973, 175, 177, 179 f. C. R. Dodwell, Peter Clemoes, The Old English Illustrated Hexateuch (E.E. MSS in facs., XVIII) 1974, 59.

67. Hanover, Kestner Museum WM XXIª 36
Gospels (Eadui Codex)
224 × 164 mm.
c. 1020. Canterbury, Christ Church.

Ills. 224–229

This splendidly decorated Gospel Book was written by Eadvius Basan (colophon f. 183ᵛ), a monk of Christ Church who may also have been the illuminator. The manuscript begins with the usual prefatory matter (ff. 1–9) headed by titles in gold capitals and initials in orange with gold blobs; these are followed by fourteen pages of Eusebian Canons (ff. 9ᵛ–16) under round or pointed and often intersecting gold arches on multicoloured columns and capitals. The tympana contain a diversity of motifs including the Hand of God, the Creator, with dividers and balance (f. 9ᵛ) and, on the opposite page, the bust figure of a blessing Christ (f. 10); on other folios are heads and faces of the Evangelist symbols (reminiscent of Insular 'Beast Canons', cf. Barberini Gospels, 8th century) and heavy acanthus foliage. The spandrels are boldly decorated with large leaf ornaments, dog's heads spitting foliage or grasping cockerels, and eagles' heads clutching knotted interlace.

The framed Evangelist portraits are facing unframed *Incipit* pages (that of Matthew is missing) with large gold initials and lines of green and blue capitals. Bulky and monumental, the Evangelist figures with large hands and feet are shown seated frontally (Luke excepted) in gold arched tabernacles, unaccompanied by their symbols, and all clad in gold mantles over white robes shaded green. Matthew (f. 17), holding a knife and a book on the right, dips his pen into an inkhorn on the left. Mark (f. 65ᵛ), seated on a high-backed knobbed throne (cf. no. 96, Hereford Gospels), knife in hand, turns slightly to the right holding up a quill over an open book on a draped stand. Luke (f. 96ᵛ) sits sideways facing right and leans forward while writing in an open book. John's portrait (f. 147ᵛ) is iconographically unusual: seated with a pen and knife in his hands, he supports a long scroll inscribed with the opening lines of his Gospel and winding down to meet the head of a figure, identified as Arius, under his feet in the right bottom corner (cf. no. 77, New Minster Offices,

f. 75^v); the heretic is provided with a scroll carrying his denial of the Godhead of Christ (cf. *English Illuminated Manuscripts, 700–1500* Brussels Exhibition Catalogue, 1973, p. 31).

The figure drawing in firm, vigorous, and varied outline is broad and forceful, a happy blend of the 'first' and the Utrecht styles and extremely close to Arundel 155 (no. 66), particularly in its animated and expressive gestures. The draperies, swinging freely at the bottom, fall in straight, firm lines, while the mantles, moulding the powerful bodies beneath, are richly patterned with soft linear folds.

The miniatures are surrounded by modified 'Winchester' borders made up of massive intersecting gold bands, heavy leafwork projecting from the centre of each side, and four corner leaf ornaments, sometimes containing animal heads (f. 96^v). The decoration also is closely related to that in no. 66 (Arundel 155) and suggests the work of the same artist.

The miniatures and the borders are painted in a remarkably wide range of chalky colours including: orange, green, light and dark blue, ochre, pale yellow, olive green, pink, mauve, and amber, with white in the highlights and a profusion of gold. Coloured backgrounds contain strong shadow outlines (deep blue on turquoise green is characteristic, cf. no. 66, Arundel 155) and orange/brown or white clouds are painted on pink or green skies (ff. 9^v, 10). Initials to sections are in gold and rubrics in blue, green, and purple. The colophon written by Eadvius (f. 183^v) is in alternating lines of the same colours.

PROVENANCE: The manuscript is an outstanding example of Christ Church, Canterbury, production. The approximate date, *c.* 1020, and origin are established from the colophon (f. 183^v, '*Liber istum monachus scripsit Eaduius cognomento Basan*'), signed by Eadvius; he was a leading scribe of the first half of the 11th century and wrote a Psalter for Christ Church (Arundel 155, no. 66) datable *c.* 1012–23, the so-called Grimbald Gospels (no. 68), a Gospel Lectionary in Florence (Laur. Plut. XVII, cod. 20, no. 69), a section in Harley 603 (no. 64, ff. 28–49^v) and two Christ Church charters; his hand appears also in parts of other manuscripts (cf. Bishop, *English Caroline*). He may have been an illuminator as well as a scribe since the decoration in Arundel 155 (no. 66), which he wrote, is in the style of the present manuscript. German additions (ff. 1, 183^v, 194) of the 11th and 12th centuries indicate that the volume left England at an early date but its destination is not known. It belonged to the Benedictine Abbey of St. Michael at Lüneburg and was kept in the so-called 'Reliquienschatz der Goldenen Tafel'. The manuscript passed to the Lüneburg Museum after 1792, and was housed for a time in the Palace Chapel at Hanover; it has been on permanent loan to the Kestner Museum since 1955.

LITERATURE: S. Beissel, *Geschichte der Evangelienbücher*, Freiburg im Breisgau 1906, 137 n. 1; A. Boutemy, 'Two obituaries', *English Historical Review*, I, 1935, 297; F. Stuttman, *Der Reliquienschatz der Goldenen Tafel des Michaelisklosters in Lüneburg*,

Berlin 1949, 39 ff.; R. Schilling, 'Carolingian and Ottonian manuscripts in the exhibition at Berne', *Burlington Magazine*, XCII, 1950, 82, fig. 22; Talbot Rice, *English Art*, 194; Bishop, *Notes*, VII, 420; A. Heimann, 'Three illustrations from the Bury St. Edmunds Psalter and their prototypes', *J.W.C.I.*, XXIX, 1966, 52 n. 1, 54, pl. 11c; J. J. G. Alexander, 'A little-known Gospel Book of the later eleventh century from Exeter', *Burlington Magazine*, CVIII, 1966, 4 nn. 44, 45 (vii); Bishop, *English Caroline*, pp. XV, XVI, XX, nos. 24, 25; J. J. G. Alexander, 'Some aesthetic principles in the use of colour in Anglo-Saxon art', *Anglo-Saxon England*, 4, 1975, 148–9, fig. V.

EXHIBITED: Bern, Kunstmuseum, 1949, *Kunst des frühen Mittelalters*, no. 160: Munich, Bayerische Staatsbibliothek, 1950, *Ars Sacra*, no. 130; Brussels, 1973, *English Illuminated Manuscripts 700–1500*, no. 10, colour pl. I.

68. London, British Library MS Add. 34890
Gospels (Grimbald Gospels)
320 × 245 mm.
c. 1020   *Ills. 215 (Colour), 218*

This finely illuminated Gospel Book introducing a number of important innovations is yet another manuscript of which the scribe has been identified by T. A. M. Bishop as Eadui Basan (cf. nos. 67, Eadui Codex; 66, Arundel Psalter; etc.). The usual prefatory matters preceding the Gospels contain gold initials to chapters and paragraphs and rubrics in lines of red, gold, and blue. At the beginning of each of the four texts there is an Evangelist portrait and a decorative initial page in matching borders (those of Mark are missing). The figures and initials are boldly silhouetted on austerely blank vellum grounds, a departure from the otherwise often elaborate surrounds (cf. no. 67), and have a good deal of space around them (one looped curtain is shown on the left behind each of the figures). The youthful Evangelists, shown seated with their filleted heads tilted to the left in an identical movement, look up at their symbols which appear above on the right and are of a type probably suggested by 9th-century models from the Metz or Rheims schools (cf. Ebbo Gospels, St. Mark). Matthew (f. 10^v) sits in profile writing at a lectern and gazing intently at the figure of an angel shown in full length standing on a column and holding a scroll, an unusual iconography probably derived from the Utrecht Psalter illustration to Psalm 60 (f. 34^v). The silver-framed borders of the missing pages of Mark have left a strong imprint on the preceding and following leaves (ff. 46^v–47) and the Evangelist's figure is faintly discernible from a hard-point impression: he is enthroned frontally accompanied by his symbol—a lion—shown on the right carrying a book and blowing a trumpet, a composition probably closely resembling the portrait of Luke (f. 73^v), where a calf is likewise portrayed with a golden horn in its mouth (cf. also nos. 23, Benedictional of St. Ethelwold, f. 19; 47, Copenhagen Gospels; 73, Pembroke Gospels). John (f. 114^v), pen in hand and a scroll across his knees, turns towards an eagle perching with a scroll in its beak on a leaf ornamenting the Evangelist's high-backed chair.

The pages for Matthew (ff. 10v–11) and Luke (ff. 74) are in narrow and rather sober 'Winchester' borders with acanthus patterns confined between silver bands, gold ornaments of stiff leaves on the corners, and foliated medallions on the four sides. The pages of John (ff. 114v–115) are within frames recalling the 'Winchester' type but their figural composition, illustrating subjects of the Last Judgement and the Incarnation, is most unusual. Both borders are made up of silver-edged panels filled with crowned half-length figures instead of foliage and of gold roundels containing choirs of adoring virgins and saints; in the centre of either side of the Evangelist's frame are two medallions, each enclosing six apostles, and at the centre of the lower frame a roundel showing two angels who hold a cluster of naked figures—souls of the departed—in a cloth; across the top are three medallions, each portraying a person of the Trinity in Majesty (cf. no. 35, Sherborne Pontifical); the medallions are held up by hovering angels whose multi-coloured, petal-like wings most effectively replace leaf decoration. The centre top roundel on the text page (f. 115), enclosing an enthroned Virgin and Child, is supported by similar angels, while the corner medallions each contain a seraph. Rickert has suggested a continental origin for the theological scheme behind the two subjects represented; their iconography, however, is a reinterpretation of themes already illustrated in the Aethelstan Psalter (no. 5, f. 21) and the Benedictional of St. Ethelwold (no. 23, ff. 1–4, with a Majesty of Christ probably among the missing miniatures).

Splendid ornamental initials introducing the Gospels contain multi-coloured leafwork within gold letter-frames and each is followed by the opening line of the text in gold capitals; the L (f. 11) and I (f. 115) are of Franco-Saxon type, while the Q (f. 74), clasped by two mask heads, has a richly foliated gold and blue tail.

The figure drawing in the firm outline of the 'first style' shows a new clarity and precision in the rhythmic linear patterns of dark and light, often rope-like, drapery folds. The figures and the borders are painted in strong opaque colours with a preponderance of silver (an innovation) now badly oxidized, an unusually intense blue, greyish to vivid green, pale purple, buff, and some brown; the features, hands, and feet of the Evangelists and saints as well as the whole group of naked souls are in red outline, a combination of painting and drawing techniques which, particularly in the latter, recalls Arundel 155 (no. 66, f. 133). The youthful Evangelist figures are closely similar in type to those in the York Gospels (no. 61).

PROVENANCE: The manuscript was generally ascribed to the New Minster, Winchester on account of a letter from Fulk, Archbishop of Rheims (ff. 158–60), recommending the monk Grimbald to King Alfred (hence Grimbald Gospels). This attribution, however, though supported by iconographical evidence (ff. 114v–115), was questioned by Homburger since the letter is a copy from the second quarter of the 11th century in the hand of the additions to the British Library manuscripts Stowe 944 (no. 78, ff. 41, 59) and Arundel 60 (no. 103, ff. 133–42) and may indicate no more than the presence of the Gospels at Winchester. Its assignment has recently become even more controversial, for T. A. M. Bishop has identified the original hand as that of Eadui Basan, the leading Christ Church, Canterbury scribe who also wrote nos. 67 (Eadui Codex) and 66 (Arundel 155), etc. The manuscript belonged to Thomas Ford, prebendary of Wells, 1721–47 (f. 161), subsequently to the Carew family, Crowcombe Court, Somerset, and was purchased of Quaritch in 1896 (f. 1).

LITERATURE: G. F. Warner, *Illuminated Manuscripts in the British Museum*, 1903, pl. 9; *id.*, *The Benedictional of St. Aethelwold*, 1910, pp. XXI, XXXIX; J. A. Herbert, *Illuminated Manuscripts*, 1911, 131, pl. XV; Homburger, 15 n. 3, 44 n. 2, 70 n. 1; British Museum, *Schools of Illumination*, I, 1914, 11, pl. 14; British Museum, *Reproductions from Illuminated Manuscripts*, ser. I, 1923, pl. V; Saunders, *English Illumination*, 21; Millar, I, 12–13, no. 23, pls. 16, 17; O. Homburger, 'Review', *Art Bulletin*, 1928, 402; G. L. Micheli, *L'Enluminure du Haut Moyen Age*, Brussels 1939, 159, pl. 249; Wormald, *Initials*, 109; Kendrick, *Late Saxon*, 10, pls. VI, VII; W. Oakeshott, *The Sequence of English Medieval Art*, 1950, 16, 30, 44, pls. 17, 19; Wormald, *English Drawings*, 17 n. 1; Talbot Rice, *English Art*, 194–6, pl. 56; Bishop, *Notes*, II, 191; A. Boutemy, 'L'enluminure anglaise de l'époque saxonne et la Flandre française, *Bull. de la Soc. Nationale des Antiquaires de France*, 1956, 47; Freyhan, 428; Ker, *Catalogue*, p. 266; Nordenfalk, *Early Medieval*, 185, pl. 181; Rickert, *Miniatura*, 13, 22, pl. 22; R. L. Bruce-Mitford, 'Decoration and miniature', *Codex Lindisfarnensis*, 1960, II, 159 n. 8, 172, 173; R. H. Randall jr., 'An eleventh-century ivory pectoral cross', *J.W.C.I.*, XXV, 1962, 169, 171, pl. 32e; F. Wormald, 'Late Anglo-Saxon Art', *Studies in Western Art. Acts of the 20th Congress of the History of Art*, ed. M. Meiss, I, Princeton 1963, 21; W. Mersmann, 'Das Elfenbeinkreuz der Sammlung Topic-Mimara', *Wallraf-Richartz-Jahrbuch*, XXI, 1963, 46, 57, figs. 35, 40, 43; Rickert, *Painting in Britain*, 41–2, 234 nn. 63–4, pl. 36; Swarzenski, *Monuments*, pl. 62, fig. 141; J. J. G. Alexander and W. Cahn, 'An eleventh-century Gospel Book from Le Cateau', *Scriptorium*, XX, 1966, 253 n. 19; M. Bourgeois-Lechartier, 'A la recherche du scriptorium de l'Abbaye du Mont Saint-Michel', *Millénaire monastique du Mont Saint-Michel*, Paris 1967, II, 195; Roosen-Runge, 56 ff., pl. III, ill. 5; W. M. Hinkle, 'The gift of an Anglo-Saxon Gospel Book to the abbey of Saint-Remi, Reims', *Journal of The British Archaeological Association*, XXXIII, 1970, 21, 22 n. 3; Alexander, *Norman Illumination*, 60 n. 4, 139–40, 160 n. 3, 169; Bishop, *English Caroline*, p. XV, no. 24; Dodwell, *Techni-*

ques, 649; *Anglo-Saxon Illumination*, 12, no. 31; G. S. Schiller, *Iconography of Christian Art*, 1971, I. 7, ills. 5, 6; *English Illuminated Manuscripts 700–1500*, Brussels Exhibition Catalogue, 1973, pp. 29, 31; Wormald, *Angleterre*, 246, ill. 245; Robb, *Illuminated Manuscript*, 152, fig. 93; C. R. Dodwell, Peter Clemoes, *The Old English Illustrated Hexateuch* (E.E. MSS in facs., XVIII) 1974, 58; H. Holländer, *Early Medieval Art*, 1974, 186.

69. Florence, Biblioteca Medicea Laurenziana MS Plut. XVII. 20
Gospel Lectionary
225 × 173 mm.
First half of 11th century. (?) Canterbury,
Christ Church   *Ill. 232*

The manuscript has been attributed by T. A. M. Bishop to Eadvius Basan, the early 11th-century scribe of Christ Church, Canterbury (cf. nos. 66, 67, 68, etc.); the date and origin of the present volume can therefore be inferred. The illumination consists of an outline drawing in the upper half of the page (f. 1) which shows a blessing Christ in a mandorla with a large book on His knee and Peter and Paul on either side of Him. Wormald has related the miniature to the drawings in two Winchester manuscripts of *c.* 1030 (nos. 77, Titus D. XXVII; 78, Stowe 944), observing, however, that the outline of the present illustration 'is much less delicate'. Lines of capitals in gold, red, and green fill the bottom part of the page. Similarly coloured initials introduce the Gospel readings. Rubrics are in red lettering.

PROVENANCE: The manuscript may have left England for the Continent at an early date since, according to T. A. M. Bishop, additional matter is in a continental 11th-century hand.

LITERATURE: A. M. Bandini, *Catalogus codicum latinorum . . . Mediceae Laurentianae . . .*, I, 1774, 343, 344; Wormald, *English Drawings*, 64, 69, no. 21; Bishop, *English Caroline*, p. XVI, no. 24.

70. London, British Library MS Royal 1. D. IX
Gospels
342 × 277 mm.
c. 1020. Canterbury, Christ Church
                                                    Ill. 222

The illumination consists of four sumptuously decorated pages with ornamental initials introducing the opening lines of each of the Gospels inscribed in gold within massive 'Winchester' frames of tightly packed foliage; the characteristic knobbed flower-leaves projecting over heavy gold bars and from gold bordered panels and corner ornaments are closely reminiscent of no. 65 (Trinity Gospels). Noteworthy also is the pearled inner edging round medallions, panels, and interlace knotwork.
The initial L to Matthew (f. 6), of Franco-Saxon type, has a blue interior ground patterned in white within a gold framework and animal-headed termi-

nals at the extremities; there are square gold medallions on the four sides of the border with bust figures of saints (Evangelists?) holding books and a cross. The initial I to Mark (f. 45) is of the same type but contains an acanthus leaf pattern in the shaft; two roundels with half-figures of saints are placed in the surrounding border. The initial Q to Luke (f. 70) is historiated with a blessing Christ in Majesty in the bowl (cf. no. 23, Benedictional of St. Ethelwold, ff. 70, 91); clothed in gold over brown, He is shown on a bright green background within a gold letter-frame filled with blue and pearled in white round the outer edge; a mask clasps the apex of the letter and its leafy gold tail is heavily outlined in black. The gold-framed initial I to John (f. 111), its stem filled with an acanthus pattern, has interlace knotwork terminals on a blue, white-spotted ground adorned with birds heads holding leaf-sprays in their beaks; it is framed by a heavy foliated border with two large medallions containing bust figures.
The colouring is extremely rich in effect; its splendour is due to the profusion of gold of a distinct reddish hue juxtaposed with heavy and muted shades of yellowish grey, brown, ochre, and dull red, and set off by touches of vivid green and blue. Initials to paragraphs and in the text are in tooled gold with gold-inscribed rubrics.

PROVENANCE: The manuscript is assigned to Christ Church, Canterbury, on the evidence of its presence in Christ Church soon after completion, a record of admission of King Cnut and his brother Harold to the confraternity, probably of Christ Church (f. 43ᵛ), and a confirmation of privileges granted by Cnut to that house and inscribed by Eadvius (f. 44), the leading Christ Church scribe active *c.* 1020 (cf. nos. 66, Arundel 155; 67, Eadui Codex; etc.). Traditionally believed to have been presented to Canterbury by Cnut, the Gospels were written in the main part (ff. 5–114; cf. Bishop, 1967) by the scribe of nos. 65 (Trinity Gospels) and 72 (Robert of Jumièges Sacramentary), both probably from Christ Church, and of additions to no. 47 (Copenhagen Gospels); the Canterbury attribution is further supported by the style of the decoration, making connections with Winchester rather unlikely. The manuscript belonged to John, Lord Lumley (f. 6), d. 1609.

LITERATURE: F. G. Kenyon, *Facsimiles of Biblical Manuscripts in the British Museum*, 1900, pl. XVII; James, *Ancient Libraries*, pp. xxv, 515; G. F. Warner and H. A. Wilson, *The Benedictional of St. Aethelwold*, 1910, p. XL; Homburger, 66; British Museum, *Schools of Illumination*, 1914, II, pl. 15; *id.*, *Reproductions from illuminated manuscripts*, ser. I, 1923, pl. VI; Millar, I, 13, no. 24, pl. 18; O. Homburger, 'Review', *Art Bulletin*, X, 1928, 402; Saunders, *English Illumination*, 18; G. L. Micheli, *L'Enluminure du Haut Moyen Age et les influences irlandaises*, Brussels 1939, 159 n. 4; Wormald, *Initials*, 132; Holmquist, *Viking Art*, 15; Talbot Rice, *English Art*, 195, pl. 58; Bishop, *Notes*, II, 186; S. Schulten, 'Die Buchmalerei des 11. Jahrhunderts im Kloster St. Vaast in Arras', *Müncher Jahrbuch der Bildenden*

Kunst, VII, 1956, 52; A. Boutemy, 'L'enluminure anglaise de l'époque saxonne', *Bull. de la Soc. Nat. des Antiquaires de France*, 1956, 48; Ker, *Catalogue*, no. 247; Rickert, *Miniatura*, 13, 22, pl. 18; *id.*, *Painting in Britain*, 38–9, 49, 224 n. 65, pl. 28b; T. A. M. Bishop, 'The Copenhagen Gospel Book', *Nordisk Tidskrift för Bok- och Biblioteksväsen*, 1967, 39, 41, fig. 2; Alexander, *Norman Illumination*, 60 n. 4; Bishop, *English Caroline*, p. XV, nos. 23, 24; *English Illuminated Manuscripts 700–1500*, Brussels Exhibition Catalogue, 1973, p. 30.

71. London, British Library MS Loan 11

Gospels (Kederminster Gospels)
305 × 205 mm.
c. 1020 (?) Canterbury, Christ Church

Ill. 223

The decoration of this sadly mutilated volume now consists of only two magnificent pages prefacing the texts of St. Mark and St. John and containing large ornamental initials and the gold-inscribed opening words of the Gospels surrounded by elaborate borders. The initial I to Mark, topped by animal-headed gold interlace on blue and ochre ground, contains in its gold-edged stem a diagonal pattern of scrolls and dots; it is shown under a splendid double gold, pink-filled, dot-patterned arch supported on columns with acanthus capitals and bases, and with foliate medallions between the gold shafts. Another medallion of stylized, sprawling foliage crowns the top of the arch which is flanked by two large gold birds (a striking and unusual feature probably inspired by Carolingian manuscripts of the Tours school) and by fleshy bunched acanthus leaves with long-stalked palmettes decorating the spandrels. The initial I to John's Gospel has interlace terminals with animal heads and foliage. Filled with a rosette pattern within a gold-panelled and pearled shaft, it is surrounded by a sumptuous rectangular 'Winchester' border of two heavy gold bars with large corner bosses and medallions of broad, flat leaves on the laterals; each of these contains a roundel with a bust-figure of a trumpeting saint (cf. no. 73, Pembroke 301, f. 3ᵛ) while the horizontals are filled with patterns of acanthus leaves curling over the edging bars.

The bold leafwork, rather static in effect, and the long-stalked palmette motifs have close analogies in the decoration of the Eadui Codex (no. 67), Arundel 155 (no. 66), and Royal 1. D. IX (no. 70), the latter also providing a parallel for the rich, opaque, and heavy colouring of the present manuscript, which includes ochre, browns, black, milky orange, and blue, and a profusion of gold. Initials to paragraphs and rubrics are in gold.

The decoration suggests connections with Christ Church, Canterbury. The manuscript was written by two hands identified by T. A. M. Bishop with the scribes of Royal 1. D. IX (no. 70). The main scribe, active *c.* 1020, was also responsible for part of no. 47 (Copenhagen Gospels) and the whole of nos. 65 (Trinity Gospels) and 72 (Robert of Jumièges Sacramentary).

PROVENANCE: The 14th-century inscription of ownership on the first leaf: *Liber Colegii de Wyndesore*, indicates that the volume belonged to Windsor College, perhaps *Unus liber Evangelii noviter ligatus* in the register of St. George's Chapel of 1384–5. Donated to the parish library of Langley Marish, Buckinghamshire, by Sir John Kederminster, the manuscript is on permanent loan to the British Museum.

LITERATURE: A. J. C., 'The Kederminster Gospels', *British Museum Quarterly*, VI, 1932, 93, pls. XXXVIII, XXXIX; Wormald, *Initials*, 132; Ker, *Catalogue*, p. LVII, i; T. A. M. Bishop, 'The Copenhagen Gospel Book', *Nordisk Tidskrift för Bok- och Biblioteksväsen*, 1967, 39, 41; *id.*, *English Caroline*, p. XV.

72. Rouen, Bibliothèque Municipale MS Y. 6 (274)

Sacramentary ('Missal') of Robert of Jumièges
342 × 220 mm.
c. 1020

Ills. 237–240

This extensively decorated Sacramentary is preceded by a calendar with KL monograms in gold and details in magenta, red, gold, and blue (ff. 5ᵛ–11ᵛ), and by paschal tables and computus matter in similar colours (ff. 12–24ᵛ). The illumination consists of thirteen full-page miniatures in sumptuous rectangular and arched frames marking each of the principal feasts, and of twelve pages with similar borders enclosing initial letters of corresponding texts or short portions of masses inscribed in gold lettering; in addition three more miniatures may have been contained on the now missing leaves, which probably preceded the elaborately framed initial pages of the Masses of Palm Sunday (f. 57), the Purification (f. 114), and the Trinity (f. 174).

The Canon of the Mass is introduced by decorative pages (ff. 25ᵛ–27ᵛ) with the opening words of the Preface headed by ornamental initials in gold and colour and with the *Vere dignum* monogram, all surrounded by borders of 'Winchester' type with gold trelliswork and multicoloured foliage. The Masses of Christmas are accompanied by two illustrations: the Nativity (f. 32ᵛ) of Anglo-Saxon type with the crib in the foreground (cf. nos. 23, Benedictional of St. Ethelwold; 44, Boulogne Gospels), and the Annunciation to the Shepherds with, below, the Flight into Egypt (f. 33). Two miniatures with four scenes mark the Epiphany, showing Herod consulting the Jewish priests (f. 36ᵛ) with, below, the Magi journeying (note the star placed on the right beyond the frame), and on the opposite page (f. 37) the Adoration and the Magi warned by an angel in their sleep. There are three illustrations for Holy Saturday: the Betrayal, a crowded scene shown under a splendid mitred arch (f. 71) with the Crucifixion (f. 71ᵛ) and the Deposition (f. 72) in richly foliated rectangular frames with medallions on each side containing bust figures; the weeping

Virgin of the Crucifixion recalls Harley 2904 (no. 41), while the moving scene of the Deposition is the earliest portrayal of that subject in English illumination. The miniature for Easter shows the Three Marys and an angel against the elaborate architecture of the Sepulchre, the whole enclosed by yet another mitre-arched frame (f. 72ᵛ). The Ascension (f. 81ᵛ) with the 'disappearing Christ' introduces an Anglo-Saxon iconographic variant where Christ's feet and legs only are shown, in this case within a mandorla, as He is ascending into heaven (cf. no. 58, 'Caedmon' Genesis; for discussion cf. Schapiro, 1943); another mandorla surrounds the Virgin standing among the Apostles below. The Pentecost representation (f. 84ᵛ) recalls those in the two Winchester Benedictionals (nos. 23, 24) for the Holy Dove is shown descending in an oval Glory, but the Apostles are seated in a row, not in semi-circle, and the Holy Spirit no longer enters their mouths but reaches the tops of their heads only as tongues of fire.

The miniatures of St. Peter (f. 132ᵛ) and St. Andrew (f. 164ᵛ) show them enthroned frontally, each surrounded by a heavy rectangular frame; St. Andrew, recalling in figure type and posture the St. Luke portrait in the Anhalt Gospels (no. 45), faces a text-page (f. 165) inscribed in gold within a matching border. The feast of All Saints is marked by a picture (f. 153ᵛ) and a similarly framed lettered page opposite (f. 150); the illustration shows a crowd of the Blessed on the ground with, above, the Holy Lamb in a circular Glory supported by two angels and medallions on each side of the frame containing bust figures.

The miniatures, probably the work of more than one hand, are in the vigorous and vivacious drawing style practised at Canterbury in the first half of the 11th century (cf. nos. 55, Royal 1. E. VI, f. 30ᵛ; 56, Arenberg Gospels; 66, Arundel 155; etc); delicate but firm, the line is extremely varied and the fine, straight strokes of the drapery folds are set off by the zigzags of the 'accordion' pleats, typical of this group of manuscripts (cf. nos. 56, Arenberg Gospels; 64, Harley 603, Hands A and B). There are also stylistic affinities with the Boulogne Gospels (no. 44) in the fluid designs of the garments and in the head types of certain figures (e.g. Christ crucified, f. 71ᵛ; the Three Marys, f. 72ᵛ), though one of the artists of the present manuscript is fond of round doll-like heads which he repeats with a monotonous insistence. The influence of the Rheims style is apparent in the lightness and spontaneity of the drawing and in the expressiveness of gestures, with a feeling of all-pervading excitement and movement which is echoed in the restlessly agitated leaf ornament of the elaborate borders. The skies are painted with streaks of thin colours in an illusionistic manner and the backgrounds of such miniatures as the Crucifixion and the Deposition (ff. 71ᵛ–72) are covered with swathes and splashes of paint; this disturbing effect enhances the dramatic context of scenes otherwise portrayed with great simplicity; similar painterly devices in the tradition of the Boulogne

Gospels are a feature of Canterbury manuscripts of the first half of the 11th century, though nowhere are they applied with the same baroque freedom. Clear but brilliant, the colours are extremely varied, and the range is enriched by overpainting and colour shading; they include blue, mauve to pink, green, yellow, reddish brown, slate-grey, and gold in details with white and yellow in the highlights. Text initials are in gold with rubrics inscribed in red and blue.

The extremely rich foliated borders are a feature of the decoration which recalls the Benedictional of St. Ethelwold (no. 23) in having frames of both rectangular and arched types, and in the system of placing matching designs on the facing pages. However, the leafwork, besides being much more varied, is also more animated, straggly, and unruly, and a flow of incessant movement seems to permeate the whole decoration which is related both in style and in certain ornamental features to the Trinity Gospels (no. 65); note the birds and plant scrolls in the spandrels of the arched frames and medallions with bust figures in the borders.

The system of marking the formulary of each of the main feasts in a sacramentary with a narrative picture, uncommon during that period (cf. Hohler, 1955), is also found in the Ethelwold Benedictional (no. 23); but in spite of certain iconographic analogies (the illustration of the Nativity and part of the Pentecost miniature) direct contacts between the two works are unlikely and the choice of subjects represented differs. The present manuscript probably derives, ultimately, from a 10th-century German or Northern French sacramentary and Hohler (1955) has shown on internal evidence (St. Gertrude invoked in the *Nobis quoque* prayer) that the archetype must have been connected with Nivelles, near Liège. There are no clear indications where in England the present manuscript may have been produced, and its attribution is highly controversial. It has been assigned to Winchester or Canterbury (Kendrick), to Peterborough and to Ely (Tolhurst, Talbot Rice), but Hohler has demonstrated that the volume was probably copied from an obsolete and defective Peterborough book, the copy having been made, however, neither at Peterborough nor at Ely, and not for use at either place. The main scribe has since been identified by Ker (*Catalogue*) and by Bishop (1967) with the scribe of the Trinity Gospels (no. 65, probably a Canterbury manuscript) who appears also as the second hand in the Copenhagen Gospels (no. 47) presumably produced at Peterborough (cf. Bishop, 1967), and in parts of two other Gospels (Royal 1. D. IX, no. 70; B.L. Loan 11, no. 71), both attributable to Christ Church, Canterbury. Stylistic evidence also weighs heavily in favour of a Canterbury origin.

The Sacramentary is datable to after 1015 on account of the name of St. Florentinus invoked in the litany for the sick (f. 207ᵛ), the translation of his relics to Peterborough having taken place that year.

PROVENANCE: The manuscript was given to Jumièges Abbey by Robert of Jumièges whilst Bishop of London (1044–51), the gift being recorded possibly in his own hand (f. 228). It passed from Jumièges into the Rouen Library at the dissolution of the monastery in 1791.

LITERATURE: T. F. Dibdin, *A bibliographical, antiquarian and pictorial tour in France and Germany*, 1821, I, 165; E. Frère, *Manuel de bibliographie normande*, Rouen 1860, II, 310 ff.; Westwood, *Facsimiles*, 136–8, pl. 40; W. G. Henderson, 'The York Manual', *S.S.* LXIII, 1875, 131–4; F. E. Warren, *The Leofric Missal*, 1883, 275–93; L. Deslisle, *Mémoire sur d'anciens sacramentaires*, Paris 1886, 220–1; H. A. Wilson, 'The Missal of Robert of Jumièges', *H.B.S.*, LXXXV, 1896, pls. I–XV; F. A. Gasquet and E. Bishop, *The Bosworth Psalter*, 1908, 160–1 and *passim*; J. A. Herbert, *Illuminated Manuscripts*, 1911, 128; Homburger, 2, 10 n. 4, 13 n. 1, 17 n. 1, 21 nn. 1 and 3, 24, 49 n. 2, 55, 60 n. 3, 61, 65, 67, pl. XII; V. Leroquais, *Les Sacramentaires et les missels manuscrits des bibliothèques publiques de France*, Paris 1924, I, 99, IV, pls. XX–XXII; J. Brønsted, *Early English ornament*, 1924, 259, 293 n. 1; P. Blanchon-Laserrve, *Écriture et enluminure des manuscrits*, Solesmes, St. Pierre 1926, 52–3, pl. XVII; Millar, I, 11–12, no. 21, pls. 12, 13; Sir Ivor Atkins, 'An Investigation of two Anglo-Saxon Calendars', *Archaeologia*, 2nd ser., XXVIII, 1928, 219 ff.; Saunders, *English Illumination*, 18, 23; A. Boeckler, *Abendländische Miniaturen*, Berlin 1930, 55, pl. 46; J. B. L. Tolhurst, 'An Examination of two Anglo-Saxon Manuscripts of the Winchester School', *Archaeologia*, 2nd ser., XXXIII, 1933, 27–44; G. L. Micheli, *L'Enluminure du Haut Moyen Age*, Brussels 1939, 159 n. 6; W. Weisbach, *Manierismus in mittelalterlicher Kunst*, Basle 1942, 22, pl. 13; M. Schapiro, 'The image of the disappearing Christ', *Gazette des Beaux Arts*, 6e sér. XXII, 1943, 149 n. 45, fig. 5; Wormald, *Initials*, 132; Kendrick, *Late Saxon*, 14 n. 1, 103, 130, pl. XI; Talbot Rice, *English Art*, 190–4, 212, pls. 53–5; J. B. L. Tolhurst, 'Le Missel de Robert de Jumièges, sacramentaire d'Ely', *Jumièges. Congrés scientifiques du XIIIe centenaire*, Rouen 1955, I, 287–93; E. C. Hohler, 'Les Saints insulaires dans le missel de L'Archevêque Robert', *ib.* 293–303; M. M. Dubois, 'Les rubriques en vieil anglais du missel de Robert de Jumièges', *ib.*, 305–8; Ker, *Catalogue*, no. 377; Nordenfalk, *Early Medieval*, 183; Rickert, *Miniatura*, 15, 20, 22, pl. II; *St. Albans Psalter*, 54, 55, 83, 97, pls. 102a, 103 c, d, 105 a, b, 131a; W. Mersmann, 'Das Elfenbeinkreuz der Sammlung Topic-Mimara', *Wallraf-Richartz-Jahrbuch*, XXV, 1963, 24–5; Rickert, *Painting in Britain*, 28, 39, 223 n. 50, pl. 31; A. Boutemy, 'Les Feuillets de Damme' *Scriptorium*, 1966, 6; T. A. M. Bishop, 'The Copenhagen Gospelbook', *Nordisk Tidskrift för Bok- och Biblioteksväsen*, 1967, 41; F. Avril, 'La decoration des manuscrits au Mont Saint-Michel (XIe–XII siècles)', *Millénaire monastique du Mont Saint-Michel*, Paris, 1967, II, 220 n. 45; F. Deuchler, *Der Ingeborg Psalter*, Berlin 1967, 62; G. Duby, *The Making of the Christian West*, 1967, pl. 30; *Roosen-Runge*, 56, 58–9; Alexander, *Norman Illumination*, 114, 130, 132, 137, 152, 154 n. 2, 160, 164, 167 n. 1, 169, 237, pls. 30c, 37d; Bishop, *English Caroline*, p. XV; *English Illuminated Manuscripts 700–1500*, Brussels Exhibition Catalogue, 1973, p. 30; Wormald, *Angleterre*, 244, ill. 242, pl. 243; H. Holländer, *Early Medieval Art*, 1974, 186; J. J. G. Alexander, 'Some aesthetic principles in the use of colour in Anglo-Saxon art', *Anglo-Saxon England*, 4, 1975, 149–50, 153, figs. VI, VII.

73. Cambridge, Pembroke College MS 301
Gospels
292 × 215 mm.
c. 1020, additions second quarter 11th century
Ills. 233–236

The four Gospels are preceded by fifteen pages of Canon Tables (ff. 1ᵛ–8ᵛ) shown in frames of great diversity under a series of small round or pointed and often intersecting arches on colonettes and columns and surmounted by triangular pediments or larger arches. The tympana contain the Holy Lamb and Evangelists' symbols, half-figures of a blessing Christ and the Virgin, St. Michael, saints, Apostles, and angels (one blowing a horn, f. 3ᵛ), with dragons, lions, architectural motifs, and plant scrolls decorating the spandrels. The choice of subjects and richness of ornament recall no. 65 (Trinity Gospels), but the strapwork motifs in roundels and the stiffness of foliage are a distinctive feature. The change from the originally soft colourings of pink, light orange, pale ochre, and green to heavier shades with predominance of deep blue and magenta brown (f. 7) indicates that the decoration of the Canon Tables must have been completed by another artist.

The four Evangelist portraits, facing the opening lines of their Gospels on the opposite pages, were executed by various illuminators and at various dates. The miniature of St. Matthew (f. 10ᵛ), stylistically reminiscent of no. 58 ('Caedmon' Genesis), though its outline is more delicate and nervous, is by the original hand. Surrounded by a late 'Winchester' border of stiff foliage confined between two gold bars with two medallions containing half-length figures, it shows the Evangelist enthroned frontally, pen in hand, with an open book on a stand (supported, unusually, by a bird perching on a leafy plant motif, cf. Innsbruck, Universitätsbibl., Cod. 484, f. 110ᵛ, 9th century). He looks up towards an angel flying down to him, scroll in hand, from a hemisphere above. A large initial L of Franco-Saxon type and the opening lines of Matthew's Gospel on the facing page (f. 11) are in a similar border.

An unfinished miniature in a different style (f. 44ᵛ), partly painted in opaque blue, green, and ochre, shows St. Mark seated in frontal view under a gold arch filled not with the usual leaf pattern but adorned with three medallions of stiff foliage; the Evangelist turns towards a draped lectern with a book on the right but holds no pen in his blessing hand; his symbol—a winged lion—is shown flying over his head from left to right and blowing a trumpet, a feature traceable to the Lindisfarne Gospels, c. 700 (cf. also nos. 23, Benedictional of St. Ethelwold; 47, Copenhagen Gospels; 68, Grimbald Gospels). The initial I introducing Mark's text (f. 45) is unframed and, made up of massive gold, blue-filled panels with interlace and foliage terminals, is heavily outlined in black.

The unfinished portraits of SS. Luke (f. 70^v) and John (f. 108^v) represent the Evangelists without symbols but, unusually, each accompanied by the 'inspiring' figure of a sceptred angel standing on the left, an iconography derived from the Utrecht Psalter (frontispiece, f. 1^v; cf. also no. 76, Besançon Gospels, f. 58^v). The figure drawing, delicate and sensitive, and in parts coarsely overlaid with opaque blue, green, and ochre, is executed in long, swift strokes which recall the marginal illustrations in no. 64 (Harley 603, Hand 'E'); the expressive gestures and the heads eagerly thrust forward also point to the impact of the Utrecht Psalter style. Initials Q (f. 71) and I (f. 109) are made up of heavy gold panels and large, bunched coloured leaves. The miniatures and initials are in matching borders (ff. 70^v–71, 108^v–109), composed of massive gold bars and containing panels or stripes of various colours with roundels (note the Insular strapwork ornament) and foliated squares or bunched leaves at the angles. They probably conceal original designs of 'Winchester' type since leaf motifs in faint brown outline can be perceived jutting out around the edges (ff. 108^v–109). Initials to paragraphs standing in the margins are in gold.

PROVENANCE: Of uncertain origin and showing some stylistic connections with Canterbury, the manuscript was written by the scribe responsible for Bodleian Library MS Bodley 163 of a known Peterborough provenance and presumed origin (cf. Bishop, *Notes*; also *Nordisk Tidskrift*). The assignment of the present volume to Peterborough is doubtful, however, because the scribe of Bodley 163, which is unilluminated, also reappears briefly in nos. 70 (Royal 1. D. IX) and 71 (Loan 11), both attributable to Canterbury. T. A. M. Bishop quotes Ker, moreover, as saying that owing to the fire at Peterborough in 1116, the 'Peterborough' manuscripts of earlier date may be of external origin (cf. *Notes*). The present manuscript is inscribed 'Andrewe Jenour' (f. 1), 17th century.

LITERATURE: M. R. James, *A descriptive catalogue of the Manuscripts in the Library of Pembroke College, Cambridge*, 1908, 263–6, 2 pls; Burlington Fine Arts Club, *Exhibition of Illuminated Manuscripts*, 1908, no. 12, pl. 13; G. F. Warner and H. A. Wilson, *The Benedictional of St. Aethelwold*, 1910, p. XLI; Homburger, 21 n. 3, 23 n. 1, 44 n. 2, 68; Millar, I, 16, no. 32; W. Weisbach, *Manierismus in mittelalterlicher Kunst*, Basle 1942, 18, pl. 17; Talbot Rice, *English Art*, 207; Bishop, *Notes*, I, 441; Dodwell, *Canterbury School*, 14, pl. 6c; R. L. S. Bruce-Mitford, 'Decoration and Miniatures', *Codex Lindisfarnensis*, ed. T. D. Kendrick, Olten and Lausanne 1960, II, 159 n. 9, pl. 28 (b), (c); J. J. G. Alexander, 'A little-known Gospel Book of the late eleventh century from Exeter', *Burlington Magazine*, CVIII, 1966, 14 n. 45 (iv); T. A. M. Bishop, 'The Copenhagen Gospel Book', *Nordisk Tidskrift för Bok- och Biblioteksväsen*, 1967, 41; id., *English Caroline*, nos. 13, 23: C. Nordenfalk, 'The Draped Lectern', *Intuition und Kunstwissenschaft: Festschrift für Hans Swarzenski*, Berlin 1973, 86, fig. 6.

74. Cambridge, Trinity College MS B. 15. 34 (369)
Homilies in Anglo-Saxon
248 × 161 mm.
c. 1020–30. Canterbury, Christ Church   *Ill. 241*

The illumination consists of a full-page drawing (f. 1) showing an imposing figure of Christ the Judge, seated within a mandorla, blessing, with His left hand resting on an open and inscribed book (cf. James, 1900). He has 'iustus iudex' written on His breast and 'Rex Regum' inscribed on the knees (Revelation, XIX, 16; cf. no. 23, Benedictional of St. Ethelwold, f. 9^v). The drawing, in fine yet firm outline tinted green and red, with the drapery folds softly marked by light brushstrokes, is related to no. 66 (Arundel 155) and anticipates the style of no. 106 (Caligula A. XV) though it is more delicate and less mannered than the latter. The markedly elongated figure with a stiffly erect torso is somewhat like no. 84 (Bury Psalter), while Christ's filleted head recalls that of the Creator in no. 67 (Eadui Codex, f. 10). Principal initials are in olive green and red with titles in red rustic capitals. Marks at the end of each homily are made up of strokes radiating from a group of four or five dots (cf. no. 80, Winchcombe Psalter).

The manuscript, written by the scribe of British Library Harley 2892 which is assigned to Christ Church, Canterbury on internal evidence (cf. R. M. Wooley, 'The Canterbury Benedictional', *H.B.S.*, 1917) may also have been produced at Canterbury. This attribution is supported by stylistic connections of the drawing with Canterbury illumination of the earlier eleventh century. Ker observed the similarity of the script with that of no. 80 (Winchcombe Psalter).

PROVENANCE: The manuscript probably belonged to Archbishop Parker, and later to his son John, being identified as no. 45 in the list of his manuscripts in Lambeth Palace Library MS. 737; given to Trinity College by John Whitgift, Archbishop of Canterbury (1583–1603/4) whose arms are stamped on the 16th-century binding, it was formerly Trinity College Library MS. B. 9. 26.

LITERATURE: M. R. James, *The Western Manuscripts in the Library of Trinity College, Cambridge*, 1900–4, I, no. 369, IV, pl. XI; Millar, I, no. 46; Wormald, *English Drawings*, 63, no. 15; Talbot Rice, *English Art*, 200, pl. 61b; C. R. Dodwell, *The Canterbury School*, 1954, 34, 24b; Ker, *Catalogue*, no. 86.

75. London, British Library, MS Harley 76
Gospels (Bury Gospels)
265 × 200 mm.
c. 1020–30. Canterbury, Christ Church

Ills. 221, 230, 231

This sadly mutilated Gospel Book which no doubt originally contained Evangelist portraits and ornamental initial pages (now only one, f. 45, is extant, leaves being removed at the beginning of each Gospel), is preceded by fourteen splendidly decorated pages with Canon Tables. These are shown under intersecting round or pointed gold arches on heavy, colour-filled columns with acanthus or mask-head capitals and bases. The tympana contain varied decoration recalling in richness that of no. 65 (Trinity Gospels) and 73 (Pembroke 301) and including: a Christ blessing, standing in an oval-shaped Glory (f. 6); SS. Peter and Paul enthroned within ornate quatrefoils (7ᵛ–8); bust-figures of Christ and the Virgin flanked by angels and saints in the spandrels (ff. 8ᵛ–9), and of sceptred angels with scrolls shown in elaborately gabled architectural surrounds (ff. 9ᵛ–10); on other pages are lions and dragons, heavy leaf motifs, and plant scrolls, while beasts' heads in the bases of some of the columns are reminiscent of the Evangelist symbols in the Canon Tables of no. 67 (Eadui Codex).

The gold-inscribed opening of St. Matthew's Gospel (f. 45) is headed by a large initial I made up of two heavy yellow and green panels framed in gold, a foliage terminal with a long-eared dragon's head at the bottom, and animal-headed interlace knotwork on the top. The whole is surrounded by a frame similar in structure and shape to those in nos. 66 (Arundel 155, cf. in particular f. 93) and 67 (Eadui Codex): they are made up of two heavy gold bands enclosing pink and blue leaf patterns, interlaced on the corners, and ornamented round the outer edge with animal and bird heads nibbling at fruit on fine hair-like stalks (cf. no. 66, Arundel 155, f. 12).

Both the decoration and the figure drawing in firm, swift strokes, are close in style to nos. 66 and 67 (Arundel 155 and Eadui Codex), a similarity which extends to the heavy opaque colours (mainly green, blues, purplish, brown, yellow, and greenish-grey), and to the painting technique with emphatic coloured shadow outlines and zigzags of clouds in the backgrounds (e.g. f. 7ᵛ). Initials to paragraphs are in red or green with rubrics in red.

PROVENANCE: The manuscript, of uncertain origin, was at Bury St. Edmunds in the late 11th century as shown by the additional matter (f. 137ᵛ) written in the hand of a Bury scribe (cf. Bishop, *Notes*). It is unlikely, however, to have been produced there since Bury Abbey, founded in 1020 and consecrated in 1032, could hardly have had a workshop organized for the production of luxury manuscripts *c*. 1030. The evidence of the style and certain ornamental details favour an origin at the same scriptorium as nos. 66 and 67 (Arundel 155 and Eadui Codex), and the Gospels probably belong to a group of manuscripts which were executed at Canterbury to be sent elsewhere (cf. nos. 35, Sherborne Pontifical; 68, Grimbald Gospels?; 84, Bury Psalter; etc.). On the 17th-century binding are the arms of Sir Simonds d'Ewes.

LITERATURE: M. R. James, *On the Abbey of St. Edmund at Bury* (Cambridge Bibliographical Society Publ.), 1895, 89, no. 269; G. F. Warner and H. A. Wilson, *The Benedictional of St. Ethelwold*, 1910, p. XLI; J. A. Herbert, *Illuminated Manuscripts*, 1911, 130–1; Homburger, 21 n. 3, 23 n. 1, 44 n. 2; Millar, I, 15–16, no. 27, pl. 21; Homburger, 'Review', *Art Bulletin*, X, 1928, 400; Saunders, *English Illumination*, 23, pl. 23; Kendrick, *Late Saxon*, 103, pl. LXXI, 2, 3; Talbot Rice, *English Art*, 207; Bishop, *Notes*, II, 185, pl. Xb; J. J. G. Alexander, 'A little-known Gospel Book of the later eleventh century from Exeter', *Burlington Magazine*, CVIII, 1966, 14 nn. 44, 45, 47; *id.*, *Norman Illumination*, 107 n. 1; Bishop, *English Caroline*, p. XIII.

76. Besançon, Bibliothèque Municipale MS 14
Gospels
253 × 190 mm.
Late 10th century, addition *c*. 1020–30.
(?)Winchester

Ill. 242

The Gospels, whose original decoration was never completed, are preceded by ten pages of Canon Tables (ff. 8ᵛ–13ᵛ) shown under a series of arches, mainly of Nordenfalk's type 'm' (cf. *Die spätantiken Kanontafeln*, 1938), resting on architraves and slender columns. Two pages (ff. 10ᵛ, 11ᵛ) contain roundels with half-length figures of Christ and the Apostles, perhaps inspired by the 'Apostolic' Canon Tables of certain 8th-century Insular Gospels; they are superimposed, unusually, one above the other between the last two columns of the framework. The only decorative page (f. 14) with a large initial L in gold, accompanied by the opening words of the text and surrounded by a foliate border, introduces St. Matthew's Gospel. Light and rather narrow and reminiscent of no. 25 (Bibl. Nat., lat. 987), the border is of a simplified 'Winchester' type with meagre foliage, square corner ornaments, and a roundel on each of the laterals. A drawing in red outline added in the 11th century on the verso of a blank leaf (f. 58ᵛ) precedes St. Mark's Gospel which is headed by an initial I in gold (f. 59). The drawing represents a seated Evangelist writing at a draped lectern on the right, with an angel standing behind him, an iconographic derivation from the Utrecht Psalter (frontispiece, f. 1ᵛ). According to Wormald, the miniature is stylistically related to no. 78 (New Minster Register, B.L. Stowe 944) and is somewhat later in date (cf. also Homburger, p. 67), but the influence of its Rheims model predominates in the broken and more sketchy outline. Iconographically the drawing also recalls portraits of St. Luke and St. John added in the second quarter of the 11th century to no. 73 (Pembroke 301), where an 'inspiring' angel is shown standing on the left, behind each seated Evangelist.

A plain, gold initial Q (f. 88) introduces St. Luke's Gospel while the text of St. John has the first three lines inscribed in gold lettering (f. 132). Red or green initials to verses stand in the margins with rubrics inscribed in the same colours.

PROVENANCE: The manuscript, whose script has been related by T. A. M. Bishop to that of no. 23 (Benedictional of St. Ethelwold) and to the early part of no. 25 (Bibl. Nat., lat. 987) and which, according to Homburger recalls the hand of B.L. MS Royal 15. C. VII (Vita S. Swithuni, early 11th century, Old Minster, Winchester), was most probably itself also produced at Winchester. This attribution is supported by the decoration of the border (f. 14) and by the added Evangelist portrait (f. 58ᵛ), which, though its iconography and style depend on the Utrecht Psalter (cf. also no. 77, Titus D. XXVII, f. 75ᵛ), is generally related to the drawings produced at Winchester c. 1020-30. The manuscript appears to have been at the Abbey of Saint-Claude (Condat) in the Jura by the end of the 12th century.

LITERATURE: A. Castan, 'La bibliothèque de l'abbaye de Saint-Claude', *Bibliothèque de l'École des Chartes*, 1889, 329; *Catalogue général des manuscrits des bibliothèques publiques de France*, XXXII, 1897, 13; Homburger, 21 n. 3, 60, 65, 67, pl. X; Millar, I, 16, no. 34; Wormald, *English Drawings*, 59, 69, 73, no. 1; Talbot Rice, *English Art*, 194; Paris, Bibliothèque Nationale, *Les manuscrits à peintures en France du VIIe au XIIe siècles*, 1954, no. 276; A. Boutemy, 'L'enluminure anglaise de l'époque saxonne', *Bull. de la Société nationale des Antiquaires de France*, 1956, 48; D. Tselos, 'English manuscript illustration and the Utrecht Psalter', *Art Bulletin*, XLI, 1959, 141 n. 4; J. J. G. Alexander, 'A little-known Gospel Book from the later eleventh century from Exeter', *Burlington Magazine*, CVIII, 1966, 14 n. 45; J. J. G. Alexander and W. Cahn, 'An eleventh-century Gospel Book from Le Cateau', *Scriptorium*, XX, 1966, 252 n. 18; Bishop, *English Caroline*, no. 12; C. Nordenfalk, 'The Draped Lectern', *Intuition und Kunstwissenschaft: Festschrift für Hans Swarzenski*, Berlin 1973, 86, fig. 7.

77. London, British Library MS Cotton, Titus D. XXVI & D. XXVII

Prayers, Church Offices, Miscellanea, etc. (in Latin and Anglo-Saxon)

128 × 93 mm.

c. 1023-35. Winchester, New Minster

Ills. 243, 245, 246

Originally one manuscript, now bound in two separate parts containing full-page drawings which precede each of the principal liturgical texts.

A miniature in Part I, Titus D. XXVI, shows St. Peter enthroned under a trefoiled canopy on columns and adored by a monk, the donor Aelfwine (f. 19ᵛ); the drawing is executed in fine brown outline, shaded green and blue with touches of yellow in details.

Two illustrations are contained in Part II, Titus D. XXVII. The first shows a Crucifixion (f. 65ᵛ) with Christ alive on the cross flanked by the Virgin and St. John, the latter bearded and writing his testimony on a tablet (cf. nos. 41, Harley 2904; 80, Winchcombe Psalter; 93, Morgan 709), and above, the blessing Hand of God. A late antique motif of personifications of Sol and Luna, here shown in half-length figures above the cross bar, is novel in this context in English illumination (it occurs prominently in no. 64, Harley 603). The miniature, inscribed across the top '*Hec crux consignet Aelfwinum corpore mente*', also contains inscriptions in the background identifying the figures and has spindly plant motifs at the bottom of the picture, both characteristic of Winchester manuscripts (cf. nos. 5, Aethelstan Psalter; 78, New Minster Register; 98, Tiberius C. VI). An unusual representation of the Trinity (f. 75ᵛ), surrounded by a circular Glory, shows the first two Persons seated on a fragment of the firmament with the Enemy crouching under Christ's feet and the Virgin standing on the left holding the Christ Child in her arms while the Holy Dove perches on her head—an iconographic derivation from the Utrecht Psalter (cf. Kantorowicz, 'The Quinity', 1947). Below the circle of the Glory an open Hellmouth is shown with Arius and Judas, identified by inscriptions, on either side. The two illustrations are in brown ink with parts in red outline and a green shadow round the contours isolating the figure of Christ and the Hand of God above (f. 65ᵛ) and lining the rim of the Glory (f. 75ᵛ); there are also touches of blue in both pictures.

The miniatures in I and II are all by one artist and possibly, being closely allied in style to no. 78 (New Minster Register), by the same man. The impact of the Utrecht Psalter illustrations, evident in the delicate, animated, and expressive drawing, is tempered by the influence of the 'first style' apparent in the firmness of both the contour line and the long strokes marking the drapery folds. The initials are plain red, blue, purple, and, occasionally, green, with rubrics in red rustic capitals.

PROVENANCE: In the original binding Part II preceded Part I; the whole was written at the New Minster, Winchester, for Aelfwine while he was a deacon (he became Abbot between 1032 and 1035) as shown by obits in the Calendar (ff. 3–8ᵛ) of II. The latter contains also a cryptogram (f. 13ᵛ) recording his ownership ('*Aelwino monacho aeque decano . . . me possidet*') and the name of one of the scribes, a New Minster monk Aelsinus (ff. 68–75) who was also the main hand of no. 78 (New Minster Register). Annals accompanying an Easter table (f. 16ᵛ) in II are written in his hand up to 1023, while obits of Aelfwine's mother, 1029, and of Abbot Byrthmear,

1030, in a different hand, seem to indicate that the manuscript was completed by then. A prayer added to II in the 12th century (f. 74) suggests subsequent ownership by a woman. The manuscript belonged to Sir Robert Cotton (d. 1631) in 1621. His library, presented to the nation by his grandson, Sir John Cotton, in 1700 was incorporated in the British Museum in 1753.

LITERATURE: R. T. Hampson, *Medii Aevi Kalendarium*, 1847, I, 435; Westwood, *Facsimiles*, 112, 123–4; *Pal. Soc.*, I, pl. 60; W. de Gray Birch, *Early Drawings and Illumination*, 1878, XIX, pl. XI; *id.*, 'On Two Anglo-Saxon Manuscripts', *Royal Society of Literature Transactions*, 1878, 463–512; *id.*, 'Liber Vitae of New Minster and Hyde Abbey', *Hampshire Record Society*, 1892, App. D, 251 (Titus D. XXVI), App. E, 269 (Titus D. XXVII); Homburger, 21 n. 3, 67; F. A. Gasquet and E. Bishop, *The Bosworth Psalter*, 1908, 19–20, 48–50 and *passim*; British Museum, *Schools of Illumination*, I, 1914, pl. 12 b, c; Millar, I, 19, nos. 42, 43, pl. 24 a, b; O. Homburger, 'Review', *Art Bulletin*, X, 1928, 401; British Museum, *Reproductions from Illuminated Manuscripts*, IV, 1928, pl. 6; Saunders, *English Illumination*, 26, pl. 26b; F. Wormald, 'English Kalendars before 1100', *H.B.S.*, LXXII, 1934, no. 9; C. Niver, 'The Psalter in the British Museum, Harley 2904', *Medieval Studies in Memory of A. Kingsley Porter*, ed. W. R. W. Koehler, Cambridge, Mass. 1939, II, 670, 686 n. 77; E. Kantorowicz, 'The Quinity of Winchester', *Art Bulletin*, XXIX, 1947, 73–85, fig. 1; Kendrick, *Late Saxon*, 20; Wormald, *English Drawings*, 33–4, 59, 65, 69, 73, 76, 79, no. 33, pl. 16 a, b; Talbot Rice, *English Art*, 165, 213 n. 3, 217, pl. 82; Dodwell, *Canterbury School*, 23, pl. 13c; Ker, *Catalogue*, no. 202, p. 438; D. Tselos, 'English manuscript illustrations and the Utrecht Psalter', *Art Bulletin*, XLI, 1959, 139–40, 147, fig. 7; Rickert, *Miniatura*, 22, pl. 26–7; F. Wormald, 'Late Anglo-Saxon Art', *Studies in Western Art: Acts of the 20th Congress of the History of Art*, ed. M. Meiss, I, Princeton 1963, 20; W. Mersmann, 'Das Elfenbeinkreuz der Sammlung Topic-Mimara', *Wallraf-Richartz-Jahrbuch*, XXV, 1963, 45, 73, ill. 34; Rickert, *Painting in Britain*, 42–3, 227 n. 24, pl. 37b; Roosen-Runge, I, 58; Gneuss, 112–13; Bishop, *English Caroline*, p. XX, no. 26; G. Schiller, *Iconography of Christian Art*, 1971, I, 8, ill. 7; Wormald, *Angleterre*, 250, ill. 247.

EXHIBITED: Brussels, 1973, *English Illuminated Manuscripts 700–1500*, no. 11.

78. London, British Library MS Stowe 944
New Minster Register (Liber Vitae)
255 × 150 mm.
1031 (?). Winchester, New Minster

Ills. 244, 247, 248

This composite volume contains in its original part the Register and Martyrology of the New Minster and Hyde Abbey with lists of the brethren, monks, and benefactors, alive or deceased, whose names were to be commemorated during the services. The decoration of the manuscript consists of a frontispiece showing King Cnut and his Queen presenting an altar cross to the Abbey (f. 6) and of a vast composition extending over two pages portraying the Last Judgment (ff. 6v–7).

The first miniature, in type and details recalling the frontispiece of the King Edgar Charter (no. 16; cf. also an ivory plaque, *c.* 960 (?), Talbot Rice, pl. 32), represents Cnut and his wife Ælfgyfu, identified by inscriptions and attended by two angels, placing the cross on the altar in the presence of Christ in Majesty above, seated between the two patron saints of the New Minster, the Virgin and St. Peter; the scene is watched by a group of monks shown in their stalls at the bottom of the picture. Vivid and animated, the figure drawing is related to Wormald's 'first style' and the long, firm strokes marking the drapery folds contrast vigorously with the zigzagging hemlines; but there is a lightness and freshness in the drawing and a spontaneity of gestures, with the heads eagerly thrust forward, that reflect the Utrecht Psalter style. The miniature is in brown outline with certain details picked out by coloured washes, and the whole is enclosed within a plain linear frame of red and green.

The dramatic representation of the Last Judgment shows (f. 6v) a crowd of the Blessed headed by a haloed archbishop, and two angels conducting them towards Heaven on the opposite page (f. 7), with two more nimbed figures, a monk and a bishop in the forefront. The three-tiered composition on the next page has in the top part St. Peter welcoming the Blessed into Heaven—a walled city—where Christ is shown adored by His saints, and, below, the Apostle rescuing a soul from the devil, whom he strikes with his huge key, while on the right two despairing souls are rounded up by a winged demon; at the bottom of the picture the Damned are rushed into the gaping jaws of Hades and the angel on the left locks up Hell's door, a motif repeated in the twelfth-century Winchester Psalter (British Library, Cotton Nero C. IV). In its iconography, the miniature vaguely recalls the Last Judgment scenes carved on the 10th-century Irish stone crosses (cf. F. Henry, *Irish Art*, II, 1967, 173 n. 1), where, however, the head of Hades devouring the Damned is not shown; the motif belongs to the early Anglo-Saxon tradition for it appears on an 8th- or 9th-century ivory panel assigned to England, the earliest fully developed representation of the Last Judgment in the West (cf. J. Beckwith, *Ivory Carvings*, 1972, 22, ills. 1, 16). The head of Hades was, incidentally, to become a characteristic feature of English depictions of Hell (cf. nos. 58, the 'Caedmon' Genesis; 98, Tiberius C. VI).

The miniature is in the same style as the frontispiece (f. 6) but, though more delicate, the drawing is more free and lively. A sense of movement and drama runs through the whole frieze-like composition, the garments flare out excitedly at the hemlines, and the figures, admirably grouped in a series of vividly, and, at times, movingly expressive scenes, show an exuberant vitality and eagerness in gestures and postures that find the closest comparison in the drawings of the Utrecht Psalter. Tselos has shown (1959), in fact, that certain figures and details, otherwise without parallel, can be traced to the latter, and a direct connection between the two manuscripts is not unlikely (cf. also no. 77, New Minster Offices). As the Register was produced at the New Minster, Winchester, the scribe being Aelsinus, a monk of that house, it is highly probable that the Utrecht Psalter may have been at Winchester at some time.

Initials are plain blue or green and rubrics inscribed in red and green.

PROVENANCE: Additions apart, the manuscript was written at New Minster, Winchester, by Aelsinus (see above) identified as one of the scribes of no. 77 (New Minster Offices) and other Winchester manuscripts of the first half of the 11th century. It contains, besides the *Liber Vitae* of New Minster, miscellanea in Latin and Old English of various dates and of mainly domestic interest (cf. *Catalogue of Stowe MSS*, 1895, I, 623–30), among them charters of the second half of the 11th century (ff. 41, 59) in favour of Hyde Abbey in the hand of the copyist of Fulk's letter which was added to no. 68 (Grimbald Gospels). The manuscript, assigned to various dates between 1020 and 1030, was, however, probably produced in 1031, a date inscribed in the main hand over an erasure in a passage on the six ages of the world (f. 33ᵛ; cf. Ker, *Catalogue*). It belonged to Walter Clavel in 1710, then to George North and to his executor Michael Lort, who presented it to Thomas Astle in 1770 (f. 69); it was transferred with Astle's collection to Stowe in 1804 and acquired by the British Museum from Lord Ashburnham in 1883.

LITERATURE: *Pal. Soc.*, II, pls. 16, 17; W. G. Birch, 'Liber Vitae of New Minster and Hyde Abbey', *Hampshire Record Society*, 1892, frontispiece, pls. pp. VI, VII; J. A. Herbert, *Illuminated Manuscripts*, 1911, 117–18, pl. 13; Homburger, 21 n. 3, 57, 67; British Museum, *Schools of Illumination*, I, 1914, 19–20, pl. 13; H. P. Mitchell, 'Flotsam of Later Anglo-Saxon Art', *Burlington Magazine*, XLII, 1923, 64, 167, pl. II; *ib.*, XLIII, 1923, 108; British Museum, *Reproductions from Illuminated Manuscripts* 1924, II, pl. IV; Millar, I, 19–20, no. 51, pl. 25; Saunders, *English Illumination*, 24–6; A. Boeckler, *Abendländische Miniaturen*, Berlin 1930, 55; W. Weisbach, *Manierismus in mittelalterlicher Kunst*, Basle 1942, 23, pl. 15; Kendrick, *Late Saxon*, 18, 108, pls. XVIII, XX, 2; W. Oakeshott, *The Sequence of English Medieval Art*, 1950, 45, pls. 4, 22; Talbot Rice, *English Art*, 203–4, 217–18, 232, pls. 81, 84; Wormald, *English Drawings*, 17, 34, 39, 59, 64–5, 69, 72, no. 42, pl. 15; T. A. M. Bishop, *Notes*, II, 191; S. Schulten, 'Die Buchmalerei des 11. Jahrhunderts im Kloster St. Vaast in Arras', *Münchner Jahrbuch der bildenden Kunst*, VII, 1956, 56, 76, fig. 15; Ker, *Catalogue*, no. 274; W. Oakeshott, *Classical Inspiration in Medieval Art*, 1959,

59–60, pl. 82 (A), (B); Rickert, *Miniatura*, 22, pl. 28; D. Tselos, 'English manuscript illustration and the Utrecht Psalter', *Art Bulletin*, XLI, 1959, 191; W. Mersmann, 'Das Elfenbeinkreuz der Sammlung Topic-Mimara', *Wallraf-Richartz-Jahrbuch*, XXV, 1963, 13, fig. 6; F. Wormald, 'Late Anglo-Saxon Art: some questions and suggestions', *Studies in Western Art. Acts of the 20th Congress of the History of Art*, ed. M. Meiss, I, Princeton 1963, 21; Rickert, *Painting in Britain*, 42, pl. 37a; Bishop, *English Caroline*, no. 26; *English Illuminated Manuscripts 700–1500*, Brussels Exhibition Catalogue, 1973, p. 32; Wormald, *Angleterre* 250, ill. 251; R. Deshman, 'Anglo-Saxon Art After Alfred', *Art Bulletin*, LVI, 1974, 181.

79. Oxford, Bodleian Library MS Douce 296 (S.C. 21870)
Psalter
264 × 160 mm.
Second quarter of 11th century. (?) Crowland
Ill. 259, 260

The Psalms are preceded by a calendar and tables (ff. 1–8) with KL monograms and details in blue, red, and green, and are followed by canticles (f. 106), a litany (f. 117) and prayers. The gold-inscribed opening lines of Psalm 1 (f. 9) are introduced by a large initial B of a type derived from the great B of Harley 2904 (no. 41) but modified by the omission of animal heads from the interlace knotwork terminals adorning the shaft, and by the simplified designs of plant scrolls filling the bows which are clasped by a mask head; the interstices of the letter contain patterns of blue acanthus foliage within a gold framework and the whole is surrounded by a plain rectangular border in blue, green, and gold.

A full-page miniature (f. 40) prefacing Psalm 51 (f. 40ᵛ) shows Christ treading upon a dragon and a lion whose characteristically up-turned head He is transfixing with a cross-staff. This is the first example of a psalter illustration with a triumphant Christ (referring to Psalm 90, v. 13). The iconography, which belongs to the Early Christian tradition, was however established in the British Isles in the 7th to 8th centuries (cf. carved stone Bewcastle and Ruthwell crosses); it recurs in manuscript painting (cf. no. 56, Arenberg Gospels; 80, Winchcombe Psalter; 84, Bury Psalter) and ivory carvings (e.g. the Alcester Tau-Cross). The tall, small-headed figure of Christ, shown in a swift movement towards the left, is set on blank vellum ground and painted in soft washes of pale blue on the mantle, which is patterned rhythmically by broad, dark blue brush-strokes marking the folds, with pale ochre on the undergarment and gold in details, this free, vivacious style being a development from the painterly manner of such manuscripts as no. 66 (Arundel 155) and no. 72 (Robert of Jumièges Sacramentary). The miniature is enclosed by a modified 'Winchester' border of two gold bars supporting rather straggly and agitated blue, pink, and green foliage which projects outwards only. The first verse of Psalm 51 in gold, green, red, and blue capitals (f. 40ᵛ) is headed by a large, panelled initial Q topped by a mask head and containing in the bowl a figure in chain mail, probably St. Michael (though without wings), who, armed with a sword and shield, fights a winged dragon forming the tail of the letter. The composition is painted in pale blue, pink, orange, and gold. Psalm 101, of which the beginning is missing (after f. 72), was, no doubt, introduced by an ornamental initial and possibly a picture, to mark the tripartite division of the Psalter. A large gold initial D and the first verse in gold capitals emphasize Psalm 109 (f. 82), while a scrolled initial B followed by gold lettering introduces Psalm 118 (f. 86). An *explicit* (f. 105ᵛ) and the title to the first canticle (f. 106) are in alternating lines of red, green, and blue capitals.

PROVENANCE: The Psalter is attributable to Crowland in the Fens on the evidence of the calendar (ff. 1–6ᵛ) and the litany (f. 117) in both of which St. Guthlac is especially honoured. The name of St. Florentinus (relics in Peterborough from 1015) invoked in the litany, and the entry for Ælfred, brother of Edward the Confessor (d. 1036), an addition in the calendar (f. 5), suggest a date for the manuscript between 1013 and 1036. The 12th-century obits (f. 2ᵛ) seem to indicate that by that time the Psalter had probably reached St. Pancras, Lewes. Sale of John Jackson, 28 April 1794, lot 364; entered the Bodleian Library in 1834 with the bequest of Francis Douce.

LITERATURE: G. F. Waagen, *Kunstwerke und Künstler in England*, Leipzig 1854, III; 90; Westwood, *Facsimiles*, 122; F. A. Gasquet and E. Bishop, *The Bosworth Psalter*, 1908, 34 n. 1, and *passim*; Homburger, 55, 60 n. 1, 62, 67, pl. XI; Sir Ivor Atkins, 'An Investigation of Two Anglo-Saxon Calendars', *Archaeologia*, LXXVIII, 1928, 22 n. 5, 225, 239; Millar, I, no. 35; Saunders, *English Illumination*, 26–7, pl. 27; F. Wormald, 'English Kalendars before A.D. 1100', *H.B.S.*, LXXII, 1933, xiii, no. 20; C. Niver, 'The Psalter in the British Museum, Harley 2904', *Medieval Studies in Memory of A. Kingsley Porter*, ed. W. R. W. Koehler, Cambridge, Mass. 1939, II, 679, 684 n. 72, 687 n. 81; F. Saxl and R. Wittkower, *British Art and the Mediterranean*, 1948, pl. 21 (7); *Scenes from the Life of Christ in English Manuscripts*, (Bodleian Library Picture Book no. 5), 1951, pl. 23; Talbot Rice, *English Art*, 200, 210, pl. 75a; Freyhan, 426–6, pl. XXXVI, fig. 9; Rickert, *Miniatura*, 22, pl. 24; *id.*, *Painting in Britain*, 52, 226 n. 16, pl. 42; Roosen-Runge, I, 67 ff., ills. 9, 10; Gneuss 113; Alexander, *Norman Illumination*, 121 n. 3, 148 n. 3, 150, 169 n. 3; *Anglo-Saxon Illumination*, pls. 24–5; Pächt and Alexander, no. 43, pl. V; Wormald, *Angleterre*, 251.

80. Cambridge, University Library MS Ff. I. 23

Psalter. Roman version with Old English gloss
270 × 160 mm.
c. 1030–50. Winchcombe Abbey, Gloucestershire
Ills. 249–53

This copiously illuminated Psalter contains four full-page, framed drawings and corresponding decorative pages with large initials to Psalms 1, 51, 101, and 109; in addition, a remarkable series of ornamental initials introduces all psalms, canticles, and prayers; all of these are in dark sepia outline with some brown and green washes and details in green, minium orange, and yellow.

The first miniature (f. 4ᵛ) shows David harping, enthroned under a trilobed architectural canopy and accompanied by his four musicians identified by inscriptions; the whole, a crowded and compartmented composition recalling 8th-century Insular manuscripts in its 'horror vacui', is surrounded by a 'Winchester' frame with foliated corner bosses and panels of emaciated tree-type acanthus on a dark sepia ground. A large Beatus initial on the opposite page (f. 5), having interlace terminals on the shaft and a mask head joining the bows, derives structurally from the great B of no. 41 (Harley 2904) but contrasts with the lushness of the latter's foliage by having scrolls of wiry, long-tendrilled acanthus leaves; the frame is composed of four round corner bosses and panels with foliage on dark sepia ground spilling in straggly and unruly curls either outwards or inwards over the edging bars.

The Crucifixion (f. 88) which precedes Psalm 51 (f. 88ᵛ), shows Christ dead on the cross blessed by the Hand of God above and flanked by Mary and John, the latter writing his testimony on a tablet, a coarsened version of an Anglo-Saxon iconographic feature first occurring in the Harley Crucifixion (no. 41, f. 3ᵛ; cf. also nos. 77, New Minster Offices; 93, Morgan 709). The weeping personifications of Sol and Luna in roundels are placed over the cross bar (cf. nos. 77 and, particularly, 93, where they are also weeping). Christ's nimbus is green with an orange cross, those of the Virgin and John are yellow and inscriptions in the background are in green lettering; the miniature is enclosed by a narrow border of contained acanthus patterns. An initial 'q' (f. 88ᵛ) with an interlace knotwork terminal and an acanthus scroll in the bowl is partly painted in green and orange and surrounded by a panelled frame with square ornaments on the angles and two roundels containing bust figures.

A miniature (f. 171) shows Christ seated in a mandorla held by four angels; His right hand raised in blessing, His left resting on a book, He is supporting an inscribed scroll laid across His arms, and the whole is enclosed by a frame with acanthus medallions and contained leaf patterns on dark ground. There is more colour in the details of this drawing as well as in the shading of the draperies. The particularly prominent circular marking of the angels' shoulders recalls St. Matthew's portrait in no. 73 (Pembroke College 301; cf. also Bristol slab, *c.* 1020, Talbot Rice, *English Art*, pl. 12). A large initial D (f. 171ᵛ) heading Psalm 101 is made up of scroll-filled panels with animal-headed interlace terminals and is surrounded by a border of confined leaf motifs. The last full-page drawing (f. 195ᵛ), framed by lines of sepia and orange, prefaces Psalm 109. It represents Christ triumphant treading the beasts and thrusting His cross shaft into the dragon's mouth (cf. no. 79, Douce 296). The opening verses of the Psalm are headed by a scroll-filled initial D.

The decoration of the small initials introducing all psalms, canticles, etc., displays a great diversity of motifs and a remarkable ingenuity in their application. There are scroll and foliage initials, often with animal heads; Wormald Type I initials made up of dragons (some with fat, solid bodies and ridged backs recalling no. 18, Salisbury Psalter, others turned into abstract ornament), and a number of initials composed of human figures. These anthropoid letters anticipate the twelfth-century Romanesque decorative style not only by the dynamic treatment of the human figure (e.g. two nudes forming an M by the curves of their bodies) but also by the artist's lighthearted, humorous delight in his portrayals. The leaf ornament is of a distinct, often extremely attenuated type, the culmination of a trend running through Anglo-Saxon decoration from the later tenth century onwards, and the foliage turns into de-leaved tendrils and scrolls with hooked ends and a straggly and dishevelled appearance that have a 'Scandinavian' flavour about them. The 'Scandinavianisms' in English art were hitherto credited to the influence of the Scandinavian Jellinge and Ringerike styles (cf. no. 58, 'Caedmon' Genesis), but Holmquist has shown that they are a development from native southern English sources and that, on the evidence of datable monuments, the Scandinavian styles in question were, in fact, inspired by English art.

Probably both miniatures and initials copy models of various styles and from various periods. Wormald has suggested a model related to the York Gospels for the flowing drapery designs in the miniature of David (f. 4ᵛ) and he distinguishes two hands in the decoration of the Psalter: one working in the 'first style', responsible for the David drawing, and the other, who did the remaining pictures and all the initials, showing connections with the 'Utrecht' style. The two hands are extremely close, however, and it is likely that the whole decoration was executed by one man—note the little lion at David's feet (f. 4ᵛ), which reappears above the frame of Christ in Majesty (f. 171), the stylistic disparities being perhaps due to differences in the models copied. It is a coarsened and eclectic style in which new and bold interpretations (figure initials) of known but rare features mingle with motifs of a rather retrospective character (dragonesque initials, foliage initials combining wiry interlace knotwork, etc.).

The Old English gloss is written throughout in red ink, aligned with the text: the script of both recalls that of no. 74 (Trinity B. 15. 34, cf. Ker, *Catalogue*). Marks composed of strokes radiating from the centre of a few circlets after some psalms and prayers also occur in the latter. Titles are in green rustic capitals and verse initials in red.

PROVENANCE: The manuscript, whose origin is uncertain, has been assigned to Winchcombe Abbey, Glos., on account of the prominence given to St. Kenelm in the litany (f. 175), his name being inscribed in capitals in the main hand at the head of the English martyrs. The Psalter, which may have been in the library of Christ Church, Canterbury, (cf. James, *Ancient Libraries*), was given by Archbishop Parker to his friend, Sir Nicholas Bacon. He in turn presented the volume to the Cambridge Library in 1574 (f. 1), and his armorial book-plate and date are on the front paste-down with old Cambridge marks, 'D. 3. 4.' and '256' inscribed above.

LITERATURE: J. O. Westwood, *Paleographia Sacra*, 1849, no. 41, figs. 1, 2; James, *Ancient Libraries*, App. D, no. 527; Millar, I, no. 55; C. Niver, 'The Psalter in the British Museum, Harley 2904', *Medieval Studies in Memory of A. Kingsley Porter*, ed. W. R. W. Koehler, Cambridge, Mass. 1939, II, 679 n. 50, 686, fig. 4; T. D. Kendrick, 'The Viking Taste in Pre-Conquest England', *Antiquity*, XV, 1941, 125–41; F. Wormald, 'The Survival of Anglo-Saxon Illumination', *Proceedings of the British Academy*, XXX, 1944, 129; id., *Initials*, 109 n. 2, 110–11, 119 n. 4, 125 n. 1, 133, pls. Ib, VId, VII b, c; Kendrick, *Late Saxon*, 34, 105, pls. LXXIII (1), LXXIV; C. E. Wright, 'The dispersal of the monastic libraries and the beginning of Anglo-Saxon studies', *Transactions of the Cambridge Bibliographical Society*, 1949–53, 225; Holmquist, *Viking Art*, 15–24, 48, 55, figs. 9–11, 17, 20, 21, 22; Wormald, *English Drawings*, 40–1, 59, 60–1, no. 2, pls. 20, 21; Talbot Rice, *English Art*, 129, 220; Dodwell, *Canterbury School*, 10–13, 20, 26, 31, pls. 5e, 8a, 9b, 10c; S. Schulten, 'Die Buchmalerei des 11. Jahrhunderts im Kloster St. Vaast in Arras', *Münchner Jahrbuch der bildenden Kunst*, VII, 1956, 52, 76, fig. 4; H. Steger, *David Rex et Propheta*, Nürnberg, 1961, pl. 12, fig. 26; Ker, *Catalogue*, no. 13; Alexander, *Norman Illumination*, 61, n. 1, 63 n. 1, 64, 70, 73, 148 n. 3, 171 n. 6, 189; Wormald, *Angleterre*, 235, fig. 229.

81. Cambridge, Corpus Christi College MS 41

Bede, Historia ecclesiastica. In Anglo-Saxon
349×215 mm.
First half of 11th century

Ill. 255, 258, 261

The illumination consists of numerous initials mainly in brown outline with occasional faint red washes. Some initials are in pencil sketch only and some were never inserted, leaving a number of spaces blank. The decoration of uneven quality contains a remarkable diversity of motifs and is in various hands. It includes Wormald Type I initials of excellent workmanship largely formed of dragons (a B, p. 246, with two dragons in the loops and a mask head, recalls the Roman capital letters in no. 18, Salisbury Psalter); Type II(b) initials with heads and interlace of a mixed type; some initials inhabited by beasts or figures or containing figures in their structure, while a D is historiated with a delicate drawing of Christ on the cross blessed by the Hand of God above, its bow made of two dragons (p. 410); and a few initials of a rudimentary 'clambering' type (cf. nos. 18, Salisbury Psalter; 65, Trinity Gospels). A fine full-page, unfinished drawing of Christ crucified (p. 484) is surrounded by text-lines written around and over it. The manuscript also contains some rough marginal sketches and various liturgical texts added in blank spaces and in the margins in the early or mid 11th century, and including part of a verse dialogue between Solomon and Saturn.

Wormald has related the style and type of decoration to that of the Winchcombe Psalter (no. 80), observing that the initials in the present volume are more delicate than those in the latter.

PROVENANCE: The manuscript is of unknown origin and was, in spite of the scribe's assertion that he wrote it 'with his two hands' (p. 483, 4; cf. James, *Catalogue*), apparently written in two main portions by two scribes simultaneously. The volume was given to St. Peter's, Exeter, by Bishop Leofric, 1046–72, as recorded in Latin and Anglo-Saxon (p. 488). It was bequeathed to Corpus Christi College by Archbishop Parker in 1575.

LITERATURE: M. R. James, *A descriptive catalogue of manuscripts in the Library of Corpus Christi College, Cambridge*, 1909, I, 82; Wormald, *Initials*, 119 n. 4, 125 n. 6, 133; Kendrick, *Late Saxon*, 33; Wormald, *English Drawings*, 60, no. 5; Dodwell, *Canterbury School*, 12; Ker, *Catalogue*, n. 32.

82. Cambridge, Corpus Christi College MS 421 (pp. 1, 2)

Anglo-Saxon Homilies
200 × 125 mm.
Second quarter of 11th century

Ill. 254

The manuscript contains a frontispiece (p. 1) showing the crucified Christ blessed by the Hand of God and accompanied by the Virgin and St. John. Two plant scrolls fill the space above the bar of the cross which has stepped extremities and a dragon (serpent?) at its foot, a motif uncommon in this context in Anglo-Saxon illumination (cf. Bury Psalter, no. 84, f. 35), suggesting a model in Carolingian ivory carvings (cf. Goldschmidt, *Elfenbeinskulpturen*, I, 41, 43, etc.; cf. also the Drogo Sacramentary, f. 43ᵛ). The drawing, in brown outline heavily washed in red, has been related stylistically by Wormald to no. 80 (Winchcombe Psalter) and manuscripts connected with it. Initials are in red or blue with rubrics inscribed in red.
The leaf with the drawing (pp. 1, 2), which originally belonged to a companion volume, Cambridge, Corpus Christi College MS 419, has been detached and, according to Ker (cf. *Catalogue*), bound up reversed with the present manuscript. The scribe of Corpus Christi College 419 also wrote part of Corpus Christi College 421; the rest consists of additions in

a somewhat later hand, mid 11th century or soon after, probably written at Exeter in a distinctively 'Exeter' type of script (cf. Ker, *Medieval Libraries*).

PROVENANCE: The present manuscript and its companion volume were both bequeathed to Corpus Christi College by Archbishop Parker in 1575.

LITERATURE: Wormald, *English Drawings*, 62 no. 13; Bishop, *Notes*, II, 198; Ker, *Catalogue*, nos. 68, 69; *id.*, *Medieval Libraries of Great Britain*, 1964, p. XXI n. 8.

83. Paris, Bibliothèque Nationale MS lat. 8824

Psalter. Roman version. In Latin and Anglo-Saxon
526 × 186 mm.
Second quarter of 11th century

Ills. 208, 209

The Psalter is written in two narrow, parallel columns in Latin and Old English. As recorded in the 1402 inventory of the Duc de Berry's possessions, besides the remaining drawings (all but one of which refer to the Latin text), it originally contained a frontispiece with David harping, pages with coloured decoration prefacing Psalms 26, 38, 51, 68, 80, 97, 109, and a similar page between the end of the Psalms and the beginning of the canticles (after f. 175). All have been removed. The thirteen tiny drawings—one, two, or three to a page—illustrate quite literally certain verses of Psalms 1 to 7 (ff. 1–6). They are placed within the text column of the Latin version (except on f. 4), thus establishing a close relationship between script and image which derives from the Late Antique tradition. They represent:

1. River god, flowering tree on the right (f. 1);
2. Bust figure of Christ, cluster of heads below (f. 1ᵛ);
3. Christ breaking a potter's vessel with a long rod (f. 2);
4. Hand of God supporting the head of a kneeling figure (f. 2ᵛ);
5. Hand of God emerging from the clouds towards a man in prayer (f. 3);
6. Man approaching an altar holding a cup and a ram (f. 3);
7. Figure carrying a sack followed by another with a vessel (f. 3);
8. Hand of God with dividers, psalmist below appealing to the Lord (f. 3ᵛ);
9. Hell's mouth filled with heads (f. 3ᵛ);
10. Two men fighting (f. 4);
11. Lion standing over a fallen figure (f. 5);
12. Psalmist praying before the Hand of God (f. 5);
13. Embracing couple shot at by the devil (f. 6).

All but four drawings (nos. 4, 7, 8, 13) belong iconographically to the Utrecht Psalter tradition, corresponding more or less closely to its illustrations; no. 8 has parallels in Anglo-Saxon illumination (cf. nos. 67, Eadui Codex; 98, Tiberius C. VI;

102, Royal I. E. VII), while no. 13, though inserted in the Latin column, illustrates the Old English paraphrase and is probably an original invention of the artist. The drawings which are stylistically connected with Canterbury manuscripts (cf. no. 66, Arundel 155) closely recall the sketchy vignettes inserted by Hand E into blank spaces of the text-column in Harley 603 (no. 64), and may possibly be by the same artist. A plain gold initial B introduces Psalm 1 (f. 1); other initials are in gold, blue, and green with Latin headings in red rustic capitals.

The Psalter contains a unique copy of a prose paraphrase in Old English of Psalms 1 to 50, followed by Psalms 51 to 150 in Anglo-Saxon metrical translation. The manuscript was written by a scribe naming himself in the colophon (f. 186) as Wulfsin ('*id est cognomento cada*'); his handwriting and an invocation to St. Martial in the litany as the last of the Apostles (ff. 183v–4), point to a date after 1030. Certain prayers (ff. 185–6) mainly in the singular with some in the feminine form, and a clause (f. 184v): '*ut episcopum (nostrum)* . . .' suggest that the manuscript, possibly produced at Canterbury (stylistic and iconographic evidence), was probably destined for a lady not connected with the Canterbury diocese.

PROVENANCE: The volume belonged to the Duc de Berry (1340–1416) being inscribed '*Ce livre est au duc de Berry*', with a signature 'Jehan' beneath it (f. 186). It was described in the inventories of his possessions (print. J. J. Guiffrey, *Inventaires de Jean duc de Berry* (1401–1416), II, 131, no. 1027), and given by him to the Sainte-Chapelle at Bourges in 1406; offered by the Chapter to Louis XV, it entered the Bibliothèque Nationale with the royal collection.

LITERATURE: Comte A. de Bastard, *Librairie de Jean de France, Duc de Berry*, Paris 1834, drawings reproduced; L. Delisle, 'Notes sur la Bibliothèque de la Sainte-Chapelle de Bourges', *Bibl. de l'École des Chartes*, 4e série, Paris 1856, 147–51; *id., Cabinet des manuscrits*, Paris 1868, I, 58, 65, 420, III, 172, 173 n. 18; Westwood, *Facsimiles*, 121; A. Goldschmidt, *Der Albani Psalter in Hildesheim*, Berlin 1895, 17; Homburger, 22 n. 2; *New Pal. Soc.*, II, pls. 123, 124; Millar, I, no. 56; G. Haseloff, *Die Psalterillustration im 13. Jahrhundert*, Kiel 1938, 3; V. Leroquais, *Les Psautiers manuscrits des bibliothèques de France*, Paris 1940–1, II, 76; Wormald, *English Drawings*, 43, 78, no. 55; Talbot Rice, *English Art*, 219; Ker, *Catalogue*, no. 367; Nordenfalk, *Early Medieval*, 186; B. Colgrave, *The Paris Psalter* (E.E.MSS in facs., 1958), with full bibliography; D. Tselos, 'English manuscript illustration and the Utrecht Psalter', *Art Bulletin*, XLI, 1959, 149; R. M. Harris, 'The marginal drawings of the Bury St. Edmunds Psalter' (Princeton Univ. Phil.D., 1960, Univ. Microfilms), 28–9, figs. 1–13; *id.*, 'An illustration in an Anglo-Saxon Psalter in Paris', *J.W.C.I.*, XVI, 1963, 255–63, pl. 316; Rickert *Painting in Britain*, 224 n. 60; M. Meiss, *French Painting in the Time of Jean de Berry*, 1967, 43 n. 77, 316; J. Vezin, 'Manuscrits des dixième et onzième

siècles copiés en Angleterre en minuscule caroline et conservés à la Bibliothèque nationale de Paris', *Mélanges offerts à Julien Cain*, Paris 1968, 286, 291–2.

84. Rome, Vatican, Biblioteca Apostolica MS Reg. lat. 12

Psalter (Bury Psalter). Gallican version
326 × 244 mm.
Second quarter of 11th century. Canterbury, Christ Church

Ills. 262–264, fig. 26

The Psalter is preceded by a calendar (ff. 7–12) with KL monograms and certain Bury feasts in gold. It contains, besides 53 marginal drawings, two framed initial pages introducing Psalms 1 (f. 21) and 51 (f. 62). An initial B (f. 21), with animal-headed interlace knotwork at the top and bottom and a roundel midway up the shaft with a monk writing (portrait of the scribe?), has bows tightly filled with large-leaved scrolls terminating in griffins' heads. The opening words of Psalm 1 are inscribed in lines of coloured capitals and the whole is enclosed by a 'Winchester' border of gold-framed panels with heavy stylized foliage growing outwards only, four rosettes on the corners, and two square medallions with birds on the laterals. The initial Q (f. 62), inscribed across the top '*oliva fructifera*', contains in its bowl a crowned, enthroned Virgin holding sceptre and palm, a splendid dragon at her feet entwined into the frame of the latter and forming its tail; the border of straggly acanthus patterns between two gold bars has roundels on two sides containing female bust figures who, with books in their veiled hands, look up adoring the Virgin. A space is left for an ornamental initial to Psalm 101 (f. 104) which was meant to complete the tripartite division of the Psalter but was never executed. A large plain gold initial D (f. 117) introduces Psalm 109.

The drawings in coloured outline of brown, red, and some green, with touches of gold and, occasionally, other colours, are disposed quite freely in the margins, often running into the text column (the Crucifixion, f. 35, is partly in outline and partly in body colour; cf. nos. 23, Benedictional of St. Ethelwold, f. 118v; 58, the 'Caedmon' Genesis, p. 11; 66, Arundel 155, f. 133). They are extraordinarily varied in subject, being for the most part literal illustrations of nearby passages. They largely derive from the imagery of the Utrecht Psalter or the later drawings of its Canterbury copy, Harley 603 (no. 64, ff. 58–73v), contracted and adapted to the marginal space. Seven drawings (ff. 22v, 28, 30v, 36, 37v top, 37v bottom) correspond to the marginalia added, probably by an Anglo-Saxon artist, to the Otbert Psalter (Boulogne MS 20), c. 1000, and thereby suggest the existence in the late tenth century of an archetype that served both manuscripts. The present volume introduces a number of iconographical innovations. Some are possibly due to liturgical or ceremonial practice, e.g. f. 96v, genuflection of the anointed David; f. 22v, the psalmist (Christ) rising from a sarcophagus, thus anticipating the iconography of the Resurrection; others derive from models outside the Utrecht Psalter tradition (e.g. f. 71ᵛ, Christ rescuing a soul from purgatory and walking away as in the Byzantine Anastasis), or they are inspired by contemporary literary sources (e.g. f. 68ᵛ, a diagrammatic representation of the Creator; cf. Heimann, 1966).

Besides Old Testament subjects, the miniatures represent a cycle of New Testament scenes which include a Nativity of Anglo-Saxon type (f. 93; cf. nos. 23, Benedictional of St. Ethelwold; 44, Boulogne Gospels; etc.) and an Ascension (f. 73) with the 'disappearing Christ' (cf. nos. 58, 'Caedmon' Genesis; 72, Robert of Jumièges Sacramentary; etc.). The Crucifixion (f. 35) contains a motif extremely rare in Anglo-Saxon painting—a serpent coiled at the foot of the cross (cf. no. 82, Corpus Christi College 421; for Carolingian prototypes cf. the Drogo Sacramentary, f. 43ᵛ, also Goldschmidt, I, 41, 44, etc.). The Trinity is represented twice and both portrayals are new interpretations of a theme that was of special interest to Anglo-Saxon artists (cf. Wormald, 1963). The first (Psalm 78, f. 88) shows a sceptred God the Father, a shield-and-sword-bearing Son and the Holy Ghost as an eagle-like bird. The second (prayers to the Three Persons, ff. 168ᵛ–169), has the Lord in a mandorla, the Holy Lamb in a roundel below (cf. nos. 32, Bibl. Nat., lat. 6401; 98, Tiberius C. VI), and the Dove similarly presented on the page opposite (f. 169).

The expressive, animated, yet delicate drawings, most probably executed by the same artist, are in firm, swinging, and sweeping lines contrasting vividly with the flutter of wind-puffed drapery hemlines, and, at times, the quick, nervous strokes of the contours—a contrast imparting a buoyant vitality to the figures. This dynamic calligraphic style, with close analogies in Canterbury manuscripts of c. 1000 and soon after (cf. nos. 55, Royal 1. E. XI; 56, Arenberg Gospels; 64, Harley 603, particularly Hands E and F) is a heightened version of the style found in Arundel 155 (no. 66), a fusion of the 'first' and the 'Utrecht' styles but with a more pronounced tendency to reduce the whole to a pattern and showing 'the skilful and sensitive use of line' (cf. Wormald, *English Drawings*, p. 47) without the mannerisms occurring in the somewhat later manuscript from Christ Church, Tiberius A. III (no. 100). The similarities between the Bury drawings and those in Arundel 155 are striking (cf. figure type, postures, gestures, drapery designs, etc.); they suggest that the two manuscripts cannot be far apart in date and that on stylistic evidence the Bury Psalter ought to be assigned to a date not much later than 1030–5. The extensive use in the Bury drawings of philacteries, often inscribed (also found in the Boulogne Gospels, no. 44), is typical of Canterbury manuscripts of that period. Initials to psalms are in gold with rubrics in red.

The Psalter was written for Bury St. Edmunds Abbey as appears from the calendar (ff. 7–12), which has gold-inscribed feasts of SS. Hiurmin (Transl.), Botulf (Transl.), and Edmund (Transl. and Nat.) and a dedication of the Bury church (18 Oct.). Other evidence includes a prayer to the Virgin and St. Edmund (f. 162ᵛ), also references added in the Easter Tables (ff. 16ᵛ–19) to the new foundation of the monastic community 1020–4, and the consecration of the new church 1032–5 by Aethelnoth, Archbishop of Canterbury 1020–38. The manuscript could hardly, however, have been made at Bury since the new foundation was probably not organized in the second quarter of the 11th century for the production of richly decorated books (cf. no. 75, Bury Gospels). Moreover, stylistic considerations and links with Utrecht–Harley 603 imagery provide sufficient indications of the Psalter's origin in Christ Church, Canterbury (cf. Harris), suggesting that it may have been one of a number of important illuminated manuscripts probably produced at Canterbury to be sent elsewhere (cf. nos. 35, Sherborne Pontifical; 68, Grimbald Gospels(?); 75, Bury Gospels; etc.). The dating of the Psalter, which is highly controversial and varies from c. 1020 to mid 11th century, has been linked with the year of the translations of SS. Hiurmin and Botulf, included in the calendar. These were apparently carried out under the sanction of Cnut (d. 1035), and were probably effected in his lifetime rather than under Abbot Leofsin, 1044–65, as somewhat indefinitely indicated by the annotator of Bodleian MS Bodley 297 (cf. Atkins, *Archaeologia*, 222 n. 4). Thus the date suggested for the Psalter on stylistic grounds remains entirely plausible.

PROVENANCE: The Psalter ends incomplete in the middle of a prayer (f. 181). The next leaf (f. 182) with a list of relics of Jouarre Abbey, Meaux diocese, was added in the 12th century, and a prayer was copied for an abbess (f. 160; cf. Wilmart) at the end of the 11th century, indicating that the Psalter had left Canterbury and perhaps England by that time. The manuscript is inscribed '*Jhe(a)nne De colancourt*' (f. 94ᵛ), 15th century, and '*Madedoin*' with below '*Jacques*' (f. 40), 16th- to 17th century. A pasted-in title (f. 1) was written by a collector A. Petau from Orléans, the bulk of whose collection was sold to Queen Christina of Sweden in 1650. The volume subsequently came into the possession of Cardinal Ottobuoni, later Pope Alexander VIII, whence it entered the Vatican Library in 1690.

LITERATURE: F. A. Gasquet and E. Bishop, *The Bosworth Psalter*, 1908, 60 n. 1, 147; G. F. Warner and H. A. Wilson, *The Benedictional of St. Aethelwold*, 1910, pp. XXXI n. 4, XLI; *New Pal. Soc.*, II, pls. 166–8; Millar, I, 15, 19, no. 26, pls. 19, 20; O. Homburger, 'Review', *Art Bulletin*, X, 1928, 400; J. Atkins, 'An Investigation of Two Anglo-Saxon Calendars', *Archaeologia*, 2nd. ser., XXVIII, 1928, 222 n. 4, 223, 226, 230, 254; A. Wilmart, 'The Prayers of the Bury Psalter', *Downside Review*, 48, 1930, 198–216; F. Wormald, 'English Kalendars before A.D. 1100'. *H.B.S.*, LXXIII, 1934, no. 19; A. Wilmart, *Codices Reginenses Latini*, Vatican 1937, I, vii, 30–5; C. Niver, 'The Psalter in the British Museum, Harley 2904',

Medieval Studies in Memory of A. Kingsley Porter, ed. W. R. W. Koehler, Cambridge, Mass. 1939, II, 641; Wormald, *Initials*, 109 n. 3, 132; H. Foester, *Mittelalterliche Buch- und Urkundenschriften*, Bern 1946, 434–7, pl. XVIIa; F. Saxl and R. Wittkower, *British Art and the Mediterranean*, 1948, pl. 21 (5); Kendrick, *Late Saxon*, 18, 22, 103, pl. XIX, 1; W. Oakeshott, *The sequence of English medieval art*, 1950, 44, pls. 20, 21; Wormald, *English Drawings*, 47–8, 64, 68, 71, 79, no. 56, pls. 26–8; Talbot Rice, *English Art*, 207, pl. 71a; Dodwell, *Canterbury School*, 10, 27, 74, 79, pl. 59c, B. Raw, 'The Drawing of an Angel in MS. 28, St. John's College, Oxford', *J.W.C.I.*, XVIII, 1955, 318–19, pl. 63b; Freyhan, 430; A. Boutemy, 'L'enluminure anglaise de l'époque saxonne', *Bull. de la Soc. nationale des Antiquaires de France*, 1956, 49; Nordenfalk, *Early Medieval*, 186, ill. 185; W. Oakeshott, *Classical inspiration in medieval art*, 1959, 61, pl. 53 (B); Rickert, *Miniatura*, 14, 17, 22, pl. 20; *St. Albans Psalter*, 51 n. 2, 54 n. 3, 85, 159 n. 1, pl. 128a; R. M. Harris, 'The marginal drawings of the Bury St. Edmunds Psalter' (Princeton University Phil.D., 1960, University Microfilm); *id.*, 'An illustration in an Anglo-Saxon Psalter in Paris', *J.W.C.I.*, XVI, 1963, 257–8; W. Mersmann, Das Elfenbeinkreuz der Sammlung Topic-Mimara', *Wallraf-Richartz-Jahrbuch*, XXV, 1963, 58, fig. 48; Rickert, *Painting in Britain*, 44–5, pl. 39; A. Heimann, 'Three illustrations from Bury St. Edmunds Psalter and their prototypes', *J.W.C.I.* XXIX, 1966, 39–59, pls. 9b, 12b, 13d; Swarzenski, *Monuments*, pl. 60, fig. 134; M. W. Evans, *Medieval Drawings*, 1969, 23, pl. 21; Alexander, *Norman Illumination*, 61 n. 1, 74 n. 3, 120 n. 3, 122 n. 3, 135, 139, 148 n. 3, Dodwell, *Techniques*, 650; Wormald, *Winchester School*, 312; *id.*, *Angleterre*, 250, ill. 252; Robb, *Illuminated Manuscript*, 152, fig. 94; C. R. Dodwell, Peter Clemoes, *The Old English Illustrated Hexateuch* (E.E. MSS in facs., XVIII) 1974, 58.

85. London, British Library MS Royal 15. A. XVI (f. 84)

Drawing added to an earlier manuscript
210×145 mm.
Second quarter of 11th century.
Canterbury, St. Augustine's

Ill. 211

The drawing is added on the fly-leaf (f. 84) of a 9th/10th century manuscript, probably continental, containing miscellaneous matter. It shows a towered, elaborately roofed building which Wormald (*English Drawings*) has related to the representation of the Lord's Temple in the illustration to Psalm 26 in the Utrecht Psalter. He has also observed that the rocky landscape with dark patches at the top of some of the hummocks is paralleled in the drawings by Hand 'E' in Harley 603 (no. 64) and he has assigned the drawing, executed in vigorous, dark brown outline, to the second quarter of the 11th century. The two towers on the outside of the building are apparently a 16th-century addition.

PROVENANCE: The manuscript belonged to St. Augustine's, Canterbury, as shown by a 13th-century press-mark (f. 1). The drawing was undoubtedly added in one of the two Canterbury houses.

LITERATURE: James, *Ancient Libraries*, 342, no. 1438; Warner and Gilson, II, 146; Wormald, *English Drawings*, 44, 72, no. 41, pl. 25a; Bishop, Codex Leidensis, p. XX (19).

86. London, British Library MS Cotton, Claudius B. IV

Aelfric's Paraphrase of Pentateuch and Joshua.
In Anglo-Saxon
342×217 mm.
Second quarter of 11th century.
Canterbury, St. Augustine's

Ills. 265–272, fig. 34

This Anglo-Saxon version of the first six Books of the Bible, based in part on Aelfric's translation and in part on later anonymous work, contains a most remarkable and extensive cycle of over four hundred illustrations. These are full-page and half-page painted compositions or uncoloured drawings (ff. 21–55), often in red, blue, and purple outline, either in continuous narrative or divided into scenes by plain linear frames. Some pictures towards the end are unfinished and compositions merely laid out in blotches of colour show the progress of work in various stages with a few places for illustrations remaining blank. A number of drawings are ruined by Latin commentaries and titles added in the twelfth century.

The miniatures are probably by one artist (for a different view, cf. Ker, *Catalogue*; Wormald, 1973). He is responsible for all underdrawing and for the painting, which is in shades of milky blue, orange, pale mauve to grey, pink, brown, and some yellow, with, however, occasional overpainting and retouching in black by various later hands. The figures, with mainly blue, wig-like hair and tiny feet, are stiff in movement and have awkward gestures; but the swarming, fluttering angels (e.g. f. 29) and some female figures are more delicately portrayed and endowed with a charming lyrical quality. Preponderantly blue and orange (after f. 6), the figures are often set in strip compositions on blank vellum ground and with repetitive profiles showing the artist's interest in unfolding the story rather than representing particular episodes. Thus most of the drawings, if somewhat crude and incompetent in places, possess nevertheless a remarkable narrative quality, while a few illustrations, particularly in the series of the Creation headed by a grandiose frontispiece depicting the Fall of the rebel angels (f. 2), are strikingly monumental and expressive. These variations in the type of miniatures are probably due to differences in the models copied.

Iconographic sources of this vast pictorial cycle are complex, and it has been said that elaborately illustrated Late Antique or Greek manuscripts lay behind Aelfric's miniatures (cf. James, 1937; Wormald, *Drawings*). This is certainly true of a number of illustrations (e.g. f. 16ᵛ, God talking to Noah under the rainbow; f. 27, Abraham's vision of the fiery furnace; etc.). Henderson (1963), drawing detailed parallels between the present volume and the Genesis cycle in the Saint-Savin-sur-Gartempe frescoes, suggested that the sources of the latter may have been English manuscripts of the type of Aelfric's Pentateuch and the 'Caedmon' Genesis, for they alone preserve parts of the iconography of some ancient models. Wormald also drew attention (1965) to such details as the corpse in the burial of Joseph wrapped up to look like a mummy (f. 72ᵛ), thus indicating an acquaintance with, and probably selective borrowings from, earlier, exotic sources. But there are also other pictures which follow the Old English version instead of the biblical text and are often inspired by Anglo-Saxon literary tradition (e.g. the Fall of the Rebel Angels, f. 2), and by the commentaries (e.g. Rivers of Paradise, f. 5ᵛ). Dodwell has recently shown (1971) that the Aelfric artist probably composed his illustrations with this particular text in front of him, since the scribal errors and inaccuracies of the Anglo-Saxon translation are reflected in the drawings and may have led to such iconographic novelties as the 'horned' Moses (ff. 105–139ᵛ) and an ass's jaw-bone used by Cain (f. 8ᵛ; scholars, however, disagree on the origin of this feature, cf. Barb, *J.W.C.I.*, 1972, 386–9). The scenes of the Israelites' everyday life, moreover, depict usages and customs of 11th-century England and, often identical with representations in the Bayeux Tapestry (e.g. f. 26, Abraham scaring the birds), may be the outcome of the artist's immediate experience rather than copies of earlier illustrative cycles.

The figure drawing is extremely vigorous and lively and the miniatures, executed in the firm outline of Wormald's 'first style', remain essentially linear whether they are painted or merely drawn. The draperies, patterned with groups of vertical parallel lines and repetitive, nested 'U' motifs emphasizing the limbs, flare out stiffly at the hemlines, while the double-line folds segmenting the surfaces in hard rope-like curves recall no. 68 (Grimbald Gospels). There is a pronounced tendency to express everything in terms of an abstract, linear pattern, a tendency typical of late Anglo-Saxon art (note the sky turned into a sea of wavy lines; trees turned into a knotwork of twisting strands or into formalized candelabra-like ornaments; etc.). Thus the harshly shaded, repetitive bands of colour covering the draperies in certain pictures anticipate the 'corrugated' fold designs in the Hereford Troper (no. 97) and, together with the marked fragmentation of surfaces, foreshadow the 12th-century Romanesque.

Rubrics are in red rustic capitals with initials to chapters and paragraphs in red, green, and blue.

PROVENANCE: James (*Ancient Libraries*) has identified the manuscript by the first words of the second leaf with an entry in the late medieval catalogue of St. Augustine's, Canterbury, where the book was most probably produced. Inscribed by R. Talbot 'ca. XXXVII' (f. 53), the volume was in Cotton's possession by 1621 since the loan of the book to William Lisle 'before this April 1621' is recorded in the catalogue of the Cottonian collection, MS Harley 6018. Sir Robert Cotton died in 1631; his library presented to the nation by his grandson, Sir John Cotton, in 1700, was incorporated in the British Museum in 1753.

LITERATURE: Westwood, *Facsimiles*, 145; *Pal. Soc.*, I, pls. 71, 72; Sir E. Maune Thompson, *English Illuminated Manuscripts*, 1895, 25–6, pl. 8; F. G. Kenyon, *Facsimiles of Biblical Manuscripts*, 1900, no. XXI, plate; James, *Ancient Libraries*, pp. xxvi, lxxxiv, lxxxviii, 201, no. 95; R. Garnet and E. Goose, *English Literature*, 1903, I, 60, plate; J. A. Herbert, *Illuminated Manuscripts*, 1911, 120; S. J. Crowford, 'The Old English Version of the Heptateuch', *E.E.T.S.*, 160, 1922, 2–3, frontisp., pl. p. 96; Millar, I, 22, no. 59, pl. 28; M. R. James, 'Illustrations of the Old Testament', in *A Book of Old Testament Illustrations*, Roxburghe Club, 1927, 4, 22; M. Schapiro, 'Cain's jaw-bone that did the first murder', *Art Bulletin*, XXIV, 1942, 206; Kendrick, *Late Saxon*, 24, 131, pl. XXIV, 4; W. Holmquist, *Viking Art*, 22–3, 55, figs. 18, 19; Wormald, *English Drawings*, 39–41, 67, no. 28, pl. 19 a, b; Talbot Rice, *English Art*, 206, 229, pl. 72; Dodwell, *Canterbury School*, 82, 91 n. 1; Ker, *Catalogue*, no. 142; Nordenfalk, *Early Medieval*, 186, pl. 189; *St. Albans Psalter*, 80–1, 122, 205, pls. 109d, 168d, e; O. Pächt, 'Cycle of English Frescoes in Spain', *Burlington Magazine*, CIII, 1961, 169; *id.*, *The Rise of Pictorial Narrative in twelfth-century England*, 1962, 5 n. 1, 8–10, 25, pl. IV, 12; G. Henderson, 'Late-antique influence in some English mediaeval illustrations of Genesis', *J.W.C.I.*, XXV, 1962, 172–98, pls. 33 a, c, e, 34d, 35 b, c; *id.*, 'The sources of the Genesis cycle at Saint-Savin-sur-Gartempe', *Journal of the British Archaeological Association*, XXVI, 1963, 11–26, pls. IV (2), V (3), VII (1), IX (2), (4), X (3), XI (2), XIII (4), (5); R. M. Harris, 'An illustration in an Anglo-Saxon Psalter in Paris', *J.W.C.I.*, XXVI, 1963, 257; W. Mersmann, 'Das Elfenbeinkreuz der Sammlung Topic-Mimara', *Wallraf-Richartz-Jahrbuch*, XXV, 1963, 49, 63 n. 142, 101, fig. 59, 94, 96; Wormald, *Style and Design*, 26 n. 6, 30–2, figs. 4, 16; *id.*, 'Continental influence on English medieval illumination', *Fourth International Congress of Bibliophiles*, London 1965, 4, pl. I; Rickert, *Painting in Britain*, 41, pl. 35; Swarzenski, *Monuments*, pl. 47, fig. 106, pl. 59, fig. 132; M. W. Evans, *Medieval Drawings*, 1969, 24, pl. 26; Alexander, *Norman Illumination*, 153 n. 5, 154; C. R. Dodwell, 'L'originalité iconographique de plusieurs illustrations anglo-saxonnes de l'Ancien Testament', *Cahiers de Civilisation Médiévale*, XIV, 1971, 319–28, pls. I–VIII; *id.*, *Techniques*, 651–62, pls. I–X; R. Mellinkoff, 'The round, cap-shaped hats depicted on Jews in BM Cotton Claudius B. IV', *Anglo-Saxon England*, 2, 1973, 155–65, pl. I b-e; Wormald, *Angleterre*, 248; pl. 246; R. Green, 'Marginal Drawings in an Ottonian Manuscript',

Gatherings in honour of Dorothy Miners, Baltimore, 1974, 131–2, 138, figs. 2–3; C. R. Dodwell, Peter Clemoes, *The Old English Illustrated Hexateuch* (E.E. MSS in facs., XVIII) 1974.

87. British Library MS Cotton, Tiberius B. V (Vol. I)

(1) Calendar, computus matters, tables, etc. (ff. 2–19)
(2) Cicero, *Aratea* (ff. 32ᵛ–49ᵛ)
(3) Marvels of the East
260 × 218 mm.
Second quarter of 11th century. (?) Winchester
Ills. 273–276

This large composite volume of uncertain origin consists of a number of astronomical and other miscellaneous treatises of the 11th century with some earlier and later additions. Parts (1), (2), and (3) are illustrated with series of coloured drawings, all probably executed by one artist.

(1) The Calendar (ff. 3–8ᵛ) in metrical verse, preceded by diagrams and lunar tables (ff. 2–2ᵛ), contains miniatures with occupations of the months which are set at the head of each page while medallions with signs of the Zodiac are placed at the foot. The illustrations correspond closely to those in Julius A. VI (no. 62), and the same subjects are represented, but three occupational scenes are displaced: June—Reaping (f. 5ᵛ); July—Cutting wood (f. 6); August—Mowing (f. 6ᵛ), and some pictures contain additional figures. Stylistically the two manuscripts are vastly different, for the delicate impressionistic drawings of the earlier calendar are here replaced by framed, fully painted miniatures with figures and details firmly outlined in black on tinted backgrounds and in parts harshly modelled with white highlights, in technique rather like the painted illustrations in Tiberius C. VI (no. 98), a Winchester manuscript. The drawings, containing figures much larger than those in Julius, show a hardening of line and the compositions, from which the atmospheric depth and the landscape settings of the Utrecht Psalter tradition have disappeared, are not too well adapted to the rectangular frames which cut across details and thus suggest a somewhat insensitive copying. Iconographically the miniatures may have derived directly from the Julius illustrations (cf. Webster), or they may be rather inferior copies of a common prototype with more emphasis on the narrative quality of the pictures. The colouring includes dull blue, purplish grey, orange, brown, pale ochre, and some green. KL monograms are mainly in green with details of the calendar and tables in green and orange.

(2) A series of 27 drawings accompanies Cicero's Latin translation of a Greek astronomical poem *Aratea* (ff. 32ᵛ–49ᵛ). It represents personifications of the constellations, close copies of a 9th-century French manuscript, now British Library Harley 647 (itself depending on a Late Antique model and known to have reached Canterbury by the late 10th century; cf. also Harley 2506, no. 42). Unlike Harley 647, where the script of the commentaries fills up the figures and is part of the pictures, the same text is written in Tiberius B. V beside the drawings. These are painted in bluish green, grey, and orange with red star formations while the writing in the constellation of Deltaton is replaced by a pattern of 'elbowed' interlace (cf. 'Caedmon' Genesis, no. 58, pp. 225, 230). Occasional changes in details of the garments in the Tiberius manuscript have apparently been introduced to conform with later fashions (note e.g. the gaiters covering the legs of Perseus, f. 34, and Apollo, f. 47). The manuscript contains a full-page composition with the chariots of the Sun and Moon drawn by four horses and two oxen respectively (f. 47); this is lacking in Harley 647 but occurs in the subsequent English copies of the *Aratea* (cf. B.M. Cott. Tiberius C. I, late 11th century). The drawings, probably by the same artist, are in the style of the calendar illustrations (ff. 3–8ᵛ) described above.

(3) Marvels of the East (*De rebus ex oriente mirabilibus*, ff. 78ᵛ–87ᵛ) contains thirty-eight framed drawings illustrating each section of the Latin text with its accompanying Old English translation. According to Weitzmann, this is the most outstanding pictorial cycle among surviving early medieval copies of this late classical treatise. A full-page composition shows the magician Mambres at the mouth of Hell (f. 87). The remaining pictures, usually two to a page, represent fabulous people, monsters, and wonders, figural scenes, and decorative plant motifs. The miniatures, firmly and vividly drawn in sepia and red inks on coloured backgrounds, are painted in pale ochre, orange, greenish-grey, brown, and blue, with white in the highlights (cf. (1) and (2) above). According to James (*Marvels*), the Anglo-Saxon translation is the same as in Vitellius A. XV (no. 52), but the illustrations, though probably derived from a common archetype, follow a different tradition.

Besides the decoration in parts (1), (2), and (3) the manuscript contains a macrobian zone map (f. 29), a circular diagram ornamented with a pattern of acanthus foliage on dark ground (f. 53), and a fine 'mappa mundi' (f. 65ᵛ) in grey, green, and orange prefacing the Periegesis of Priscian (f. 57) though unrelated to it.

The script and style of parts (1), (2), and (3) suggest a date in the second quarter of the 11th century; Wormald (*Angleterre*), however, ascribed the manuscript to the end of the 10th century, while in the opinion of Dr. McGurk (for which I have to thank him) the date is *c.* 1050. The Easter Tables (f. 16) which follow the calendar are for the cycles 969–87 and 988–1006.

The manuscript is of undetermined origin. Owing to the affinity of the calendar (1) with that of Winchester (cf. nos. 5, Aethelstan Psalter; 7, Junius Psalter) and because of 'SUUIDHUN' being the only name in capitals in the list of bishops (ff. 20ᵛ–22—but this may have been taken over from an earlier model), an origin in Wessex (Winchester?) has been suggested (cf. Homburger; Saxl and Wittkower:

Ker, *Catalogue*), an attribution which has been lately supported by Wormald (*Angleterre*). Certain stylistic considerations also favour connections with Winchester, but since the calendar illustrations (1) and the Aratea (2) show links with Canterbury, the evidence is not entirely conclusive.

PROVENANCE: The manuscript was at Battle Abbey in the 12th century (except for ff. 74-6 which were probably inserted by Cotton), as shown by the donation formula (f. 88) and the annals of that Abbey written after 1119 and continued to 1206, now bound separately as Cotton MS Nero D. II. The volume belonged to Lord Lumley (d. 1607), probably entered as no. 1295 in his catalogue (a 1609 copy of a 1596 original from which it is clear that the order of contents has been rearranged by Cotton). The manuscript, bearing ownership inscription 'Robertus Cotton Bruceus' (f. 2), was in Cotton's possession by, if not before, 1621. Sir Robert Cotton died in 1631; his library was presented to the nation by his grandson, Sir John Cotton, in 1700, and was incorporated in the British Museum in 1753.

LITERATURE: S. Strutt, *Horda*, 1775-6, I, 55-8, pls. IX, fig. 1, X-XII, XIII, fig. 1; K. G. Anton, *Geschichte der deutschen Landwirthshaft*, Gorliz 1799, 46-58; W. Y. Otley, 'On a MS of Cicero's translation of Aratus', *Archaeologia*, XXVI, 1836, 146-58, pls. IX, X, XI, figs. 25-7, XIII, XV, XX, XXI; R. T. Hampson, *Medii Aevi Kalendarium*, 1841, I, 395-420; Westwood, *Facsimiles*, 109, 113, pl. 48; J. Fowler, 'On Medieval Representations of the Months and Seasons', *Archaeologia*, XLIV, 1873, 138-9; K. Miller, *Mappaemundi*, Stuttgart 1895, III, 124, fig. 58, H. II, T. 10, H. III, T. 29-31; G. Thiele, *Antike Himmelsbilder*, Berlin 1898, 152; H. O. Trail, *Social England*, 1901, II, 188, ill.; C. R. Beazley, *The Dawn of Modern Geography*, 1901, II, 559-63, 608-12, ills. pp. 560, 574; A. Ballard, *The Domesday Inquest*, 1906, 37, 167, 171, 205, ills. p. 256; J. A. Herbert, *Illuminated Manuscripts*, 1911, 114; Homburger, 68-9; E. Bishop, *Liturgica Historica*, 1918, 253 ff.; Millar, I, no. 48; O. Homburger, 'Review', *Art Bulletin*, X, 1928, 401; M. R. James, *Marvels of the East*, 1929, 2-6, pls. 51-61; A. Van de Vyver, 'Les oeuvres inédites d'Abbon de Fleury', *Revue Bénédictine*, 1935, 142; S. Rypins, 'Three Old English Prose Texts', *E.E.T.S.*, 161, 1924, pp. xliv-xlvii; G. R. Taylor, 'Some notes on Early Ideas of the Form and Size of the Earth', *Geographial Journal*, LXXXV, 1935, 65-75, pl. 1; J. C. Webster, *The Labours of the Months*, Evanston and Chicago 1938, 53-6, 99, 135-6, no. 34, pls. XIX, XX; R. Wittkower, 'Marvels of the East', *J.W.C.I.*, 1942, 172 nn. 6, 7, 173 nn. 1, 2, pl. 43a; F. Saxl and R. Wittkower, *British Art and the Mediterranean*, 1948, pls. 29, (2), (3), 30 (7); Kendrick, *Late Saxon*, 23, 26, 131, pls. XXIV, 1, 2, XXVI; Saxl and Meier, I, pp. xxix, 119-28, II, pls. LVII (146), LX (153), LXI (155), LXV (164), LXVI (165), LXVIII (170); Talbot Rice, *English Art*, 40, 219, 224-5, pls. 85b, 87, 89; Dodwell, *Canterbury School*, 18 n. 4; Sears Jayne and F. R.

Johnson, *The Lumley Library*, 1956, 162, no. 1295; F. Saxl, 'Illuminated Science Manuscripts in England', *Lectures*, 1957, I, 103, pls. 58 c, d, 59b; Ker, *Catalogue*, no. 193; Nordenfalk, *Early Medieval*, 191; K. Weitzmann, *Ancient Book Illumination*, Cambridge, Mass. 1959, 18, fig. 21; W. Mersmann, 'Das Elfenbeinkreuz der Sammlung Topic-Mimara', *Wallraf-Richartz-Jahrbuch*, XXV, 1963, 64, fig. 51; Rickert, *Painting in Britain*, 46-7, 56 n. 59, 73 n. 14, pl. 34b; Swarzenski, *Monuments*, pl. 61, figs. 145-6; Gneuss, 91-2, 94-5; Pächt and Alexander, no. 156; Wormald, *Angleterre*, 242, ill. 239.

88. Cambridge, Corpus Christi MS 198
Anglo-Saxon Homilies
266×183 mm.
Second quarter of 11th century. (?) Worcester
Fig. 58

The frontispiece (p. 1), a rather rough, unfinished drawing, shows six richly-draped Apostles standing in two rows one above the other in lively postures, some with legs crossed. St. Andrew with a cross and sceptre is in the centre of the upper row with St. Peter on the right holding a book and key. Below on the right (probably) St. John, holding a pair of tablets, is shown writing (cf. the St. John of the Crucifixion in nos. 41, Harley 2904; 80, Winchcombe Psalter; 94, Judith of Flanders Gospels). The drawing, in firm, brown and red outline shaded purple, highly patterned, is stylistically related to no. 80 (Winchcombe Psalter). Titles are in red or metallic red and silver with initials mainly in the same colours.

PROVENANCE: The manuscript, annotated throughout in the Worcester 'tremulous' hand, must have been at Worcester by the 13th century at the latest and may have been written there before the mid 11th century. The leaf with the frontispiece, however, has no connection with the rest of the volume and may have been inserted by Archbishop Parker who owned the book (cf. Ker, *Catalogue*). Inscribed *aedelric* (f. 323), 11th century, and *Aelfricus abbas transtulit* (f. 1), 16th century, the manuscript was bequeathed by Archbishop Parker to Corpus Christi College in 1575.

LITERATURE: M. R. James, *A descriptive catalogue of the Manuscripts in the Library of Corpus Christi College*, 1909, I, 475-81; Wormald, *English Drawings*, 42, 61, no. 8; Ker, *Catalogue*, no. 48; Bishop, *English Caroline*, no. 22.

89. Oxford, Bodleian Library MS Tanner 3
Gregory the Great, Dialogues
271×170 mm.
Second quarter of 11th century. (?) Worcester
Ill. 298

The frontispiece (f. 1ᵛ) represents Pope Gregory the Great in conversation with Petrus, the interlocutor of the Dialogues. The imposing figure of the Saint, mitred and enthroned by a lectern with an open book, is shown on blue ground with two looped pink curtains on either side of his head and Petrus seated at his feet in the right bottom corner. The miniature, which has been heavily retouched and partly redrawn in thick black outline (Gregory's face and gown, the curtain on the right, etc.), is surrounded by a 'Winchester' frame of contained acanthus patterns with large corner bosses of multicoloured leaves. The main colours are coral pink, blue, and soft green, with white in the highlights. The style of what remains of the original painting resembles no. 87 (Tiberius B. V) and the painted miniatures in no. 98 (Tiberius C. VI).

PROVENANCE: The manuscript, containing a 12th-century copy of a papal letter to Bishop Roger of Worcester (f. 1) and a list of books, possibly from Worcester cathedral (f. 189ᵛ), may itself have been produced at Worcester. The volume belonged to Thomas Tanner, Bishop of St. Asaph (d. 1735) 'ex dono V. R. Hugonis Lloyd vicarii de Mould' (f. 1).

LITERATURE: H. M. Bannister, 'Bishop Roger of Worcester and the church of Keynsham with a list of vestments and books probably belonging to Worcester', *English Historical Review*, XXXII, 1917, 388–9; A. Gwynn, 'The writings of Bishop Patrick 1074–84', *Scriptores Latini Hiberniae*, I, 1955, 16 n. 1; *Anglo-Saxon Illumination*, pl. 23; Bishop, *English Caroline*, no. 22; Pächt and Alexander, no. 45, pl. V.

90. Rouen, Bibliothèque Municipale MS A. 27 (368)

Pontifical (Lanalet Pontifical)
304 × 196 mm.
Second quarter of 11th century. Wessex

Ill. 256

The drawings are on two independent leaves at the beginning of the book. The first, in red and black ink with red washes in the details, shows a large figure of a bishop accompanied by a small one of an acolyte (f. 1ᵛ). The second, in black outline, represents the consecration of a church with a bishop at its entrance followed by a crowd of ecclesiastics with, below, another group of figures (f. 2ᵛ; cf. no. 23, Benedictional of St. Ethelwold). The drawings, seemingly by two different hands, are both in the firm outline of Wormald's 'first style', but the second drawing, possibly somewhat later than the first (cf. Wormald, *English Drawings*), reflects a certain degree of Rheims influence. Rubrics are in alternating lines of red and blue or red and green capitals (ff. 1–31ᵛ), with initials in the same colours.
The manuscript, of uncertain origin, contains the form of excommunication issued by the bishop of *lanaletensis monasterii* (f. 183) pointing to connections with St. Germans in Cornwall, seat of the Lanalet diocese. The invocation to St. Martial in the litany as the last of the Apostles (f. 187) suggests

a date for the manuscript after 1031 (cf. Wormald, *Analecta Boll.*, 1946).

PROVENANCE: Early ownership by Lyfing, Bishop of Crediton (1027–46), is recorded in Anglo-Saxon (f. 196). The manuscript was at Jumièges Abbey in the Middle Ages, hence removed to Rouen after the dissolution of the monastery in 1791.

LITERATURE: J. Gage, 'The Anglo-Saxon Ceremonial of the Dedication and Consecration of Churches', *Archaeologia*, XXV, 1834, 235–74; Westwood, *Facsimiles*, 143–4; H. Wilson, 'The Benedictional of Archbishop Robert', *H.B.S.*, XXIV, 1903, p. XVII; Homburger, 57; I. Gollancz, *The Caedmon Manuscript*, 1927, p. XXXVII; H. Doble, 'The Lanalet Pontifical', *H.B.S.*, LXXIV, 1937; V. Leroquais, *Les Pontificaux manuscrits des bibliothèques publiques de France*, Paris 1937, II, 287, III, pls. I, II; Wormald, *English Drawings*, 79, no. 57; Talbot Rice, *English Art*, 205, pl. 70a; Ker, *Catalogue*, 438, no. 374; Rickert, *Painting in Britain*, 226 n. 80; Alexander, *Norman Illumination*, 238; D. H. Turner, 'The Claudius Pontifical', *H.B.S.*, XCVII, 1971, pp. XXXIII–IX.

91. Oxford, Bodleian Library MS Lat. lit. F. 5 (S.C. 29744)

Gospel Lectionary (St. Margaret Gospels)
172 × 110 mm.
c. 1030–50

Ills. 277–280

The manuscript contains full-page authors' portraits preceding each of the sections of Gospel readings. The four Evangelists are shown enthroned against plain vellum curtained backgrounds (curtains omitted behind Luke, f. 21ᵛ), their names inscribed in gold overhead. Unaccompanied by their symbols, they are surrounded by rectangular frames in gold and colour and are all turning slightly to the right. Matthew (f. 3ᵛ), in blue under greenish-grey, is sitting sideways and writes in a book on an acanthus-ornamented stand. The gold initial L on the opposite page (f. 4) is of a Franco-Saxon type and contains interlace knotwork and a pattern of dots on orange ground. Mark (f. 13ᵛ), a massive figure clad in orange-brown over gold, is shown frontally, holding a pen in one hand, and a book on an acanthus-topped stand in the other. The opening words of Mark's Gospel are inscribed in large gold capitals on the facing page (f. 14). Luke (f. 21ᵛ) and John (f. 30ᵛ) are both shown under arched, gold canopies surmounted by architectural motifs. Luke, in green over orange, holds a long golden scroll and is sitting, legs crossed, on a cushioned stool at a draped lectern, his posture closely resembling that of St. Luke in no. 95 (Monte Cassino 437). John, wearing blue over pale green and seated frontally on a high-backed throne holding a pen and a book in his hands, is writing. The opening words of the Gospels of Luke and John are in large gold capitals on the opposite pages (ff. 22 and 31).

The Evangelist figures, shown in lively poses, are drawn in firm, vigorous outline, their tense animation brought out by the broad, free, rhythmic brushstrokes emphasizing the restless pattern of the drapery edges, and modelling the folds of the garments with deep shadows. This vivid, painterly style, under strong Rheims influence, is related to the style of Arundel 155 (no. 66) and technically recalls Douce 296 (no. 79, f. 40). But the figures are more solid in appearance than the Christ in the latter, and the fold patterns, less abstract in effect, are more suggestive of bodily forms under the draperies. The omission of the symbols and the Evangelists' names inscribed in the background point to ultimate Greek sources for the four portraits. The colouring with its juxtaposition of intense orange-red, soft green, pale blue, and gold in profusion recalls the Hereford Gospels (no. 97). Incipits are in red with text-initials in gold and headings in red.

The manuscript contains Latin hexameters written on the flyleaf (f. 2) in the late 11th century relating a miracle according to which the book was recovered undamaged from a stream into which it fell. An identical story told in Turgot's Life of St. Margaret (wife of King Malcolm Canmore of Scotland) identifies the present volume with her favourite Gospel Book which she bequeathed to Durham Cathedral (d. 1093; cf. Reg. Dunelm., cap. XCVIII, 218, S.S., 1835). A description in the list of Durham relics of 1383 may also refer to the present manuscript.

PROVENANCE: The Gospels belonged subsequently to Clayton Sudlow (f. 30) and John Stowe (f. 38ᵛ), 16th century; to William Howard (f. 3), 17th century; Fane Edge and Brent Ely Library (f. 3), 18th century. It was acquired for the Bodleian Library in 1887, having been added to the William Brice sale as lot 104.

LITERATURE: F. Madan, 'The Evangeliary of St. Margaret, Queen of Scotland', *Academy*, 6 Aug. 1887, 88–9; J. O. Westwood, *Academy*, 20 Aug. 1887, 120; F. E. Warren, *Academy*, 3 Sept. 1887, 151; W. Forbes-Leigh, *The Gospel book of St. Margaret*, 1896, facsimile; *Pal. Soc.*, II, pl. 131; Homburger, 67 n. 1; H. H. E. Craster, 'St. Margaret's Gospel Book', *The Bodleian Quarterly Record*, IV, 1925, 202–3; Saunders, *English Illumination*, 25, pl. 26a; Talbot Rice, *English Art*, 211, pl. 76b; Rickert, *Painting in Britain*, 53, pl. 48a; Roosen-Runge, 69 ff., pl. 8; Exh. *The Bodleian Library and its friends*, 1969–70, no. 77; Alexander, *Norman Illumination*, 121, pl. 24b; *Anglo-Saxon Illumination*, pls. 26–9; Pächt and Alexander, no. 44, pl. V; Wormald, *Angleterre*, 257.

92. Warsaw, Biblioteka Narodowa MS I. 3311

Evangeliary and Lectionary
155 × 99 mm.
c. 1000, additions second quarter of 11th century
Ills. 281–284, figs. 51–55, 59

It has been possible only recently to study this manuscript in some detail. Though datable in fact to c. 1000, it has been listed here on account of an Evangelist portrait, added later (f. 53), which, known for some time from Liebaert's photograph, has been assigned by Wormald to the second quarter of the 11th century. The manuscript contains readings from the four Gospels and lections for various feast-days. Its decoration, of a rather rough execution, now consists of three Evangelist portraits, full-page borders intended to contain ornamental initials and the opening lines of the text (the borders on ff. 1 and 4, enclose only blank spaces), and a number of other initials of various sizes. The book is not too well preserved: the portrait of Matthew is missing from the beginning, some leaves have been displaced in consecutive bindings, and the text ends abruptly at Luke, VI, v. 45.

The decoration in red and black ink with colour washes (the two additions are in brown outline) was executed by more than one artist in different periods and styles. The portrait of John (f. 83ᵛ), the borders and the initials, probably all contemporary with the script, belong to the first stage of production; the portraits of Mark (f. 15) and Luke (f. 53), in a different style, are a later addition. Some of the initials (e.g. ff. 28, 69) as well as the miniature showing St. John (f. 83ᵛ) must have been done before the writing, since lines, and sometimes words, of the text are broken up to accommodate the decoration; this suggests that the illuminator and scribe worked simultaneously, or were possibly even one and the same person.

John, dipping his pen in an inkhorn on the left, is shown seated frontally on a cushioned throne supported on two lion's legs with terminals of Franco-Saxon bird-heads holding balls in their beaks (cf. Durham Ritual, no. 3, ff. 2ᵛ, 14, etc.; this type of throne, unusual in Anglo-Saxon illumination, can be most readily associated with manuscripts of the Rheims and Tours schools, e.g. Ebbo Gospels, Epernay MS. 1, ff. 60ᵛ, 90ᵛ). The Evangelist's robe is pink, heightened with white and shaded with red, while his thickly painted mantle is bluish green, and his nimbus, book and throne are yellow; the subpedaneum, under his pink feet, is green and the carpet in the lower half of the picture is pale rose with a fringe across the front edge drawn in red. It seems likely that the artist had a late Carolingian Gospel Book at his disposal, since the figure of John, here shown on plain vellum ground, has no parallel in Anglo-Saxon painting, but in posture and movement, in the head-type, and in the emphatic side glance is closely reminiscent of a St. Mark in a Tours manuscript (Stuttgart, Landesbibliotek II, 40, f. 65ᵛ). Stylistically, the drawing, in firm outline, harks back to Wormald's 'early Winchester' group (cf. nos. 5, Aethelstan Psalter; 6, Corpus Christi College 183; 7, Junius Psalter), recalling also the drawing of an angel added in the late 10th century to St. John's College MS 28 in Oxford.

To the same school of Tours can be traced the panelled initial *I*(*n principio*) of St. John's Gospel inscribed on the opposite page (f. 84): topped by a knotwork of interlace, it terminates at the bottom in bunched acanthus leaves. Other ornamental initials are equally retrospective in style with their flat hatched palmette motifs, trefoils and sparse acanthus foliage, the latter as yet unaffected by 'Winchester' three-dimensionality; albeit much larger, they recall the initials in the Durham Ritual (no. 3). Certain letters in the present manuscript are closely dependent on Franco-Saxon work, e.g. an A (f. 69) having bird-head terminals on the horizontal bar and a knotwork of interlace at the top. There is also an M (f. 13) reminiscent of St. Gall manuscripts, an I made up of two bird-headed interlaced serpents (f. 50), two full-page bordered and painted initials, an E (f. 16ᵛ) with a mask head on the centre bar, and an S (f. 28) with knots of interlace, and a few other smaller initials with straggly tendrils, bird and mask heads. The borders have flat leaf patterns on dark ground or blank spaces between the edging bars, and, on the corners, interlace knotwork which is structurally reminiscent of Franco-Saxon manuscripts (e.g. Bibl. Nat., lat. 2, Second Bible of Charles the Bald, f. 11). The initials and the borders, so far removed from contemporary Anglo-Saxon decoration and closer in spirit to that from Northern France, must have been copied directly from late Carolingian examples; they suggest, as place of origin, a remote provincial centre, unaffected by the latest developments in English decorative forms.

The miniatures of St. Mark (f. 15) and St. Luke (f. 53) were probably added on blank leaves in the second quarter of the 11th century. They show the Evangelists enthroned under arches on columns (Mark in a round arch, Luke in a trefoiled one), both turning towards their draped lecterns on the right, Mark writing in a book, Luke examining his pen. There are wind-blown curtains in the backgrounds; Mark's lectern is supported on a bird-foot and a scrolled plant motif grows from capital of the column on the right (cf. no. 58, Junius 11); only Luke's symbol—the ox—is shown hovering over the Evangelist's head though the name *Marcum* (*Secundum Marcum*) is inscribed across the top of the picture. Both drawings are partly coloured: green curtains, bright blue robe and violet mantle in the miniature of St. Mark, and green in Luke's mantle, highlighted with white patches that seem to recall Tiberius C. VI (no. 98, ff. 18ᵛ, 30ᵛ), and with violet, blue shaded lines in the folds of his white robes. The portraits, in firm, brown outline, are probably by the same artist: that of St. Mark is reminiscent of the St. Matthew in Pembroke College MS 301 (no. 73), but the drapery folds, drawn in broad, vigorous brushstrokes with an abstract effect, show a certain affinity with the Judith of Flanders Gospels (nos. 93, 94); Luke's head (note also his enormous hands, a feature of certain Canterbury manuscripts, see nos. 84, 100, 101) and the soft treatment of his draperies have been described by Wormald (*English Drawings*) as a late derivation from the style of the St. Margaret Gospels (no. 91).

According to T. A. M. Bishop (a private communi-

cation for which my warm thanks are due) the manuscript was written by one Anglo-Saxon scribe. His hand, not so far encountered elsewhere, bears a close similarity to some of the hands in such late 10th-century manuscripts as Lincoln Cathedral 182 and Antwerp, Plantin-Moretus Museum 190, the former probably, the latter almost certainly, from Abingdon (Ker, *Catalogue*). The name Leonard, 15th century, is written in the margin of f. 47ᵛ.

PROVENANCE: The manuscript, of unknown origin, bears the inscription across the top of f. 1ᵛ *Biblia 4 Evangelia, Codex saec. X* in the hand of Jozef A. Załuski, later Bishop of Kiev (d. 1774). His collection, housed in Warsaw and made available to the public in 1747, was opened under the supervision of the Jesuit Fathers at the Warsaw Public Library in 1765. Transferred to St. Petersburg after the partition of Poland in 1795, it was for the most part incorporated into the Imperial Library and remained in Leningrad till the treaty of Riga in 1923. The present manuscript, listed as Codex Lat. O. v.I.10, was in the last batch of books returned to Poland in 1934.

LITERATURE: Dom Antonio Staerk, *Les Manuscrits Latins du V au XIII siècles conservés a la bibliothèque imperials de Saint-Petersbourg . . .*, 1910, I, 355; S. Sawicka, 'Les principaux manuscrits à peintures de la Bibliothèque Nationale de Varsovie', *Bulletin de la Société Française de Reproductions des Manuscrits à Peintures*, 19e Année, 1938, 14–22, pl. Ia; Wormald, *English Drawings*, 63, no. 23.
Reproduction of f. 53 in Liebaert Photographic Collection. Petrograd, IV, no. 1303, kept in Dept. of MSS, British Library and Oxford, Bodleian Library.

93, 94. New York, Pierpont Morgan Library MSS 709, 708
Gospels (Judith of Flanders Gospels)
Second quarter of 11th century

93. Pierpont Morgan MS 709 (Holkham Hall 16)
295 × 190 mm.   *Ills. 285, 289 (Colour)*

This important manuscript, possibly the earliest of the three Anglo-Saxon Gospel Books associated with Judith, Countess of Flanders (1032–94), contains, besides the usual Evangelist portraits with corresponding *incipit* pages, a miniature with the Crucifixion (f. 1ᵛ), preceding the text of the Gospels. It is one of the most moving renderings of that subject in English illumination, equalling in dramatic power the Crucifixion in Harley 2904 (no. 41). The full-page representation, framed by a plain band of burnished gold, shows the dead Christ on a greenish-brown tree-trunk cross, His body sagging heavily to the left. St. John, standing on the right and recording his testimony in a book (cf. nos. 41 Harley 2904; 77, New Minster Offices; 80, Winchcombe Psalter), closely recalls in posture the St. John of the Harley Crucifixion. On the left, the Virgin with book in hand lovingly raises the edge of her headcloth to wipe the wound in Christ's side, the impulsiveness of her tender gesture, unparalleled in this context, anticipating the highly emotional portrayals of the Crucifixion in the following centuries. In the heavily overcast sky above the cross bar the blessing Hand of God appears between the roundels with personifications of Sun and Moon (cf. nos. 77, New Minster Offices; 80, Winchcombe Psalter), here shown dramatically covering their faces and weeping, while below a small figure of a kneeling woman clutches the foot of the cross compulsively. Probably a patroness who commissioned the book, she is a controversial figure, for, at times believed to be Judith herself (which would postdate the manuscript to after 1051), she has nevertheless also been identified by Schiller (1971) with Mary Magdalen; on this unlikely assumption, the present portrayal of the Saint would be the earliest to show her in this particular scene and pose, precociously anticipating the 14th-century Crucifixions by Giotto and other Italian painters. The figures, painted chiefly in blue, pale ochre shaded brown (with a yellow diaper on the robes of the Virgin and the donor), red in Christ's hair, and burnished gold in details, are silhouetted sharply against plain vellum ground. The sweeping and incisive line of the drawing recalls Arundel 155 (no. 66) and the Bury Psalter (no. 84) but the soft brushstrokes marking drapery folds are reminiscent of the St. Margaret Gospels (no. 91) and Douce 296 (no. 79), the latter also providing a parallel for the swaying, exceedingly tall and small-headed figures of the Virgin and John. Iconographically, the miniature shows connections with Winchester Crucifixions (cf. Harley 2904, no. 41; New Minster Offices, no. 77) and close comparisons for the cloudy sky are found in no. 23 (Benedictional of St. Ethelwold).

The Evangelist portraits and their initial pages are all enclosed within full or half 'Winchester' frames of two burnished gold bands supporting pink and blue to green foliage on black ground; they have large corner rosettes and median medallions containing various ornamental motifs. The colouring of the miniatures, soft and harmonious, includes light ochre to tan, shades of blue to green, pink, dull orange, pale yellow, and gold in details. With the exception of John, the Evangelists, in posture and gesture alike, are seated frontally on identical cushioned thrones, their torsos stiffly erect, elbows pressed characteristically to their sides, and heads thrust forward; dipping their pens into golden ink bottles on the left, they gaze at their symbols descending from the upper right corners. Matthew (f. 2ᵛ) opens a book resting on a draped stand on the right and inscribed 'Liber generationis JHU . . .'. An angel flies down from blue clouds bearing a long golden scroll. A large gold initial L (f. 3), topped by beast-headed interlace and ornamented with a quatrefoil and leaf motifs, introduces lines of Matthew's text in gold capitals and uncials. Frames (ff. 2ᵛ–3) have quatrefoils containing angels on the laterals and roundels with birds on the top and bottom sides.

Mark (f. 48ᵛ), seated on a high-backed throne, receives a scroll from an ox (Luke's symbol) instead of a lion. An initial I (f. 49), made up of two gold-edged panels and topped by a quatrefoil with griffin's head and a fleuron, is followed by lines of gold lettering. The borders surrounding the two pages (ff. 48ᵛ–49) contain slanting outward-growing acanthus (cf. no. 79, Douce 296) and round bosses on the lateral sides.

Luke (f. 77ᵛ), holding a knife in his right hand and resting it on a golden tablet supported by a draped stand, looks up at the lion (Mark's symbol) descending with a wavy scroll. An initial Q (f. 78), made up of acanthus-filled panels, is surmounted by a mask-head (cf. Grimbald Gospels, no. 68; Douce 296, no. 79), and its tail is formed of a winged dragon. Borders (ff. 77ᵛ–78) of outward growing acanthus on these two pages are ornamented with round bosses and stiff star-like rosettes.

John (f. 122ᵛ), bearded, writes the first words of his Gospel in gold in an open book on a draped stand and seems to be listening to the eagle flying down with a long scroll from the right. An initial I (f. 123), similar to that of Mark (f. 49) but with a round boss and foliage on the shaft, introduces the opening words of the text in gold. The full 'Winchester' borders (ff. 122ᵛ–123) contain roundels with bust-figures without haloes on the laterals (cf. no. 72, Robert of Jumièges Sacramentary).

The figure drawing, in firm and vigorous outline, delineating the garments with long sweeping curves, is related to the Arundel 155 (no. 66) style, and shows affinities with Canterbury manuscripts of the second quarter of the 11th century (cf. nos. 74, Trinity B. 15. 34; 84, Bury Psalter); while the rhythmic brushstrokes deeply shading the drapery folds recall St. Margaret Gospels (no. 91) though the patterning is more abstract and more schematized. All miniatures are by the same artist but, as suggested by the Pierpont Morgan Library Catalogue (unpublished), the Crucifixion (f. 1ᵛ) may have been an addition executed especially for Judith of Flanders when the Gospel Book was procured for her after 1051. This conjecture would explain the identity of the kneeling woman. Some gold initials in the text ending in fleurons recall those in Douce 296 (no. 79).

94. New York, Pierpont Morgan MS 708 (Holkham Hall 15)

290 × 190 mm.   *Ill. 286*

The manuscript, another Gospel book possessed by, and probably written for, Judith of Flanders, is decorated with four full-page Evangelist portraits and similarly framed gold-lettered *incipit* pages.

Matthew (f. 2ᵛ), seated frontally, head resting on left hand, writes in an open book on a draped lectern on the right. A tall angel holding a long scroll stands by on green clouds (cf. no. 68, Grimbald Gospels), while a knotted curtain fills the upper left corner. The whole is enclosed by plain gold bands (cf. f. 3 and ff. 42ᵛ–43).

Mark (f. 26ᵛ), enthroned frontally in a frame of arch and columns with plant scrolls in the spandrels (cf. nos. 65, Trinity Gospels; 72, Robert of Jumièges Sacramentary), his nimbus incised with concentric circles, dips his pen into an ink bottle attached to a knotted curtain on the left; resting his left hand on an open book on a stand, he receives a scroll from a winged lion descending from the right. The Evangelist's gown is diapered with unusual, large 'x' motifs (cf. no. 95, Monte Cassino Gospels).

Luke (f. 42ᵛ), seated on a wide high-backed throne with a curtain twisted round its frame is shown in an awkwardly contorted position with feet pointing to the left, legs crossed, and torso turned to the right, holding pen and knife and writing on a golden tablet supported on a draped lectern; he gazes at a scroll lowered by an ox emerging from the upper right corner. The posture of his crossed legs is the same as that of Luke in the St. Margaret Gospels (no. 91), though in an inverse position.

John (f. 66ᵛ), his nimbus incised with concentric circles and his head filleted, is seated, a blue curtain on either side, under a trilobed arch on columns with plant scrolls in the spandrels (cf. f. 26ᵛ, above); he writes on a golden tablet supported on a draped stand on the right, while an eagle descending from above whispers into his ear, an iconography nearly identical with that in no. 95 (Monte Cassino Gospels), probably copying the same model (cf. also nos. 10 and 44, Boulogne MSS 10 and 11).

The figures, firmly outlined on plain vellum, are large, bulky, and strong. The liveliness of their postures is enhanced by broad, vigorous brushstrokes patterning the deep-folded draperies, which are reminiscent of nos. 79 (Douce 296) and 91 (St. Margaret Gospels), but are more uniform and abstract in effect. The colouring includes shades of green, rose, yellow, and light blue with a diaper of various ornamental motifs in white on the Evangelists' garments and a good deal of reddish gold in frame and details. Initials to paragraphs are in gold, but those of John's text were never filled in.

PROVENANCE: The origin of both manuscripts is uncertain. Morgan 709 (no. 93) was variously ascribed to Canterbury (Talbot Rice), Winchester (Rickert, Bräude), and an East Anglian scriptorium, either Crowland, on stylistic considerations (similarities to no. 79, Douce 296) or possibly Thorney, the latter being also suggested as the place of origin of Morgan 708 (no. 94; cf. Harssen). The work of two scribes can be distinguished in each of the manuscripts. One of them, according to T. A. M. Bishop, appears in all four Gospels possessed by Judith of Flanders (Morgan 709 and 708; Monte Cassino BB. 437—all three produced in England; Fulda, Landesbibl. Aa 21, made at St. Bertin, c. 1065), and may have been an English itinerant scribe in Judith's train. Stylistic and iconographical connections as well as the contribution by a common scribe to the three English Gospel Books of Judith suggest that they may have emanated from the same centre and are close in date. Their exact dating is controversial for although stylistically they seem to be not later

than the mid 11th century, their presumed destination suggests a date between 1051, the year of Judith's arrival in England, and 1064, the date of her departure for the Continent. Nevertheless, for Morgan 709 various dates between 1020 and 1050 have been advanced and the figure of the kneeling donor in the Crucifixion (f. 1ᵛ) explained by the miniature being a later addition.

Judith, who came to England as the bride of Tostig Godwinson, Earl of Northumbria, subsequently married Welf IV, Duke of Bavaria (1071) and donated her manuscript collection to Weingarten Abbey. The Weingarten provenance of the present volumes is attested by entries in Morgan 708 including records of dedications both of St. Leonard's chapel at Weingarten in 1124 (f. 84) and Weingarten Abbey itself in 1183 (ff. 1ᵛ–2) and a note by Berthold, Abbot of Weingarten, 1200–32 (ff. 85–6). The two Morgan Gospels and Fulda Aa 21 were identified by A. Haseloff in 1905 with Judith's gifts of manuscripts to Weingarten by an entry in the Fulda volume (f. 89ᵛ) mentioning among her donations '. . . tria plenaria cum uno textu evangelii'. The Weingarten Library was dispersed in 1805 and in 1818 the two Morgan Gospels were purchased in Paris on behalf of Thomas W. Coke, later Earl of Leicester, to become Holkham Hall MSS 15 and 16. Acquired for Pierpont Morgan Library in 1926.

BINDINGS: Both manuscripts are bound in boards with contemporary gold (Morgan 709) and silver gilt (Morgan 708) upper covers, the latter datable to the third quarter and the former to the end of the 11th century. The cover of Morgan 709 with a repoussé plaque showing Christ in Majesty and attributed to the artist of the Hadelinus shrine in Vise, Belgium, on stylistic grounds, is generally ascribed to a Flemish workshop. The cover of Morgan 708 is more controversial: bearing in its upper half a majesty of Christ between two cherubim and below a Cruxifixion, it was believed to be of English workmanship (Ross, 1940). Steenbock (1965) attributed both covers to a Flemish atelier, dating them after 1064, the year of Judith's final departure from England. Recently, however, Hinkle has convincingly shown that on account of the striking similarities between the cover of the Morgan manuscript and a cover apparently belonging to an Anglo-Saxon Gospel Book, Rheims MS 9 (no. 102), now missing but described in an inventory, 1549, the English origin of Judith's cover can be confirmed; probably contemporary with the manuscript, it is datable between 1051 and 1064. This attribution has been also accepted by Grodecki (1973).

LITERATURE: W. Roscoe, *Proof impressions of engravings . . . of the manuscript library at Holkham*, 1835, pls. 7–10; G. F. Waagen, *Treasures of Art in Great Britain*, 1854, III, 425–6; L. Dorez, 'Reliures du moyen âge', *L'Art*, LI, 1891, 182–6, fig. p. 185; A. Haseloff, 'Aus der Weingarten Klosterbibliothek', *Deutsche Literaturzeichnung*, no. 32, XXVI, 1905, cols. 1998–2000; L. Dorez, *Les manuscrits à pein-*

tures de Lord Leicester, Paris 1908, 7–10, pls. 1–3; K. Löffler, Die Handschriften des Klosters Weingarten, Leipzig 1912, 5, 44–5, 147–8; Homburger, 24, 55, 62, 67 n. 1; W. R. Lethaby, 'English Primitives', II, Burlington Magazine, XXIX, 1916, 287–8, ill. p. 288; C. James, 'Some notes on the manuscript library at Holkham', The Library, II, 1921–2, 233–7; Millar, I, 16, nos. 28, 29; O. Homburger, 'Review', Art Bulletin, X, 1928, 401; Saunders, English Illumination, 31; The Pierpont Morgan Library. A Review of the Growth . . . 1924–29, New York 1930, 20–3, pls. VII–X; M. Harssen, 'The Countess Judith of Flanders and the Library of Weingarten Abbey', Papers of the Bibliographical Society of America, XXIV, 1930, 1–13, pl. I, figs. 1, 2; M. Schott, Zwei Lütticher Sakramentare und ihre Verwandten, Strassburg 1931, 189, 206; W. L. Hildburgh, 'A mediaeval bronze pectoral cross', Art Bulletin, XIV, 1932, 92, fig. 15; The Pierpont Morgan Library. Exhibition of Illuminated Manuscripts, New York 1933–4, p. XI, nos. 19, 20, pls. 17–20; A. Goldschmidt, 'English influence on mediaeval art on the continent', Medieval Studies in Memory of A. Kingsley Porter, ed. W. R. W. Koehler, Cambridge, Mass. 1939, II, 711, fig. 5; Niver, 'The Psalter in the British Museum, Harley 2904', ib., 684, 686; M. C. Ross, 'An Eleventh-Century English Bookcover', Art Bulletin, XXII, 1940, 83–5, figs. 1, 2, 5; C. Morey, Mediaeval Art, New York, 1942, 212; W. Weisbach, Manierismus in der mittelalterlichen Kunst, Basel 1942, 20, pl. 14; H. Swarzenski, The Berthold Missal, New York 1943, 1, 3, 8, 12, 43, 56 n. 124, 66; F. Wormald, 'The survival of Anglo-Saxon illumination after the Norman Conquest', Proceedings of the British Academy, XXX, 1944, 4, pl. 3; The Pierpont Morgan Library Exhibition, The Bible IV-XIX Century, 1947, 12, no. 19; id., The First Quarter Century, New York 1949, 33, no. 13, pl. 6; The Walters Art Gallery, Illuminated Books of the Middle Ages and Renaissance, Baltimore, 1949, 8, no. 16, pl. IX; Kendrick, Late Saxon, 15, 103, pls. XII, XIII; H. Comstock, 'The Pierpont Morgan Library's Quarter Century', The Connoisseur, 1949, 42, ill.; Talbot Rice, English Art, 199 f., 210, pl. 63; W. O. Hassall, 'Holkham MSS acquired for the nation', The Connoisseur, 1952, 15; W. A. Bräude, 'The wanderings of two ancient manuscripts', History Today, 323–31, figs. pp. 323, 325, 326, 328, 330; R. W. Southern, The Making of the Middle Ages, New Haven 1953, pp. vii, 237, frontisp.; Dodwell, Canterbury School, 15, pl. 6a; Freyhan, 429, pl. XL, fig. 28; Nordenfalk, Early Medieval, 185; P. Thoby, Le crucifix des origines au Concile de Trente, Nantes 1959, 41, pl. XIII; Rickert, Miniatura, 18–19, pl. 23; W. Mersmann, 'Das Elfenbeinkreuz der Sammlung Topic-Mimara', Wallraf-Richartz-Jahrbuch, XXV, 1963, 26–7, 102, fig. 17; The Pierpont Morgan Library Exhibition, Liturgical Manuscripts, introduction J. Plummer, New York 1964, nos. 11, 12; N. R. Ker, Medieval Libraries of Great Britain, 1964, 189; Rickert, Painting in Britain, 52, 226 n. 17, pl. 43; Swarzenski, Monuments, pl. 26, figs. 145–7; K. L. Galbraith, 'The Iconography of Biblical Scenes in Malmesbury Abbey', Journal of the British Archaeological Association, III, 1965, 51, pl. XXIV, 1; Frauke Steenbock, Der Kirchliche Prachteinband im frühen Mittelalter, Berlin 1965, 168–9, pls. 104, 105; Wormald, Style and Design, 32, fig. 13; A. E. Elsen, 'The Sacred Book', Purposes of Art, New York, 1967, 96, fig. 116; Alexander, Norman Illumination, 121 n. 3, 169 n. 3; Bishop, English Caroline, p. XVI; W. M. Hinkle, 'The gift of an Anglo-Saxon Gospel Book to the Abbey of Saint-Remi, Reims', Journal of the British Archaeological Association, XXXIII, 1971, 33–5, pl. IX; G. Schiller, Iconography of Christian Art, 1971, II, 117, ill. 388; F. Wormald, The Winchester Psalter, 1973, 82, fig. 72; id., Angleterre, 251, ills. 253, 254; L. Grodecki, 'L'Angleterre', in Le siècle de l'an mil, eds. A. Malraux and A. Parrot, Paris 1973, 318, ill. 334; Robb, Illuminated Manuscript, 152, fig. 95.

95. Monte Cassino, Archivio della Badia MS BB. 437, 439

Gospels
250 × 170 mm.
c. 1050

Ills. 287, 288

This Gospel Book probably also belonged to Judith of Flanders. It contains four Evangelist portraits and corresponding *incipit* pages under matching arch-and-column frames. Splendid ornamental initials introduce the gold-inscribed opening lines of each Gospel with symbols placed above in the tympana of the arches. With the exception of John (p. 166), the Evangelists sit frontally in identical poses and write, turning towards open golden books on the right, supported on draped lecterns. Matthew (p. 2), knife in left hand and flanked by a looped curtain on either side, is shown stiffly erect on a high-backed throne against a coloured background with some shadow outline and streaky zigzags in its upper part indicating the sky. A fine initial L on the opposite page (p. 3) is made up of a bird in the vertical and a dragon in its horizontal bar. Under the arch, crowned with a roundel containing a bird (cf. 93, Morgan 709, f. 2ᵛ), the half-figure of an angel is shown on a cloudy background. The arches (pp. 2, 3) are surmounted with plant scrolls and figures, the latter recalling the decoration of Canon Tables in Carolingian manuscripts of the Metz School (cf. also Boulogne Gospels, no. 44). Mark (p. 102) sits under a round arch with scroll ornament round the top (cf. p. 103). He is flanked by two curtains looped round a golden bar with the upper part of the background painted in streaks of colour. He wears a diapered overgarment with an unusual motif of a large 'x' on his knee (cf. Morgan 708, no. 94). The initial I on the facing page (p. 103) is topped by a mask head and has a large leafy boss midway up its acanthus-filled shaft, while in the tympanum above an anthropomorphic bust-figure of a winged lion is shown against a cloudy background (cf. nos. 15, Add. 40618; 65, Trinity Gospels). Luke (p. 126) and his *incipit* page (p. 127) are placed under mitred arches richly ornamented round the top with rampant lions and a bird and with leafy scrolls in the spandrels, a type of decoration closely resembling the Trinity Gospels (no. 65). The Evangelist, holding pen and knife, is shown against a plain coloured background with a looped curtain on the left and is, most unusually, wearing shoes. A panelled initial Q (p. 127), clasped at the top by a mask head spitting leaves, has a tail in the form of a dragon whose neck is looped round the letter-frame (cf. Douce 296, no. 79). Above, under the arch on a cloudy background the half-length figure of a winged ox—Luke's anthropomorphic symbol—is depicted (cf. p. 103).

John (p. 166) sits in profile facing right and leans forward writing on a golden tablet. The Holy Dove(?) perched on the top of the Evangelist's filleted head (shown in three-quarter view) is apparently dictating his text (a composition paralleled in no. 94, Morgan 708), and probably inspired by a common model (cf. also no. 10, Boulogne 10). The background is a plain colour with streaks of a darker shade and a coloured shadow emphasizing the outlines, the whole enclosed by a round gold arch ornamented over the top with foliage and two rampant lions. An initial I on the facing page (p. 167) is composed of an upright dragon with an elaborate foliated tail, and above, against a cloudy sky, the symbol—an eagle—is shown (cf. no. 44, Boulogne 11, for the Holy Dove and the symbol simultaneously represented in John's portrait).

The placing of the Evangelist symbols over the initial pages is most unusual and may be linked with some early insular examples (cf. Royal 1. E. VI, Gospels from Canterbury, c. 800). The anthropomorphic representations of the lion and ox, an iconography perhaps ultimately of Coptic origin and transmitted by manuscripts from Gaul (cf. Ameisenowa, J.W.C.I., 1949), have few parallels in Anglo-Saxon illumination (cf. nos. 13, Oxford, St. John's College 28; 15, B.L. Add. 40618; 65, Trinity Gospels).

Stylistic and iconographical variations in the Evangelists' portraits suggest dependence on different models but the work is probably by the same artist. With the exception of John, the Evangelists recall in type and posture those of Morgan 709 (no. 93) but the figure drawing in all four representations is less mannered and the design of the draperies more flowing and less formalized. The latter, drawn in vigorous curves and long straight lines, is reminiscent of Canterbury manuscripts of c. 1050 but hemlines are scarcely agitated and the deep rhythmic shading of the folds (particularly on p. 166) recalls the painterly style of Douce 296 (no. 79). The decoration of the arched frames, related to Morgan 709 (ff. 26ᵛ–27, 66ᵛ–67) is also closely reminiscent of the Canon Tables in the Trinity Gospels (no. 65).

The colours, including a good deal of gold in frames and details, are soft and harmonious: opaque light blue, shades of green, pale pink, milky orange to rust brown, and deep indigo blue for the shadow outlines, a colour scheme recalling Arundel 155 (no. 66). Initials throughout, of excellent quality, are in gold.

PROVENANCE: According to T. A. M. Bishop (*English Caroline*), the manuscript was written by the scribe whose hand appears in three other Gospel Books owned by Countess Judith of Flanders (cf. nos. 94, 93, Morgan 709, 708; Fulda, Landesbibl. Aa 21, produced at St. Bertin) and who may have been an itinerant English scribe working among her retinue. His participation suggests that the three English manuscripts were probably especially written for Judith during her stay in this country between 1051 and 1064. On account of its style the present volume, of uncertain origin, was assigned by Homburger to the workshop which produced Douce 296 (no. 79) and Morgan 709 (no. 93). A marginal inscription listing the names of German monks (p. 238) suggests that the Gospels passed through Bavaria before being handed over to the Monte Cassino Library by Countess Matilda of Tuscany. It was probably one of the wedding presents which the latter received from Countess Judith on occasion of her marriage to Judith's son Welf in 1089.

LITERATURE: D. O. Piscicelli Taeggi, *Le miniature dei codici Cassinesi*, Monte Cassino 1887, pls. I, II; Millar, I, no. 31; O. Homburger, 'Review', *Art Bulletin*, X, 1928, 401; M. Harssen, 'The Countess Judith of Flanders and the Library of Weingarten Abbey', *Papers of the Bibliographical Society of America*, XXIV, 1930, 1–13, pl. II, fig. 3; D. Maurus Iguanez, *Codicum Casinensium Manuscriptorum Catalogus*, Monte Cassino 1940–1, 46; Kendrick, *Late Saxon*, 103; M. Bräude, 'The wanderings of two ancient manuscripts', *History Today*, 1952, 329; Talbot Rice, *English Art*, 215, pl. 75b; Rickert, *Miniatura*, 13, 22, pl. 25; *id.*, *Painting in Britain*, 52–3, pl. 45; Alexander, *Norman Illumination*, 119 n. 2; Bishop, *English Caroline*, p. XVII; C. Nordenfalk, 'The Draped Lectern', *Intuition und Kunstwissenschaft: Festschrift für Hans Swarzenski*, Berlin 1973, 86, fig. 5; Wormald, *Angleterre*, 251.

EXHIBITED: Rome, Palazzo di Venezia, *Mostra Storica Nazionale della Miniatura*, 1954, no. 145.

96. Cambridge, Pembroke College MS 302
Gospel Lectionary (Hereford Gospels)
197 × 102 mm.
c. 1050

Ills. 290–292

The Gospel Lections are preceded by twelve pages of Eusebian Canons (ff. 1–6ᵛ) under a series of round and pointed arches, mainly in gold, supported by slender shafts in gold and colour, sometimes with spiral bands about them (cf. no. 61, York Gospels). The arches are decorated at the sides with birds, cocks, acanthus scrolls, and heavy foliage and at the centre with either delicate plant motifs and tulip-shaped flowers (an innovation) or tonsured and hooded figures holding books and shown against backgrounds with characteristic zigzag motifs. The four Evangelist portraits, framed by bands of gold and colour with small ornaments at the angles' show massive monumental seated figures against curtained backgrounds, filling most of the picture space. Unaccompanied by the usual symbols, they are (with the exception of St. John) reminiscent of the Evangelists in no. 67 (Eadui Codex), in their poses and gestures and in the expanse of gold in their mantles. Unframed *incipit* pages contain ornamental initials and the beginnings of the Gospels in lines of gold, red, blue, and purple with rubrics in red rustic capitals.

Matthew (f. 9), seated frontally on a round-backed cushioned throne, dips his pen into an inkpot on the left, while his left hand holding a knife rests on an open book (cf. no. 67, f. 17). A large panelled initial L in gold and colour (f. 9ᵛ), its horizontal bar made up of a voluminous hollow leaf motif, introduces the first verses of Matthew's text.

Mark (f. 38), seated sideways with feet pointing to the left, turns to the right to sharpen his pen with a knife (cf. no. 67, f. 65ᵛ). The abrupt movement of his torso is echoed by the drapery end flying beyond the frame-bar, by the chair placed diagonally in perspective, by the emphatic twist of the curtain with its rings set aslant on the bar, and by his garments flaring widely out at the bottom. It is a crowded composition, conceived in terms of movement and countermovement heralding the oncoming Romanesque style. A golden blob entangled in red and blue lines (the sun?) is placed over the top right corner of the frame. An initial I (f. 38ᵛ) in gold and colour, topped by interlace knotwork with two griffins' heads chewing foliage, has a bunched-leaf terminal at the base.

Luke (f. 60ᵛ), closely recalling the St. Luke of no. 67 (f. 61), is shown in sideview against a red to pink curtain dotted with gold in the folds. With a knife in his hand and a quill stuck behind his ear, he bends to the right over an open book on a draped stand. A splendid initial Q on the opposite page (f. 61) contains an elaborate plant scroll with a tulip-like flower in the bowl (frequent in Carolingian manuscripts from Tours but as yet unknown in Anglo-Saxon illumination). The tail of the letter is in the form of a finned dragon fighting a basilisk.

John (f. 88ᵛ), seated sideways with legs crossed and feet in a dancing posture (cf. no. 78, Cambridge, Corpus Christi College 389), the flap of his mantle flying beyond the frame, bends to the right over an open book and, knife in hand, writes busily; two curtains looped round the inner band of the frame fill the space above. The initial I opposite (f. 89) contains pink and blue panels within gold and has, at the top and bottom, interlace knotwork terminating in animal and bird heads, the latter holding fruit in their beaks.

Colours, remarkable for their intensity, include bright orange-red, pink, mauve, green, blue, and a good deal of burnished gold. In the Evangelists' mantles the niello-like effect of the gold is due to the incised lines which were originally filled in with black. The strong colouring and hard outline of the drawing, with the drapery folds sharply and deeply shaded, are unusual in Anglo-Saxon illumi-

nation and suggest continental influences, perhaps from the German schools of Trier and Echternach or from Flanders (note the distinct upright format of the pictures). But the liveliness of the Evangelist figures and the excitement of their gestures, enhanced by the vigorous patterning of the agitated, crumpled draperies, together with the painting devices of coloured shadow outline and zigzags in the backgrounds, are unmistakably English. Stylistically and in iconographic details the miniatures show analogies with no. 97 (Hereford Troper).

PROVENANCE: The Gospels, of uncertain origin, were at Hereford as shown by the description of boundaries of that see drawn by Aethestan, Bishop of Hereford (1012–56). This was added in Old English on a blank leaf (f. 8) in the late 11th century, an addition which led to suggestions that the manuscript may have been produced at Hereford. Both the Gospels and the related so-called Hereford Troper (no. 97) were recently ascribed by Wormald (1973) to Canterbury. The present volume was given to Pembroke College by William Mundy, fellow, in 1730.

LITERATURE: Westwood, *Facsimiles*, 143; M. R. James, *A descriptive catalogue of the Manuscripts in Pembroke College, Cambridge*, 1905, 266–9, plates (ff. 60ᵛ, 61); Burlington Fine Arts Club, *Exhibition of Illuminated Manuscripts*, 1908, no. 10, pl. 16; Homburger, 6; *New Pal. Soc.*, I, pl. 238; Millar, I, 22–3, no. 61, pl. 30; O. Homburger, 'Review', *Art Bulletin*, X, 1928, 400; A. Boeckler, *Abendländische Miniaturen*, Berlin 1930, 56, 91; M. Forster, 'Der Flussname Themse und seine Sippe', *Sitzungsberichte der Bayrischen Akademie der Wissenschaften*, 1941, I, 769; Kendrick, *Late Saxon*, 21 n. 4; Talbot Rice, *English Art*, 211–12, pl. 77a; Freyhan, 429; Ker, *Catalogue*, no. 78; *St. Albans Psalter*, 105 n. 1; Rickert, *Painting in Britain*, 55–6, pl. 49b; J. J. G. Alexander, 'A little-known Gospel Book', *Burlington Magazine*, CVIII, 1966, 10 nn. 19, 28, 14 nn. 44–5; Roosen-Runge, 67–9, ills. 9, 10; Alexander, *Norman Illumination*, 164; C. Nordenfalk, 'The Draped Lectern', *Intuition und Kunstwissenschaft: Festschrift für Hans Swarzenski*, Berlin 1973; Wormald, *Angleterre*, 253, ill. 257; C. M. Kauffmann, *Romanesque Manuscripts 1066–1190*, 1975, 18.

EXHIBITED: Brussels, 1973, *English Illuminated Manuscripts 700–1500*, no. 12.

97. London, British Library MS Cotton, Caligula A. XIV (ff. 1–92)

Troper (Hereford Troper)
216 × 155 mm.
c. 1050

Ills. 293–295

This manuscript, a collection of tropes (musical interpolations in the liturgy), is illustrated with eleven full- or half-page pictures representing subjects related to Church festivals throughout the year.

The miniatures are mainly enclosed by bands of gold and colour with corner ornaments (cf. no. 96, Hereford Gospels) and have versified *tituli* inscribed around the frames; the long swinging philacteries, most often left blank, are an unusual and prominent feature (cf. no. 84, Bury Psalter).

An ornamental initial 'h' (f. 2) to the tropes for Christmas is made up of voluminous acanthus foliage in gold, brown, purple, and yellow. A full-page picture (f. 3ᵛ), an unusual hieratic representation, shows the protomartyr Stephen in priestly garments standing rigidly frontal, holding in veiled hands a flowering rod and stole on the right and an open book and censer on the left with the space above it filled by an abstract two-pronged motif. A miniature representing an Ascension of Anglo-Saxon type (f. 18) contains unusual features; it portrays 'the disappearing Christ' with only His feet shown when He ascends into a saffron yellow sky from a mountain peak inscribed *Mons Oliveti*; and, below, the Virgin with the Apostles standing under three arches of a building and looking up to heaven with gestures of amazement (cf. nos. 72, Robert of Jumièges Sacramentary; 84, Bury Psalter; 98, Tiberius C. VI; also 58, Junius 11; for literary sources cf. Schapiro, 1943). The Naming of John (f. 20ᵛ), a half-page picture framed by a heavy interlace ribbon, represents Elizabeth holding the infant in gold swaddling clothes, Zacharias writing its name on a tablet and two inquiring figures (cf. no. 23, Benedictional of St. Ethelwold, f. 92ᵛ).

The Release of St. Peter (f. 22) is shown in three registers and in continuous narrative with the top register depicting Peter in prison, addressed by an angel standing beyond the frame and holding an inscribed scroll. Below and at the bottom the Apostle is being led out and then away, and the whole picture is again enclosed by an interlace ribbon. The Martyrdom of St. Lawrence (f. 25) is represented in two scenes: above, the confrontation with Decius and below, the torture of the Saint with an angel flying down to receive his soul, a feature not usually found in other representations of this theme, but here traceable to the Utrecht Psalter and appearing in its copy, Harley 603 (no. 64, f. 71).

Joachim with his flock and an announcing angel are shown in an unframed picture (f. 26), their figures in brown and purplish-grey silhouetted sharply against a bright yellow background. A similarly coloured miniature (f. 26ᵛ) represents Joachim and Anna with the infant Mary in her arms blessed by the Hand of God and seated under an arch-and-column frame with heavily foliated spandrels.

A scene from the life of St. Martin (f. 29) shows the two figures drawn by the main artist, but with that of the Saint in monkish garb overpainted by another hand. A monumental representation of St. Andrew enthroned (f. 30ᵛ; cf. no. 72, Robert of Jumièges Sacramentary, f. 164ᵛ) is set against a reddish-brown ground with formalized, starkly yellow cloud motifs.

A half-page illustration (f. 31), showing the Apostles in two compact groups with Peter and Paul in the centre blessed by the Hand of God, probably refers to the feast of All Saints (not the Pentecost for the Holy Dove is absent; cf. Talbot Rice); it is drawn by the main artist but possibly coloured by another with light washes of red, yellow, green in the figures and pale greenish-grey in the background. A group of the Holy Virgins (f. 36) carrying lamps, torches, and flowering rods, their figures harshly silhouetted against a saffron yellow background, is shown standing and looking up to the blessing Hand of God issuing rays from a hemisphere above.

The miniatures, stylistically related, to no. 96 (Hereford Gospels) with similarities extending to a number of details, may have been executed by the same artist. They show modifications, however, in their extensive use of swinging philacteries, their extreme formalization of design with a complete absence of agitated hemlines, and their emphasis on stiffly crumpling draperies with folds incised in deeply-shaded parallel lines, which give them the look of corrugated metal sheeting. This harsh breaking up of surfaces heralds the Romanesque style and, unusual in Anglo-Saxon illumination (cf. no. 96, Hereford Gospels), it suggests fresh influences of continental manuscripts, perhaps from Echternach or Flanders (cf. Brussels, Bibl. Royale MS II. 175, from St. Bertin?) though a foretaste of this stylistic development can be seen in certain miniatures of Aelfric's Pentateuch (no. 86), a manuscript from St. Augustine's, Canterbury. Glaring and sharply contrasted, the colours include saffron yellow, dull green, mauve, grey, gold, and silver in the highlights (now oxidized). The features of the squat, large-headed and solemn figures are modelled in red or brown on a thick, flesh-tinted paste. Large gold initials introduce the tropes, rubrics are in red, and initials in the text deep red, mauve, and green.

Some of the illustrated subjects find parallels in the Sacramentary of Drogo (Bibl. Nat., lat. 9428), the Benedictional of St. Ethelwold (no. 23), and the Sacramentary of Robert of Jumièges (no. 72); their iconography, however, bears little resemblance to that of the three manuscripts mentioned above. In one case only—the Martyrdom of St. Lawrence—the unusual presence of an angel may perhaps be linked with the imagery of the Utrecht Psalter. This lack of correlation and the inclusion of illustrations without known parallels in manuscript painting (cf. ff. 22, 26, 26ᵛ, 29, 36), suggest not only a dependence on different models, perhaps metalwork or ivory carvings from Byzantium, but also a possible inspiration from literary sources (such as the Apocryphal Gospels of Pseudo-Matthew for the Joachim and Anna episode, ff. 26, 26ᵛ; and Anglo-Saxon literature on Holy Places reflected in the Ascension, f. 18, cf. Schapiro, 1943).

PROVENANCE: Bearing similarities to no. 96 (Hereford Gospels) the manuscript was ascribed to Hereford on stylistic grounds. There is apparently some liturgical evidence, however, indicating Christ Church, Canterbury, as a likely place of origin (Frere, 1894), an attribution tentatively accepted by

Ker (*Medieval Libraries*, 1964, 35), and lately also supported by Wormald (*Angleterre*). The manuscript belonged to Sir Robert Cotton (d. 1631). His library, presented to the nation by his grandson, Sir John Cotton, in 1700, was incorporated in the British Museum in 1753.

LITERATURE: W. H. Frere, 'The Winchester Troper', *H.B.S.*, VIII, 1894, p. XXX n. 1; C. Wordsworth and H. Littlehales, *The old service books of the English Church*, 1904, 207, 210, pl. XXIV; Homburger, 6, 21 n. 1; Millar, I, 22–3, no. 60, pl. 29; O. Homburger, 'Review', *Art Bulletin*, X, 1928, 400; A. Boeckler, *Abendländische Miniaturen*, Berlin 1930, 56, 91; M. Schapiro, 'The image of the disappearing Christ', *Gazette des Beaux Arts*, 6e sér. XXIII, 1943, 142, fig. 6; Kendrick, *Late Saxon*, 21, 131, pl. XXII; H. Swarzenski, 'Der Stil der Bibel Carilefs von Durham', *Form und Inhalt. Kunstgeschichtliche Studien für Otto Schmitt*, Stuttgart 1951, 91; Talbot Rice, *English Art*, 212, pl. 67b; Freyhan, 429, pl. XL, fig. 26; *St. Albans Psalter*, 105 n. 1; W. Mersmann, 'Das Elfenbeinkreuz der Sammlung Topic-Mimara', *Wallraf-Richartz-Jahrbuch*, XXI, 1963, 102, fig. 50; Rickert, *Painting in Britain*, 55–6, 70, 227 n. 32, pl. 49a; Swarzenski, *Monuments*, 26, pl. 66, figs. 152–3; Alexander, *Norman Illumination*, 119, 152, 164, pl. 37a; *English Illuminated manuscripts 700–1500*, Brussels Exhibition Catalogue, 1973, p. 33; Wormald, *Angleterre*, 253, ill. 256; C. M. Kauffmann, *Romanesque Manuscripts 1066–1190*, 1975, 18, fig. 6.

98. London, British Library MS Cotton, Tiberius C. VI

Psalter. Gallican version with Old English gloss
248 × 146 mm.

c. 1050   *Ills. 297, 302–311, fig. 37*

This richly illuminated manuscript is the earliest surviving example of a psalter which contains a prefatory pictorial cycle of sixteen full-page drawings with explanatory inscriptions illustrating the lives of David (ff. 8–10) and of Christ (ff. 10v–15). In addition there are various groups of diagrams, three illustrations in the text, and two fully painted miniatures. Framed initial pages preceding Psalms 1, 51, 101 (ff. 31, 72, 115) mark the three-fold division of the Psalter, while elaborate coloured initials introduce Psalms 26, 38, 52, 68, 80, 97, and 109 (the latter surrounded by a full page border) belonging to the liturgical eight-fold system. All diagrams and drawings are in brown and red outline shaded blue, green, and red with orange and red in details. The decoration can be roughly divided into four groups: the first connected with computus matter (ff. 2–7v); the second comprising the pictorial series; the third with representations of musical instruments; the fourth illustrating the text (ff. 30v, 71v, 114v, 126v).

To the first group belong: angels and plant motifs decorating arch-and-column frames of computistic tables (ff. 2v, 3) with beasts and birds at the base (ff. 4v, 5); a miniature of a feast at the head of the last table (f. 5v) which probably comes from a series

of occupational calendarial illustrations and may represent January; a diagrammatic representation (f. 6v) of Christ–*Vita* holding a scroll with numbers for calculation of chances of recovery or death, and below *Mors–Superbia*, a winged figure with a similar scroll, six small dragons—the vices—springing from its wings, the whole surrounded by inscriptions (cf. no. 17, Leofric Missal); a page with diagrams separated by a band inscribed '*Dextera iam dni fulget cum floribus paschae*' (f. 7; cf. no. 17), showing above *Horologium*, below *Dextera dni* with dates written on each of its fingers (for discussion see Heimann, 1966); and a diagrammatic representation of the Creation (f. 7v) with the head of the Almighty over the circle of the world, two trumpets (or horns) —the breath of God—issuing from His mouth, a pair of dividers and scales in His hand, and the Holy Dove emerging from the waters (Heimann has suggested that the diagram is, in fact, a representation of the Trinity, with the two trumpets standing for the Second Person, cf. no. 102, Royal 1. E. VII; cf. also nos. 84, Bury Psalter; 67, Eadui Codex).

The cycle from David's life is introduced by a drawing of David rescuing a lamb from the lion (f. 8; cf. no. 7, Junius Psalter, f. 118). It is followed by the David and Goliath episode shown on two pages (ff. 8v–9) in three scenes which are in the wrong sequence: on the left David is slinging a stone and, below, piercing Goliath with the latter's own sword; on the right, Goliath threatens David with a spear while the Philistines turn away in flight. Wormald (1962) has observed that the whole episode was probably originally a single, horizontal composition with the beheading of Goliath shown as the last scene. Representations of this kind occur in early Byzantine art, as is shown by a 7th-century silver dish from Cyprus, now in the Metropolitan Museum in New York. Illustrations from David's life were also current in Insular art from the 8th century onwards, e.g. in initials of the Vespasian Psalter (Cotton Vesp. A. 1), in the drawings on a leaf in Leningrad (see Wormald, 1962), and in carvings on certain 10th-century Irish crosses (see Henry, Irish Art, II, 1967). The next scene in the present manuscript, the Anointing of David by Samuel (f. 9v), whose names are inscribed over their heads, is witnessed by a group of David's followers on the left (note the spindly plant motifs typical of 10th- to 11th-century Winchester manuscripts). The last picture shows David enthroned harping, with the Holy Dove perched on his sceptre, while the Hand of God emerges from clouds with a horn emitting green rays (f. 10).

The christological series, which refers to the liturgical cycle from Lent to Whitsun, may have largely derived, according to Wormald, from Sacramentary illustrations (e.g. no. 72, Robert of Jumièges Sacramentary). It opens with the Third Temptation (f. 10v) representing Christ on a hillock on the left, worldly treasures piled up at His feet, rebuking the Devil shown with many-eyed wings. The Entry into Jerusalem (f. 11) portrays Christ, book in hand, astride a donkey in Western fashion and acclaimed by a group of Israelites on the left. The Washing of the Feet (f. 11ᵛ), is the earliest example of the Anglo-Saxon iconographic formula with Christ kneeling on both knees in front of St. Peter (cf. Schapiro, 1943; cf. also no. 64, Harley 603, f. 66ᵛ, showing a monk washing the feet of the poor) and unique in having an angel flying down from heaven on the right with a towel. The Betrayal (f. 12) shows Christ in the centre, Judas on the left embracing Him, while a crowd approaches from the right with torches to apprehend Him. The next scene represents Christ before Pilate (f. 12ᵛ), His wrists bound by a rope; He is led by a servant towards Pilate enthroned under a canopy on the left. The Crucifixion (f. 13) shows the Dead Christ on a tree-trunk cross (cf. nos. 93, Morgan 709; 104, Corpus Christi College 422; 103, Arundel 60) between Longinus piercing His side with a spear on the left and Stephaton handing up a sponge on the right (recalling the figure of Orion in no. 42, Harley 2506, f. 38), an iconography without parallel in Anglo-Saxon illumination but not uncommon on ivories and stone carvings. The Resurrection (f. 13ᵛ) portrays the Three Marys carrying ointments and a censer, approaching from the left, and an angel with a book seated by a Sepulchre of a Late Antique type (cf. Ascension panel in Munich, 5th century). The Harrowing of Hell (f. 14) shows a towering figure of Christ trampling upon the bound Hades and stooping down in the Utrecht Psalter manner to deliver the souls from the mouth of Hell in the bottom right corner. In the Incredulity of Thomas (f. 14ᵛ) Christ raises His arm to show the wound in His side to the doubting Apostle, a representation identical with that in no. 23 (Benedictional of St. Ethelwold, f. 56ᵛ) but here limited to the two main figures. The scene of the Ascension (f. 15) contains the so-called 'disappearing Christ', an iconographic variant of Anglo-Saxon origin (cf. nos. 58, 'Caedmon' Genesis; 72, Robert of Jumièges Sacramentary; 97, Hereford Troper), and below two groups of Apostles in the centre of which stand Peter and another Apostle holding a crown, unique in this context. The Pentecost (f. 15ᵛ) shows unusually the Holy Dove being held by the Hand of God while descending upon the Apostles in two groups below, headed on the left by Peter with a book in veiled hand, and an Apostle on the right holding a crown. St. Michael (f. 16) carrying a shield (cf. no. 79, Douce 296) is throwing a spear into the mouth of a dragon standing on the right (for sources of the iconography see Alexander, *Norman Illumination*), a representation probably at one time also included in no. 23 (Benedictional of St. Ethelwold).

The diagrammatic representations of musical instruments (ff. 16ᵛ, 17, 18), each accompanied by a descriptive commentary, are centred round the miniature with David playing the psaltery (f. 17ᵛ; cf. Otbert Psalter, Boulogne MS 20) and linked with the preface of the Psalter (f. 19) where the instruments of David's musicians are mentioned. A full-page painted miniature (f. 18ᵛ) shows Christ in Majesty holding a flaming horn and a cross and seated in a yellow mandorla delicately patterned in red and flanked by trumpeting angels with many-eyed wings, while below an archangel with similar wings supports a scroll held on either side by a tonsured haloed ecclesiastic. The miniature, painted in soft clear blue, pale mauve, pink, grey, and green, high-lighted with white and yellow in ovals and circles, is framed by pale pink and ochre bands with delicate scroll pattern. An initial D to the first Preface on the opposite page (f. 19), painted in similar colours, is made up of panels and animal-headed interlace knotwork and surrounded by a late 'Winchester' border of interlacing bands with foliage spreading outwards only.

Another painted miniature representing David and the Musicians (f. 30ᵛ) marks the beginning of the Psalter text, facing the great B initial on the opposite page (f. 31). David, enthroned, harping, the Holy Ghost descending to touch his crown, is accompanied by his four musicians (the names Ethan, Iduthin, David are still visible, others, presumably Asaph and Eman as in no. 80, Winchcombe Psalter, f. 4ᵛ, no longer legible). The miniature in a similar late 'Winchester' border as described above (f. 19) is also similarly coloured with figures and details emphasized by a purple shadow outline on pale pink ground. The initial B to Psalm 1 (f. 31), made up of coloured panels, interlace knotwork terminals on the shaft, and a mask head clasping the bows (cf. no. 41, Harley 2904), is accompanied by alternating lines of coloured lettering, the whole enclosed by a full 'Winchester' border of multicoloured foliage. A full-page drawing prefacing Psalm 51 (f. 71ᵛ) shows a tonsured ecclesiastic in Mass vestments, probably St. Jerome (cf. *Psalterium aureum* of St. Gall, p. 14; Lothair Psalter, B.L. Add. 37768, f. 6, both 9th cent.) standing under an arch-and-column frame. On the opposite page (f. 72) the initial Q to Psalm 51 contains coloured acanthus leaves in the bowl composed of two dragons, while a third dragon forms the tail of the letter. A full-page drawing (f. 114ᵛ) under arch and columns prefacing Psalm 101 shows Christ treading upon a lion and dragon (cf. no. 80, Winchcombe Psalter). The opening lines of the Psalm on the opposite page (f. 115), headed by an ornamental initial D with foliage on dark ground, are surrounded by a full border of 'Winchester' type. A half-page drawing of the Trinity (f. 126ᵛ), preceding Psalm 109, is enclosed in a quatrefoil within a circle and shows the Lord blessing, Alpha and Omega on either side of His head, the *Agnus Dei* with a book and cross on the left, and a cross-haloed Dove on the right, the iconography related to nos. 32 (B.N. lat. 6401, f. 159) and 84 (Bury Psalter, ff. 168ᵛ–169). The opening verses of Psalm 109 (f. 127) are introduced by an ornamental initial D and surrounded by a modified 'Winchester' frame with mask heads spitting leaves on the two laterals. Large plain initials to psalms are in blue, green, or metallic red with similar smaller initials to verses and rubrics in red capitals. Each psalm is followed by a collect (cf. Stowe 2, no. 99) and the text ends imperfectly in Psalm 113, v. 11.

The decoration is probably executed by one artist. Wormald has suggested that the archetype of the drawings may have been a set of illustrations executed in the style of Harley 2904; but in the Tiberius manuscript the flickering outline has been hardened and illusionistic elements have been stylized into decorative conventions (note the trefoils of the bunched drapery ends, the heart-shaped pattern of the elbow joints of Christ crucified, etc.). But despite this advanced stylization and reduction of design into pattern, there is a remarkable lightness in the drawing as well as verve and vigour in the swift, incisive strokes of the contours; and figures with their conventionalized features, wig-like hair set into series of knobby curls, and stiff angular movement, are nevertheless sensitive and expressive. The pattern of the ample draperies is rich in effect and has a rhythm about it but the all-pervading ornamental tendency destroys any notion of body-forms beneath. The garments are often diapered or ornamented with quatrefoils and bands of strokes and dots, while the white and yellow highlights distributed in circles, ovals, and lozenges over the painted as well as the merely drawn figures create a curious dichotomy with the intricate linear arabesques of the folds. In the head-types, certain drapery patterns, and a number of details, the drawings hark back to no. 23 (Benedictional of St. Ethelwold).

Homburger assigned the manuscript to Winchester on account of the script and decoration. This attribution has been supported by Wormald (1962) on internal evidence, Psalm 77 being divided at v. 40 by means of a large initial, a peculiarity limited, as observed by Sisam (1959), to four other psalters, all fairly certainly from Winchester (Harley 2904, no. 41; Cotton, Vitellius E. XVIII; Stowe 2, no. 99; Arundel 60, no. 103). Moreover, the ornamental initials in the present volume are strikingly similar to those in two mid 11th-century Winchester manuscripts, Bodleian MS Bodley 775 and British Library MS Stowe 2 (no. 99), and were probably executed by the same illuminator. Lastly, T. A. M. Bishop's recent identification of the scribe with the one who wrote part of Bodley 775 confirms the Winchester origin of the Tiberius Psalter, together with its dating on stylistic considerations to c. 1050.

PROVENANCE: The Psalter, which belonged to Thomas Cotton (f. 2), 1594–1662, the only surviving child of Robert, was damaged by fire in 1731 and the leaves are now mounted on sheets of paper. Sir Robert Cotton died in 1631; his library, presented to the nation by his grandson, Sir John Cotton, in 1700, was incorporated in the British Museum in 1753.

LITERATURE: Westwood, *Facsimiles*, 118, pl. 46; *Pal. Soc.*, I, pl. 98; J. A. Herbert, *Illuminated Manuscripts*, 1911, 119, pl. 14; Homburger, 21 nn. 1, 3, 25, 68, 69; H. P. Mitchell, 'Flotsam of Later Anglo-Saxon Art', *Burlington Magazine*, XLIII, 1923, 107–8, pl. VIIc; Millar, I, 21–2, no. 57, pl.

27a; M. R. James, 'Illustrations of the Old Testament', in *A Book of Old Testament Illustrations*, Roxburghe Club, 1927, 26; O. Homburger, 'Review', *Art Bulletin*, X, 1928, 401; Saunders, *English Illumination*, 24, 27, pls. 28, 29; A. Boeckler, *Abendländische Miniaturen*, Berlin, 1930, 56; W. Weisbach, *Manierismus in mittelalterlicher Kunst*, Basle 1942, 23, pl. 16; F. Wormald, 'The development of English Illumination in the twelfth century', *Journal of the British Archaeological Association*, VIII, 1943, 32, pl. XII; M. Schapiro, 'The image of the disappearing Christ', *Gazette des Beaux Arts*, XXIII, 1943, 150; Wormald, *Initials*, 126; F. Saxl and R. Wittkower, *British Art and the Mediterranean*, 1948, pls. 21 (6), 22 (4, 5), 23 (5); Kendrick, *Late Saxon*, 17, 131, pl. XVI; Wormald, *English Drawings*, 50–3, 57, 64, 68, 71, 76, no. 32, pls. 30–2; Talbot Rice, *English Art*, 96, 219, pl. 83; R. Loewe, 'Herbert Bosham's Commentary on Jerome's Hebrew Psalter', *Biblica*, 1953, 166 n. 5, pl. facing p. 166; F. Behn, *Musikleben im Altertum und frühen Mittelalter*, Stuttgart 1954, 157, pl. 202; Dodwell, *Canterbury School*, 5, 18, 23, pls. 10a, 14d; Ker, *Catalogue*, no. 199; Nordenfalk, *Early Medieval*, 190, pl. 186; C. and K. Sisam, 'The Salisbury Psalter', *E.E.T.S.*, no. 242, 1959, 4, 5; D. Tselos, 'English manuscript illustration and the Utrecht Psalter', *Art Bulletin*, XLI, 1959, 149; Rickert, *Miniatura*, 14, 22, pl. 29; *St. Albans Psalter*, 51, 53, 56, 86, 88, 93, 143 n. 3, 204, 206, pls. 101 c, d, 106b, 127c, 167b; H. Steger, *David Rex et Propheta*, Nürnberg 1961, pl. 15, fig. 27; F. Wormald, 'An English eleventh-century Psalter with pictures', *Walpole Society*, XXXVIII, 1962, 1–13, pls. 1–30; R. H. Randall jr., 'An eleventh-century ivory pectoral cross', *J.W.C.I.* XXV, 1962, 165, 167–8, pls. 32a, 32b; W. Mersmann 'Das Elfenbeinkreuz der Sammlung Topic-Mimara', *Wallraf-Richartz-Jahrbuch*, XXV, 1963, 28, 40, 102, figs. 20, 31, 52; Rickert, *Painting in Britain*, 51, 53–4, 55, pls. 50, 51; F. Wormald, 'Continental Influence on English Medieval Illumination', *Fourth International Congress of Bibliophiles*, London 1965, 10, pl. II; id., *Style and Design*, 31, fig. 11; A. Heimann, 'Three illustrations from the Bury St. Edmunds Psalter and their prototypes', *J.W.C.I.*, XXIX, 1966, 39, 43 ff., pls. 9a, 10a, 12a; Swarzenski, *Monuments*, pl. 60, fig. 133; M. W. Evans, *Medieval Drawings*, 1969, 24, pl. 23; Alexander, *Norman Illumination*, 60–1, 91, 92 n. 4, 93, 120, 133, 148 n. 3, 152, 193, pls. 140, 18d; Bishop, *English Caroline*, no. 27; G. Schiller, *Iconography of Christian Art*, 1971, II, 46, 55, ills. 134, 168; J. Beckwith, *Ivory Carvings in Early Medieval England*, 1972, 34, fig. 34; F. Wormald, *The Winchester Psalter*, 1973, 70, ills. 45, 46, 49; id., *Angleterre*, 252, pl. 219, ill. 255; C. M. Kauffmann, *Romanesque Manuscripts 1066–1190*, 1975, 17, 18, fig. 4.

99. London, British Library MS Stowe 2
Psalter. Gallican version with Old English gloss
278 × 180 mm.
c. 1050–75. (?) Winchester, New Minster

Ill. 296

The decoration of the Psalter consists of large, ornamental initials heading Psalms 1, 51, and 101, with smaller and less elaborate ones introducing other psalms and canticles. Their close similarities to the initials of no. 98 (Tiberius C. VI), noted by Homburger, suggest not only their origin from the same or a closely related scriptorium but also most likely a common illuminator. He was probably responsible likewise for the only initial, an O, in the so-called 'Aethelred Troper', Bodleian MS Bodley 775 from Winchester, written in part by the scribe of no. 98 (Tiberius C. VI; cf. Bishop, *English Caroline*).

The initial B to Psalm 1 (f. 1), rather conservative in style, is a simplified and cruder version of the one in Harley 2904 (no. 41) and is composed of acanthus-filled panels, interlace terminals with beasts' heads, and floriated plant scrolls filling the bows, with a mask head where they join. The Q (f. 56) to Psalm 51 is clasped on the top by a mask head spitting foliage, with the tail of the letter in the form of a dragon. The D (f. 111ᵛ) to Psalm 101 is composed of panels containing acanthus patterns and of beast-headed interlace terminals. The colouring (pale pink, mauve, blue, ochre, and yellow) closely recalls that of no. 98 (Tiberius C. VI). Other initials are in red, green, blue, and mauve, with red or silvery rubrics.

The Psalter contains the same series of collects, one after each psalm, as does Tiberius C. VI (no. 98; cf. Wormald, 1962) and Psalm 77 is similarly divided at v. 40, a peculiarity found in four other examples from Winchester. The scribe of the present volume is, according to T. A. M. Bishop, a New Minster, Winchester, scribe responsible for three more manuscripts with the same origin (cf. *English Caroline*).

PROVENANCE: The manuscript belonged to Kateryn Rudston (f. 9) in the 16th century and subsequently to Henry Spelman (f. 1), whose name accompanies the *imprimatur* of 17 May, 1638 (f. 183ᵛ) for the edition of the Psalter brought out by his son, John Spelman, in 1640. In the sale of W. Clavell, 1742, as lot 18, it belonged successively to Thomas Astle (d. 1803), to the Marquis of Buckingham who formed the Stowe collection (d. 1849), and to the Earl of Ashburnham (d. 1879). It was purchased for the British Museum with other Stowe manuscripts in 1883.

LITERATURE: Homburger, 64, 68; Ker, *Catalogue*, no. 271; F. Wormald, 'An English eleventh-century Psalter with pictures', *Walpole Society*, XXXVIII, 1962, 1–13; Bishop, *English Caroline*, p. XV.

100. London, British Library MS Cotton, Tiberius A. III

(1) Regularis concordia (ff. 3–27ᵛ)
(2) Rule of St. Benedict (ff. 118–63)
240 × 177 mm.
c. 1050. Canterbury, Christ Church

Ills. 313, 314

This composite volume the leaves of which were damaged by the fire of 1731, contains besides (1) and (2), miscellaneous contemporary prayers, homilies, and other matter, and is illustrated by two full-page miniatures.

The first (f. 2ᵛ) preceding the *Regularis concordia* (1), shows King Edgar, a palm in his hand, seated with SS. Dunstan and Ethelwold under three arcades. They all support a long scroll which undulates across the picture. Below in the forefront, a genuflecting monk holding a similar wavy scroll (he seems to be a standard Canterbury figure, cf. f. 117ᵛ, and no. 101, Durham B. III. 32) is looking eagerly up at them. The drawing, in fine, crisp sepia outline shaded brown, green, mauve, and ochre, is stylistically a development from Arundel 155 (no. 66) and closely reminiscent of the Bury Psalter (no. 84), but, particularly in the monk's figure, it is more stylized and mannered.

The second, fully-painted, miniature (f. 117ᵛ), prefacing the Rule of St. Benedict (2) shows three monks approaching from the right and presenting a copy of the Rule, displayed on a draped stand, to the Saint. He is enthroned on the left, with, below, the tiny figure of a monk embracing his feet, a group copied from a similar representation in Arundel 155 (no. 66, f. 133). Another monk falling to his knees in fervent adoration of the Saint and holding an exceedingly long, winding scroll is shown in the foreground on the right (cf. f. 2ᵛ). This highly dramatized composition, divided into clearly defined compartments, is conceived in terms of contrast between, on the one hand, the long vertical curves of the swaying, small-headed monks' figures and on the other hand, the bold S-motif, a powerful 'key-note' of the picture (Dodwell, *Canterbury School*), which is formed by whorls and tumbles of draperies on the knees of the frontally enthroned, majestic St. Benedict, looming large on the left. The apotheosis of the Saint is staged with an amazing virtuosity and vigour. Iconographically and stylistically a development from Arundel 155 (no. 66), the miniature shows a culmination of trends apparent in Canterbury work of the second quarter of the eleventh century. The dynamic qualities of the picture are brought out by the extremely free, broad brushstrokes of opaque colours (shades of grey, olive to sea green, ochre, brown, and orange) and by a firm, sweeping black outline softened by coloured shadows around figures and details. The illustration is enclosed within a trellis-like sparsely foliated 'Winchester' border (badly damaged by fire), with bars interlacing on the corners and closely reminiscent of the framework in no. 67 (Eadui Codex). The initials are in red, brown, and green, with rubrics in red.

PROVENANCE: The manuscript, written in Christ Church, Canterbury, is identifiable by a table of contents (f. 117), 12th century, with a volume described in the medieval catalogue of the Christ Church library (cf. James, *Ancient Libraries*). Inscribed across the top of the same page (f. 117)

'Eluricus Bate' in a hand possibly earlier than the table below, the volume may have been owned or assembled by Bate (cf. Ker, *Catalogue*. p. 241). As appears from the order of the entries listed in the said table part (2) originally preceded part (1). The manuscript, containing a list of contents inscribed by Cotton (f. 2ᵛ), was in his possession by 1621. Sir Robert Cotton's library, presented to the nation by his grandson, Sir John Cotton, in 1700, was incorporated in the British Museum in 1753.

LITERATURE: Westwood, *Facsimiles*, 129; James, *Ancient Libraries*, pp. xxiii, 508, no. 296; Homburger 25 n. 1; Millar, I, 49; O. Homburger, 'Review', *Art Bulletin*, X, 1928, 401; F. Wormald, 'Two Anglo-Saxon Miniatures Compared', *British Museum Quarterly*, 1935, 113-15, pl. XXXV, a; R. A. B. Mynors, *Durham Cathedral Manuscripts*, 1939, 28; Wormald, *English Drawings*, 45-7, 49, 51, 53, 57, 64, 68, 71, no. 31, pl. 23; Dodwell, *Canterbury School*, 3 ff., 37, 120, pls. 2b, 3a; Ker, *Catalogue*, no. 186; *St. Albans Psalter*, 205, pl. 168a; Rickert, *Painting in Britain*, 48; Gneuss, 45 n. 14, 89, 101, 110-11, 118-19, 161-2, 180, 189, 230-40, 382; C. Nordenfalk, 'The Draped Lectern', *Intuition und Kunstwissenschaft: Festschrift für Hans Swarzenski*, Berlin 1973, 87.

The manuscript was assigned by Wormald to Christ Church, Canterbury, on account of the drawing (f. 56ᵛ), and on stylistic and internal evidence (the occurrence of three hymns for St. Augustine of England in the Hymnal).

PROVENANCE: The volume belonged to Thomas Aynesworth in the 16th century (f. 1) and was lent by Richard Shuttleworth to George Davenport in 1676 (f. 127ᵛ). Recorded in the Catalogue of the Cathedral MSS by Thomas Rud, it must have come to Durham before 1775, as a gift, according to Rud, of Thomas Wharton (d. 1714).

LITERATURE: R. Surtees, *History and Antiquities of the County Palatine of Durham*, 1816-40, III, 300-1; F. Wormald, 'Two Anglo-Saxon Miniatures Compared', *British Museum Quarterly*, IX, 1935, 113-15, pl. XXXV, b; R. A. B. Mynors, *Durham Cathedral Manuscripts*, 28-9, no. 22, pl. 15a; Wormald, *English Drawings*, 45, 47, 50, 64, 68, no. 20, pl. 29; C. R. Dodwell, *Canterbury School*, 5, 120, pl. 3b; Ker, *Catalogue*, no. 107; Rickert, *Painting in Britain*, 48; Gneuss, 40 n. 48, 50 n. 32, 55, 85-90, 122, 198, 241, 246, 248 and *passim*; P. M. Korhammer, 'The origin of the Bosworth Psalter', *Anglo-Saxon England*, 2, 1973, 180.

101. Durham, Cathedral Library MS B. III. 32
(1) Hymnal (ff. 1-55), with Latin and Old English gloss
(2) Aelfric's grammar (ff. 56-127)
235 × 156 mm.
c. 1050. Canterbury, Christ Church

Ill. 315

The volume consists of two manuscripts bound together at an early date, as indicated by a 13th-century inscription (f. 2).
(1) This part contains an initial O (f. 2), drawn in fine, firm outline and historiated with a personification of Light represented by a half-length female figure holding two torches, her head-type closely recalling no. 75 (Harley 76). Initials to the hymns and canticles are in red, green, or blue.
(2) A full-page drawing (f. 56ᵛ) prefacing Aelfric's grammar copies the frontispiece in no. 100 (Tiberius A. III, f. 2ᵛ) but the omission of the central figure of King Edgar, leaving only the two secondary figures, changes its subject into a disputation picture of rare occurrence in Anglo-Saxon illumination. The two haloed ecclesiastics are shown seated under an arcade of two arches talking together; they are supporting a long undulating scroll which extends across the composition, while in the foreground, a genuflecting monk holding a similar scroll looks up at them. The drawing has lost some of its delicacy and sensitiveness in the copying and the contour lines have become both hardened and devitalized by the uniformly heavy deep blue shadow outline. Main initials are in green and others in red with titles in red rustic capitals.

102. London, British Library MS Royal 1. E. VII (f. 1ᵛ)
Bible. 2 vols.
550 × 348 mm.
c. 1050-70. Canterbury, Christ Church

Ill. 319

The drawing was added *c.* 1050-70 at the beginning of a tenth-century Bible as a frontispiece to Genesis and its subject is a diagrammatic representation of the Creation. It shows the head of the Almighty over the circle of the world, two long trumpets—the breath of God—issuing from His mouth. The miniature is based on the same model as the illustration in no. 98 (Tiberius C. VI, f. 7ᵛ; cf. also no. 84, Bury Psalter, f. 68ᵛ), a model which probably goes back to an Early Christian prototype (for iconographic sources cf. Heimann, 1966). But this representation differs from the Tiberius drawing in a few details: the Hand of God likewise holding a scale and dividers is shown here within the rim of the circle and in addition it holds a short cross-shaft. The Holy Dove emerging from the waters at the bottom of the circle is enclosed within a hemisphere and the sky in the background is filled with clouds and stars. Heimann has suggested that diagrammatic drawings of this type may represent the Trinity, with the two trumpets symbolizing the Second Person (cf. no. 98, Tiberius C. VI). The drawing is partly coloured blue for the Lord's hair and beard, and also for the sky and the waters; there are touches of green for the land, and silver (now oxidized) for the rim of the circle. The Almighty's head and the long-fingered hand are closely reminiscent of no. 100 (Tiberius A. III, f. 2ᵛ).

The Bible, bearing a 14th-century marginal inscription 'Biblioteca ecclesie Christi', f. 193, vol. II, was probably produced at Christ Church. The drawing was also most likely added at Canterbury, an attribution suggested by stylistic evidence.

LITERATURE: James, *Ancient Libraries*, p. lxiv; Warner and Gilson, I, 20; Wormald, *English Drawings*, 63, 68, 71, no. 37; A. Heimann, 'Three illustrations from the Bury St. Edmunds Psalter and their prototypes', *J.W.C.I.*, XXIX, 1966, 53 n. 78, pl. 11a.

103. London, British Library MS Arundel 60
Psalter. Gallican version with Old English gloss
306 × 192 mm.
c. 1060, add. c. 1080. Winchester, New Minster
Ill. 311

The Psalter is preceded by a calendar and computistic tables (ff. 1–12) decorated in red and blue, the former containing KL monograms and drawings of the signs of the Zodiac in red outline; they belong, together with a full-page Crucifixion (f. 12ᵛ), to the original decoration of the manuscript, the remainder (ff. 13, 52ᵛ, 53, 85) being executed by a different, probably a late eleventh-century hand (cf. Dodwell, *Canterbury School*).

The Crucifixion (f. 12ᵛ) prefacing Psalm 1 shows the dead Christ on a tree-trunk cross (cf. nos. 93, 98, 104) between the Virgin and St. John, who both hold books and who, turning towards the Crucified Christ with stiff, conventionalized gestures, are shown in the attitude of witnesses. The Hand of God emerges from the clouds above, and heads of the personifications of the Sun and Moon in roundels are set over the cross bar (cf. no. 93, also nos. 77, 80). The representation of Christ recalls the Christ in no. 77 (Titus D. XXVII) but the figure, presented in strict frontality and clad in a richly diapered, symmetrically disposed perizoma, has become remote and hieratic. The drawing is highly formalized with the drapery folds 'frozen into stillness' (Wormald, *Walpole Soc.*, 6), while the coloured shadow of green, red, and blue, heavily and uniformly reinforcing the fine brown outline, is hard and deadening in effect.

Framed initial pages executed by the later hand mark the three-fold division of the Psalter introducing Psalms 1, 51, and 101. Red and blue brush-work initials head all other psalms, with titles in red rustic capitals.

The Calendar, which is nearly identical with that of no. 77 (Titus D. XXVII), and in which the feast of St. Grimbald, the first abbot of the New Minster, is marked with a red cross, indicates that the manuscript was probably produced at that house (cf. Wormald, *Drawings*, no. 25). This attribution, supported by iconographic considerations, is confirmed by the additions of the late 11th century (ff. 133–42) which are in the same hand as the copy of Fulk's letter added to no. 68 (Grimbald Gospels, ff. 158–60) and additions to no. 78 (Stowe 944, ff. 41, 59).

LITERATURE: Westwood, *Facsimiles*, 121, pl. 49; Sir E. M. Thompson, *English Illuminated Manuscripts*, 1895–6, 24, pl. 7; G. F. Warner, *Illuminated Manuscripts in the British Museum*, 1903, pp. IV–V, pl. 11; F. A. Gasquet and E. Bishop, *The Bosworth Psalter*, 1908, 76–119 and *passim*; G. Oess, *Der altenglische Arundel-Psalter* (Anglistische Forschungen, H. 30), Heidelberg 1910; J. A. Herbert, *Illuminated Manuscripts*, 1911, 132–3; Homburger, 24, 64, 68, 69; British Museum, *Schools of Illumination*, I, 1914, pl. 16; British Museum, *Reproductions from Illuminated Manuscripts*, II, 1923, pls. VII, VIII; Millar, I, 23, no. 63, pl. 31; O. Homburger, 'Review', *Art Bulletin*, X, 1928, 401; Saunders, *English Illumination*, 26, pls. 24, 25; A. Boeckler, *Abendländische Miniaturen*, 1930, 56, pl. 48; F. Wormald, 'English Kalendars before A.D. 1100', *H.B.S.*, LXXII, 1934, no. 11; C. Niver, 'The Psalter in the British Museum, Harley 2904', *Medieval Studies in Memory of A. Kingsley Porter*, ed. W. R. W. Koehler, Cambridge, Mass. 1939, II, 678, 686; F. Wormald, 'The Survival of Anglo-Saxon illumination after the Norman Conquest', *Proceedings of the British Academy*, XXX, 1944, 131 n. 2, 132, 134, no. 2, pl. 3; *id.*, *Initials*, 126, 129, pl. Ic; *id.*, 'English saints in the litany of Arundel 60', *Analecta Bollandiana*, 64, 1946, 72–86; F. Saxl and R. Wittkower, *British Art and the Mediterranean*, 1948, pl. 23 (3); Kendrick, *Late Saxon*, 19, 25, 133, 136, pls. XXI, LXXXIX, 2; Wormald, *English Drawings*, 47, 50, 52, 66, 78, no. 25, pl. 33; Talbot Rice, *English Art*, 191, 213 n. 3, 216–17, 219, 223, pls. 74b, 79; Dodwell, *Canterbury School*, 11 n. 3, 118 f., pl. 72 f; Freyhan, 431, pl. XL, fig. 30; Ker, *Catalogue*, no. 134; Rickert, *Miniatura*, 13, pl. 30; F. Wormald, 'An English eleventh-century Psalter with pictures', *Walpole Society*, XXXVIII, 1962, 3 n. 1, 6, 10; Rickert, *Painting in Britain*, 55, 227 n. 27, pls. 52, 53; J. J. G. Alexander, 'A little-known Gospel Book of the later eleventh century from Exeter', *Burlington Magazine*, CVIII, 1966, 13, fig. 13; Roosen-Runge, 71 ff., pl. IV, ill. 11; Wormald, *Angleterre*, 253–4, ill. 258.

104. Cambridge, Corpus Christi College MS 422 (pp. 27–586)
Missal (Red Book of Darley)
190×130 mm.
c. 1061. Winchester

Ills. 300, 301

The prefatory matter of this Missal (pp. 27–50) includes a calendar and computistic tables. The former, written in black, red, and green, contains red and green KL monograms. The same shades appear on the first page of the order of the Mass (p. 51) inscribed in alternating lines of coloured capitals headed by a fine, large initial P(er omnia . . .) with beast-headed interlace and knotwork at the extremities. A drawing in the upper half of the page (p. 52) is in green and brown outline with heavy green washes and touches of red and represents a blessing Christ in a mandorla supported by two angels with flowering sceptres. The text of the Preface, written round the mandorla in red and green capitals, continues below in minuscule with neumes. The initial T(e igitur . . .) to the Canon of the Mass (p. 53) is formed by a sprouting green tree-trunk cross bearing Christ crucified, clad in a diapered perizoma (cf. no. 103, Arundel 60). The Virgin on the left, holding her robe to her face and bowing to the right, recalls by her posture the Virgin in the Harley Crucifixion (Harley 2904, no. 41). An ornamental tree motif, placed between the cross and Mary, is unusual in this context (cf. Romsey stone panel, Talbot Rice, pl. 18a). The Hand of God appears on the right above, and on the left a dove holding a wreath (or the Crown of Thorns) in its beak is flying down. The drawing, in firm red outline with green washes, is stylistically related to no. 80 (Winchcombe Psalter), but is a coarsened version of the latter.

The Missal was apparently written in Winchester (cf. Bishop, *English Caroline*), probably for Sherborne Abbey, Dorset, since the calendar was identified by E. Bishop (*Bosworth Psalter*) as being that of Sherborne. The manuscript is datable soon after 1061, as shown by the table of years which is for 1061–98. The Missal (pp. 27–586) is preceded by an Anglo-Saxon poem of Salomon and Saturn (pp. 1–26), 10th century, the two parts having been bound together at an early date since both contain additions in the same twelfth-century hand (cf. Ker, *Catalogue*).

PROVENANCE: The manuscript was known in the 16th century as 'the rede boke of Dareley' (Darley, near Matlock, Derbyshire) and was held there in great reverence as recorded on the last page (p. 586). The volume, inscribed 'Margaret Rollesleye wydowe' (pp. 130–1), 16th century, was given to Archbishop Parker by Richard Wendesley (p. 586). It was bequeathed by Parker to Corpus Christi College in 1575.

LITERATURE: F. A. Gasquet and E. Bishop, *The Bosworth Psalter*, 1908, 34 n. 1, 60–1, etc.; M. R. James, *A descriptive Catalogue of the Manuscripts in the Library of Corpus Christi College, Cambridge*, 1909, II, 315–22; Homburger, 69 n. 2; F. Wormald, 'English Kalendars before A.D. 1100', *H.B.S.*, LXXII, 1934, no. 14; *id.*, *English Drawings*, 62, no. 14; Talbot Rice, *English Art*, 191–2; Ker, *Catalogue*, no. 70; Bishop, *English Caroline*, p. XV n. 2.

105. Rheims, Bibliothèque Municipale MS 9
Gospels
320×238 mm.
c. 1062

Ills. 299

The manuscript has recently been identified by Hinkle as the Anglo-Saxon Gospels given to Saint-Remi of Rheims between 1062–5 by Aelfgar, count of Mercia, in memory of his son Burchard who was buried in that Abbey. It contains four Evangelist portraits which are preceded by Canon Tables (ff. 18–22ᵛ) shown under a series of simple gold arch-and-column frames filled with multicoloured acanthus patterns. The full-page Evangelist portraits are painted on plain vellum ground within late 'Winchester' borders containing friezes of stylized foliage between the gold bars; the frames of medallions and rosettes of stiff foliage on the corners are often interlaced with the bars of the borders. Stylistically and structurally, the borders recall those in no. 68 (Grimbald Gospels).

The Evangelists are enthroned beside their desks which support gold-framed tablets set parallel to the picture plane and inscribed in gold with the opening lines of their Gospels. They are shown writing or pointing to their texts, an unprecedented device eliminating the necessity for the usual *incipit* pages. The nimbed symbols (with the lion and ox wingless) are placed over the Evangelists' heads and isolated from them by horizontal gold bars suggesting a model in the Ada Court school of Charlemagne (cf. also no. 65, Trinity Gospels, ff. 59, 89). Matthew (f. 23), wearing milky blue over red, is shown in side-view bending to the right, a gold pen in his hand, between two multicoloured curtains in the background. Mark (f. 60), in pale green under greenish-grey with yellow highlights and enthroned frontally between two red curtains in the background, turns to inscribe a large cartouche on the right. Luke (f. 88), in pale purple gown diapered with pink, his blue mantle highlighted with white, is shown sideways on a throne draped in greenish-grey with two griffins' heads for finials; he is turning to the right and points to the text of his Gospel. John (f. 128), in blue over red, is seated full-face on a throne with two lions' heads, and, holding a pen in one hand, points to the text of the Gospel.

The figures are in firm and uniformly thick, rather insensitive outline. The draperies are covered with flowing yet highly formalized surface patterns marking the folds with white and yellow underlining that give them the appearance of having been chiselled in stone. The designs of the folds are reminiscent of those in no. 68 (Grimbald Gospels) but are more complex, repetitive, and abstract. There is also an affinity with no. 96 (Hereford Gospels, cf. the curtains, hemlines of the Evangelists' gowns, etc.). Gold is used profusely in the details of the frames and figures. Plain gold initials head the chapters; those introducing the Passion Readings for Holy Week (ff. 53, 119, 194ᵛ), however, are more elaborate, while some capital I's have fleur-de-lis finials at top and bottom.

T. A. M. Bishop attributed the script to the second half of the 11th century (see Hinkle), an attribution supported by stylistic as well as historical evidence.

PROVENANCE: Possibly no. 1 in the Abbey's inventory of 1549, the manuscript, having survived the disastrous fire at Saint-Remi in 1774, must have remained at Rheims throughout the Middle Ages. This is also indicated by the additions (ff. 1–9), probably of the second quarter of the 17th century, containing readings for the feast of St. Gibrian, patron saint of the Abbey (relics at Saint-Remi), and a frontispiece inscribed '. . . *ad usum Archimonasterii S. Remigi Remensis . . .*'. The inventory contained a description of the manuscript whose binding, probably original, was decorated with two subjects: a Majesty and a Crucifixion, both paralleled on the cover of the Gospels of Judith of Flanders (no. 94, Morgan 708). The choice of subjects and close similarities in the details suggest an English origin for the covers of both volumes.

LITERATURE: *Catalogue général des manuscrits des bibliothèques publiques de France*, XXXVIII, Reims 1904, 14–15; A. Boutemy, 'Notes de voyage sur quelques manuscrits de l'ancien archidiocèse de Reims', *Scriptorium*, II, 1948, 123–9; R. Laslier, *Les plus beaux manuscrits de la Bibliothèque de Reims*, Exhibition Catalogue, Reims 1967, no. 45; W. M. Hinkle, 'The gift of an Anglo-Saxon Gospel Book to the Abbey of Saint-Remi, Reims', *Journal of the British Archaeological Association*, XXXIII, 1970, 21–35.

106. London, British Library MS Cotton, Caligula A. XV (ff. 120–43)

Paschal tables, annals, etc.
217×165 mm.
c. 1073. Canterbury, Christ Church

Ills. 317, 318

The manuscript, a composite volume with miscellaneous texts, contains a collection of tables and tracts for the calculation of Easter (ff. 120–41), the former illustrated with drawings set across the top of two pages (ff. 122ᵛ, 123). Though the manuscript was produced after the Conquest, the illustrations are evidence of the tenacity of the Anglo-Saxon style, epitomizing as they do the characteristics of the highly animated figure drawing typical of Canterbury manuscripts of the earlier eleventh century.

The illustrations, drawn in swift, impressionistic strokes, are in the 'revived Utrecht' style; they closely recall the later drawings in no. 64 (Harley 603, Wormald's Hand F and Group II), and show a marked tendency towards suggesting bodily forms beneath the garments. The figures are softly modelled under the clinging draperies and their frantic animation is forcefully brought out by the flowing yet vigorous patterns marking the folds in broad green washes with touches of red. A sense of excitement and urgency is also conveyed by the wildly gesticulating hands, the heads poked forward, and the impatient eagerness of the postures. The drawing is rather mannered and conventional, however, and the figure of Pachomius, thrusting himself rapturously forward, is a variant of another popular Canterbury representation, a monk genuflecting at the feet of St. Benedict (cf. no. 100, Tiberius A. III).

The manuscript (ff. 120–43) was produced at Christ Church, Canterbury, as shown by the annals (ff. 133–7) attached to the table of years and relating to the affairs of that house. Extending from 988 to 1193, they are written up to 1073 in the same ink as this part of the manuscript, and in the same hand as the Canterbury privileges, the first of the series in the earlier 11th century (cf. Ker, *Catalogue*).

PROVENANCE: The manuscript was in Sir Robert Cotton's possession by 1621. His library, presented to the nation by his grandson, Sir John Cotton, in 1700, was incorporated in the British Museum in 1753.

LITERATURE: Westwood, *Facsimiles*, 112; *Pal. Soc.*, I, pl. 145; James, *Ancient Libraries*, 508, 516 no. 330; J. A. Herbert, *Illuminated Manuscripts*, 1911, 120–1; Millar, I, no. 62; Kendrick, *Late Saxon*, 17, pl. XVII; Wormald, *English Drawings*, 45, 47, 50, 64, 68, no. 20, pl. 29; Talbot Rice, *English Art*, 170, 205, pl. 67a; Dodwell, *Canterbury School*, 21, 47, 120, pl. 12 a, b; Ker, *Catalogue*, no. 139; F. Wormald, *Style and Design*, 31, 32, 34; Dodwell, *Techniques*, 649; id., Peter Clemoes, *The Old English Illustrated Hexateuch* (E.E. MSS in facs., XVIII) 1974. 58, pl. Vd.

ILLUSTRATIONS

The author and publishers are grateful to all institutions, museums, and libraries who have helped with illustrations for this publication, including the Master and Fellows of Corpus Christi College, Cambridge; the Master and Fellows of Trinity College, Cambridge; His grace the Archbishop of Canterbury and the Trustees of Lambeth Palace Library, London; the College of Arms, London; the President and Fellows of St. John's College, Oxford.

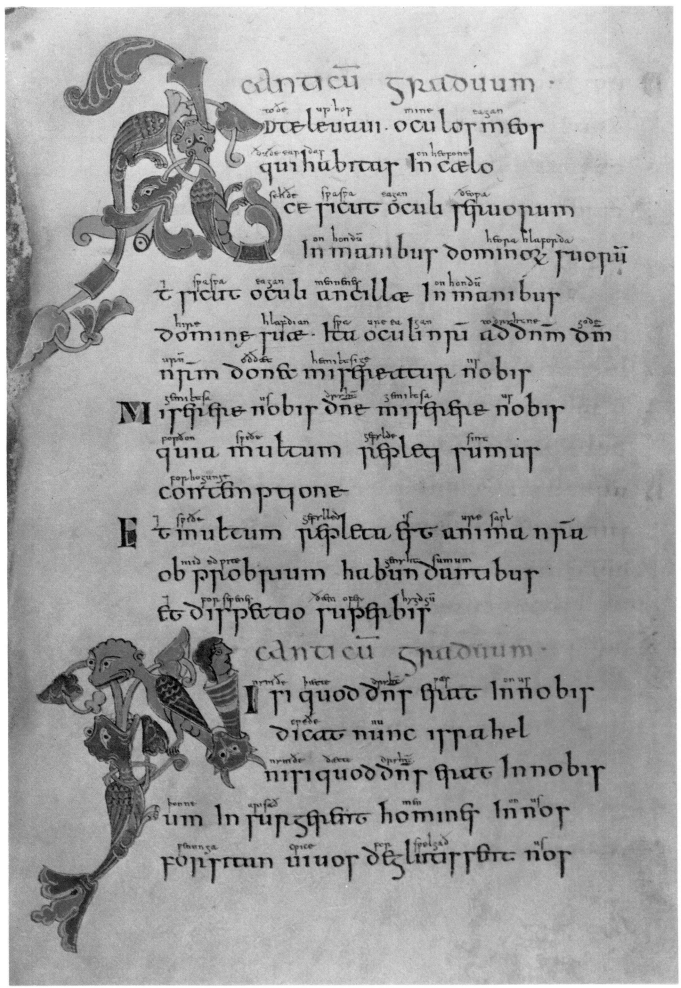

1. Oxford, Bodl. Lib., Junius 27, f. 135ᵛ (Cat. 7)

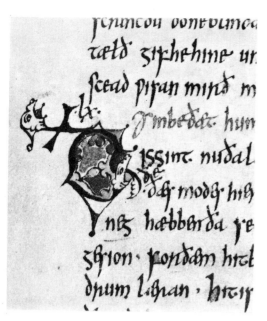

2. Initial.
Oxford, Bodl. Lib., Hatton 20, f. 6ᵛ (Cat. 1)

3. Initial.
Oxford, Bodl. Lib., Hatton 20, f. 93ᵛ (Cat. 1)

4. Initials.
Oxford, Bodl. Lib., Hatton 20, f. 11ᵛ (Cat. 1)

5. Initial N.
London, B.L., Royal 5. F. III, f. 6ᵛ (Cat. 2)

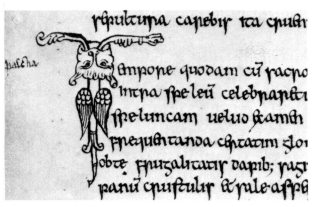

6. Initial T.
London, B.L., Royal 5. F. III, f. 32ᵛ (Cat. 2)

7. Initial 'h'.
Durham, Cathedral Lib., A. IV. 19, f. 2ᵛ (Cat. 3)

8. Marginal Drawing.
Durham, Cathedral Lib., A. IV. 19, f. 57 (Cat. 3)

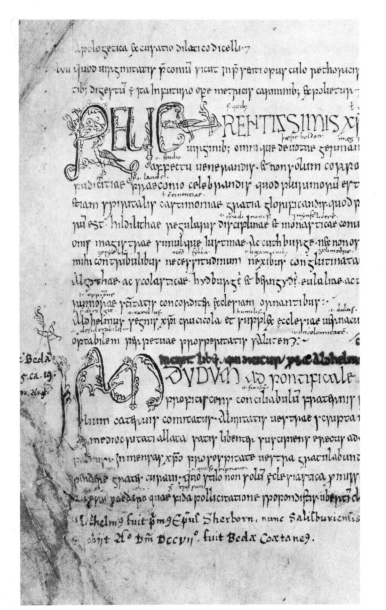

9. Initials.
London, B.L., Royal 5. F. III, f. 2ᵛ (Cat. 2)

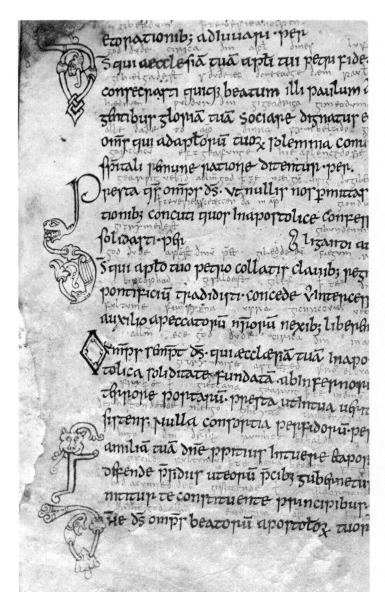

10. Initials.
Durham, Cathedral Lib., A. IV. 19, f. 28ᵛ (Cat. 3)

11–14. Initials. London, B.L., Royal 7. D. XXIV, f. 138, f. 147ᵛ, f. 104ᵛ, f. 86 (Cat. 4)

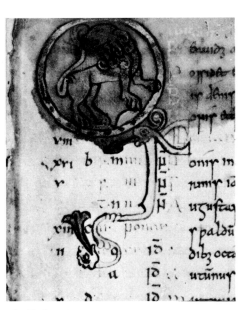
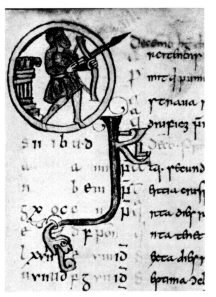

15. Saint. London, B.L.,
Cotton, Galba A. XVIII, f. 9ᵛ (Cat. 5)

16. Zodiac Sign. London, B.L.,
Cotton, Galba A. XVIII, f. 10 (Cat. 5)

17. Zodiac Sign. London, B.L.,
Cotton, Galba A. XVIII, f. 14 (Cat. 5)

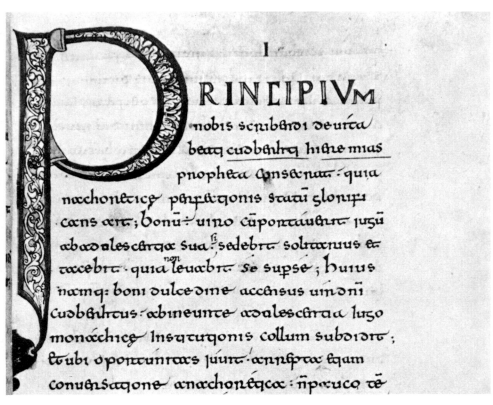

18. Initial P.
Cambridge, Corpus Christi College 183, f. 6 (Cat. 6)

19. Initial 'd'. Cambridge,
Corpus Christi College 183, f. 42ᵛ (Cat. 6)

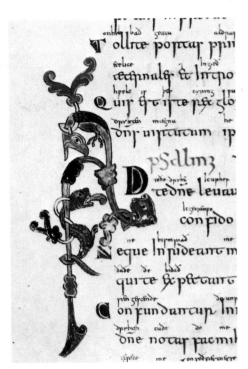

20–22. Initials. Oxford, Bodl. Lib., Junius 27, f. 20, f. 27ᵛ, f. 136 (Cat. 7)

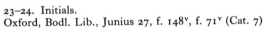

23–24. Initials.
Oxford, Bodl. Lib., Junius 27, f. 148ᵛ, f. 71ᵛ (Cat. 7)

25. Initial A.
London, B.L., Add. 47967, f. 94 (Cat. 8)

26. Initial D.
Oxford, Bodl. Lib., Junius 27, f. 118 (Cat. 7)

27. Aldhelm Seated (*enlarged*).
London, B.L., Royal 7. D. XXIV, f. 85ᵛ (Cat. 4)

28. Evangelist Symbols. London, B.L., Add. 47967, Fly-leaf (iii) (Cat. 8)

29. Aethelstan offering a Book of St. Cuthbert.
Cambridge, Corpus Christi College 183, f. 1ᵛ (Cat. 6)

30. Nativity.
Oxford, Bodl. Lib., Rawlinson B. 484, f. 85 (Cat. 5)

31. Ascension.
London, B.L., Cotton, Galba A. XVIII, f. 120ᵛ (Cat. 5)

32. Christ in Majesty with Angels and Prophets.
London, B.L., Cotton, Galba A. XVIII, f. 2ᵛ (Cat. 5)

33. Christ Enthroned with Martyrs, Confessors and Virgins.
London, B.L., Cotton, Galba A. XVIII, f. 21 (Cat. 5)

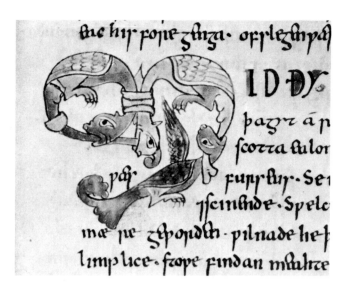

34. Initial.
Oxford, Bodl. Lib., Tanner 10, f. 131 (Cat. 9)

35. Initial M.
Oxford, Bodl. Lib., Tanner 10, f. 43 (Cat. 9)

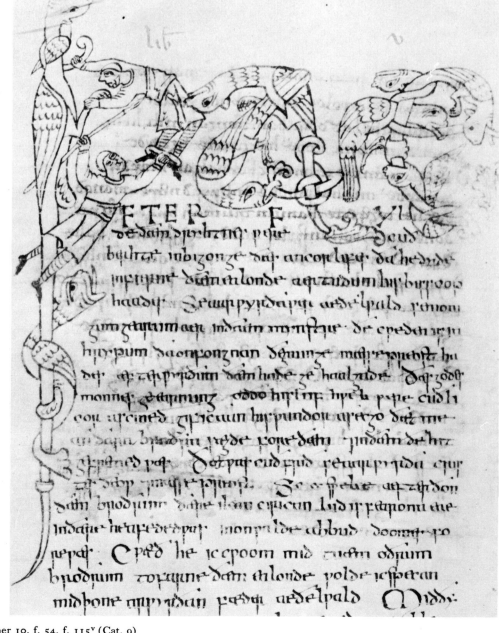

36–37. Initials. Oxford, Bodl. Lib., Tanner 10, f. 54, f. 115ᵛ (Cat. 9)

38. Initial Q.
Boulogne, Bibl. Mun. 10, f. 8 (Cat. 10)

39–40. Initials. Oxford, Bodl. Lib., Tanner 10, f. 42ᵛ, f. 79 (Cat. 9).

41. Christ adored by St. Dunstan.
Oxford, Bodl. Lib., Auct. F. 4. 32, f. 1 (Cat. 11)

miserere pax misericors iuuenu
&eox q̄f infide rudes nen os
acillos m̄t infidelū ēbines
desttuos relinquas. Tunc
petrus roganab: se ait.
fugiendū suadeas. &u
uenū acq; infirmox cor
dib: exéplo n̄o metu
passionis maiere. cū
uerbū di ēstanē debe
am̄ asserere. & sc̄a
castamonie funda
mta q; iecum̄ ēser
uare. fugiendū pu
taus. ut morcē decli
nem. quā multas
suspirus & gemi
ab: diutnus
ut ingressū
uiro ex   peam̄
qua di   sc̄m̄
illius   ueue
latione   dn̄m
clarificare   debem̄
trs̄ ū hec au di encs̄:
louauer planctum̄
dicentes. O pax uera
cissimo: ubi sē uerba
mode q̄b: diecebas
qm̄ putta n̄ra more
esses succúbere.
&n̄c impetrare

ñ possum. uepn̄ra saluce donec corro
boreū pataris aliquatculū uiuere.
Adolescenctes quoq: quos ipse sollicite
custodiens. infide & castucate sedulo
educabat: mari p̄endences incelū
& porreca, ance facē illuf uelut subtto
morau   cadences m̄trā. uocifera
bant nimio h̄ulacu
clamantes. O bono petre:
pastor & pax. p̄ tuū dn̄m indemia
singularis: cur nos affecu maeno
nouit psacrū fonte dn̄o pe
pisti. quos̄tā m̄maturo solacio
& animo crudeli q̄te nūquā
antea atangerat. In mans
simox morsib: lupox exponis.
Clamabant auē & maerone:
pulue   re ēsp̄s capiab: Hec eino est
miscdia quā desaluacoreauo pdicare
solebas. q̄ turs lacrims se quē adcēpus
negauerit meē nū pietace mo
indulserac. Et cuiranus lacrimarū
fluminib: te ut paruo tēpore non
ēcedis. p̄serū cū & dn̄o possis munistrare
incarue. & ē reseruatā coronā adipisci
ppecuā. Sed & custodes carceris pro
cessus & maratuari. cū reliquis ma
gistuanis exofficio uinceis: postulabdl
eū dicentes. D̄ie quouus abscede: quia
impacoreē obliruau iā credim̄: scd
iste iniquissim̄ agrippa peu cūamore
& incēpantia sue libidinis inflāmax̄
pdere te festinac. Si enū te regis iussione

43. Two Figures and Angel.
Oxford, St. John's College 28, f. 81ᵛ (Cat. 13)

44. Philosophy.
Cambridge, Trinity College O. 3. 7, f. 1 (Cat. 20)

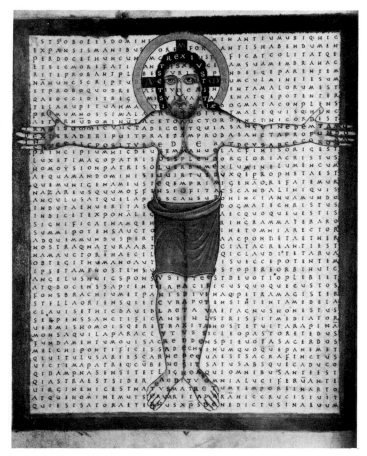

45. Christ with outstretched arms.
Cambridge, Trinity College B. 16. 3, f. 3 (Cat. 14)

46. Rabanus Maurus adoring the Cross.
Cambridge, Trinity College B. 16. 3, f. 30ᵛ (Cat. 14)

47. St. Matthew.
Oxford, St. John's College 194, f. 1ᵛ (Cat. 12)

48. Rabanus Maurus offering his book to Pope Gregory.
Cambridge, Trinity College B. 16. 3, f. 1ᵛ (Cat. 14)

50. Initial S.
Cambridge, Corpus Christi College 23, f. 2 (Cat. 48)

49. St. Luke. London, B.L., Add. 40618, f. 22ᵛ (Cat. 15)

51–52. St. John; Opening to St. John's Gospel. London, B.L., Add. 40618, f. 49ᵛ, f. 50 (Cat. 15)

53. Initial E.
Oxford, Bodl. Lib., Bodley 579, f. 154ᵛ (Cat. 17)

54. Paschal Hand.
Oxford, Bodl. Lib., Bodley 579, f. 49 (Cat. 17)

55. Vita.
Oxford, Bodl. Lib., Bodley 579, f. 49ᵛ (Cat. 17)

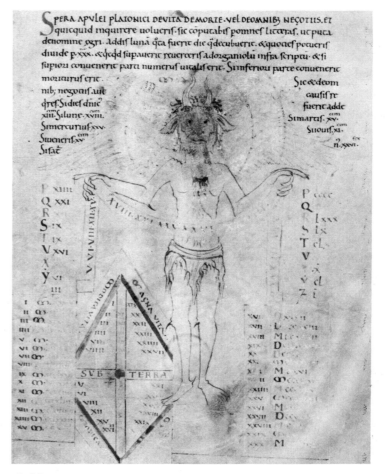

56. Mors.
Oxford, Bodl. Lib., Bodley 579, f. 50 (Cat. 17)

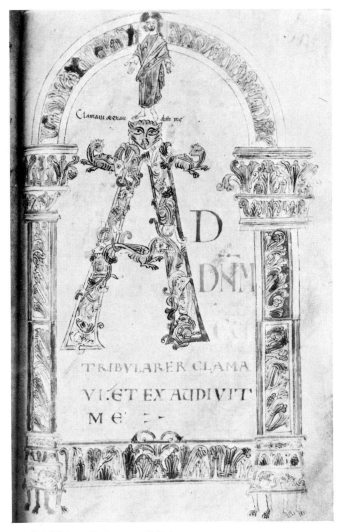

57. Initial A to Psalm 119. Salisbury,
Cathedral Lib. 150, f. 122 (Cat. 18)

58–59. Initials. Salisbury,
Cathedral Lib. 150, f. 60ᵛ, f. 64ᵛ (Cat. 18)

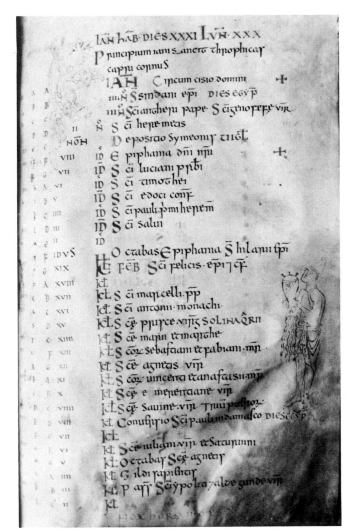

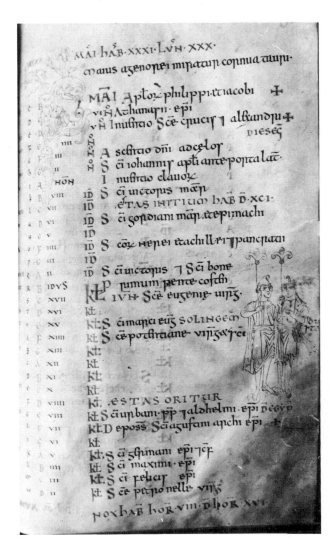

60–61. Calendar Pages. Salisbury, Cathedral Lib. 150, f. 3, f. 5 (Cat. 18)

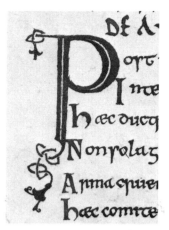

62. Initial P.
Oxford, Bodl. Lib., Bodley 49,
f. 67ᵛ (Cat. 19.i)

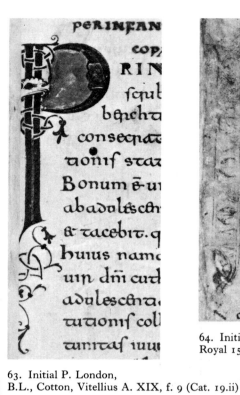

63. Initial P. London,
B.L., Cotton, Vitellius A. XIX, f. 9 (Cat. 19.ii)

64. Initial P. London, B.L.,
Royal 15. B. XIX, f. 1 (Cat. 19.iii)

65–67. Initials. Salisbury, Cathedral Lib. 38, f. 46ᵛ, f. 19ᵛ, f. 7ᵛ (Cat. 19.v)

68. Initial 'h'. Salisbury,
Cathedral Lib. 38, f. 37ᵛ (Cat. 19.v)

69. Initial 'h'. London,
B.L., Harley 110, f. 3 (Cat. 19.vii)

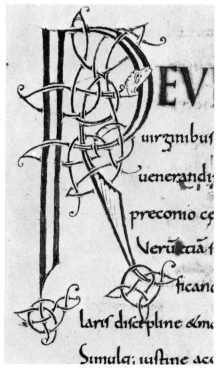

70. Initial R. Oxford, Bodl. Lib.,
Digby 146, f. 7 (Cat. 19.vi)

71–72. Initials P. Oxford, Oriel College 3, f. 70, f. 6 (Cat. 19.viii)

73. Initial P. Oxford, Bodl. Lib., Bodley 708, f. 1 (Cat. 19.xi)

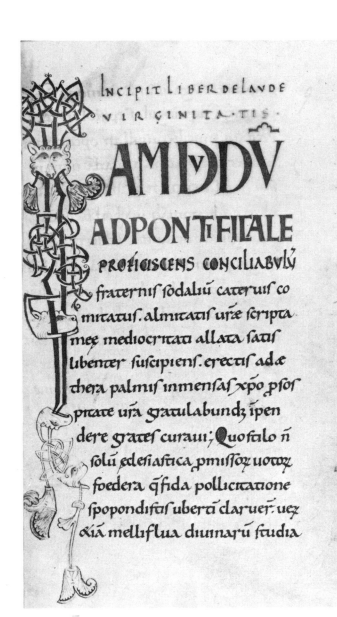

74. Initial I. London, B.L., Royal 5. E. XI, f. 9 (Cat. 19.ix)

75. Initial R. London, B.L., Royal 5. E. XI, f. 7ᵛ (Cat. 19.ix)

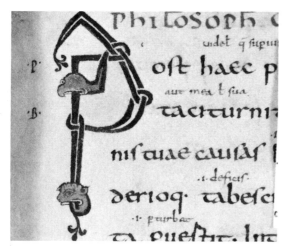

76. Initial P. Cambridge,
Trinity College O. 3. 7, f. 9 (Cat. 20)

77. Initial 'h'. Cambridge,
Trinity College O.. 3. 7, f. 31 (Cat. 20)

78. Initial C. Cambridge,
Trinity College O. 3. 7, f. 2 (Cat. 20)

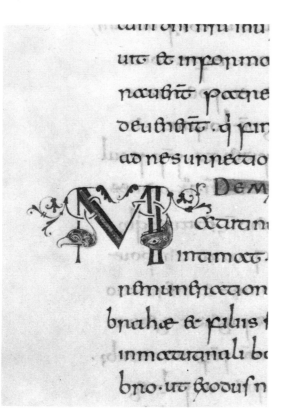

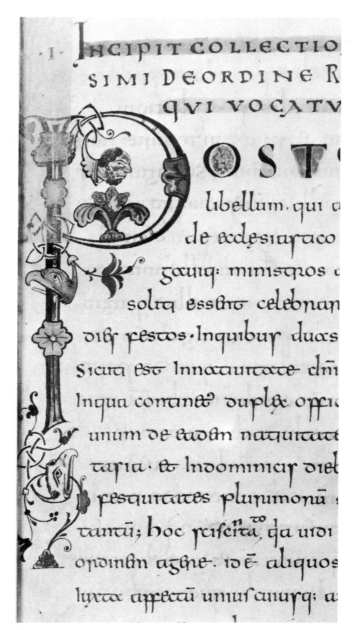

79–80. Initials M and P. Cambridge, Trinity College B. 11. 2, f. 106ᵛ, f. 4 (Cat. 21)

81. Initial D.
London, B.L., Add. 37517, f. 74 (Cat. 22)

82. Initial L.
London, B.L., Add. 37517, f. 94ᵛ (Cat. 22)

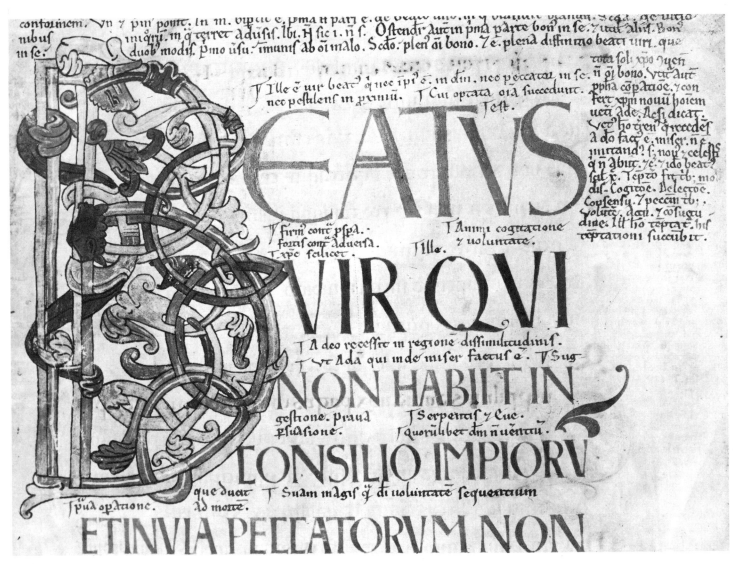

83. Beatus Initial. London, B.L., Add. 37517, f. 4 (Cat. 22)

84. King Edgar offering the Charter to Christ.
London, B.L., Cotton, Vespasian A. VIII, f. 2ᵛ (Cat. 16)

85. Baptism of Christ.
London, B.L., Add. 49598, f. 25 (Cat. 23)

86. The Incredulity of Thomas.
London, B.L., Add. 49598, f. 56ᵛ (Cat. 23)

87. Dormition. Rouen, Bibl. Mun. Y. 7, f. 54ᵛ (Cat. 24)

88. St. John.
London, B.L., Add. 49598, f. 19ᵛ (Cat. 23)

89. The Holy Women at the Sepulchre.
Rouen, Bibl. Mun. Y. 7, f. 21ᵛ (Cat. 24)

90. Nativity.
London, B.L., Add. 49598, f. 15ᵛ (Cat. 23)

91. Consecration of a Church.
London, B.L., Add. 49598, f. 118ᵛ (Cat. 23)

92. Ornamental Page.
Paris, Bibl. Nat., lat. 987, f. 41 (Cat. 25)

93. Ornamental Page.
Paris, Bibl. Nat., lat. 987, f. 43 (Cat. 25)

94–95. Apotheosis of Boethius; Initial I with Trinity (*enlarged*).
Paris, Bibl. Nat., lat. 6401, f. 158ᵛ, f. 159 (Cat. 32)

97. Initial M. Vercelli, Cathedral, Codex CVII, f. 112 (Cat. 28)

96. Initial. London, B.L.,
Cotton, Cleopatra A. VI, f. 19ᵛ (Cat. 27)

98–99. Initial 'h'; Tailpiece.
Vercelli, Cathedral, Codex CVII, f. 49, f. 49ᵛ (Cat. 28)

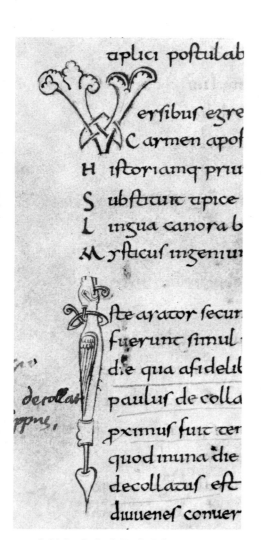

100. Initials. Oxford, Bodl. Lib.,
Rawlinson C. 570, f. 44ᵛ (Cat. 30.iv)

101–102. Initials. Boulogne, Bibl. Mun. 82, f. 7, f. 65 (Cat. 29)

103. Initial D.
Cambridge, Trinity College O. 1. 18, f. 12 (Cat. 30.i)

104. Initial T. Paris, Bibl. Nat., lat. 7585, f. 164 (Cat. 30.ii)

105. Initial G. Leiden, University Lib., Codex Scaligeranus 69, f. 17 (Cat. 30.v)

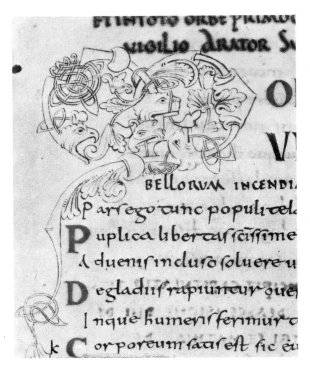

106. Initial M. Oxford, Bodl. Lib.,
Rawlinson C. 570, f. 2 (Cat. 30.iv)

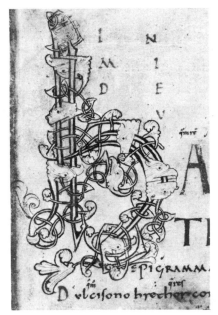

107. Initial 'h'. Cambridge,
Trinity College O. 2. 31, f. 1 (Cat. 30.vi)

108–109. Initials D and M. London, B.L., Harley 1117, f. 45 (Cat. 30.vii)

110. Initial I.
Paris, Bibl. Nat., lat. 17814,
f. 46 (Cat. 30.xii)

111. Initial I. Oxford, Bodl. Lib.,
Bodley 718, f. 1 (Cat. 30.xiv)

112. Initial M. New York,
Pierpont Morgan Lib. 333, f. 25 (Cat. 30.xiii)

113. Initial P. London, B.L.,
Royal 12. C. XXIII, f. 6ᵛ (Cat. 30.iii)

114. Initial C. Oxford, Bodl. Lib.,
Auct. F. 1. 15, f. 5 (Cat. 37)

115. Initial H. London, B.L.,
Harley 5431, f. 38ᵛ (Cat. 38)

116. Initial C.
London, B.L., Cotton, Tiberius B. I,
f. 7ᵛ (Cat. 30.xviii)

117. Initial D.
London, B.L., Royal 6. A. VI, f. 5 (Cat. 30.xi)

118. Initial A. Oxford, Bodl. Lib.,
Bodley 342, f. 1 (Cat. 30.xvii)

119. Initial 'h'.
Paris, Bibl. Nat., lat. 6401A,
f. 57ᵛ (Cat. 30.viii)

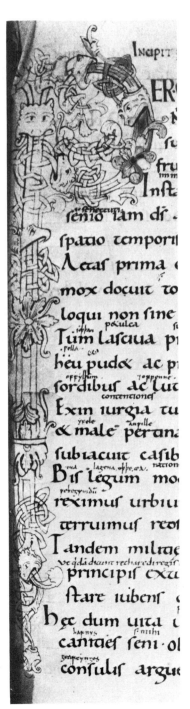

120. Initial I. London, B.L.,
Harley 5431, f. 54ᵛ (Cat. 38)

121. Initial P. Boulogne,
Bibl. Mun. 189, f. 4 (Cat. 30.xv)

122. Initial P. Paris,
Bibl. St. Geneviève 2410, f. 126 (Cat. 30.xvi)

123–124. Initials M and 'h'. London, B.L., Cotton, Caligula A. VII, f. 11, f. 21ᵛ (Cat. 33)

125. Initial Q. Cambridge,
Trinity College B. 14. 3, f. 5 (Cat. 34)

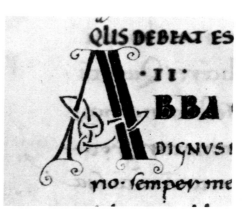

126–127. Initial 'd'; Initial A. London, B.L., Harley 5431, f. 101, f. 16ᵛ (Cat. 38)

128. Initial Q to Psalm 51. Cambridge,
Corpus Christi College 411, f. 40 (Cat. 40)

129. David (?). Cambridge,
Corpus Christi College 411, f. 1ᵛ (Cat. 40)

130. Initial F. Cambridge,
Corpus Christi College 389, f. 22ᵛ (Cat. 36)

131. Initial S.
London, Lambeth Palace Lib. 200, f. 80ᵛ (Cat. 39)

EVERENTISSIMIS
XPI VIRGINIBVS OMNIQV

deuotæ germanitatis affectu uenerandis. & non
solum corporalis pudiciciæ preconio celebrandis
quod plurimorum est: uerum etiam spiritalis castimo
integra nia glorificandis. quod paucorum est. Hildelithe
regulariſ disciplinæ. & monasticæ conuersationiſ magistrae
simulque iustinæ ac cuthburgæ. necnon & osburgæ. mihi
contribulibuſ. necessitudinum nexibuſ conglutinatæ.
aldgythæ. ac scolasticæ. hydburgæ. & byrngythæ. eulaliæ ac teclæ.
rumore scitatis concorditer æcclesiam ornantibuſ Aldhelmuſ
segniſ xpi cyraicola & supplex æcclesiæ uernaculuſ. optabilem per
petuæ prosperitatis salutem;

132. Aldhelm presenting his Book to the Nuns of Barking. London, Lambeth Palace Lib. 200, f. 68ᵛ (Cat. 39)

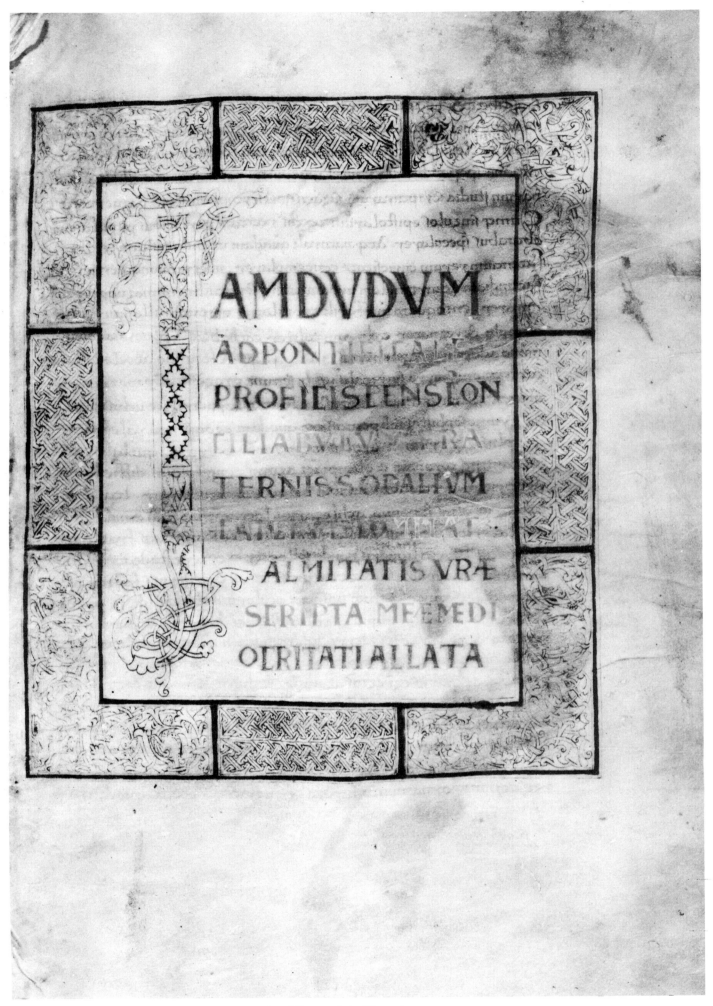

133. Title-page with Initial I. London, Lambeth Palace Lib. 200, f. 69 (Cat. 39)

134. Crucifixion. Paris, Bibl. Nat., lat. 943, f. 4ᵛ (Cat. 35)

135. God the Father. Paris, Bibl. Nat.,
lat. 943, f. 5ᵛ (Cat. 35)

136. God the Son. Paris, Bibl. Nat.,
lat. 943, f. 6 (Cat. 35)

137. The Holy Ghost. Paris, Bibl. Nat.,
lat. 943, f. 6ᵛ (Cat. 35)

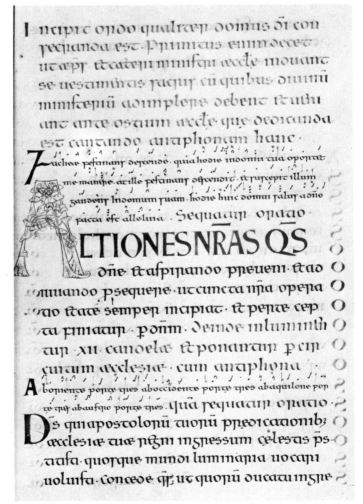

138. Initial A. Paris, Bibl. Nat.,
lat. 943, f. 10 (Cat. 35)

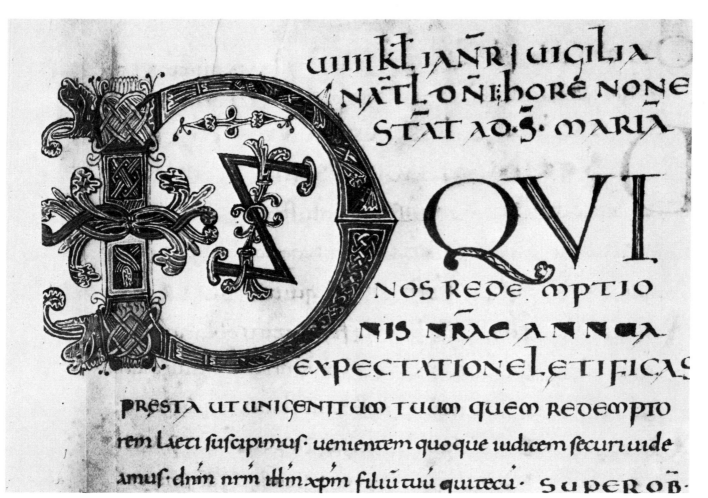

uiiii kt̄ ianr̄ i uiqilia
nāt̄l oñi hore none
stat ad·s̄· maria
Dqui
nos redempt̄io
nis n̄r̄ac annua
expectatione letificas
presta ut unicentitum tuum quem redempto
rem l̄ieti suscipimus· uenientem quoque iudicem securi uide
amus· dn̄m n̄r̄m ih̄m xp̄m filiū tuū quitēcu· super ob·

139. Initial D. Orléans, Bibl. Mun. 105, p. 8 (Cat. 31)

Dne
ex
audi orati

140. Initial D. London, B.L., Harley 2904, f. 125 (Cat. 41)

141. Initial B. London, B.L., Harley 2904, f. 4 (Cat. 41)

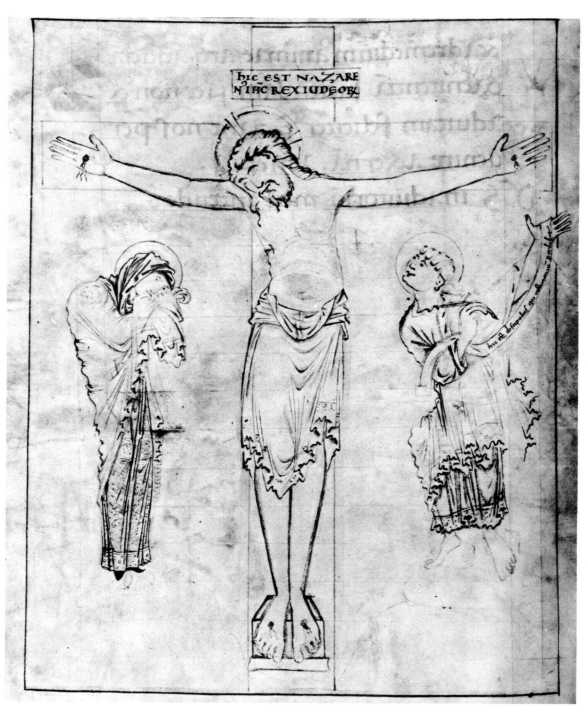

142. Crucifixion. London, B.L., Harley 2904, f. 3ᵛ (Cat. 41)

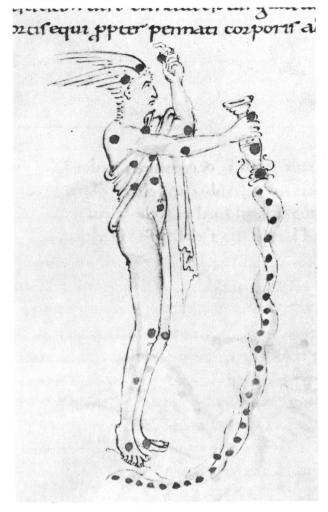

143. Aquarius. London, B.L.,
Harley 2506, f. 38ᵛ (Cat. 42)

144. Christ with St. Gregory and St. Benedict.
Orléans, Bibl. Mun. 175, f. 149 (Cat. 43)

145. St. John. Boulogne, Bibl. Mun. 11, f. 107 (Cat. 44)

146. St. John. New York, Pierpont Morgan Lib. 827, f. 98ᵛ (Cat. 45)

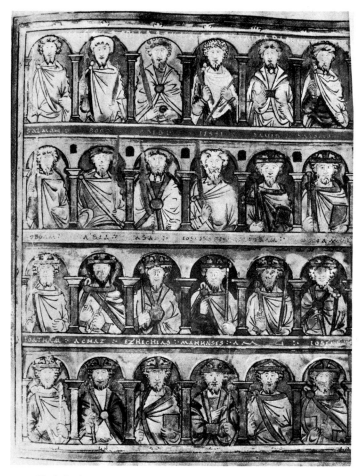

147. Christ's Ancestors.
Boulogne, Bibl. Mun. 11, f. 11 (Cat. 44)

148. Nativity and Annunciation to the Shepherds.
Boulogne, Bibl. Mun. 11, f. 12 (Cat. 44)

149. St. Mark.
Boulogne, Bibl. Mun. 11, f. 55ᵛ (Cat. 44)

150. Opening to St. Mark's Gospel.
Boulogne, Bibl. Mun. 11, f. 56 (Cat. 44)

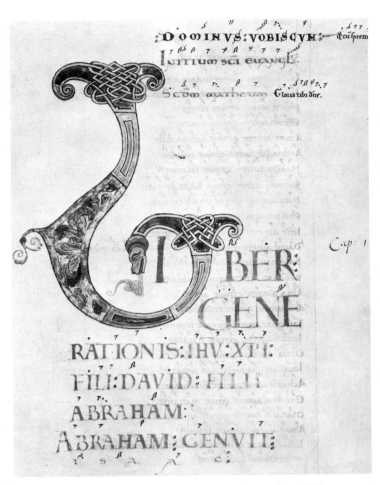

151. Canon Table. Copenhagen, Royal Lib.,
G.K.S. 10, 2⁰, f. 2ᵛ (Cat. 47)

152. Opening to St. Matthew's Gospel. Copenhagen, Royal Lib.,
G.K.S. 10, 2⁰, f. 18 (Cat. 47)

153. St. Luke. Copenhagen, Royal Lib.,
G.K.S. 10, 2⁰, f. 82ᵛ (Cat. 47)

154. St. Matthew. Copenhagen, Royal Lib.,
G.K.S. 10, 2⁰, f. 17ᵛ (Cat. 47)

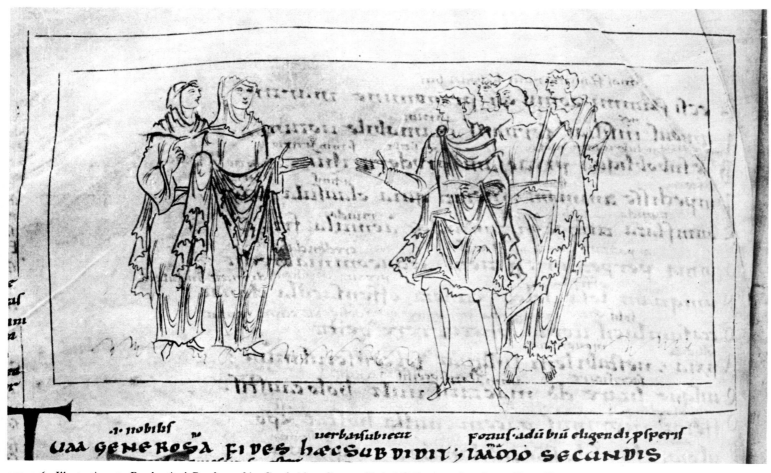

155–156. Illustrations to Prudentius' *Psychomachia*. Cambridge, Corpus Christi College 23, f. 2, f. 37ᵛ (Cat. 48)

157–158. Illustrations to Prudentius' *Psychomachia*. Cambridge, Corpus Christi College 23, f. 17ᵛ (Cat. 48)

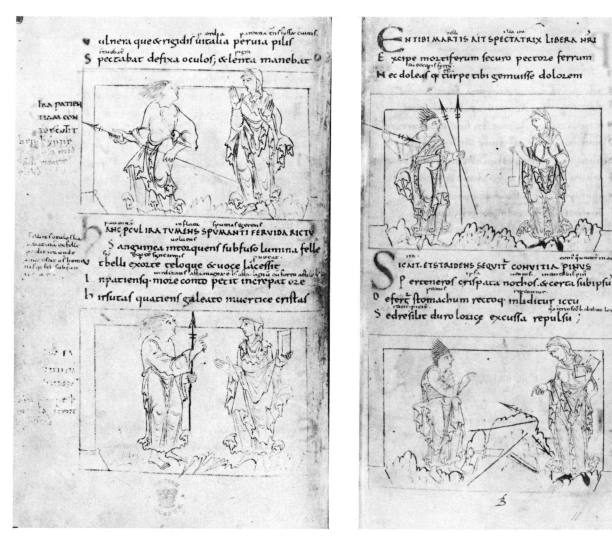

159–160. Illustrations to Prudentius' *Psychomachia*. London, B.L., Cotton, Cleopatra C. VIII, f. 10ᵛ, f. 11 (Cat. 49)

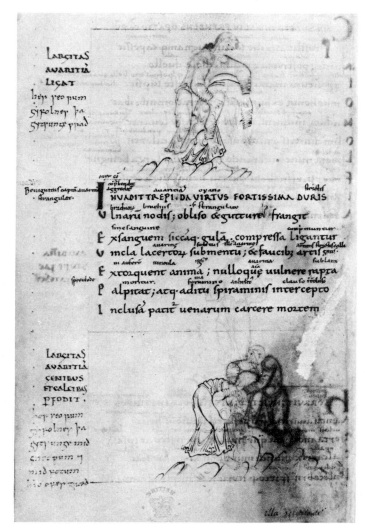
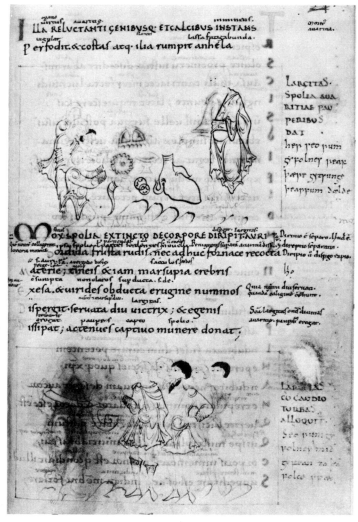

161–162. Illustrations to Prudentius' *Psychomachia*. London, B.L., Cotton, Cleopatra C. VIII, f. 28ᵛ, f. 29 (Cat. 49)

163. Illustration to Prudentius' *Psychomachia*.
London, B.L., Add. 24199, f. 17 (Cat. 51)

164. Initial S. London, B.L.,
Royal 6. B. VIII, f. 1ᵛ (Cat. 54)

165. Illustrations to Prudentius' *Psychomachia*.
Munich, Staatsbibliothek, CLM 29031b, f. 1ᵛ (Cat. 50)

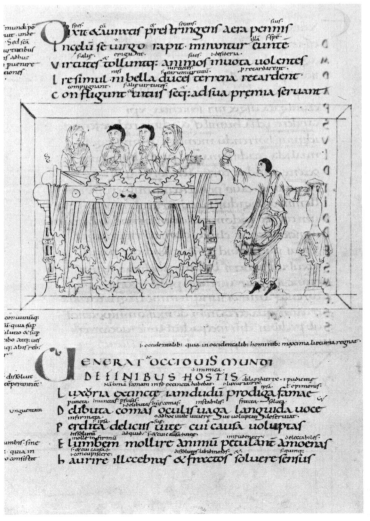

166. Illustration to Prudentius' *Psychomachia*.
London, B.L., Add. 24199, f. 16ᵛ (Cat. 51)

167–168. Canon Tables. New York, Pierpont Morgan Lib. 869, f. 11ᵛ, f. 13ᵛ (Cat. 56)

169–170. St. Matthew; St. Luke. New York, Pierpont Morgan Lib. 869, f. 17ᵛ, f. 83ᵛ (Cat. 56)

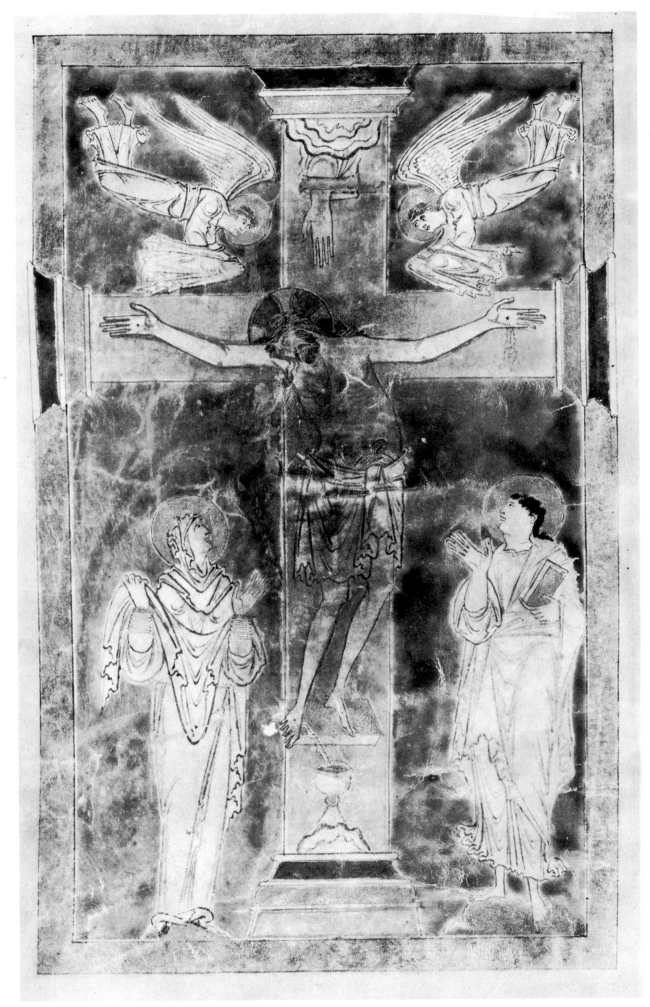

171. Crucifixion. New York, Pierpont Morgan Lib. 869, f. 9ᵛ (Cat. 56)

172. St. Mark. London, B.L.,
Royal I. E. VI, f. 30ᵛ (Cat. 55)

173. Christ and Apostles. Damme, Musée van Maerlant,
Fragment (Cat. 53)

174. Miracle of the Gadarene Swine.
Damme, Musée van Maerlant, Fragment (Cat. 53)

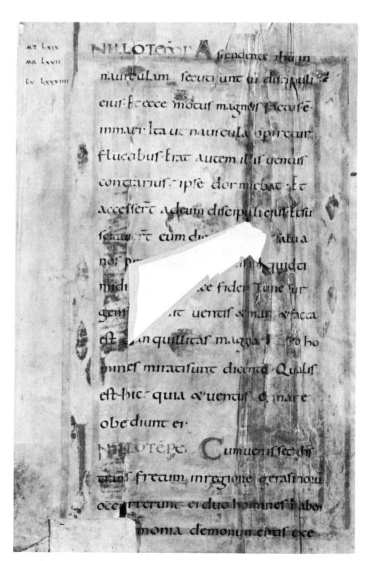

175. Gospel Lections.
Damme, Musée van Maerlant, Fragment (Cat. 53)

176. Miracle of the Tribute Money. Damme, Musée van Maerlant, Fragment (Cat. 53)

177–178. Angels. Oxford, Bodl. Lib., Bodley 155, f. 93ᵛ, f. 146ᵛ (Cat. 59)

179–180. St. Aldhelm; St. Aldhelm presenting his Book to the Nuns of Barking.
Oxford, Bodl. Lib., Bodley 577, f. 1 and f. 1ᵛ (Cat. 57)

181–182. St. Matthew; Opening to St. Matthew's Gospel, York Minster, Chapter Lib., Add. 1, f. 22ᵛ, f. 23 (Cat. 61)

183–184. St. Mark; St. Luke. York Minster, Chapter Lib., Add. 1, f. 60ᵛ, f. 85ᵛ (Cat. 61)

185. Marvels of the East. London, B.L.,
Cotton, Vitellius A. XV, f. 101 (Cat. 52)

186. Page from Herbal. London, B.L.,
Cotton, Vitellius C. III, f. 56ᵛ (Cat. 63)

187–188. Illustrations to Apuleius' *Herbarium*. Cotton, Vitellius C. III, f. 11ᵛ, f. 19 (Cat. 63)

189. The Translation of Enoch. Oxford, Bodl. Lib., Junius 11, p. 61 (Cat. 58)

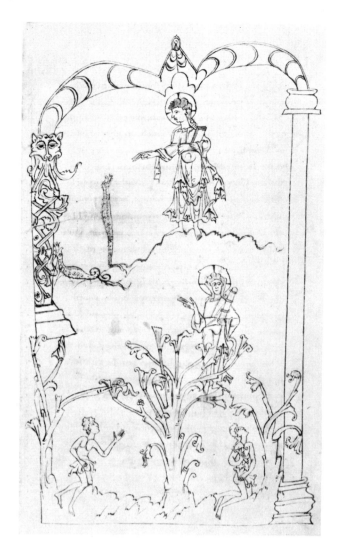

190–191. Adam and Eve; God condemning the Serpent. Oxford, Bodl. Lib., Junius 11, p. 11, p. 41 (Cat. 58)

192–193. Cain Enthroned; Malalehel before an Altar. Oxford, Bodl. Lib., Junius 11, p. 57, p. 58 (Cat. 58)

þa noe ongan nifiglnde lac. nð fæft neðnan ꝼne

194. Noah offering a Sacrifice. Oxford, Bodl. Lib., Junius 11, p. 74 (Cat. 58)

195–196. Calling of Abraham and Departure for Canaan; Abraham offering Incense. Oxford, Bodl. Lib., Junius 11, p. 84, p. 87 (Cat. 58)

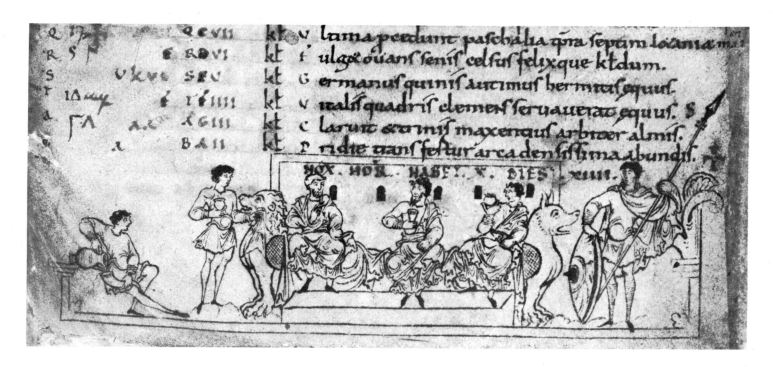

Q 17		Q. VII	kt	v	luna perdunt paschalia qua septem locania m
R S		6 RVI	kt	f	ulgæ ouans senis celsus felixque ktdum.
S	V k VI	SEU	kt	G	ermanus quinis aurimus hermitas equus.
T	ID aug	6 TIIII	kt	v	italis quadris clemens seruauerat equus. S
a	ΓΛ	A.E. XGIII	kt	c	laruit eximis maxentius arbiter almis.
a		B AII	kt	p	ridie transfertur arca densissima abundis.

MOX · HOR · HABET · X · DIES · XIIII.

w H S	kk v	HF VII		A	tque agustinus septenis qui euenit urchus.
t mis	kt 6	VI	kt	T	errigena ingreditur arcu deuerace sonas. A A
iiii k A		k A V			
l ΓΛΙ A KG 8	IIIIkt			M	aximianus agens querit celestia regna.
M		XE III		A	tque saturninus ternis prostrauit olimpum.
XI M ID B	HE B II		kt	T	u pateris nella pia sinus discrimine sim

NOX · HOR · HABET · VIII · DIES · XII

T mi	6 T XII	kt		I	ohannis senis rutilant paulusque kalendis. S
A A A A	6 EOVI	kt		I	cce celebramus fratrum natalia quinis.
B	HE B IIII	kt		I	nuigilant populi quadris leoque repausat. S
c B	6 EIII	kt		I	nternis gaudent patris paulusque kalendis.
B	6 I EEII			M	arcialis reunge pridias idemque kalendas.

197–199. April; May; June. London, B.L., Cotton, Julius A. VI, f. 4ᵛ, f. 5, f. 5ᵛ (Cat. 62)

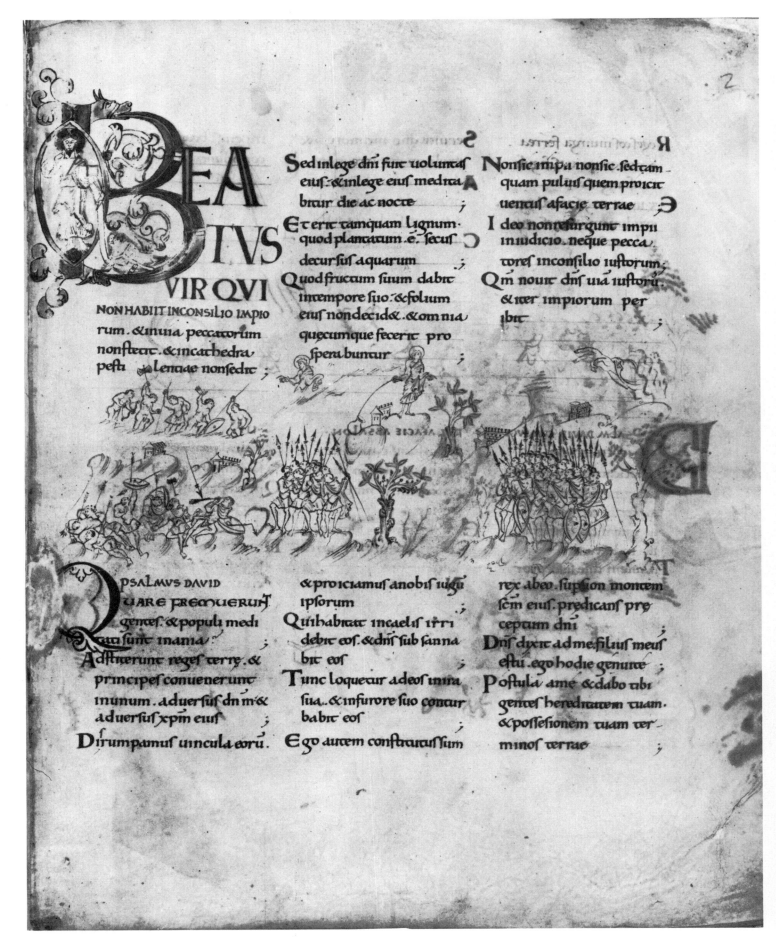

BEA
TVS
VIR QVI
NON HABIIT INCONSILIO IMPIO
rum. &inuia peccatorum
nonstetit. &incathedra
pesti lentiae nonsedit

Sed inlege dni fuit uoluntas
eius. &inlege eius medita
bitur die ac nocte

Et erit tamquam lignum.
quod plantatum .e. secus
decursus aquarum

Quod fructum suum dabit
intempore suo. &folium
eius non decidet. &omnia
quecumque fecerit pro
sperabuntur

Non sic impii non sic. sed tam
quam puluis quem proicit
uentus afacie terrae

Ideo non resurgunt impii
iniudicio. neque pecca
tores inconsilio iustorum

Qm nouit dns uia iustoru.
&iter impiorum per
ibit

PSALMVS DAVID
QVARE FREMUERUNT
gentes. &populi medi
tati sunt inania:

Adstiterunt reges terre. &
principes conuenerunt
inunum. aduersus dnm &
aduersus xpm eius

Dirumpamus uincula eoru.

&proiciamus anobis iugu
ipsorum

Qui habitat incaelis irri
debit eos. &dns sub sanna
bit eos

Tunc loquetur adeos inira
sua.. &infurore suo contur
babit eos

Ego autem constitutus sum

rex abeo. supsion montem
scm eius. predicans pre
ceptum dni

Dns dixit adme. filius meus
estu. ego hodie genuite

Postula ame. &dabo tibi
gentes hereditatem tuam.
&possesionem tuam ter
minos terrae

200. Psalm 1. London, B.L., Harley 603, f. 2 (Cat. 64)

201. Psalm 20.
London, B.L., Harley 603, f. 12 (Cat. 64)

202. Psalm 23.
London, B.L., Harley 603, f. 13ᵛ (Cat. 64)

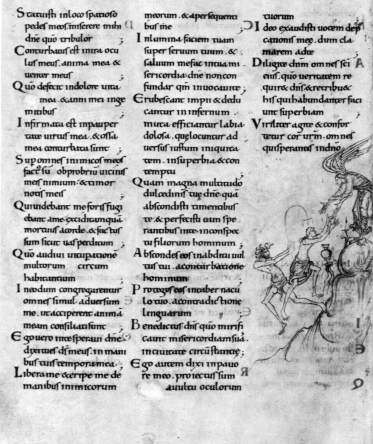

203. Psalm 26.
London, B.L., Harley 603, f. 15 (Cat. 64)

204. Psalmist between Angel and Devil.
London, B.L., Harley 603, f. 17ᵛ (Cat. 64)

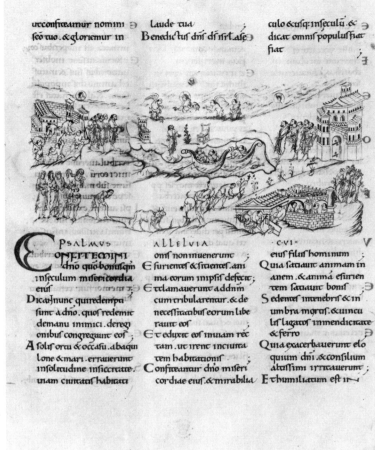

205. Psalm 103.
London, B.L., Harley 603, f. 51ᵛ (Cat. 64)

206. Psalm 106.
London, B.L., Harley 603, f. 54ᵛ (Cat. 64)

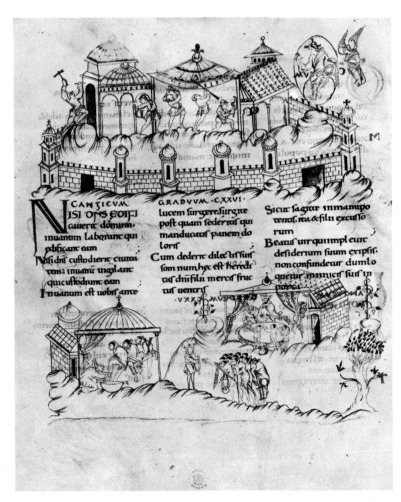

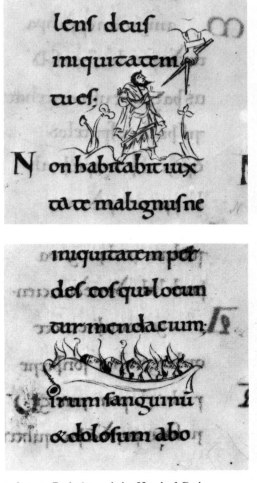

207. Psalm 126.
London, B.L., Harley 603, f. 66ᵛ (Cat. 64)

208–209. Psalmist and the Hand of God;
Mouth of Hell. Paris, Bibl. Nat.,
lat. 8824, f. 3ᵛ (Cat. 83)

210. Trinity. London B.L., Harley 603, f. 1 (Cat. 64)

211. Towered Building. London, B.L., Royal 15. A. XVI, f. 84 (Cat. 85)

212. Christ in Majesty. Cambridge, Trinity College B. 10. 4, f. 16ᵛ (Cat. 65)

213. Monks presenting the Rule to St. Benedict. London, B.L., Arundel 155, f. 133 (Cat. 66)

214. St. Matthew. Cambridge, Trinity College B. 10. 4, f. 17ᵛ (Cat. 65)

215. St. Matthew. London, B.L., Add. 34890, f. 10ᵛ (Cat. 68)

216. Initial B. London, B.L.,
Arundel 155, f. 12 (Cat. 66)

217. Initial Q. London, B.L.,
Arundel 155, f. 53 (Cat. 66)

218. Initial I. London, B.L.,
Add. 34890, f. 115 (Cat. 68)

219. Initial I. Cambridge,
Trinity College B. 10. 4, f. 60 (Cat. 65)

220. Initial D. London, B.L.,
Arundel 155, f. 93 (Cat. 66)

221. Initial I. London, B.L.,
Harley 76, f. 45 (Cat. 75)

222. Initial I. London, B.L.,
Royal 1. D. IX, f. 111 (Cat. 70)

223. Initial I. London, B.L.,
Loan 11 (Cat. 71)

224–225. Canon Tables. Hanover, Kestner Museum WM XXIᵃ 36, f. 9ᵛ, f. 10 (Cat. 67)

226–227. St. Mark; St. John. Hanover, Kestner Museum WM XXIᵃ 36, f. 65ᵛ, f. 147ᵛ (Cat. 67)

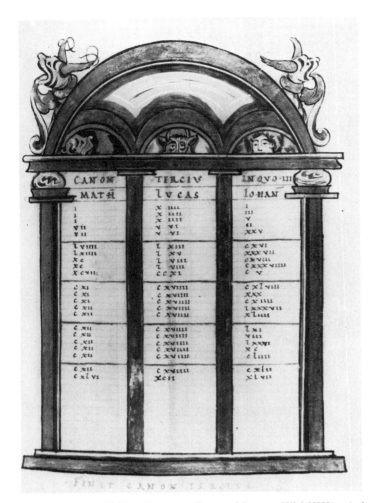

228–229. Canon Tables. Hanover, Kestner Museum WM XXIᵃ, 36, f. 12, f. 14 (Cat. 67)

230–231. Canon Tables. London, B.L., Harley 76, f. 8ᵛ, f. 10 (Cat. 75)

232. Christ Enthroned with Peter and Paul. Florence, Bibl. Medicea-Laurenziana, Plut. XVII. 20. f. 1 (Cat. 69)

233–234. Canon Table; St. Matthew. Cambridge, Pembroke College 301, f. 2ᵛ f. 10ᵛ, (Cat. 73)

235–236. St. Luke; Initial Q. Cambridge, Pembroke College 301, f. 70ᵛ f. 71, (Cat. 73)

237–238. Herod consulting Priests; Deposition. Rouen, Bibl. Mun. Y. 6, f. 36ᵛ, f. 72 (Cat. 72)

239–240. Ascension; St. Andrew. Rouen, Bibl. Mun. Y. 6, f. 81ᵛ, f. 164ᵛ (Cat. 72)

241. Christ the Judge. Cambridge, Trinity College B. 15.34, f. 1 (Cat. 74)

243. St. Peter. London, B.L.,
Cotton, Titus D. XXVI, f. 19ᵛ (Cat. 77)

242. Evangelist with Angel.
Besançon, Bibl. Mun. 14, f. 58ᵛ (Cat. 76)

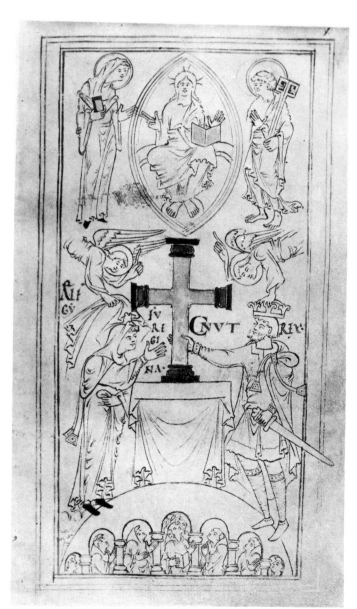

244. King Cnut and his Queen
presenting an Altar Cross to Christ.
London, B.L., Stowe 944, f. 6 (Cat. 78)

245. Quinity. London, B.L.,
Cotton, Titus D. XXVII, f. 75ᵛ (Cat. 77)

246. Crucifixion. London, B.L.,
Cotton, Titus D. XXVII, f. 65ᵛ (Cat. 77)

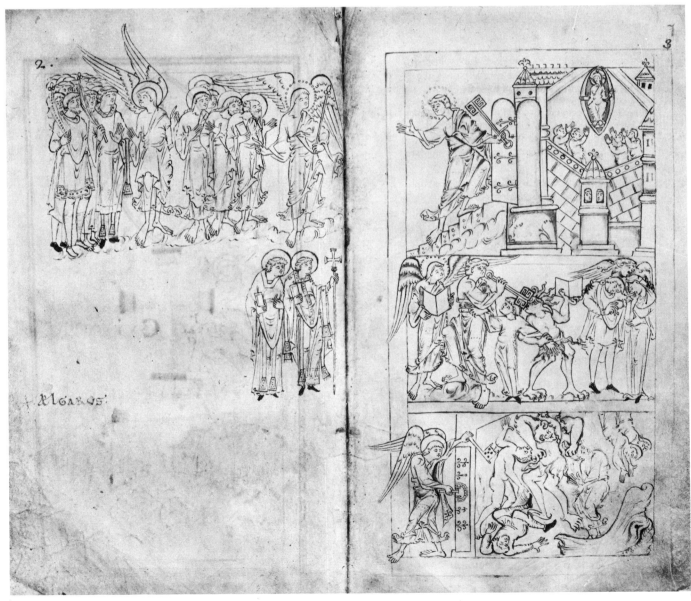

247–248. Last Judgment. London, B.L., Stowe 944, f. 6ᵛ, f. 7 (Cat. 78)

249. David Harping. Cambridge, University Lib., Ff. I. 23, f. 4ᵛ (Cat. 80)

re ne ge pat mgebeahte
quinon abiit inconsilio
anlcaepa   jonpege pyn
impiorum   & inuia pec
pulpa na ytod jonbpy
catorii nonstetit & inca
rede cpylder   na pat
thedra pestilenae iisedit;

250. Beatus Page. Cambridge, University Lib., Ff. I. 23, f. 5 (Cat. 80)

251–252. Initials B and I. Cambridge, University Lib., Ff. I. 23, f. 226, f. 169 (Cat. 80)

253. Christ with Angels.
Cambridge, University Lib., Ff. I. 23, f. 171 (Cat. 80)

254. Christ with Virgin and St. John.
Cambridge, Corpus Christi College 421, p. 1 (Cat. 82)

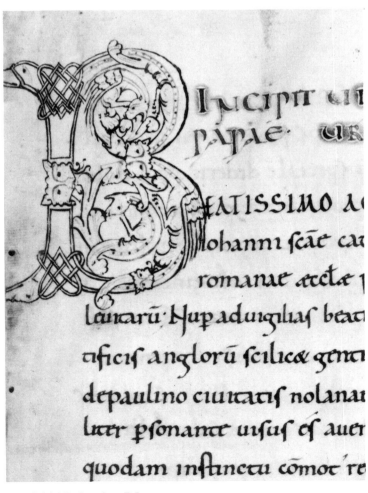

255. Christ Crucified. Cambridge,
Corpus Christi College 41, p. 484 (Cat. 81)

256. Bishop and Acolyte.
Rouen, Bibl. Mun. A. 27, f. 1ᵛ (Cat. 90)

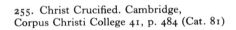

257. Initial B. London, B.L.,
Royal 6. A. VII, f. 2 (Cat. 60)

258. Initial B. Cambridge,
Corpus Christi College 41, p. 246 (Cat. 81)

259. Christ Triumphant. Oxford, Bodl. Lib.,
Douce 296, f. 40 (Cat. 79)

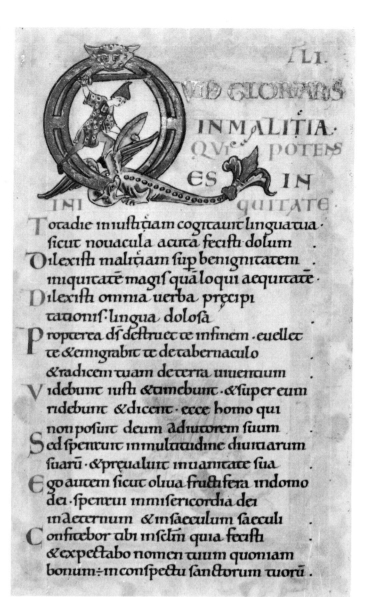

260. Initial Q. Oxford, Bodl. Lib.,
Douce 296, f. 40ᵛ (Cat. 79)

261. Initial D. Cambridge, Corpus Christi College 41, p. 410 (Cat. 81)

262. Initial Q. to Psalm 51. Rome, Vatican, Biblioteca Apostolica, Reg. lat. 12, f. 62 (Cat. 84)

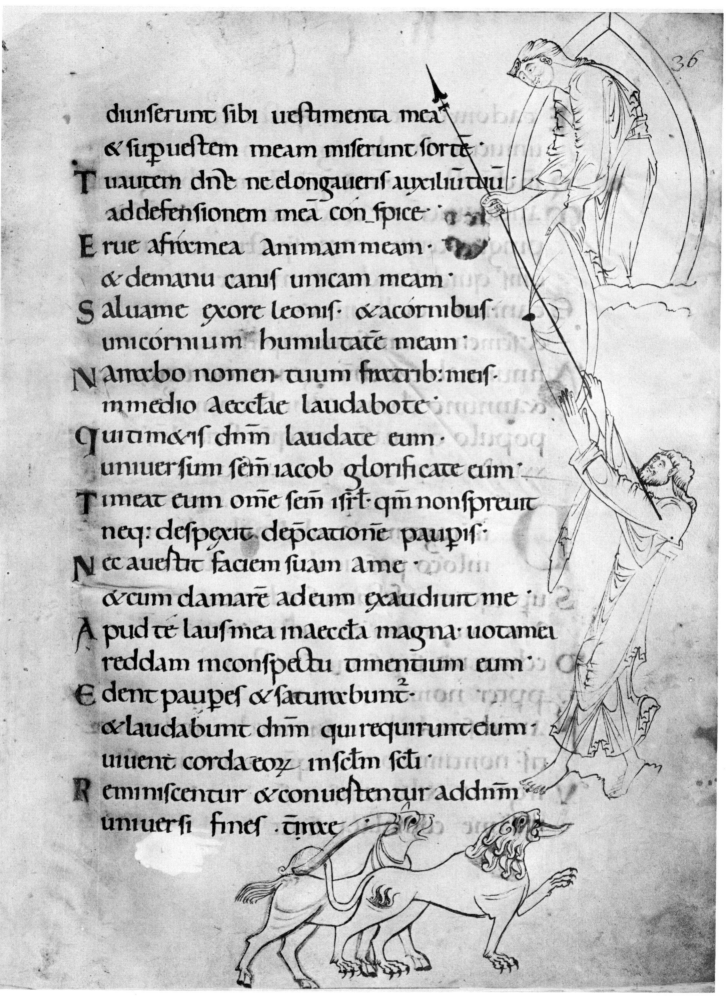

diuiserunt sibi uestimenta mea

& sup uestem meam miserunt sorte·

T u aut dñe ne elongaueris auxiliu tuu

ad defensionem mea con spice·

E rue a frãmea Animam meam·

& de manu canis unicam meam·

S alua me ex ore leonis· & a cornibus

unicornium humilitate meam·

N arrabo nomen tuum frãtrib; meis·

in medio æcclae laudabo te·

Q ui timetis dñm laudate eum·

uniuersum sem iacob glorificate eum·

T imeat eum oñe sem isrl· qm non spreuit

neq; despexit deprecatione paupis·

N ec auertit faciem suam a me·

& cum clamare ad eum exaudiuit me·

A pud te laus mea in æccla magna· uota mea

reddam in conspectu timentium eum·

E dent paupes & saturabunt·

& laudabunt dñm qui requirunt eum·

uiuent corda eor in sclm scli·

R eminiscentur & conuertentur ad dñm

uniuersi fines trre·

263. Illustration to Psalm 21. Rome, Vatican, Biblioteca Apostolica, Reg. lat. 12, f. 36 (Cat. 84)

Oum difcernit caeleftif regef fup eam·
niue dealba buntur infelmon
monf dei monf pinguif·
onf coagulatuf monf pinguif· utquid
fufpicamini montef coagolatof
Monf inquo bene placitum eft deo·habi
tare ineo· & enī dnf habitabit infinem·
Curruf dei decem milib: multiplex milia
loeantium dnf meif infyna infancto·
Afcendifti inaltum cepifti captuitate·
accepifti dona inhominibuf·
Etenim non credentef inhabitare
dominum deum·
Benedictuf dnf die cotidie·pfpum facia
nob df falutarium noftrorum·
Df nr df faluof faciendi
& dnī domini exituf mortif·
Verumptamen deuf confringa capita
inimicorum fuorum uerticem capilli
per ambulantium indelic tiffuif·
Dixit dnf exbafan conueftam·
conueftam inp fundum marif·
Vt intinguatur pef tuuf infanguine

264. Ascension. Rome, Vatican, Biblioteca Apostolica, Reg. lat. 12, f. 73ᵛ (Cat. 84)

265. Fall of the Rebel Angels. London, B.L., Cotton, Claudius B. IV, f. 2 (Cat. 86)

. dūs.

.ñoñba . cccxc̄ . tū . annoꝛ .

. moꝛſeſ obiſt .

Cãiꝯ moab . q̄d m̄tp̄ uallıſ moab nıxta fogoꝛ . ⁊ ſepul̄ꝯ ⁊ moꝛſeſ . ꝉ Gader . ⁊ huꝯ regē m̄ſter iſc . Turrıſ ubı habıtante ıacob ruben pat̄ſ ſuı uıolauıt thoꝛū . ⁊ abſq̄ ḡ lıcıa ın hebᵒ ader ſebꝛcıa ꝫ;

266. Death of Moses. London, B.L., Cotton, Claudius B. IV, 139ᵛ (Cat. 86)

Þabe realı lothıf vıſ ıınpırlıce unoth bæc. ıreand rona apꝥıo to

de god ſã ne   pdtthı ꝑꝗt ꝓdhıonꝛlını. ꝥheo oꝼꝥã real de ꝥã enãpan dꝛınꝗan ꝛ́ınꝓ
                                        Lꝥheo ꝑıınode ꝛ́ıo lnıı:
        o' et ſedıt   pꜹl·euanꝛı́ arcuſ ıacere potell. ne ıderet lilı
                                        ꝿoꝛıenꝛem·ꝗ ꝼ́euıt:

267–268. The Destruction of Sodom; Hagar in the Wilderness.
London, B.L., Cotton, Claudius B. IV, f. 32, f. 36 (Cat. 86)

269–270. Disembarkation of Noah; Abraham's Sacrifice. London, B.L., Cotton, Claudius B. IV, f. 15ᵛ, f. 38 (Cat. 86)

271–272. Illustrations to the story of Moses. London, B.L., Cotton, Claudius B. IV, f. 110ᵛ, f. 111 (Cat. 86)

273-274. May; August. London, B.L., Cotton, Tiberius B.V, f. 5, f. 6ᵛ (Cat. 87)

275. Marvels of the East. London, B.L., Cotton, Tiberius B. V, f. 85ᵛ (Cat. 87)

ula

...q; pseus extendit adsoceri ... abstulit cominerue tradidi
...uidelicet pa ...tris androme ... qd illo insuo pectore · Perseu
...dibus capu ... prefati psei aut ... uero intersidera collocasse op
...rum ordi ...ne constitui ... habet autem singulas s
...r dure ...fa ...bulose ... insingulis humeris · lun
...conlocatus eo ... dextera nicida una · h
...er insimilitudinem aurei ... sinistra una · incub
...ransformans delusa deang... ... sinistro · i ·
...rto · Qui missus apoli decto ... capite · i ·
...turi accepta auulca ... indextra
...damantina pdera ... lumboru
...s adgorgonas phi ... Inder ...ro femore
...e dum tres sorores ... Ingenu · i · Insinistra t
...o oculo una uidelicet ... Ingorgonis crinib: iii · Inabi
...line utebantur· Equib... ... Insinistro femore unam i
...edusa dicebatur caput ... sunt insumma decem
... nonam · caput et fal
... absque · astris

276. Perseus. London, B.L., Cotton, Tiberius B. V, f. 34 (Cat. 87)

277–278. St. Matthew; St. Mark. Oxford, Bodl. Lib., Lat. lit. F. 5, f. 3ᵛ, f. 13ᵛ (Cat. 91)

279–280. St. Luke; St. John. Oxford, Bodl. Lib., Lat. lit. F. 5, f. 21ᵛ, f. 30ᵛ (Cat. 91)

281–282. St. John; Initial A. Warsaw, Biblioteka Narodowa I. 3311, f. 83ᵛ, f. 69 (Cat. 92)

283–284. St. Mark; St. Luke. Warsaw, Biblioteka Narodowa I. 3311, f. 15, f. 55 (Cat. 92)

285. St. Matthew. New York.
Pierpont Morgan Lib. 709, f. 2ᵛ (Cat. 93)

286. St. Matthew. New York,
Pierpont Morgan Lib. 708, f. 2ᵛ (Cat. 94)

287. St. Luke. Monte Cassino, Archivio della Badia,
BB. 437, 439, p. 126 (Cat. 95)

288. Opening of St. Luke's Gospel. Monte Cassino, Archivio della Badia,
BB. 437, 439, p. 127 (Cat. 95)

289. Crucifixion. New York, Pierpont Morgan Lib. 709, f. 1ᵛ (Cat. 93)

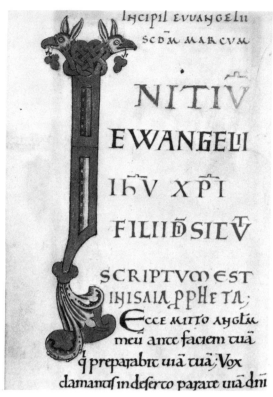

INCIPIT EVVANGELII
SCDM MARCVM

NITIV
EWANGELII
IHV XPI
FILIIDSIEV

SCRIPTVM EST
IN ISAIA PPHETA;
Ecce mitto angtm̄
meu ance faciem tuā
q̄ preparabit uiā tuā. Vox
damanaf in deserto parare uiā dn̄i

290. Initial I. Cambridge,
Pembroke College 302, f. 38ᵛ (Cat. 96)

INCIPIT EVVANGT SCDM LVCAM.

QVIDEM
MVLTICONATI
SUNT ORDINARE NARRATIOHE
QVE IN NOBIS COMPLETE
SUNT RERVM SICVT TRADIDE
runt nobif qui abinitio ipf̄i
uiderunt & miniftri fuerunt
sermonif. uifum est & mihi ad

291. Initial Q. Cambridge,
Pembroke College, 302 f. 61 (Cat. 96)

292. St. Mark. Cambridge,
Pembroke College 302, f. 38 (Cat. 96)

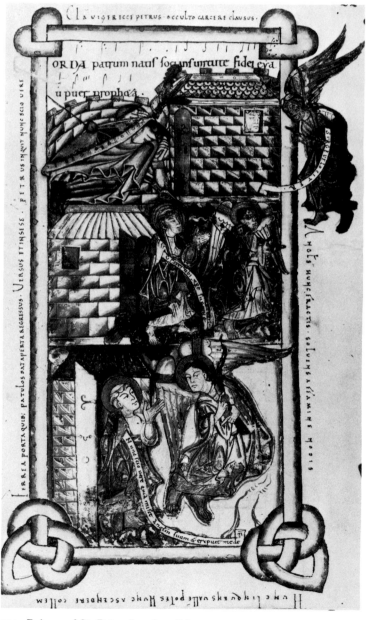

293. Release of St. Peter. London, B.L.,
Cotton, Caligula A. XIV, f. 22 (Cat. 97)

294–295. Annunciation to Joachim; Apostles blessed by the Hand of God.
London, B.L., Cotton, Caligula A. XIV, f. 26, f. 31 (Cat. 97)

296. Beatus Page. London, B.L., Stowe 2, f. 1 (Cat. 99)

297. Psalm 51. London, B.L., Cotton, Tiberius C. VI, f. 72 (Cat. 98)

298. St. Gregory.
Oxford, Bodl. Lib., Tanner 3, f. 1ᵛ (Cat. 89)

299. St. Luke. Rheims, Bibl. Mun. 9, f. 23, f. 88 (Cat. 105)

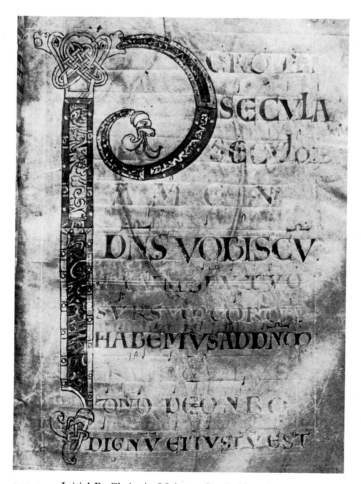

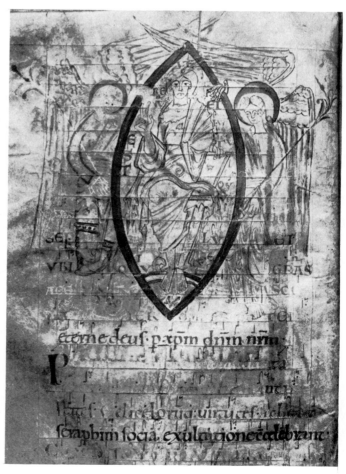

300–301. Initial P; Christ in Majesty, Cambridge, Corpus Christi College 422, p. 51, p. 52 (Cat. 104)

302. Christ in Majesty. London, B.L., Cotton, Tiberius C. IV, f. 18ᵛ (Cat. 98)

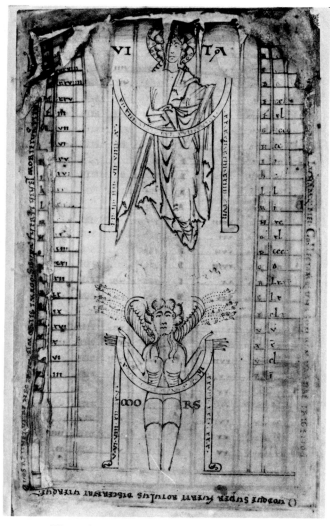
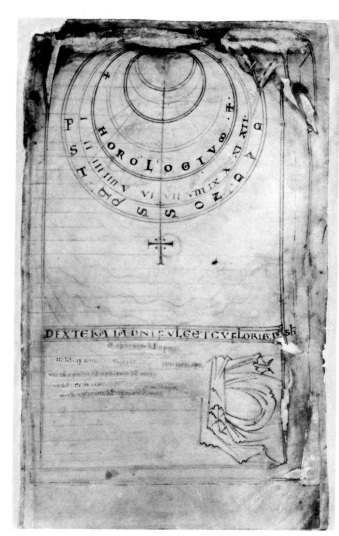

303–304. Vita and Mors; Diagram with *Horologium*. London, B.L., Cotton, Tiberius C. VI, f. 6ᵛ, f. 7 (Cat. 98)

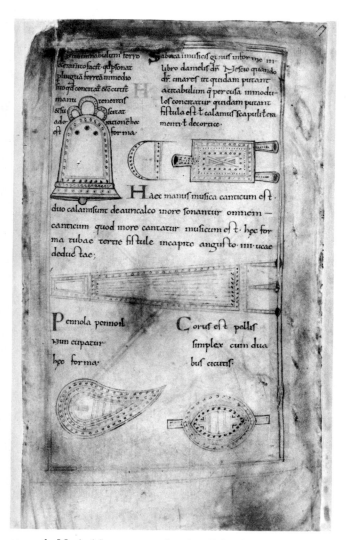
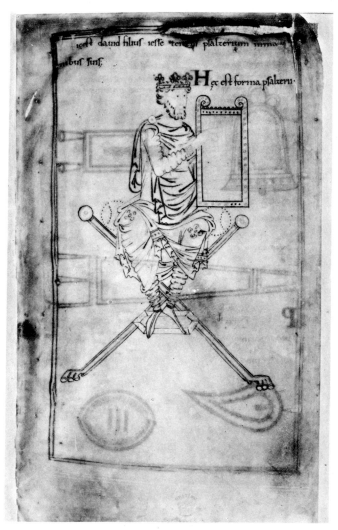

305–306. Musical Instruments. London, B.L., Cotton, Tiberius C. VI, f. 17, f. 17ᵛ (Cat. 98)

307-308. David and Goliath. London, B.L., Cotton, Tiberius C. VI, f. 8ᵛ, f. 9 (Cat. 98)

309-310. Entry into Jerusalem; St. Michael. London, B.L., Cotton, Tiberius C. VI, f. 11, f. 16 (Cat. 98)

311. Crucifixion. London, B.L., Cotton, Tiberius C. VI, f. 13 (Cat. 98)

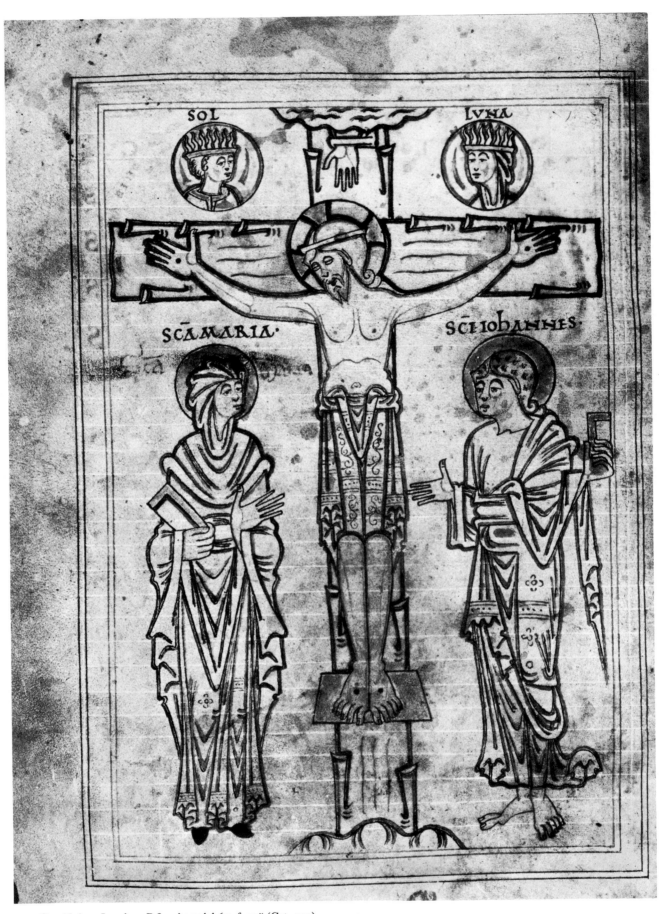

312. Crucifixion. London, B.L., Arundel 60, f. 12ᵛ (Cat. 103)

313. King Edgar with SS. Dunstan and Ethelwold.
London, B.L., Cotton, Tiberius A. III, f. 2ᵛ (Cat. 100)

314. Monks presenting the Rule of St. Benedict.
London, B.L., Cotton, Tiberius A. III, f. 117ᵛ (Cat. 100)

315. Two Ecclesiastics with kneeling Monk.
Durham, Cathedral Lib., B. III. 32, f. 56ᵛ (Cat. 101)

316. St. Jerome. Cambridge,
Corpus Christi College 389, f. 1ᵛ (Cat. 36)

317–318. St. Pachomius receiving the Easter Tables; Christ and Angels.
London, B.L., Cotton, Caligula A. XV, f. 122ᵛ, f. 123 (Cat. 106)

319. Creation. London, B.L.,
Royal 1. E. VII, f. 1ᵛ (Cat. 102)

INDEX

INDEX OF MANUSCRIPTS

References are to page numbers; figures in italics refer to illustrations and figures preceded by 'no.' refer to the numbered entry in the Catalogue of Manuscripts

Aachen
Cathedral Treasury
Otto III Gospels: 72

Amiens
Bibliothèque Municipale
18 (Corbie Psalter): 12, 40; *figs. 7, 8*
223: 42; *fig. 32*

Antwerp
Plantin-Moretus Museum
190: 108

Arras
Bibliothèque Municipale
559 (St. Vaast Bible): 24, *fig. 22*

Avranches
Bibliothèque Municipale
59: *fig. 24*

Berlin
Staatsbibliothek
lat. theol. 2° 733: *fig. 14*

Besançon
Bibliothèque Municipale
14 (Gospels): no. 76; 20, 92, 110; *242*

Boulogne
Bibliothèque Municipale
10 (Gospels): no. 10; 12, 110, 112; *38*
11 (Boulogne Gospels): no. 44; 19, 64, 67–8, 74, 75, 84, 89, 90, 101, 110, 111, 112; *145, 147–50*
20 (Otbert Psalter): 23, 67, 100, 116; *fig. 27*
82 (Amalarius): no. 29; *101–2*
107: *fig. 20*
189 (Prudentius, Carmina, Misc.): no. 30(xv); 79; *121*

Brussels
Bibliothèque Royale
II. 175: 114

Cambridge
Corpus Christi College
2 (Bury Bible): *fig. 35*
23 (Prudentius): no. 48; 17–18, 43, 60, 70, 73, 74, 77, 82; *50, 155–8*
41 (Bede): no. 81; 78, *255, 258, 261*
57 (Rule of St. Benedict, Martyrology, etc.): no. 30(x)
173 (Anglo-Saxon Chronicle): 39, 40
183 (Bede: Lives of St. Cuthbert): no. 6; 11, 12, 36, 37, 39, 40, 42, 47, 63, 107; *18, 19, 29*
198 (Anglo-Saxon Homilies): no. 88, *fig. 58*
214: 64
307: 63
326 (Aldhelm): no. 19(iv)
389 (St. Paul the Hermit; Felix, Life of St. Guthlac): no. 36; *130, 316*
411 (Psalter): no. 40; *128, 129*
419: 99
421 (Anglo-Saxon Homilies): no. 82; 101; *254*
422 (Missal - Red Book of Darley): no. 104; 116; *300–1*

Pembroke College
301 (Gospels): no. 73; 20, 50, 69, 75, 86, 93, 97, 108; *233–6*
302 (Hereford Gospels): no. 96; 23, 85, 114, 121; *290–2*
Sidney Sussex College
100 (ii): 64
Trinity College
B. 10. 4 (Trinity Gospels): no. 65; 12, 19–20, 43, 45, 53, 59, 66, 69, 88, 89, 90, 91, 93, 99, 110, 111–12, 121; *212, 214, 219*
B. 11. 2 (Amalarius): no. 21; 12, 43, 47, 62, 73; *79, 80*
B. 14. 3 (Arator, Historia Apostolica): no. 34; 57; *125*
B. 15. 34 (Anglo-Saxon Homilies): no. 74; 98, 109; *241*
B. 16. 3 (Rabanus Maurus): no. 14; 12; *45, 46, 48*
O. 1. 18 (Enchiridion Augustini): no. 30(i); *103*
O. 2. 31 (Prosper, Cato, etc.): no. 30 (vi); *107*
O. 3. 7 (Boethius): no. 20; 18, 70; *44, 76–8*
University Library
Ff. 1. 23 (Winchcombe Psalter): no. 80; 23, 64, 73, 92, 94, 96, 99, 105, 108, 109, 116, 120, 121; *249–53*
Ll. 1. 10 (Book of Cerne): 55; *fig. 5*

Chantilly
Musée Condé
1695 (Ingeborg Psalter): *fig. 39*

Coburg
Landesbibliothek
Gandersheim Gospels: 12

Copenhagen
Royal Library
G.K.S. 10, 2° (Copenhagen Gospels): no. 47; 20, 50, 83, 86, 88, 89, 90, 92; *151–4*

Damme (nr. Bruges)
Musée van Maerlant
Gospel Lectionary (fragment): no. 53; 20, 77; *173–5, 176 (colour)*

Dublin
Trinity College Library
A. 1. 6 (Book of Kells): 66

Durham
Cathedral Library
A. IV. 19 (Durham Ritual): no. 3; 11, 107, 108; *7, 8, 10*
B. III. 32 (Hymnal; Aelfric's grammar): no. 101; 23, 108, 118; *315*

Épernay
Bibliothèque Municipale
1 (Ebbo Gospels): 19, 86, 107; *fig. 15*

Florence
Biblioteca Laurenziana
Codex Amiatinus I (Bible): 69
Laur. VI. 23: 72, 73
Plut. I, 56: 72, 73
Plut. XVII. 20 (Gospel Lectionary): no. 69; 85, 86; *232*

Fulda
Landesbibliothek
Aa 6: *fig. 49*
Aa 21: 110, 112

Hanover
Kestner Museum
WM XXIᵃ 36 (Eadui Codex): no. 67; 22, 67, 74, 79, 82, 84, 85, 86, 88, 89, 92, 93, 99, 113, 115, 118; *224–9*

Hildesheim
Cathedral Library
18: *fig. 42*

Innsbruck
Universitätsbibliothek
Cod. 484: 91

Leiden
Rijksuniversiteit
Codex Scaligeranus 69 (Aethici, Istrici, Cosmographia): no. 30 (v); *105*

Lincoln
Cathedral Library
182: 108

Lille
Bibliothèque Municipale
479 (Cysoing Gospels): 24; *fig. 46*

London
British Library
Add. 9381 (Bodmin Gospels): 73
Add. 11850: 29; *figs. 21, 48*
Add. 17739: *fig. 50*
Add. 24199 (Prudentius): no. 51; 18; *163, 166*
Add. 34890 (Grimbald Gospels): no. 68; 20, 23, 50, 60, 67, 69, 79, 85, 86, 88, 93, 96, 101, 103, 109, 120, 121; *215 (colour), 218*
Add. 37517 (Bosworth Psalter): no. 22; 12, 57, 62, 63, 72, 75, 77; *81–3*
Add. 37768 (Lothair Psalter): 116
Add. 40618 (Gospels): no. 15; 70, 83, 111, 112; *49, 51–2*
Add. 47967 (Orosius): no. 8; 39, 43; *25, 28*
Add. 49598 (Benedictional of St. Ethelwold): no. 23; 18–19, 37, 53, 54, 59, 63, 66, 67, 69, 71, 76, 84, 86, 88, 89, 90, 92, 94, 100, 101, 106, 109, 114, 116, 117; *85, 86, 88, 90, 91*
Add. 54180: *fig. 36*
Arundel 60 (Psalter): no. 103; 23, 64, 116, 117, 121; *312*
Arundel 155 (Psalter): no. 66; 22, 23, 51, 67, 74, 76, 82, 86, 88, 89, 90, 92, 93, 96, 100, 101, 107, 109, 112, 118; *213, 216, 217, 220, fig. 56*
Cotton Calig. A. VII (Heliand): no. 33; *123–4*
Cotton Calig. A. XIV (Hereford Troper): no. 97; 23–4, 103, 107, 113, 116; *293–5*
Cotton Calig. A. XV (Pascal tables, etc.): no. 106; 23, 61, 82, 92; *317–18*
Cotton Claud. B. IV (Aelfric's Pentateuch): no. 86; 18, 71, 76, 114; *265–72, fig. 34*
Cotton Cleop. A. VI (Grammatical treatises, miscellanea): no. 27; *96*
Cotton Cleop. C. VIII (Prudentius): no. 49; 18, 76, 77, 81; *159–62*
Cotton Galba A. XVIII (Aethelstan Psalter): no. 5; 11, 39, 42, 44, 48, 49, 94, 104, 107; *15–17, 31–3*
Cotton Jul. A. VI (Calendar: Hymnal): no. 62; 22, 70, 73, 104; *197–9*
Cotton Nero C. IV (Winchester Psalter): 95; *fig. 45*
Cotton Nero D. IV (Lindisfarne Gospels): 20, 36, 40, 50, 69, 91–2
Cotton Otho B. II (Gregory the Great): no. 46; *fig. 57*
Cotton Otho B. VI (Cotton Genesis): 76
Cotton Tib. A. II: 11, 41; *fig. 30*

Cotton Tib. A. III (Regularis Concordia; Rule of St. Benedict): no. 100; 23, 74, 82, 101, 108, 119, 120; *313, 314*
Cotton Tib. B. I (Orosius, Menologium, etc., Anglo-Saxon Chronicle): no. 30(xviii); *116*
Cotton Tib. B. V, Vol. I (Calendar, computus matters, Aratea, Marvels of the East): no. 87; 22, 72, 106; *273–6*
Cotton Tib. C. I: 104
Cotton Tib. C. VI (Psalter): no. 98; 23, 45, 50, 64, 94, 95, 99, 101, 104, 106, 108, 114, 118, 119; *297, 302–11, fig. 37*
Cotton Titus D. XXVI and D. XXVII (Prayers, Church Offices, misc.): no. 77; 22, 64, 75, 86, 88, 94, 96, 97, 108, 109, 120; *243, 245–6*
Cotton Vesp. A. I: 39, 115
Cotton Vesp. A. VIII (New Minster Charter): no. 16; 18, 51, 52, 53, 83; *84*
Cotton Vit. A. XV (Marvels of the East): no. 52; 22, 104; *185*
Cotton Vit. A. XIX (Bede, Lives of St. Cuthbert); no. 19(ii); *63*
Cotton Vit. C. III (Herbal, Dioscorides): no. 63; 22; *186–8*
Cotton Vit. E. XVIII: 64, 117
Harley 76 (Bury Gospels): no. 75; 23, 101; *221, 230–1*
Harley 110 (Prosper, Isidore, etc.): no. 19(vii); *69*
Harley 603 (Utrecht Psalter copy): no. 64; 22, 61, 75, 86, 90, 92, 94, 100–1, 102, 114, 116; *200–7, 210, fig. 1*
Harley 647 (Aratus): 22, 65, 104
Harley 1117 (Bede, Lives of St. Cuthbert): no. 30(vii); 60; *108–9*
Harley 2506 (Cicero, Aratea): no. 42; 19, 64, 66, 67, 104, 116; *143*
Harley 2788: 43, 67
Harley 2892: 92
Harley 2897: *fig. 43*
Harley 2904 (Psalter): no. 41; 19, 44, 58, 65, 66, 67, 78, 84, 90, 94, 96, 97, 105, 108, 109, 116, 117, 118, 121; *140–2*
Harley 5431 (St. Benedict, statutes, etc.): no. 38; 62; *115, 120, 126, 127*
Loan 11 (Kedarminster Gospels): no. 71; 20, 90, 92, 96; *223*
Royal 1. D. IX (Gospels): no. 70; 20, 83–4, 89, 90, 92; *222*
Royal 1. E. VI (Gospels): no. 55; 90, 101, 112; *172*
Royal 1. E. VII: no. 102; 100, 110, 115; *319*
Royal 2. A. XX: *fig. 4*
Royal 5. E. XI (Aldhelm): no. 19(ix); *74–5*
Royal 5. F. III (Aldhelm): no. 2; 11; *5, 6, 9*
Royal 6. A. VI (Aldhelm): no. 30(xi); 62; *117*
Royal 6. A. VII (Life of St. Gregory): no. 60; *257*
Royal 6. B. VIII (Isidore): no. 54; *164*
Royal 7. D. XXIV (Aldhelm): no. 4; 38, 40, 44; *11–14, 27*
Royal 12. C. XXIII (Julian, Aldhelm, etc.): no. 30(iii); *113*
Royal 15. A. XVI: no. 85; *211*
Royal 15. B. XIX (Sedulius): no. 19(iii); *64*
Royal 15. C. VII (Vita S. Swithuni): 94
Stowe 2 (Psalter): no. 99; 64, 116, 117; *296*
Stowe 944 (New Minster Register): no. 78; 22, 88, 93, 94, 113, 120; *244, 247–8*
College of Arms
Arundel 22 (Fragment of Gospel Lectionary): no. 26; *p. 21 (colour)*
Lambeth Palace Library
200 (Aldhelm): no. 39; 11, 17, 76; *131–3*
204 (Gregory the Great, Ephrem): no. 19(x); *fig. 2*

Monte Cassino
Archivio della Badia
BB. 437, 439 (Gospels): no. 95; 23, 40, 43, 66, 83, 106, 110; *287–8*

Moscow
Historical Museum
Hist. Cod. Gr. 129 (Chludoff Psalter): 50

Munich
Staatsbibliothek
CLM. 290316 (Prudentius fragment): no. 50; 18; *165*

New York
Pierpont Morgan Library
M. 333 (Otbert Gospels): no. 30(xiii); 11, 12, 67; *112, fig. 41*
M. 641 (Mont St. Michel Sacramentary): 29; *fig. 23*
M. 708 (Holkham Hall 15) (Judith of Flanders Gospels): no. 94; 23, 105, 108, 111, 112, 122; *286*
M. 709 (Holkham Hall 16) (Judith of Flanders Gospels): no. 93; 23, 64, 94, 97, 108, 111, 112, 116, 120; *285, 289 (colour)*
M. 827 (Anhalt-Morgan Gospels): no. 45; 19, 64, 66, 67, 90; *146*
M. 869 (Arenberg Gospels): no. 56; 20, 60, 73, 74, 79, 90, 96, 101; *167–71*

Orléans
Bibliothèque Municipale
105 (Winchcombe Sacramentary): no. 31; *139*
175 (St. Gregory, Homilies on Ezekiel): no. 43; 19, 64, 67; *144*

Oxford
Bodleian Library
Auct. D. 2. 16 (Breton Gospel Book): 78
Auct. D. inf. 2. 9: 62
Auct. F. 1. 15 (Boethius): no. 37; 12, 56, 60, 62, 77; *114*
Auct. F. 4. 32 ('St. Dunstan's Classbook'): no. 11; 12, 17, 35, 42; *41*
Bodley 49 (Aldhelm): no. 19(i); *62*
Bodley 155 (Gospels): no. 59; 17, 20; *177–8*
Bodley 163: 92
Bodley 297: 101
Bodley 340, 342 (Homiliary): no. 30(xvii); *118*
Bodley 577 (Aldhelm): no. 57; 17, 36, 70; *179–80*
Bodley 579 (Leofric Missal): no. 17; 17, 47, 48, 49, 70, 81, 82, 115; *53–6*
Bodley 708 (Gregory the Great): no. 19(xi); *73*
Bodley 718 (Penitential of Egbert, Halitgar): no. 30(xiv); 60–1; *111*
Bodley 775: 117, 118
Bodley 819: 36
Digby 146 (Aldhelm): no. 19(vi); *70*
Douce 176: 40; *fig. 10*
Douce 296 (Psalter): no. 79; 23 79, 98, 107, 109, 110, 112, 116; *259–60*
Hatton 20 (Gregory the Great): no. 1; 11, 68; *2–4*
Junius 11 (Caedmon Genesis): no. 58; 18, 51, 59, 70, 72, 84, 90, 91, 95, 98, 100, 103, 104, 108, 114, 116; *189–96*
Junius 27 (Junius Psalter): no. 7; 12, 37, 38, 39, 40, 41, 45, 47, 55, 59, 62, 76, 77, 104, 107, 115; *1, 20–4, 26*
Lat. lit. f. 5 (St. Margaret Gospels): no. 91; 23, 108, 109, 110; *277–80*
Laud misc. 126: 40
Rawl. B. 484 (Aethelstan Psalter): no. 5; 11, 76; *30*
Rawl. C. 570 (Arator): no. 30(iv); 63; *100, 106*
Tanner 3 (Gregory the Great): no. 89; *298*
Tanner 10 (Bede, Historia ecclesiastica): no. 9; 41, 45, 55, 59, 62, 73; *34–7, 39–40*
Tanner 10*: 40

Oriel College
3 (Prudentius, Peristephanon, etc.): no. 19(viii); *71, 72*
St. John's College
28 (misc. texts, Gregory the Great): no. 13; 17, 22, 47, 60, 61, 107, 112; *42, 43*
194 (Gospels): no. 12; 12; *47*
University College
165: *fig. 38*

Paris
Bibliothèque Nationale
gr. 74: *72*
lat. 2 (Second Bible of Charles the Bald): 108; *fig. 13*
lat. 4: 43
lat. 261 (Le Mans Gospels): 72
lat. 943 (Sherborne Pontifical): no. 35; 17, 19, 42, 49, 59, 71, 73, 74, 93, 101; *134–8*
lat. 987 (Benedictional): no. 25; 19, 93, 94; *92, 93*
lat. 1141 (Coronation Sacramentary): 37
lat. 6401 (Boethius): no. 32; 19, 101, 116; *94–5*
lat. 6401A (Boethius): no. 30(viii); *119*
lat. 7585 (Isidore): no. 30(ii); *104*
lat. 8824 (Psalter): no. 83; 22; *208–9*
lat. 9338 (Evangeliary): 39
lat. 9428 (Drogo Sacramentary): 49, 50, 51, 99, 101, 114; *fig. 28*
lat. 12048 (Gellone Sacramentary): *fig. 9*
lat. 17814 (Boethius): no. 30(xii); 70, 73; *110*
Bibliothèque Ste. Geneviève
2410 (Iuvencus, Sedulius, etc.): no. 30(xvi); *122*

Poitiers
Bibliothèque Municipale
17: 39

Rheims
Bibliothèque Municipale
9 (Gospels): no. 105; 23, 36; *299*

Rome
S. Paolo fuori le Mura
San Paolo Bible: 11, 38, 44, 66, 73; *fig. 12*

Rouen
Bibliothèque Municipale
A. 27 (Lanalet Pontifical): no. 90; *256*
Y. 6 (274) (Sacramentary of Robert of Jumièges): no. 72; 19, 69, 83, 88, 89, 101, 109, 110, 114, 115, 116; *237–40*
Y. 7 (369) (Benedictional of Archbishop Robert): no. 24; 19, 63; *87, 89*

St. Gall
Stiftsbibliothek
22 (Psalterium Aureum): 116

St. Lô
Archives Départmentales de la Manche
1: *fig. 25*

St. Omer
Bibliothèque Municipale
56: 11; *fig. 19*

Salisbury
Cathedral Library
38 (Aldhelm): no. 19(v); *65–8*
150 (Psalter): no. 18; 12, 55, 78, 83, 98, 99; *57–61*

Stuttgart
Landesbibliothek
II: 107
Cod. Bibl. 4° 7: *fig. 47*

Trier
Stadtbibliothek
    24 (Egbert Codex): 50
    Codex 22: 59

Utrecht
University Library
    32 (Utrecht Psalter): 22, 75, 82, 92, 94, 95, 99, 100-1,
      114; *fig. 11*

Vatican
Biblioteca Apostolica
    Barb. lat. 570 (Barberini Gospels), 35, 37, 41, 43, 85;
      fig. 6
    Pal. lat. 834: 42, 60; *fig. 31*
    Reg. lat. 12 (Bury Psalter): no. 84; 23, 51, 74, 76, 84,
      92, 93, 96, 99, 108, 109, 114, 115, 116; *262-4, fig. 26*
    Reg. lat. 1671 (Virgil): no. 30(ix); 55

Vercelli
Cathedral
    Codex CVII (Homilies and Poems): no. 28; *97-9*

Vienna
Nationalbibliothek
    Cod. 652 (theo. 39): *fig. 33*
    271: 59

Warsaw
Biblioteka Narodowa
    I. 3311 (Evangeliary and Lectionary): no. 92; *281-4*,
      figs. 51-5, fig. 59

York Minster
Chapter Library
    Add. 1 (York Gospels): no. 61; 75, 82, 85, 112; *181-4*

Fig. 58. Apostles. Cambridge, Corpus Christi College, 198, p. 1 (Cat. 88)

ANALYSIS OF MANUSCRIPTS IN THE CATALOGUE

I. TYPES OF BOOK

Aelfric's Grammar: no. 101
Benedictionals: nos. 23, 24, 25
Bible: no. 102
Caedmon (Genesis): no. 58
Calendars: nos. 62, 87
Charter (New Minster): no. 16
Church Fathers
   Enchiridion Augustini: no. 30(i)
   Gregory the Great (Pastoral Care): nos. 1 (Alfred's translation), 13, 19(xi), 64 (Alfred's translation) (Dialogues): nos. 19(x), 89
Classical Authors
   Aratea (Latin poems translated from the Greek of Aratus by Cicero): nos. 42, 87(2)
   Boethius: no. 30(viii), 30(xii), 37
   Cato: no. 30(vi)
   Cicero: nos. 42, 87(2)
   Dioscorides: no. 63
   Iuvencus: no. 30(xvi)
   Prudentius (Peristephanon): no. 19(viii) (Psychomachia): nos. 48, 49, 50, 51
   Sedulius: no. 19(iii)
   Virgil: no. 30(ix)
Collectar: no. 3
Evangeliary: no. 92
Gospels: nos. 10, 12, 15, 30(xiii), 32(xvi), 44, 45, 47, 55, 56, 59, 61, 65, 67, 68, 70, 71, 73, 75, 76, 93, 94, 95, 105
Grammatical treatises. nos. 27, 101 (Aelfric)
Heliand (Life of Christ): no. 33
Herbal: no. 63
Homiliary: no. 30(xvii)
Homilies and poems: nos. 28, 43, 74, 82, 88
Hymnal: no. 62, 101

Lectionaries: nos. 26 (fragment), 53, 69, 91, 96
Lives of Saints: nos. 36, 60
Marvels of the East: nos. 52, 87
Medicinal: no. 63
Medieval Theologians and Scholars
   Aelfric, Pentateuch and Joshua: no. 86
   Aethicus, Istricus: no. 30(v)
   Aldhelm: nos. 2, 4, 19(i), 19(iv), 19(v), 19(ix), 30(iii), 30(ix), 39, 57
   Amalarius: nos. 21, 29
   Arator: nos. 30(iv), 34
   Bede: nos. 6, 19(ii), 30(vii)—*Lives of St. Cuthbert* nos. 9, 81—*Historia Ecclesiastica*
   Dunstan: no. 11
   Felix: no. 36—*Vita S. Guthlaci*
   Isidore: no. 19(vii), 30 (ii)—*Ethymologia Isidorii*, 54—*De fide catholica*
   Istricus: no. 30(v)
   Julian: no. 30(iii)
   Orosius: nos. 8, 30(xviii)
   Prosper: no. 19(vii), 30(vi)
   Rabanus Maurus: no. 14
Missal: no. 104
Pascal Tables, annals, etc.: 106
Prayers, Church Offices, Miscellanea: no. 77
Penitential of Egbert: no. 30(xiv)
Pontifical: nos. 24, 35, 90
Psalters: nos. 5, 7, 18, 22, 40, 41, 64, 66, 79, 80, 83, 84, 98, 99, 103
Regularis Concordia: no. 100
Rule of St. Benedict: nos 30(x), 38, 100
Sacramentaries: nos. 17, 31, 72
Troper: no. 97

II. PLACES OF ORIGIN

Abingdon: nos. 30(x), 30(xviii)
Canterbury: no. 53(?)
   Christ Church: nos. 12, 14, 19(iii), 19(iv), 19(v), 19(vii), 19(viii), 19(ix), 19(x), 19(xi), 22, 30(vi), 30(vii), 30(xi), 30(xii), 30(xv), 30(xvi), 34, 35, 48, 49, 56, 57, 58, 61, 62, 63, 64, 65, 66, 67, 69, 70, 71, 74, 75, 84, 86, 100, 101, 102, 103, 106
   St. Augustine's: nos. 13, 19(ii), 20, 21, 30(i), 30(ii), 30(iii), 30(iv), 30(v), 36, 37, 38, 39, 40, 54(?), 55, 85
Chester le Street: no. 3
Crowland: no. 79 (?)
Exeter: no. 30(xiv)

Fleury: nos. 32, 42, 43
Glastonbury: no. 11, 17
Mercia: no. 2
Rochester: no. 30(xvii)
St. Bertin: nos. 30(xiii), 44
Southern England: no. 3
Wessex: no. 90
Winchcombe: nos. 31(?), 80
Winchester: nos. 4(?), 5, 6, 7, 8, 25, 26(?), 41, 47(?), 76(?), 87(?), 104
   New Minster: nos. 16, 24, 77, 78, 99(?)
   Old Minster: no. 23
Worcester: nos. 28(?), 30(ix), 60, 88(?), 89(?)

GENERAL INDEX

Abbo of Fleury, 65
Ada Court School, 17, 41, 43, 57, 59, 66
Aelfgar, Count of Mercia, 23, 121
Aelfgiva, Abbess of Barking, 78
Aelfleda, Queen, 11
Aelfric, Archbishop of Canterbury, 61
Aelfric's Pentateuch see London, British Library MS Cotton Claud. B. IV
Aelfwin, Abbot, 22, 94
Aelfwine, 77
Aelsinus, monk of Winchester, 96
Aelwald, King of the East Angles, 61
Aethelgar, Abbot, 20
Aethelstan, King, 11, 12, 36, 37, 41, 76
Aethestan, Bishop of Hereford, 113
Aldhelm, St., 70 (see also Analysis of Manuscripts)
Alfred, King, 11, 35, 37, 39, 87
Anhalt-Morgan Gospels see New York, Pierpont Morgan Library M. 827
Arenberg Gospels, see New York, Pierpont Morgan Library M. 869
Arras, St. Vaast, 68
Athelward, Abbot of Malmesbury, 70

Baldwin II, Count of Flanders, 11
Battle Abbey, 105
Bede, 11 (see also Analysis of Manuscripts)
Berno, monk of Fleury, 65
Bosworth Psalter see London, British Library MS. Add. 37517
Bristol Cathedral, Stone relief of Christ, 97
Brunswick Museum, Ivory casket, 49, 50
Burchard, Son of Aelfgar, 121
Bury Gospels see London, British Library MS Harley 76
Bury Psalter see Vatican, Biblioteca Apostolica MS Reg. lat. 12
Bury St. Edmunds, 71, 93

Caedmon Genesis see Oxford, Bodleian Library MS Junius, 11
Charlemagne, Court School of, 48
Charles the Bald, Court School of, 38, 44, 73
Citeaux, Stephen Harding MSS, 73
Cnut, King, 79, 88, 101
Crowland, 22, 97, 110
Cuthbert, St., 11, 38
  vestments of, 36, 37, 38, fig. 3

Dunstan, St., 12, 17, 41, 60
Durham Ritual see Durham, Cathedral Library MS A. IV. 19

Eadui Codex see Hanover, Kestner Museum MS WM XXIª, 36
Eadvius Basan (Eadui), scribe, 22, 79, 82, 84, 85, 86
Ealswith, Queen, 37, 39
Ebbo Gospels see Épernay, Bibliothèque Municipale MS 1
Edgar, King, 18, 44
Eduardus diaconus, scribe, 43
Edward the Confessor, 42
Ethelwold, Bishop of Winchester, 17, 18, 52, 53
  Benedictional of, see London, British Library MS Add. 49598

Fleury, 67
Frithestan, Bishop of Winchester, 11
Fulk, Archbishop of Rheims, 87

Gauzlin, Abbot of Fleury, 58, 59
Giotto, 109
Glastonbury, 44–5
Godefredus, Archbishop of Rouen, 53
Godeman, scribe, 18, 52, 54
Godwinson, Tostig, 110
Grimbald Gospels see London, British Library MS Add. 34890
Grimbald, monk, 11, 20, 87

Hadelinus Shrine, Vise, 110
Hehstan, Bishop of London, 68
Helmingham Orosius, see London, British Library MS Add. 47967
Hereford Gospels see Cambridge, Pembroke College MS 302
Hereford Troper see London, British Library MS Cotton Calig. A. XIV
Hugh, Duke of the Franks, 36
Hyde Abbey, 96

Ivory Carvings, 49, 50, 51, 60, 95, 116

John XII, Pope, 60
Jouarre Abbey, Diocese of Meaux, 101
Judith, Countess of Flanders, 23, 29, 108–10, 111, 112
  Gospels see New York, Pierpont Morgan Library MSS 708, 709
Judith, daughter of Charles the Bald, 11
Junius Psalter see Oxford, Bodleian Library MS Junius 27

Knook, Wilts, tympanum, 63

Lanalet Pontifical see Rouen, Bibliothèque Municipale MS. A. 27
Leofric, Bishop of Exeter, 45, 62, 99
Leofric Missal see Oxford, Bodleian Library MS Bodley 579
Lindisfarne Gospels see London, British Library MS Cotton Nero D. IV
Lobbes, 41
Lorsch, 42
Lyfing, Bishop of Crediton, 106

Malmesbury Abbey, 70
Margaret, St., 107
Matilda, Countess, 112
Metz School, 12, 18–19, 66, 73, 86, 111
  Ivories, 49, 51
Munich, Nationalmuseum, Ivory panel (Ascension), 50, 116

New Minster Register see London. British Library MS Stowe 944
Nivelles, nr. Liège, 90

Oswald, St., 17
Otbert, Abbot, 19, 29, 57, 67
Otto I, Emperor, 41

Prudentius Psychomachia, *see* Cambridge, Corpus Christi
   College MS 23; London, British Library MS Cotton,
   Cleop. C. VIII; Munich, Staatsbibliothek MS CLM.
   29031b; London, British Library MS Add. 24199

Remi, St., of Rheims, 23, 121
Rheims School, 45, 46, 63, 64, 66, 74, 86, 90, 107
Richard, Count of Avranches, 58
Robert of Jumièges, 19, 53, 91
   Benedictional of, *see* Rouen Bibliothèque Municipale
     MS Y. 7 (369)
   Sacramentary of, *see* Rouen, Bibliothèque Municipale
     MS Y. 6 (274)
Roger of Worcester, 106
Robert, Archbishop of Rouen, 53

St. Gall, 18
   MSS from, 108
St. Germans, Cornwall, 106
St. Margaret Gospels *see* Oxford, Bodleian Library MS
   Lat. lit. F. 5
Saint-Savin-sur-Gartempe
   Genesis cycle, 76, 77, 103

St. Vaast Bible *see* Arras, Bibliothèque Municipale,
   MS 559
Shaftesbury Abbey, 47
Sherborne Pontifical *see* Paris, Bibliothèque Nationale
   MS lat. 943
Stigand, Bishop of Winchester, 37

Thorney Abbey, 40, 52, 110
Tours, school of, 38, 107
   MSS, 113
Trier MSS, 66, 113
Trinity Gospels *see* Cambridge, Trinity College MS
   B. 10. 4

Utrecht Psalter *see* Utrecht University Library MS 32 and
   copy *see* London, British Library MS Harley 603

Weingarten Abbey, 24
Welf IV, Duke of Bavaria, 110
Werferth, Bishop of Worcester, 35
William, Abbot of Thorney, 40
Wulfsin, Bishop of Sherborne, 6
Wulfstan, Archbishop, 35

York Gospels *see* York, Chapter Library, MS Add. 1

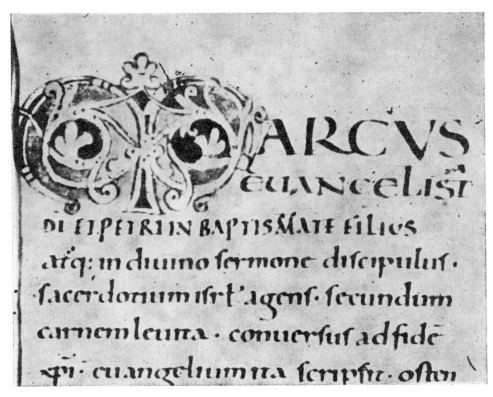

Fig. 59. Initial M. Warsaw, Biblioteka Narodowa I. 3311, f. 13 (Cat. 92)